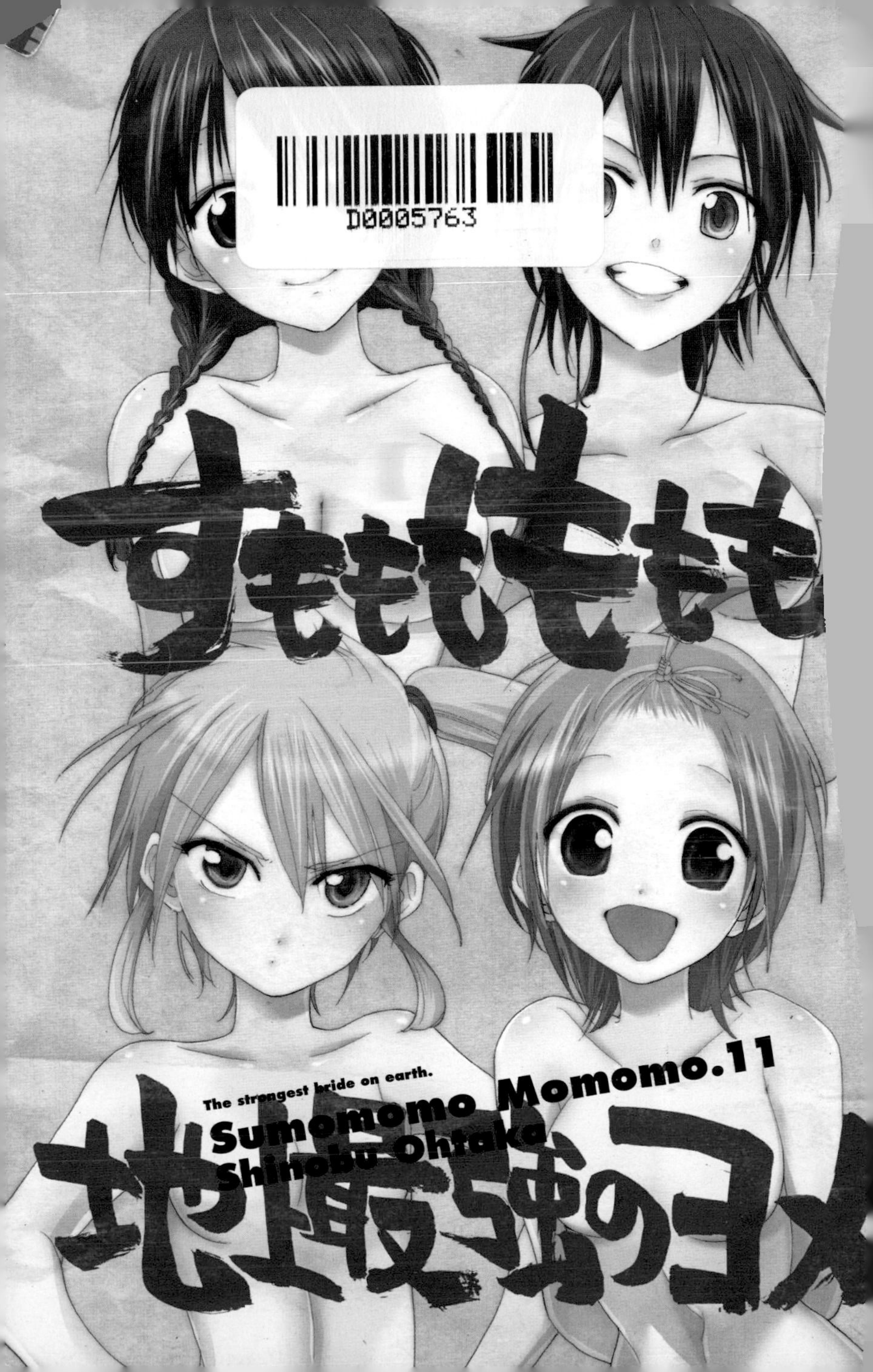
すもももももも
The strongest bride on earth.
Sumomomo Momomo.11
Shinobu Ohtaka
地上最強のヨメ

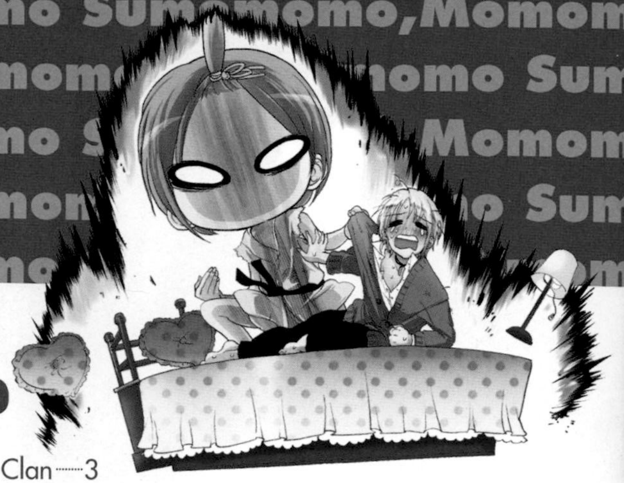

CONTENTS

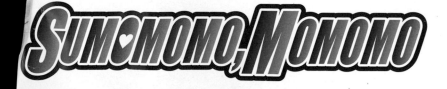

SUMOMOMO, MOMOMO

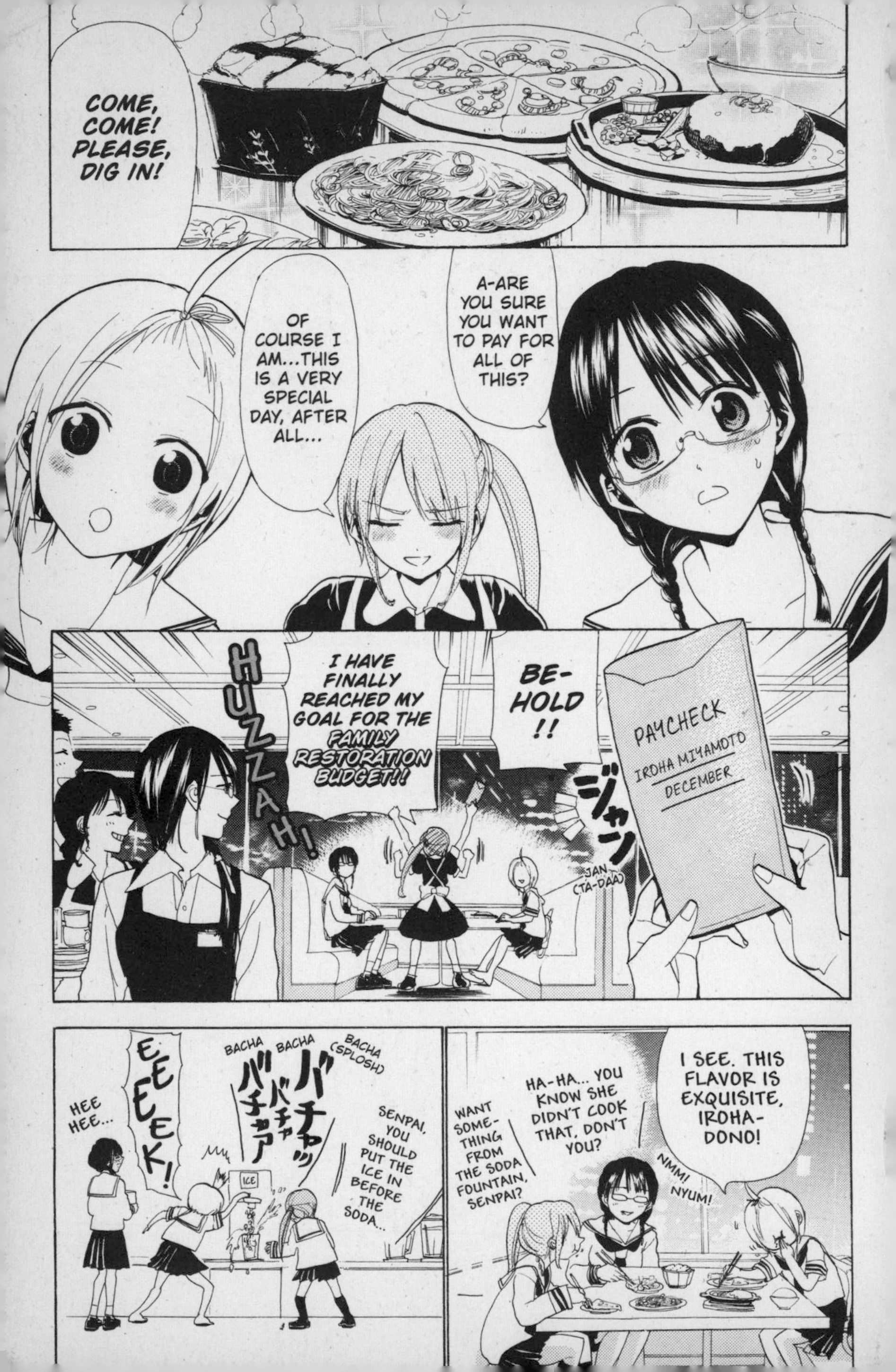
COME, COME! PLEASE, DIG IN!
A-ARE YOU SURE YOU WANT TO PAY FOR ALL OF THIS?
OF COURSE I AM...THIS IS A VERY SPECIAL DAY, AFTER ALL...
PAYCHECK
IROHA MIYAMOTO
DECEMBER
ジャン
JAN (TA-DAA)
BE-HOLD!!
I HAVE FINALLY REACHED MY GOAL FOR THE FAMILY RESTORATION BUDGET!!
HUZZAH!
I SEE. THIS FLAVOR IS EXQUISITE, IROHA-DONO!
NMM! NYUM!
HA-HA... YOU KNOW SHE DIDN'T COOK THAT, DON'T YOU?
WANT SOME-THING FROM THE SODA FOUNTAIN, SENPAI?
SENPAI, YOU SHOULD PUT THE ICE IN BEFORE THE SODA...
バチャッ バチャ バチャア
BACHA BACHA BACHA (SPLOSH)
EEEEK!
ICE
HEE HEE...

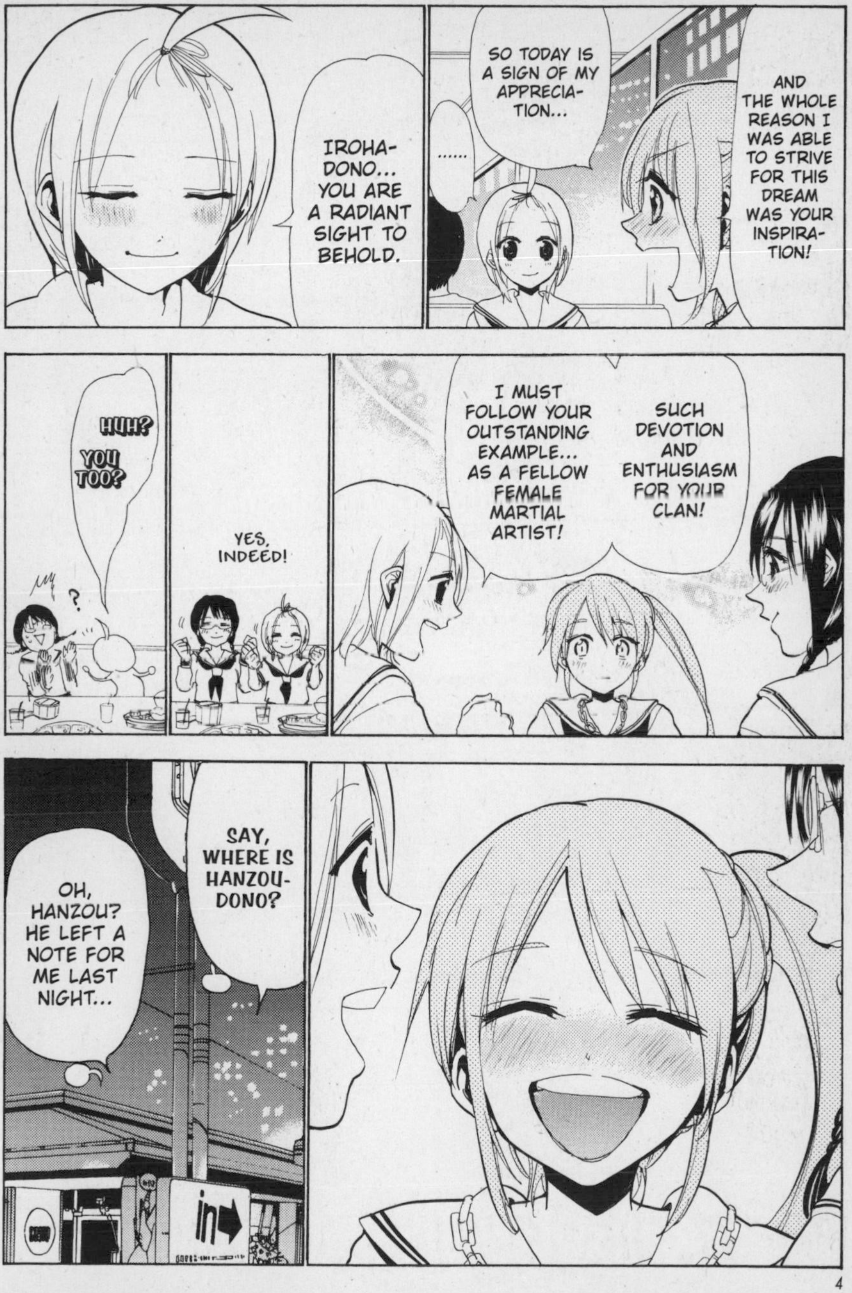
AND THE WHOLE REASON I WAS ABLE TO STRIVE FOR THIS DREAM WAS YOUR INSPIRATION!
SO TODAY IS A SIGN OF MY APPRECIATION...
......
IROHA-DONO... YOU ARE A RADIANT SIGHT TO BEHOLD.
SUCH DEVOTION AND ENTHUSIASM FOR YOUR CLAN!
I MUST FOLLOW YOUR OUTSTANDING EXAMPLE... AS A FELLOW FEMALE MARTIAL ARTIST!
YES, INDEED!
HUH?
YOU TOO?
?
SAY, WHERE IS HANZOU-DONO?
OH, HANZOU? HE LEFT A NOTE FOR ME LAST NIGHT...
in

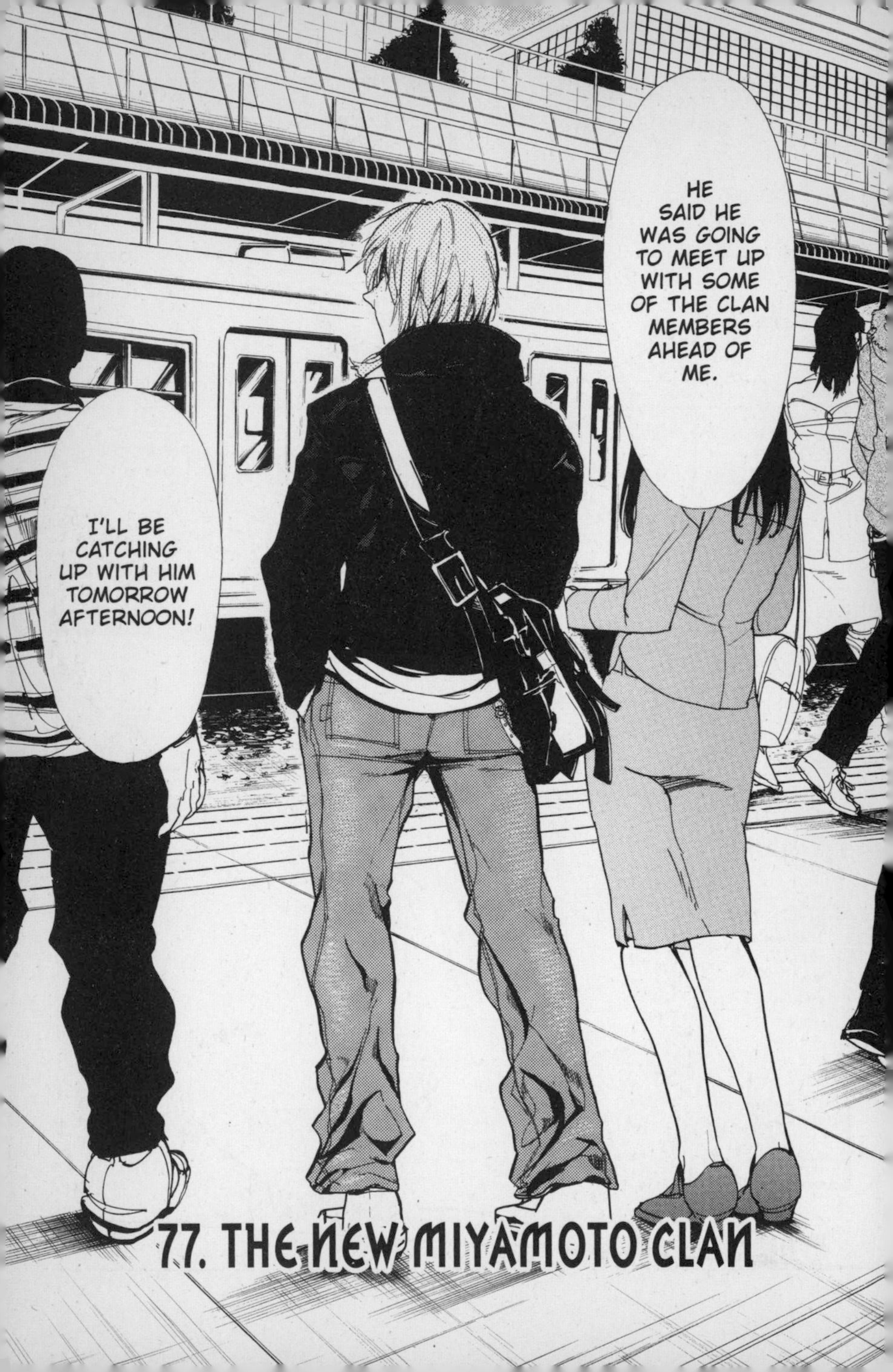
HE SAID HE WAS GOING TO MEET UP WITH SOME OF THE CLAN MEMBERS AHEAD OF ME.
I'LL BE CATCHING UP WITH HIM TOMORROW AFTERNOON!
77. THE NEW MIYAMOTO CLAN

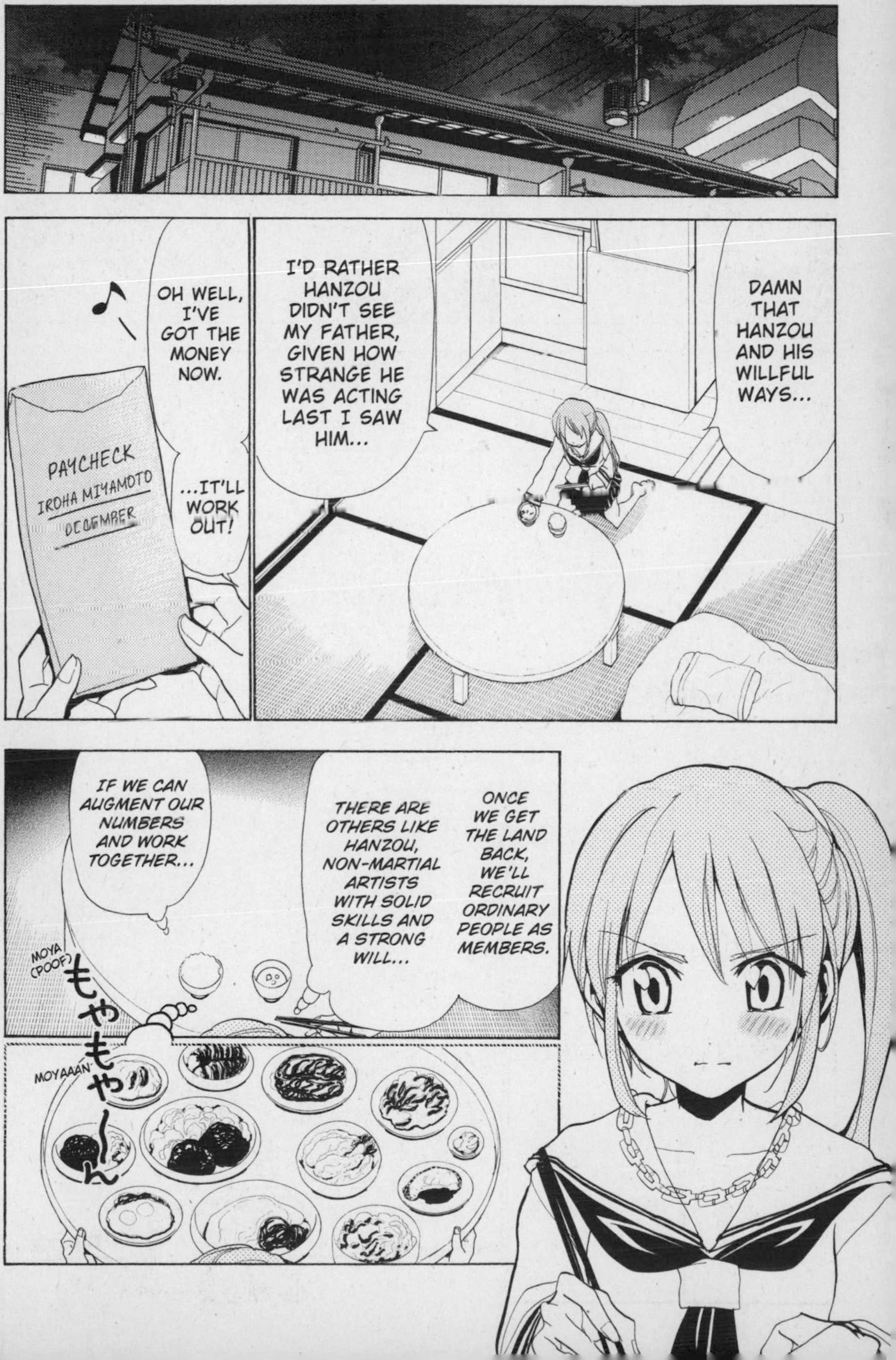
DAMN THAT HANZOU AND HIS WILLFUL WAYS...
I'D RATHER HANZOU DIDN'T SEE MY FATHER, GIVEN HOW STRANGE HE WAS ACTING LAST I SAW HIM...
OH WELL, I'VE GOT THE MONEY NOW.
PAYCHECK
IROHA MIYAMOTO
DECEMBER
...IT'LL WORK OUT!
ONCE WE GET THE LAND BACK, WE'LL RECRUIT ORDINARY PEOPLE AS MEMBERS.
THERE ARE OTHERS LIKE HANZOU, NON-MARTIAL ARTISTS WITH SOLID SKILLS AND A STRONG WILL...
IF WE CAN AUGMENT OUR NUMBERS AND WORK TOGETHER...
MOYA (POOF)
もや
MOYAAAN
もや〜ん

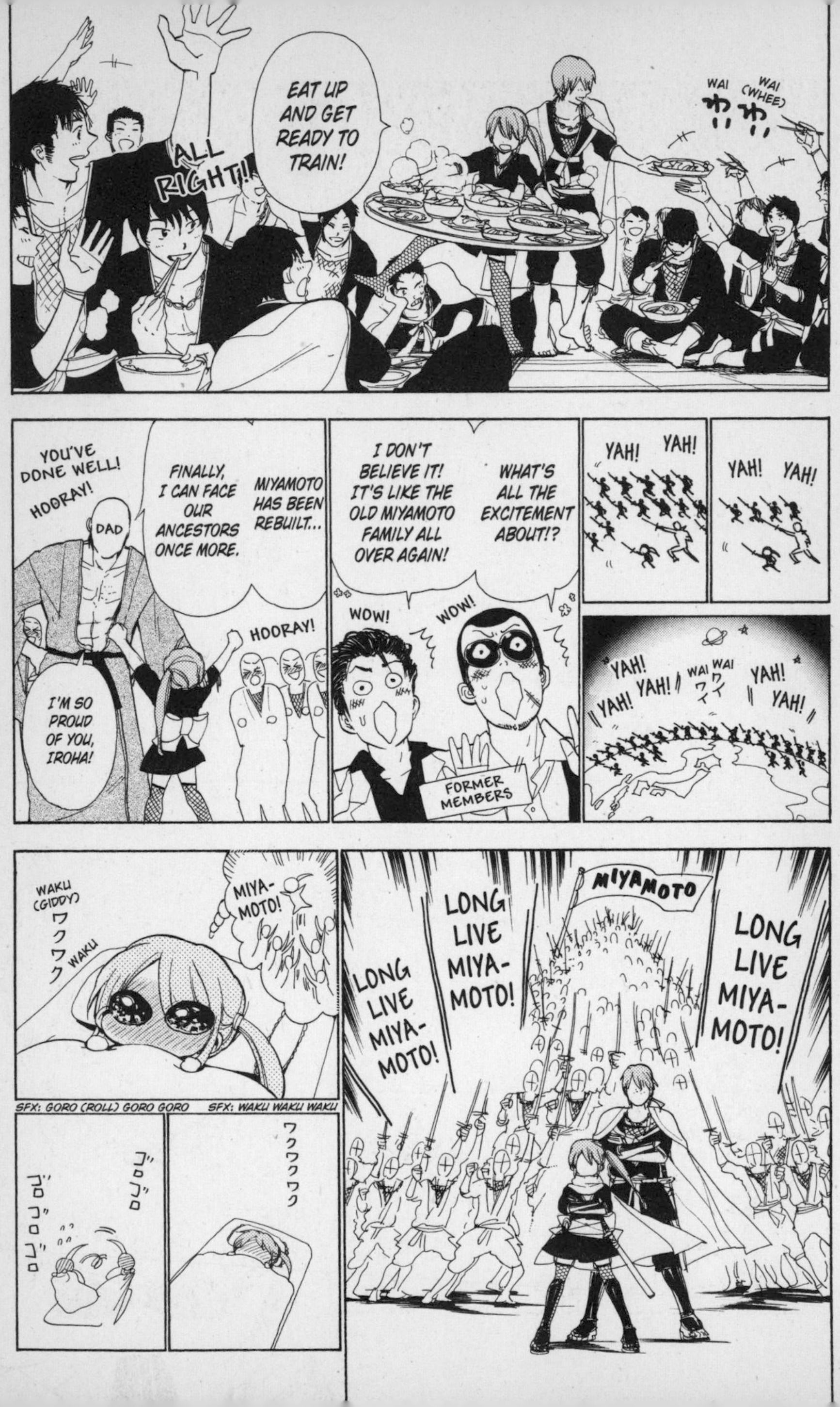
WAI WAI (WHEE)
ワイワイ
EAT UP AND GET READY TO TRAIN!
ALL RIGHT!!
YAH! YAH!
YAH! YAH!
YAH! YAH! YAH!
WAI WAI
ワイワイ
YAH! YAH! YAH!
WHAT'S ALL THE EXCITEMENT ABOUT!?
I DON'T BELIEVE IT! IT'S LIKE THE OLD MIYAMOTO FAMILY ALL OVER AGAIN!
WOW!
WOW!
FORMER MEMBERS
MIYAMOTO HAS BEEN REBUILT...
FINALLY, I CAN FACE OUR ANCESTORS ONCE MORE.
YOU'VE DONE WELL! HOORAY!
DAD
HOORAY!
I'M SO PROUD OF YOU, IROHA!
MIYAMOTO
LONG LIVE MIYAMOTO!
LONG LIVE MIYA-MOTO!
LONG LIVE MIYA-MOTO!
MIYA-MOTO!
WAKU (GIDDY) ワクワク WAKU
SFX: WAKU WAKU WAKU
SFX: GORO (ROLL) GORO GORO
ワクワクワク
ゴロゴロ
ゴロゴロゴロ

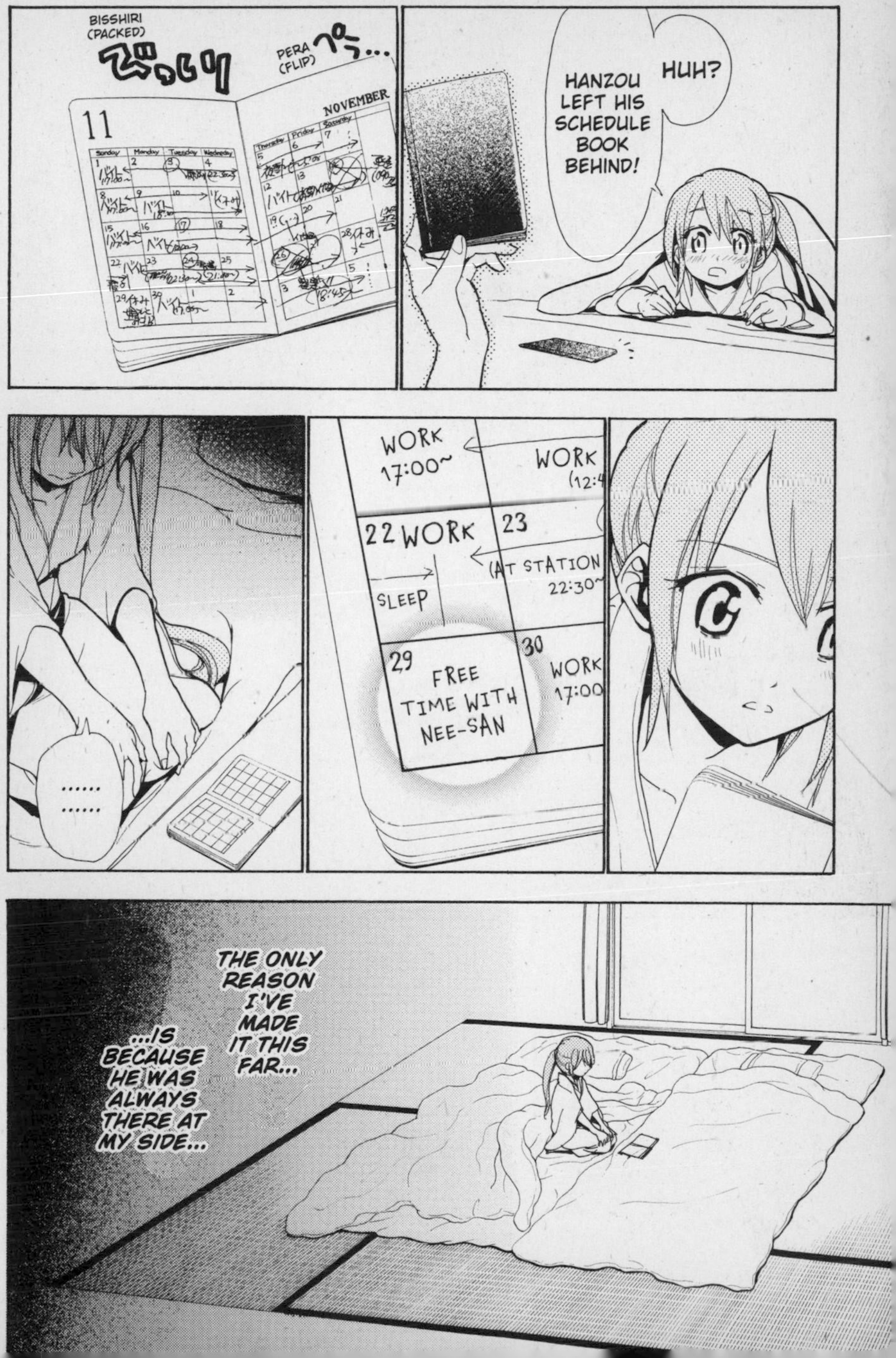
HUH?
HANZOU LEFT HIS SCHEDULE BOOK BEHIND!
BISSHIRI (PACKED)
PERA (FLIP)
11
NOVEMBER
WORK 17:00~
WORK (12:4
22 WORK
23
(AT STATION 22:30~
SLEEP
29 FREE TIME WITH NEE-SAN
30 WORK 17:00
....
THE ONLY REASON I'VE MADE IT THIS FAR...
...IS BECAUSE HE WAS ALWAYS THERE AT MY SIDE...

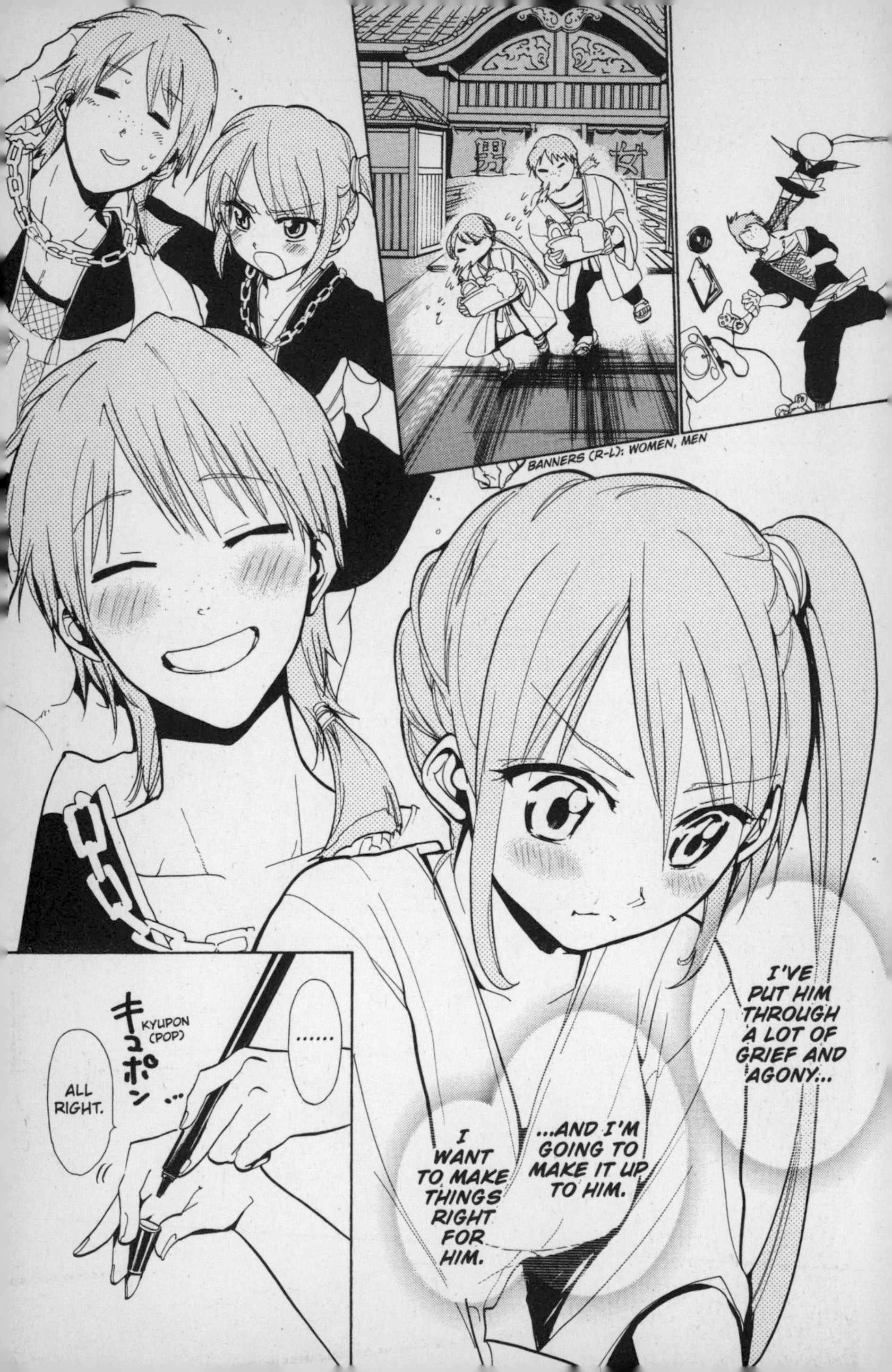
女
男
BANNERS (R-L): WOMEN, MEN
I'VE PUT HIM THROUGH A LOT OF GRIEF AND AGONY...
...AND I'M GOING TO MAKE IT UP TO HIM.
I WANT TO MAKE THINGS RIGHT FOR HIM.
......
キュポン
KYUPON (POP)
ALL RIGHT.

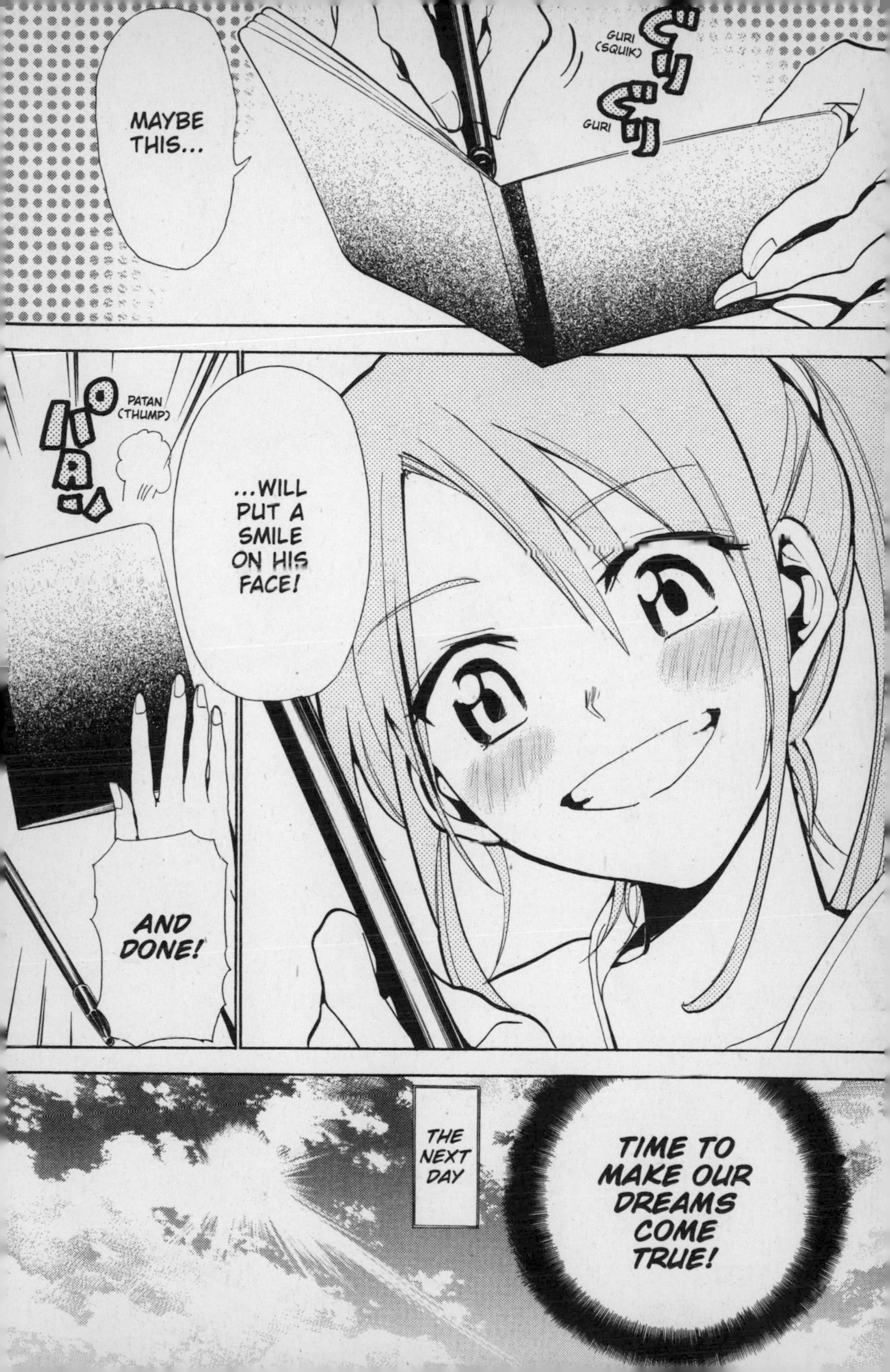
GURI (SQUIK)
GURI
MAYBE THIS...
...WILL PUT A SMILE ON HIS FACE!
PATAN (THUMP)
AND DONE!
TIME TO MAKE OUR DREAMS COME TRUE!
THE NEXT DAY

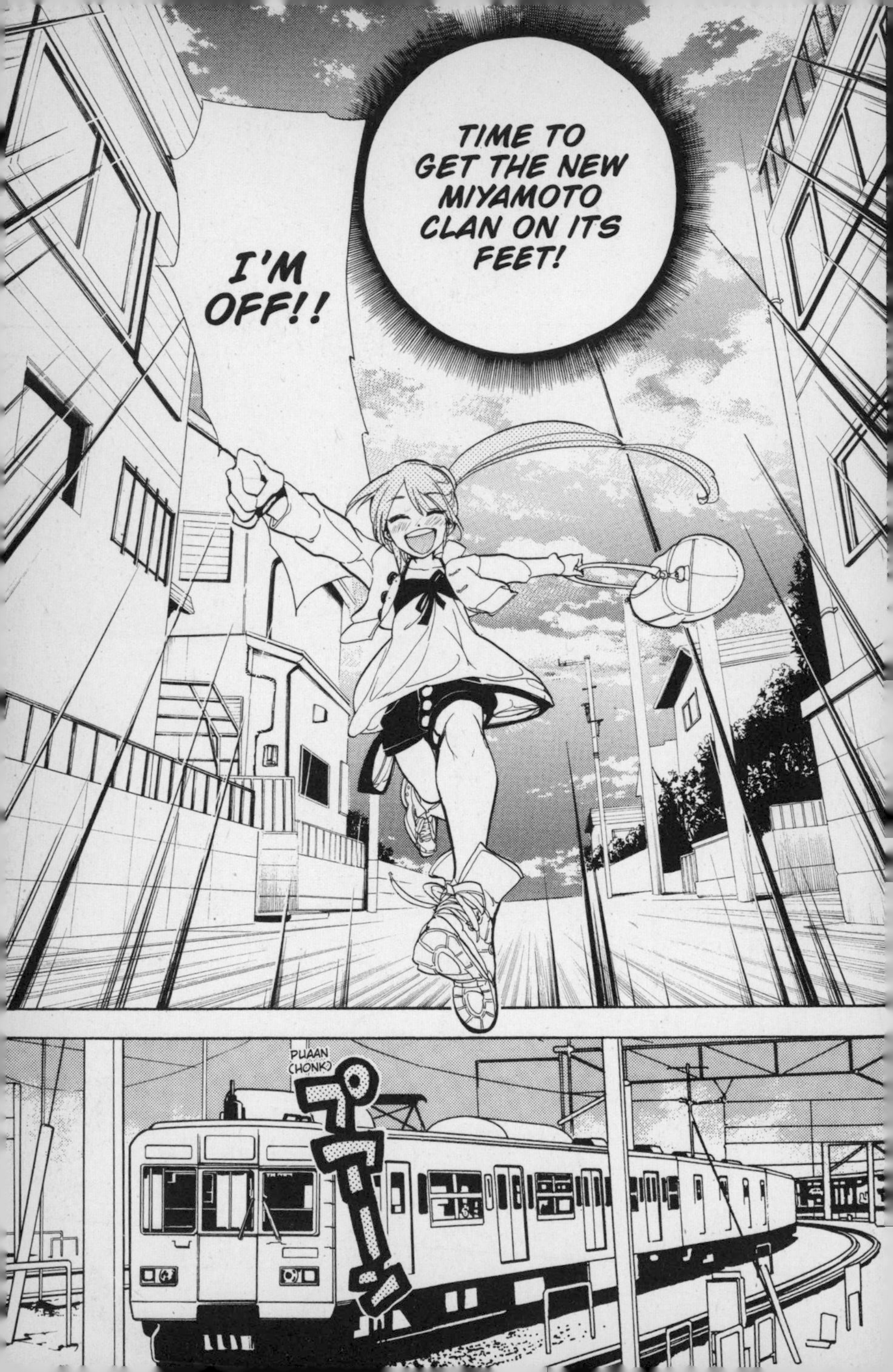
TIME TO GET THE NEW MIYAMOTO CLAN ON ITS FEET!
I'M OFF!!
PUAAN (HONK)

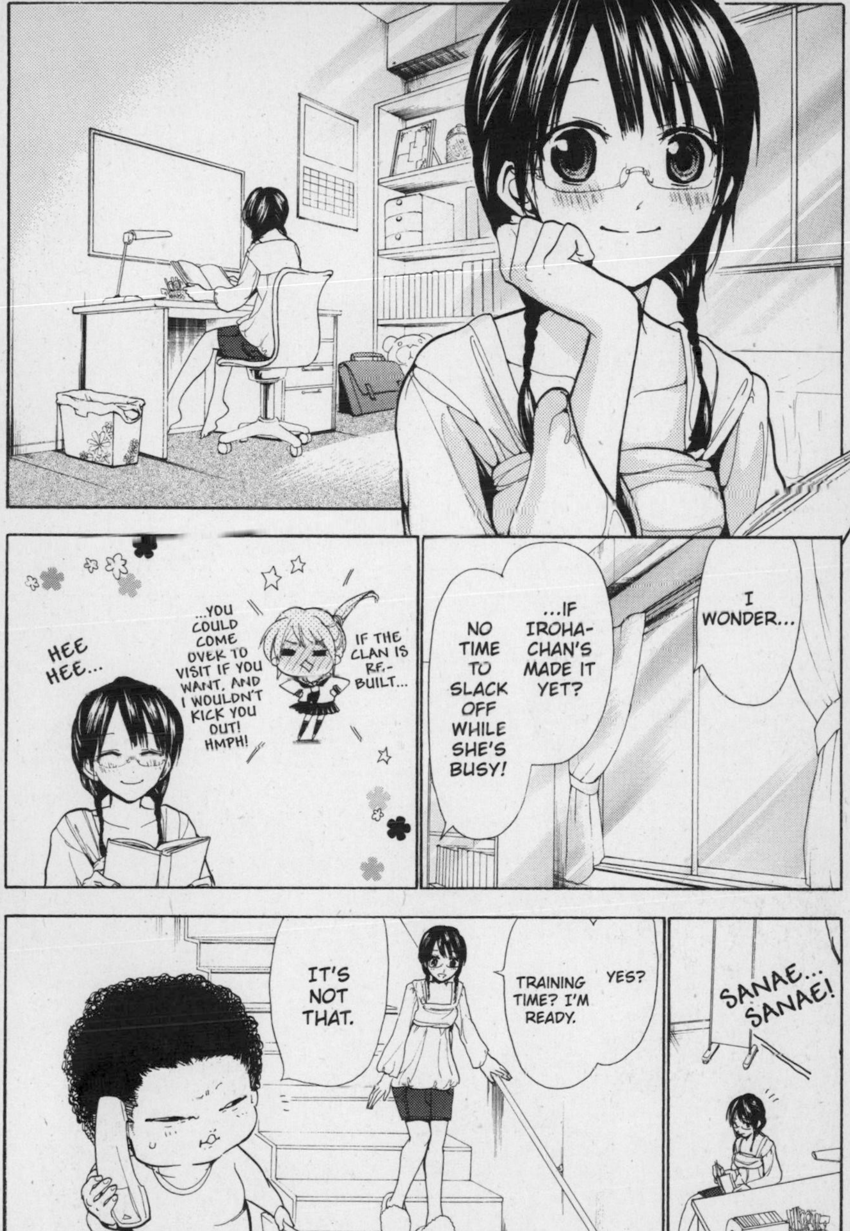
I WONDER...
...IF IROHA-CHAN'S MADE IT YET?
NO TIME TO SLACK OFF WHILE SHE'S BUSY!
IF THE CLAN IS RE-BUILT...
...YOU COULD COME OVER TO VISIT IF YOU WANT, AND I WOULDN'T KICK YOU OUT! HMPH!
HEE HEE...
SANAE... SANAE!
YES?
TRAINING TIME? I'M READY.
IT'S NOT THAT.

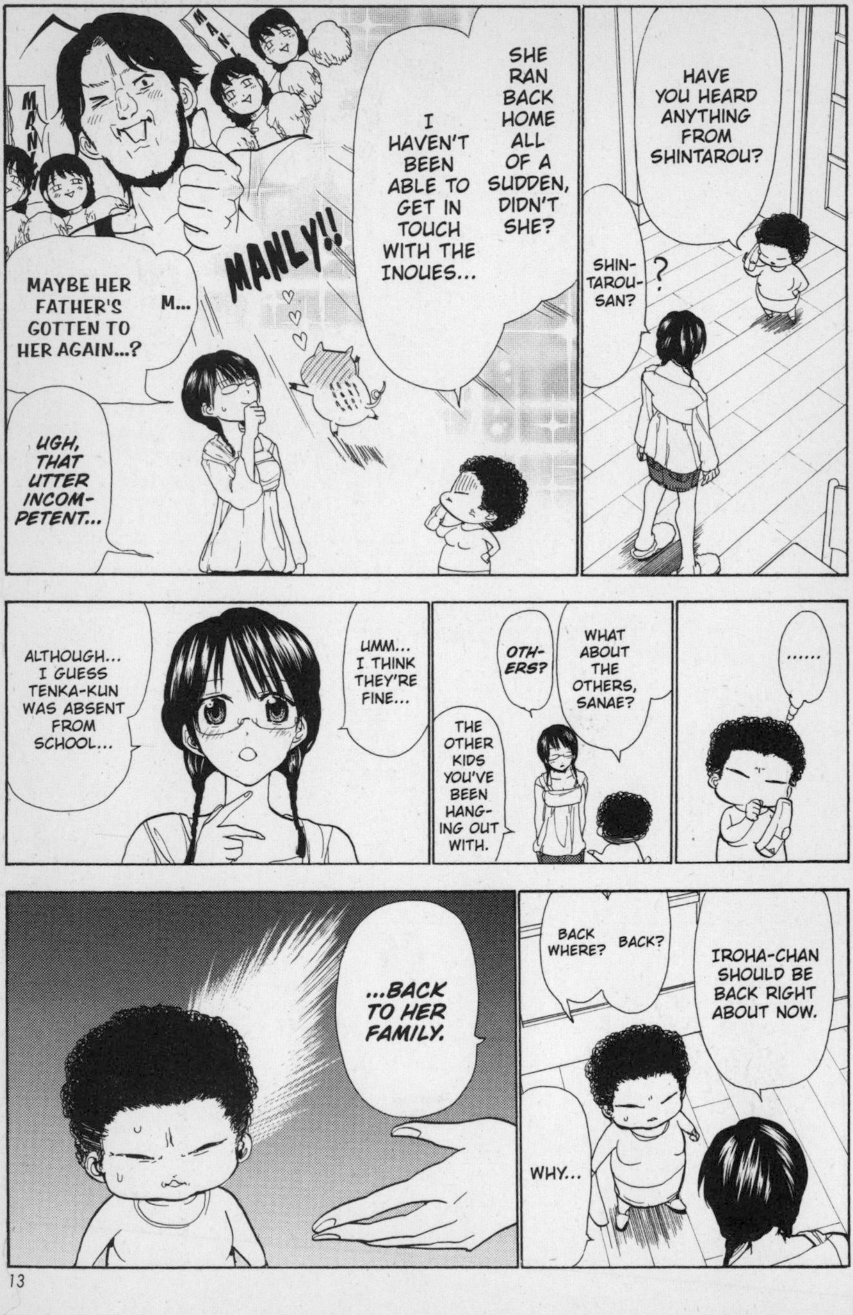
HAVE YOU HEARD ANYTHING FROM SHINTAROU?
SHIN-TAROU-SAN?
?
SHE RAN BACK HOME ALL OF A SUDDEN, DIDN'T SHE?
I HAVEN'T BEEN ABLE TO GET IN TOUCH WITH THE INOUES...
MANLY!!
M...
MAYBE HER FATHER'S GOTTEN TO HER AGAIN...?
UGH, THAT UTTER INCOMPETENT...
......
WHAT ABOUT THE OTHERS, SANAE?
OTHERS?
THE OTHER KIDS YOU'VE BEEN HANGING OUT WITH.
UMM... I THINK THEY'RE FINE...
ALTHOUGH... I GUESS TENKA-KUN WAS ABSENT FROM SCHOOL...
IROHA-CHAN SHOULD BE BACK RIGHT ABOUT NOW.
BACK?
BACK WHERE?
WHY...
...BACK TO HER FAMILY.

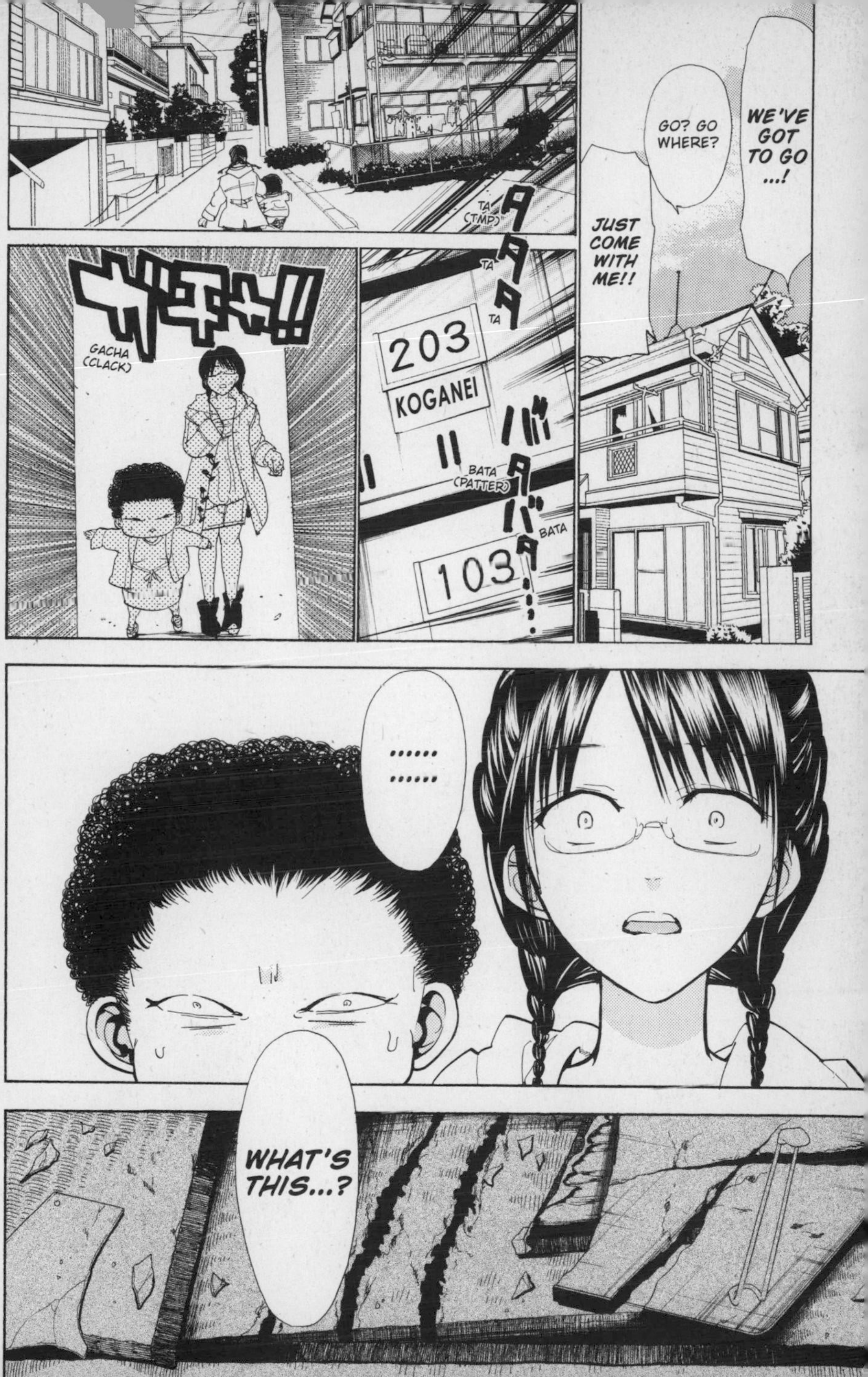
WE'VE GOT TO GO ...!
GO? GO WHERE?
JUST COME WITH ME!!
TA (TMP)
TA
TA
203
KOGANEI
BATA (PATTER)
BATA
103
GACHA (CLACK)
......
......
WHAT'S THIS...?

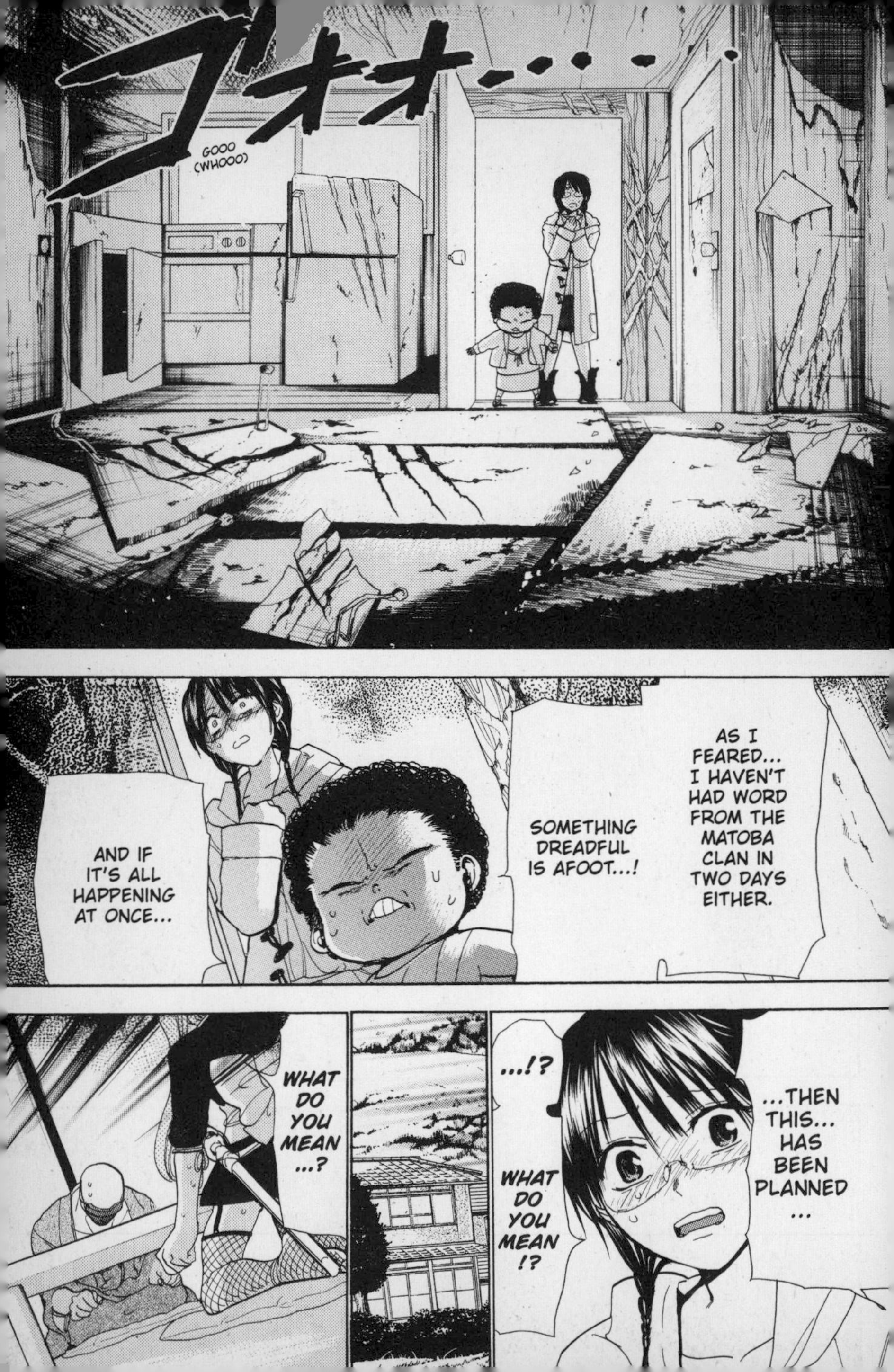
ゴオオ……
GOOO (WHOOO)
AS I FEARED... I HAVEN'T HAD WORD FROM THE MATOBA CLAN IN TWO DAYS EITHER.
SOMETHING DREADFUL IS AFOOT...!
AND IF IT'S ALL HAPPENING AT ONCE...
...THEN THIS... HAS BEEN PLANNED...
...!?
WHAT DO YOU MEAN!?
WHAT DO YOU MEAN...?

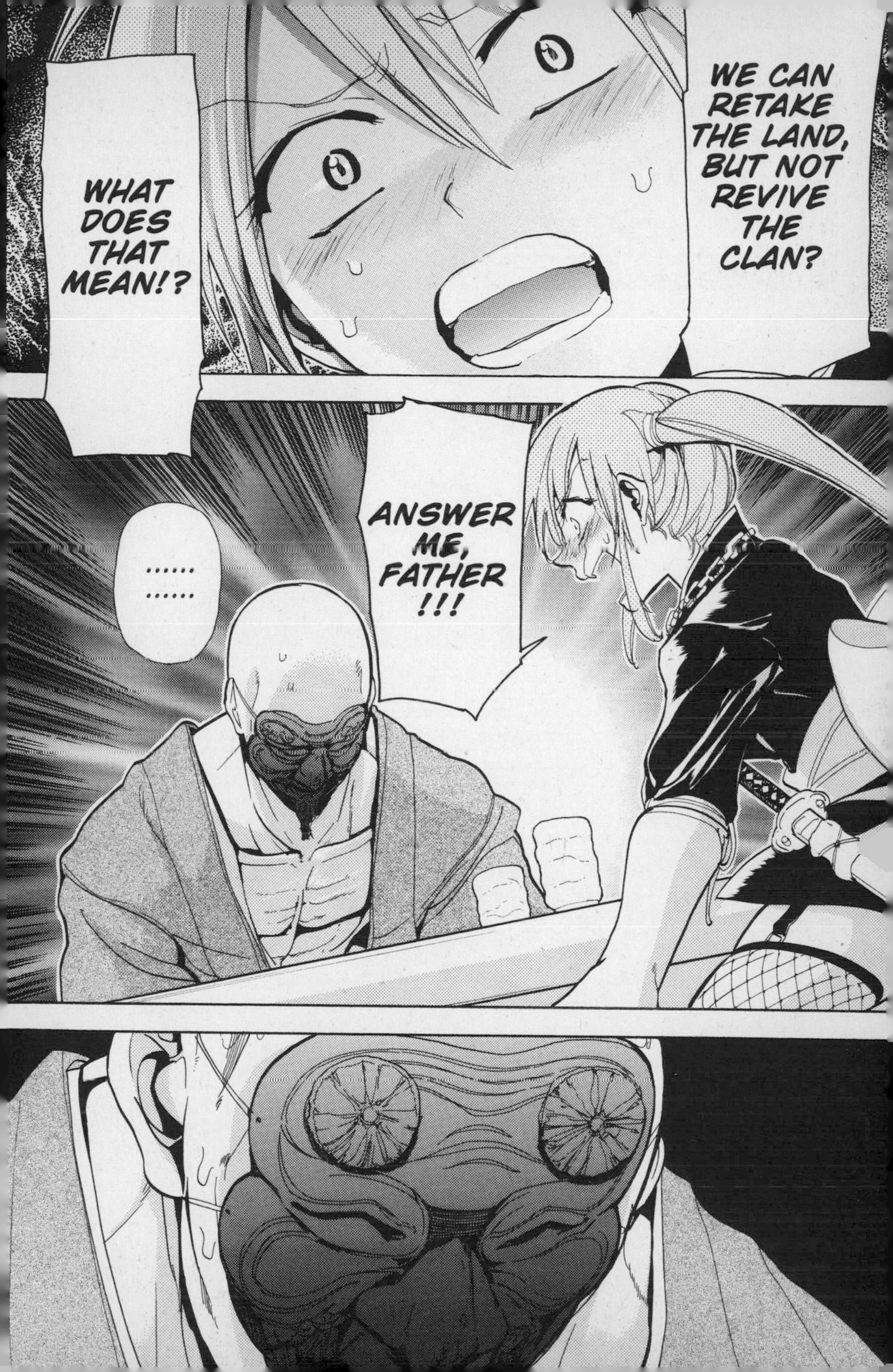
WE CAN RETAKE THE LAND, BUT NOT REVIVE THE CLAN?
WHAT DOES THAT MEAN!?
ANSWER ME, FATHER!!!
......
......

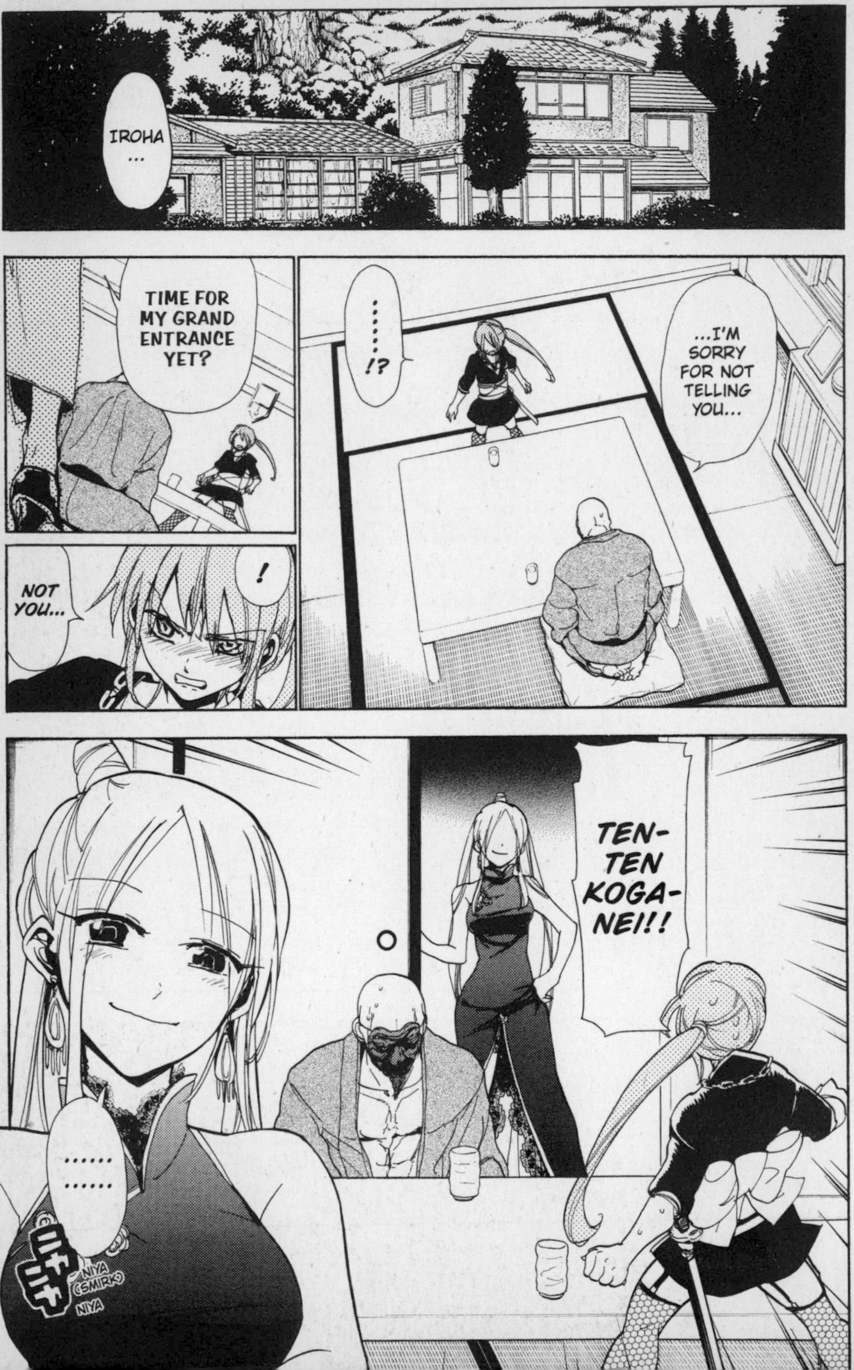
IROHA ...
...I'M SORRY FOR NOT TELLING YOU...
......!?
TIME FOR MY GRAND ENTRANCE YET?
!
NOT YOU...
TEN-TEN KOGANEI!!
....
NIYA (SMIRK) NIYA

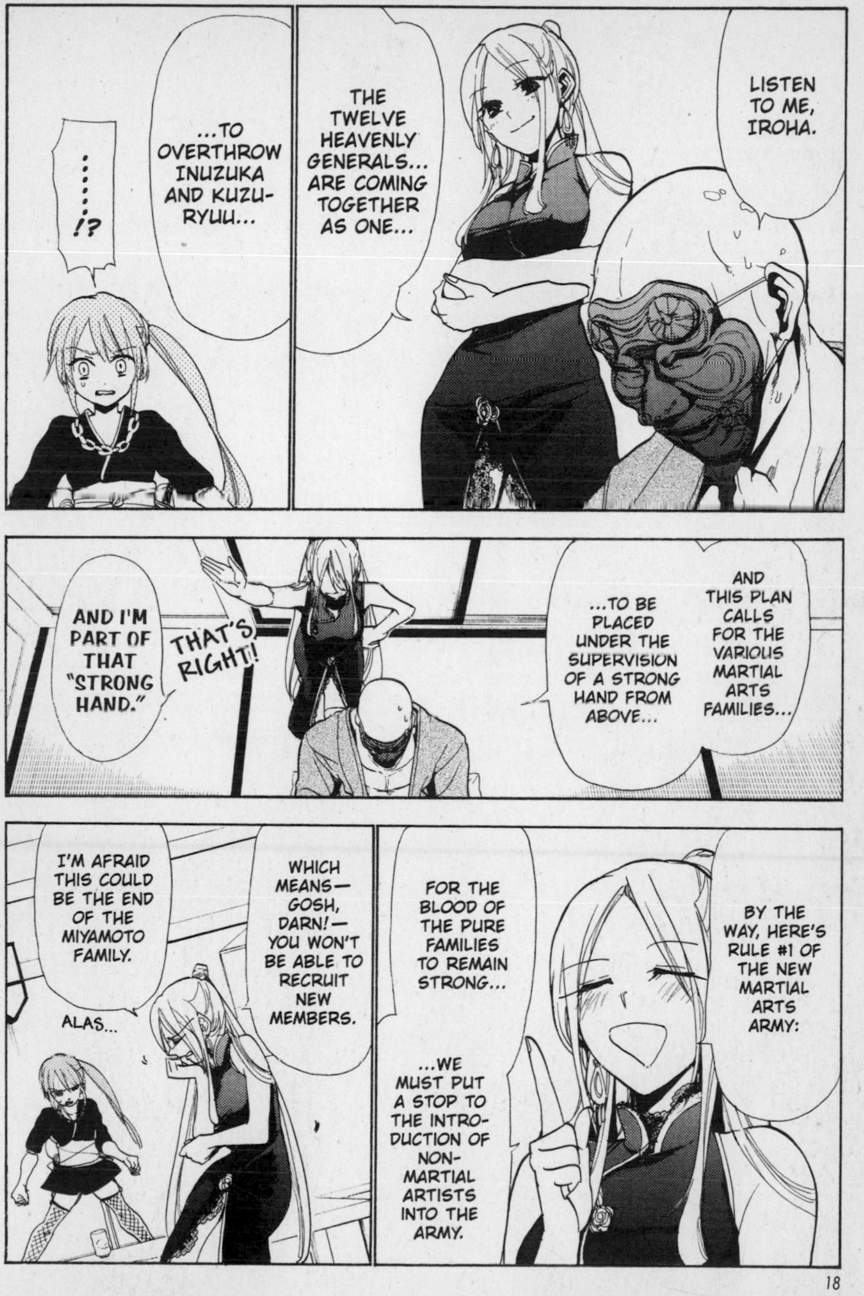
LISTEN TO ME, IROHA.
THE TWELVE HEAVENLY GENERALS... ARE COMING TOGETHER AS ONE...
...TO OVERTHROW INUZUKA AND KUZU-RYUU...
......!?
AND THIS PLAN CALLS FOR THE VARIOUS MARTIAL ARTS FAMILIES...
...TO BE PLACED UNDER THE SUPERVISION OF A STRONG HAND FROM ABOVE...
THAT'S RIGHT!
AND I'M PART OF THAT "STRONG HAND."
BY THE WAY, HERE'S RULE #1 OF THE NEW MARTIAL ARTS ARMY:
FOR THE BLOOD OF THE PURE FAMILIES TO REMAIN STRONG...
...WE MUST PUT A STOP TO THE INTRODUCTION OF NON-MARTIAL ARTISTS INTO THE ARMY.
WHICH MEANS—GOSH, DARN!—YOU WON'T BE ABLE TO RECRUIT NEW MEMBERS.
I'M AFRAID THIS COULD BE THE END OF THE MIYAMOTO FAMILY.
ALAS...

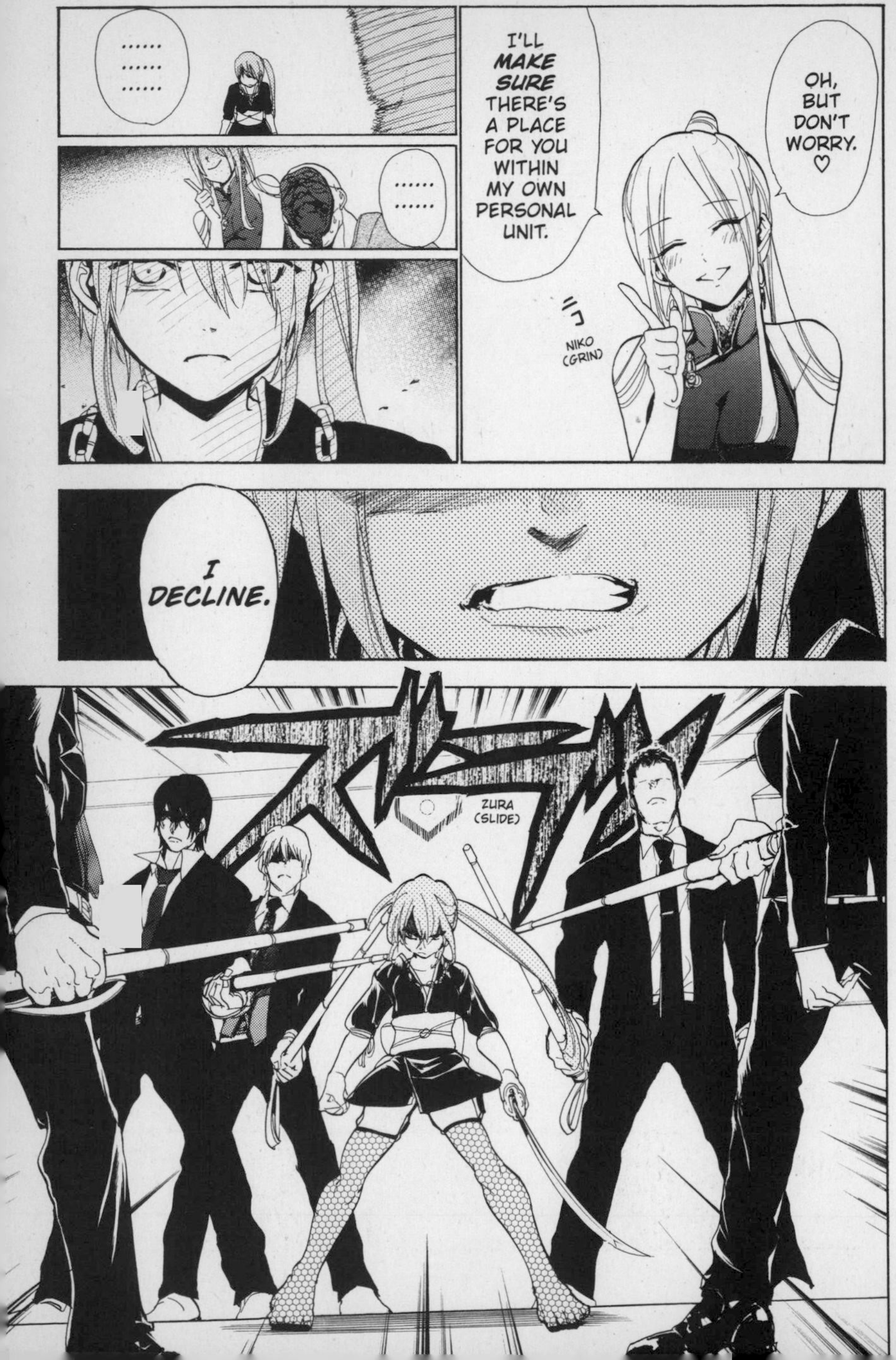
OH, BUT DON'T WORRY. ♡
I'LL MAKE SURE THERE'S A PLACE FOR YOU WITHIN MY OWN PERSONAL UNIT.
ニコ
NIKO (GRIN)
....
....
I DECLINE.
ZURA (SLIDE)

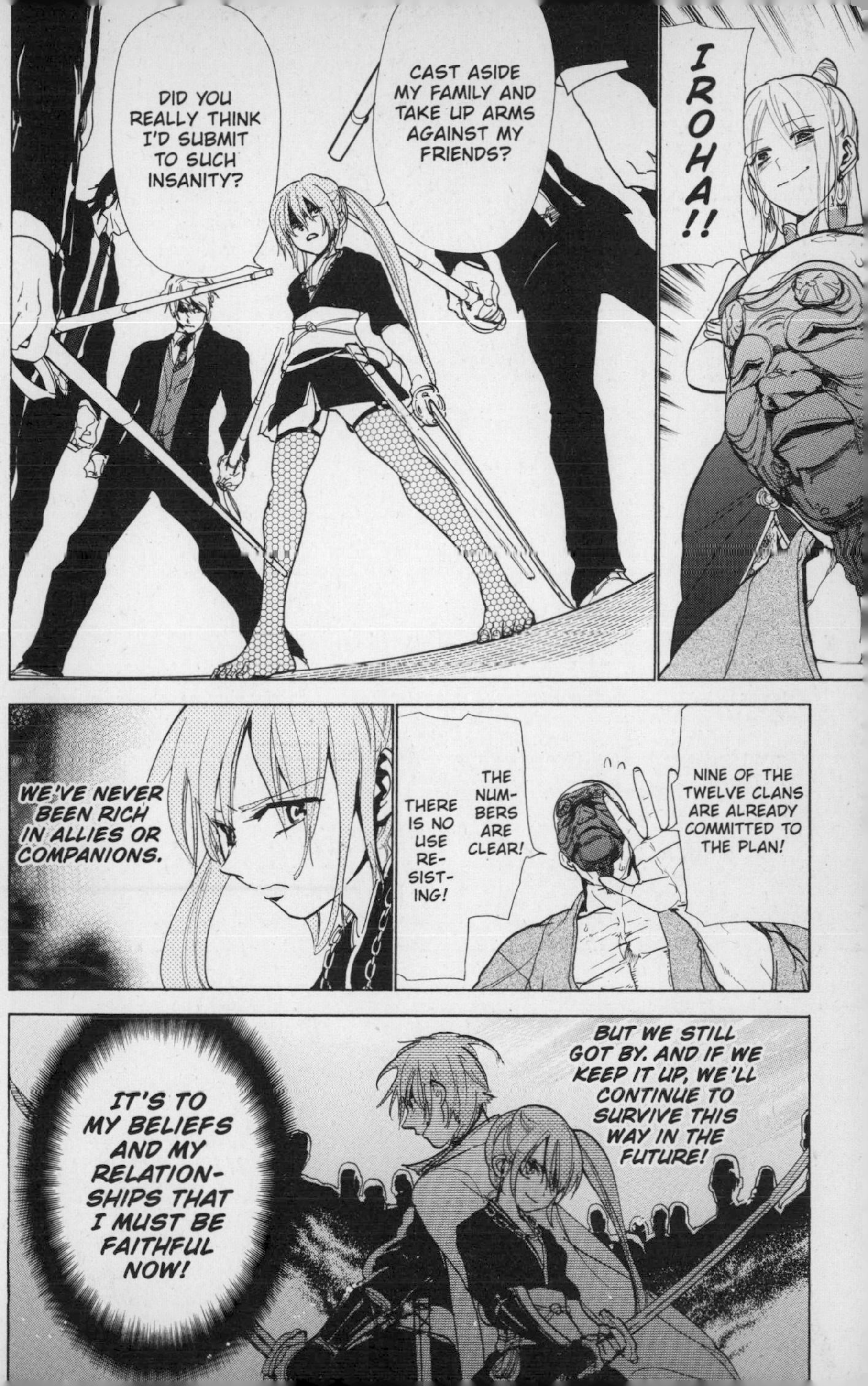
IROHA!!
CAST ASIDE MY FAMILY AND TAKE UP ARMS AGAINST MY FRIENDS?
DID YOU REALLY THINK I'D SUBMIT TO SUCH INSANITY?
NINE OF THE TWELVE CLANS ARE ALREADY COMMITTED TO THE PLAN!
THE NUM-BERS ARE CLEAR!
THERE IS NO USE RE-SIST-ING!
WE'VE NEVER BEEN RICH IN ALLIES OR COMPANIONS.
BUT WE STILL GOT BY. AND IF WE KEEP IT UP, WE'LL CONTINUE TO SURVIVE THIS WAY IN THE FUTURE!
IT'S TO MY BELIEFS AND MY RELATION-SHIPS THAT I MUST BE FAITHFUL NOW!

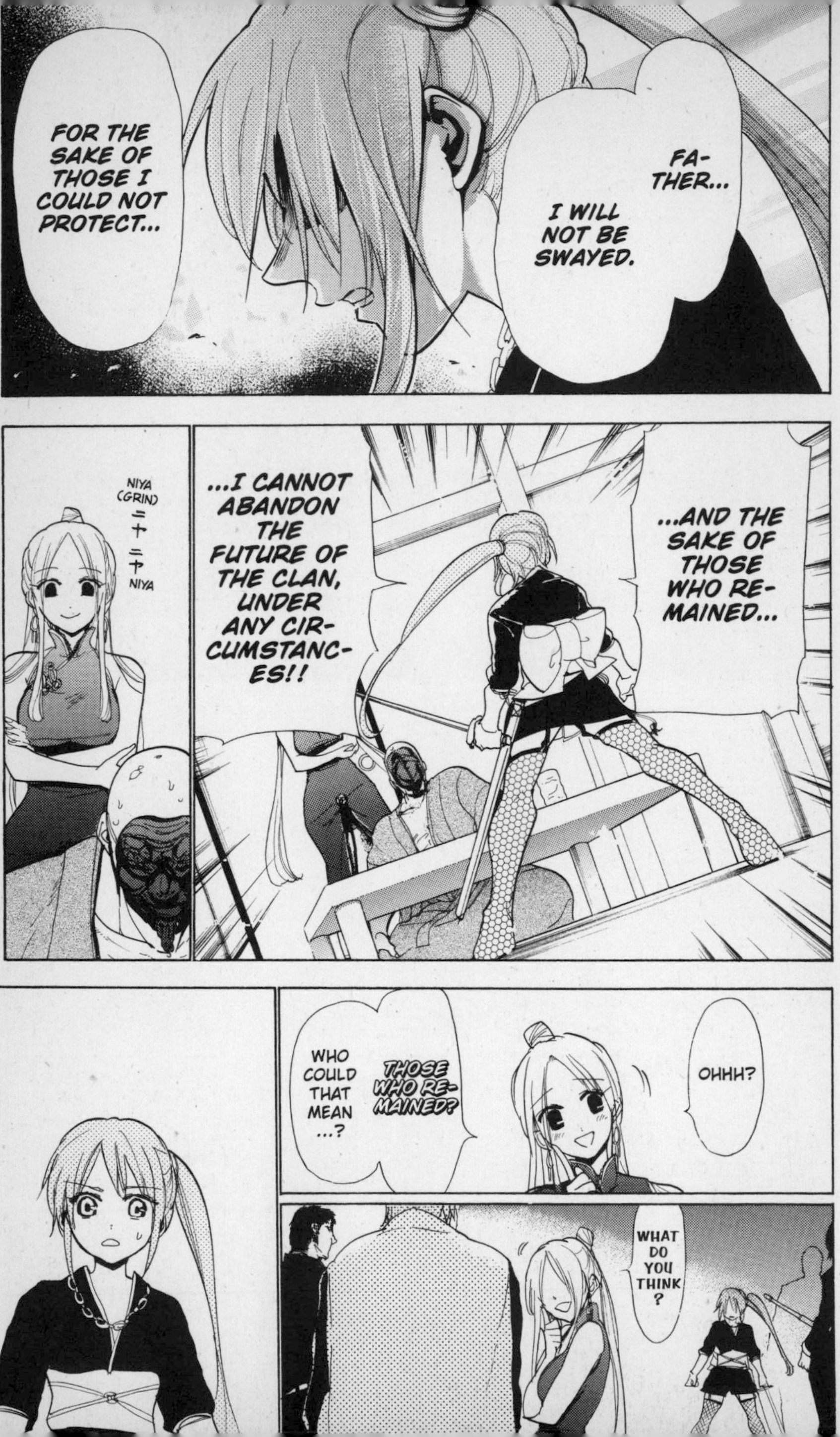
FA-THER...
I WILL NOT BE SWAYED.
FOR THE SAKE OF THOSE I COULD NOT PROTECT...
...AND THE SAKE OF THOSE WHO RE-MAINED...
...I CANNOT ABANDON THE FUTURE OF THE CLAN, UNDER ANY CIR-CUMSTANC-ES!!
NIYA (GRIN) ニヤニヤ NIYA
OHHH?
THOSE WHO RE-MAINED?
WHO COULD THAT MEAN ...?
WHAT DO YOU THINK?

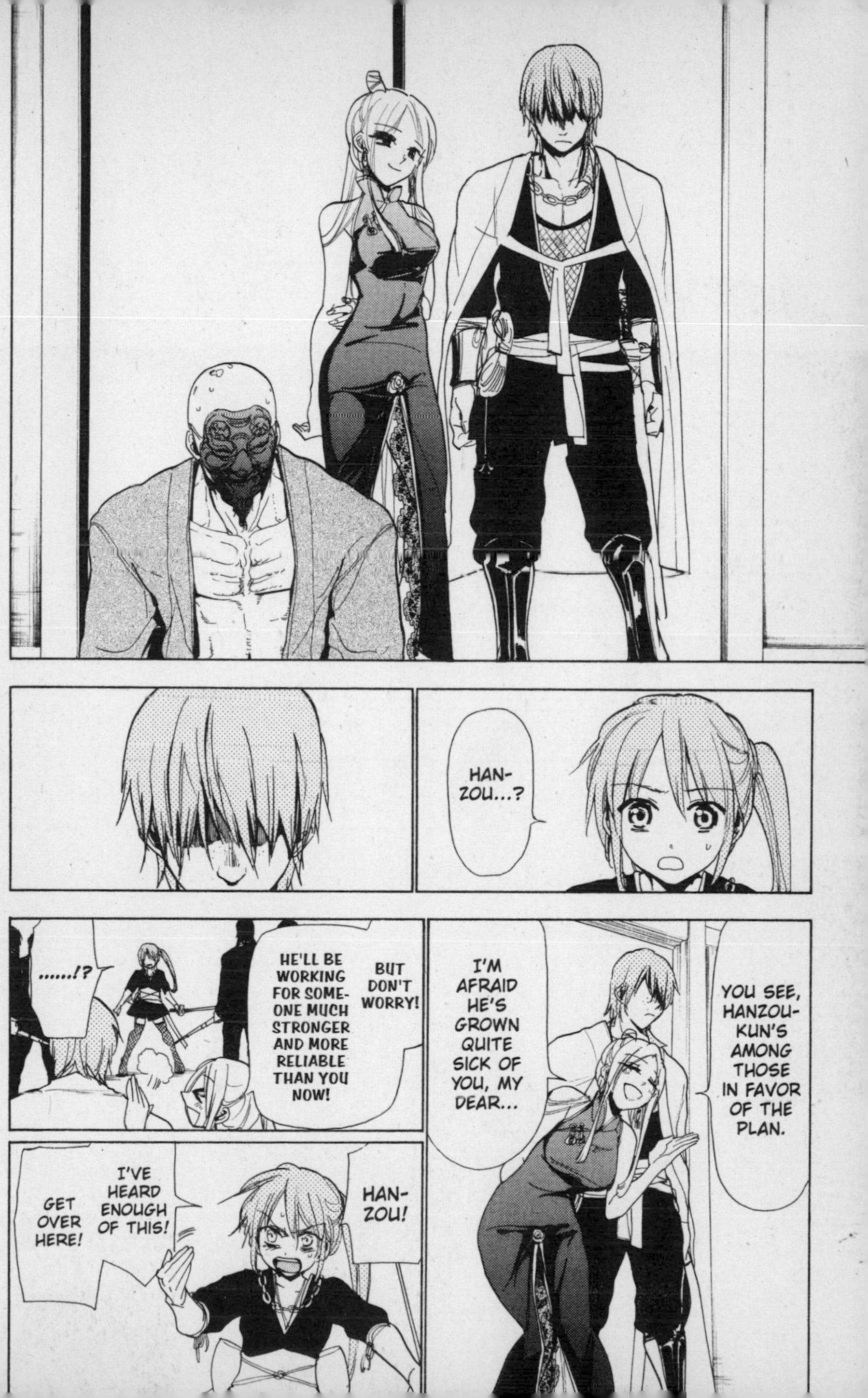
HAN-ZOU...?
YOU SEE, HANZOU-KUN'S AMONG THOSE IN FAVOR OF THE PLAN.
I'M AFRAID HE'S GROWN QUITE SICK OF YOU, MY DEAR...
BUT DON'T WORRY!
HE'LL BE WORKING FOR SOME-ONE MUCH STRONGER AND MORE RELIABLE THAN YOU NOW!
......!?
HAN-ZOU!
I'VE HEARD ENOUGH OF THIS!
GET OVER HERE!

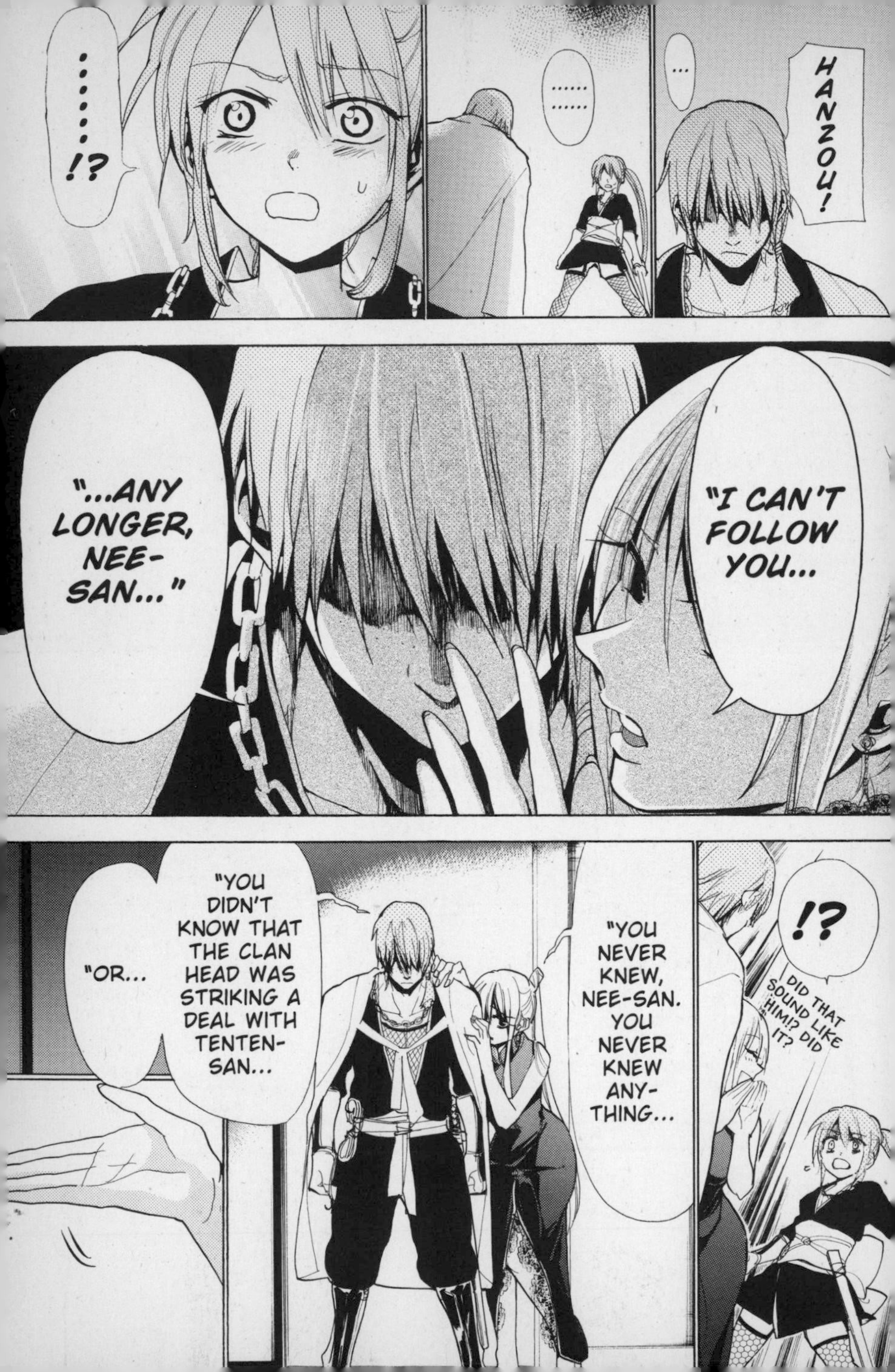
HANZOU!
...
......
......
......!?
"I CAN'T FOLLOW YOU...
"...ANY LONGER, NEE-SAN..."
!?
DID THAT SOUND LIKE HIM!? DID IT?
"YOU NEVER KNEW, NEE-SAN. YOU NEVER KNEW ANYTHING...
"YOU DIDN'T KNOW THAT THE CLAN HEAD WAS STRIKING A DEAL WITH TENTEN-SAN...
"OR...

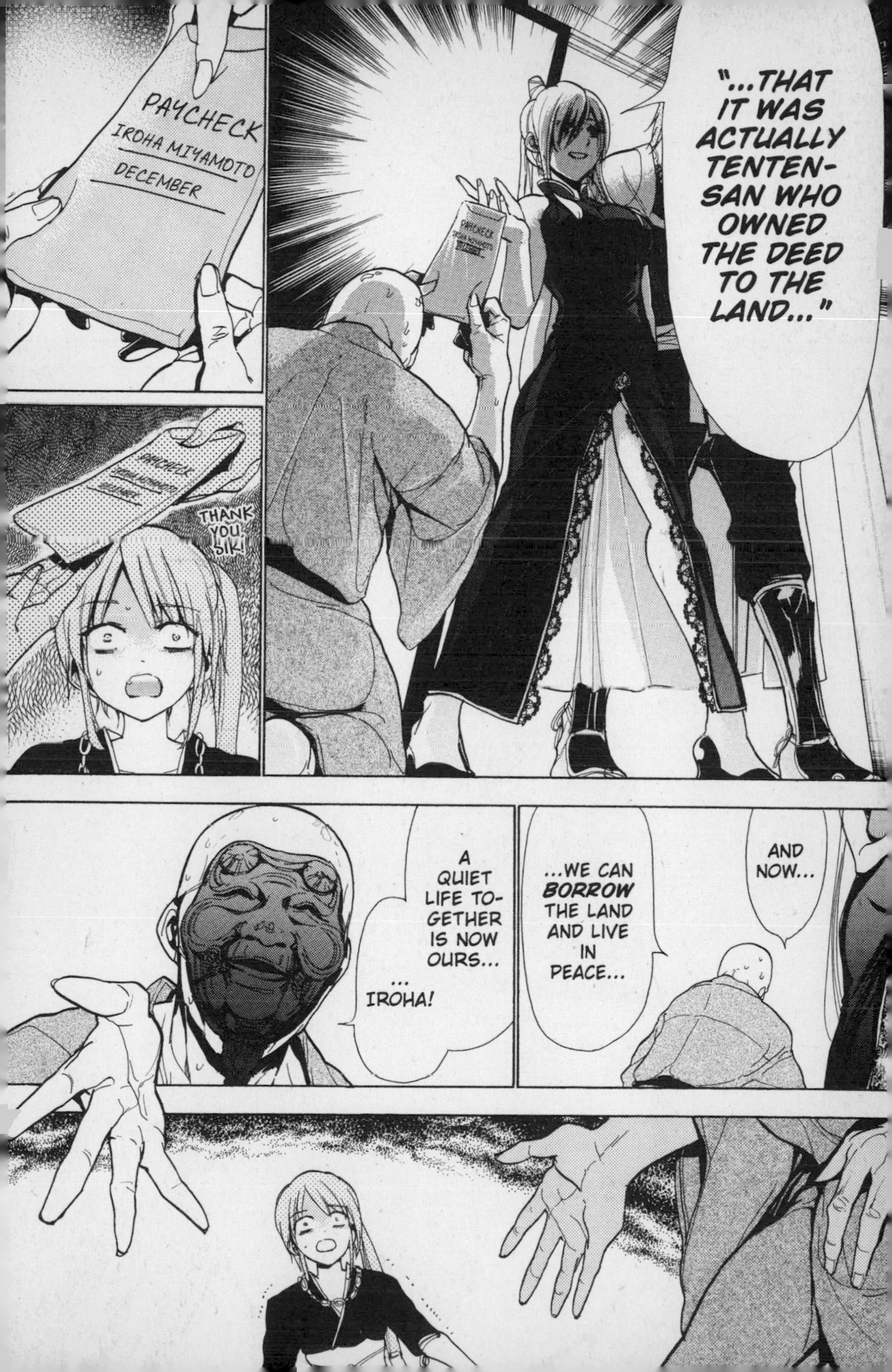
"...THAT IT WAS ACTUALLY TENTEN-SAN WHO OWNED THE DEED TO THE LAND..."
PAYCHECK
IROHA MIYAMOTO
DECEMBER
THANK YOU, SIR!
AND NOW...
...WE CAN **BORROW** THE LAND AND LIVE IN PEACE...
A QUIET LIFE TOGETHER IS NOW OURS...
...IROHA!

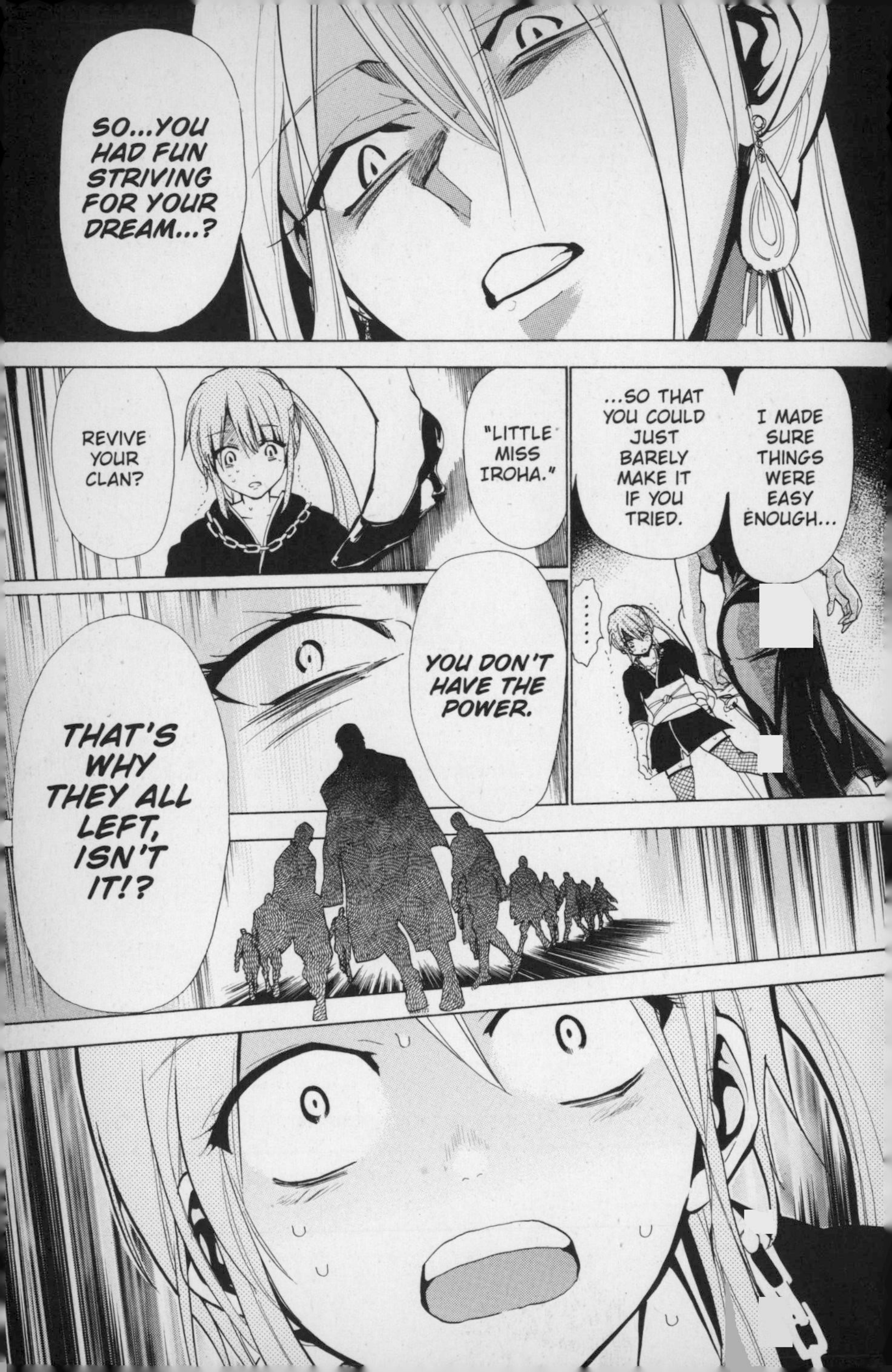
SO...YOU HAD FUN STRIVING FOR YOUR DREAM...?
I MADE SURE THINGS WERE EASY ENOUGH...
...SO THAT YOU COULD JUST BARELY MAKE IT IF YOU TRIED.
......
"LITTLE MISS IROHA."
REVIVE YOUR CLAN?
YOU DON'T HAVE THE POWER.
THAT'S WHY THEY ALL LEFT, ISN'T IT!?

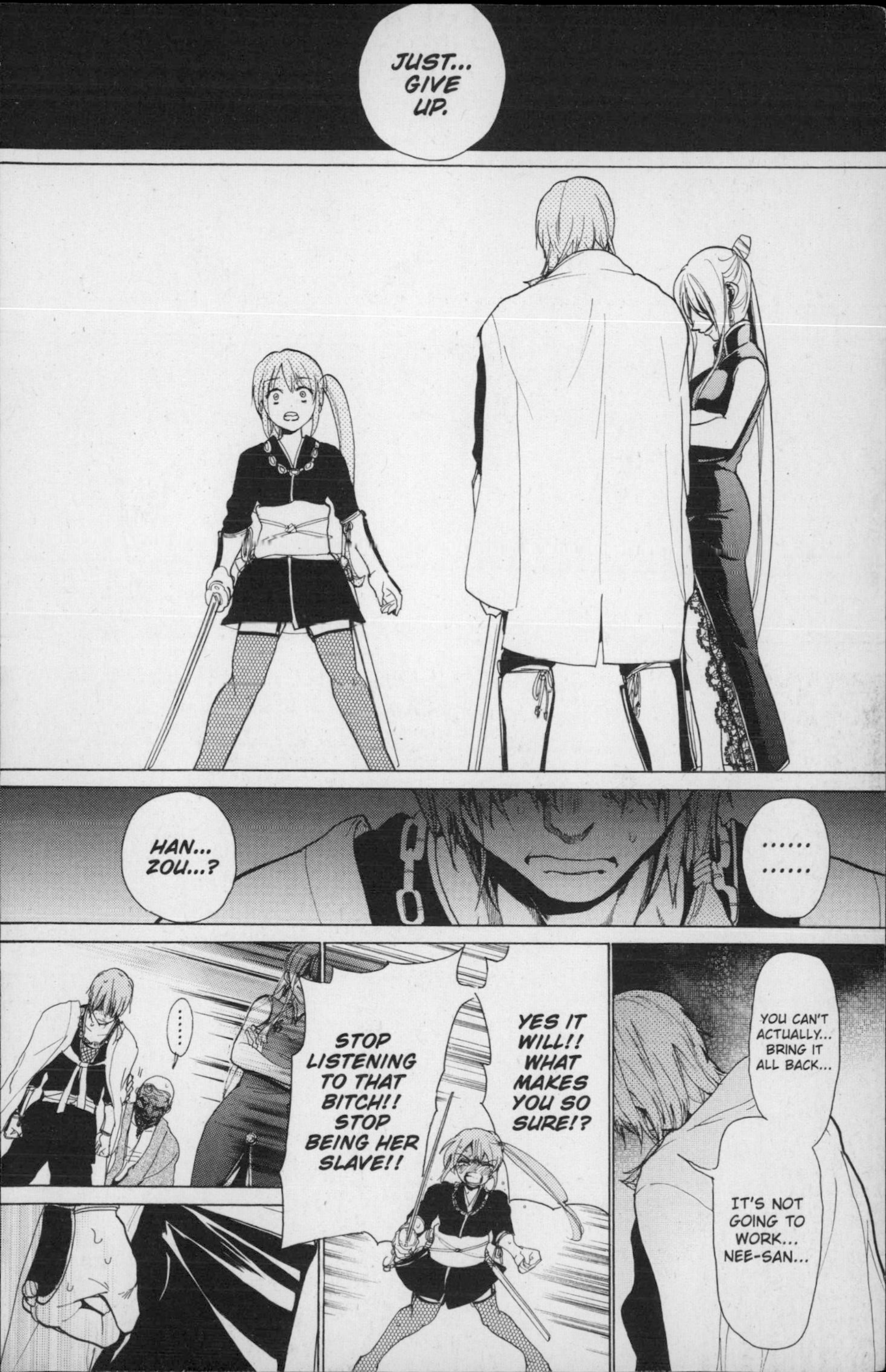
JUST... GIVE UP.
......
......
HAN... ZOU...?
YOU CAN'T ACTUALLY... BRING IT ALL BACK...
IT'S NOT GOING TO WORK... NEE-SAN...
YES IT WILL!! WHAT MAKES YOU SO SURE!?
STOP LISTENING TO THAT BITCH!! STOP BEING HER SLAVE!!
......

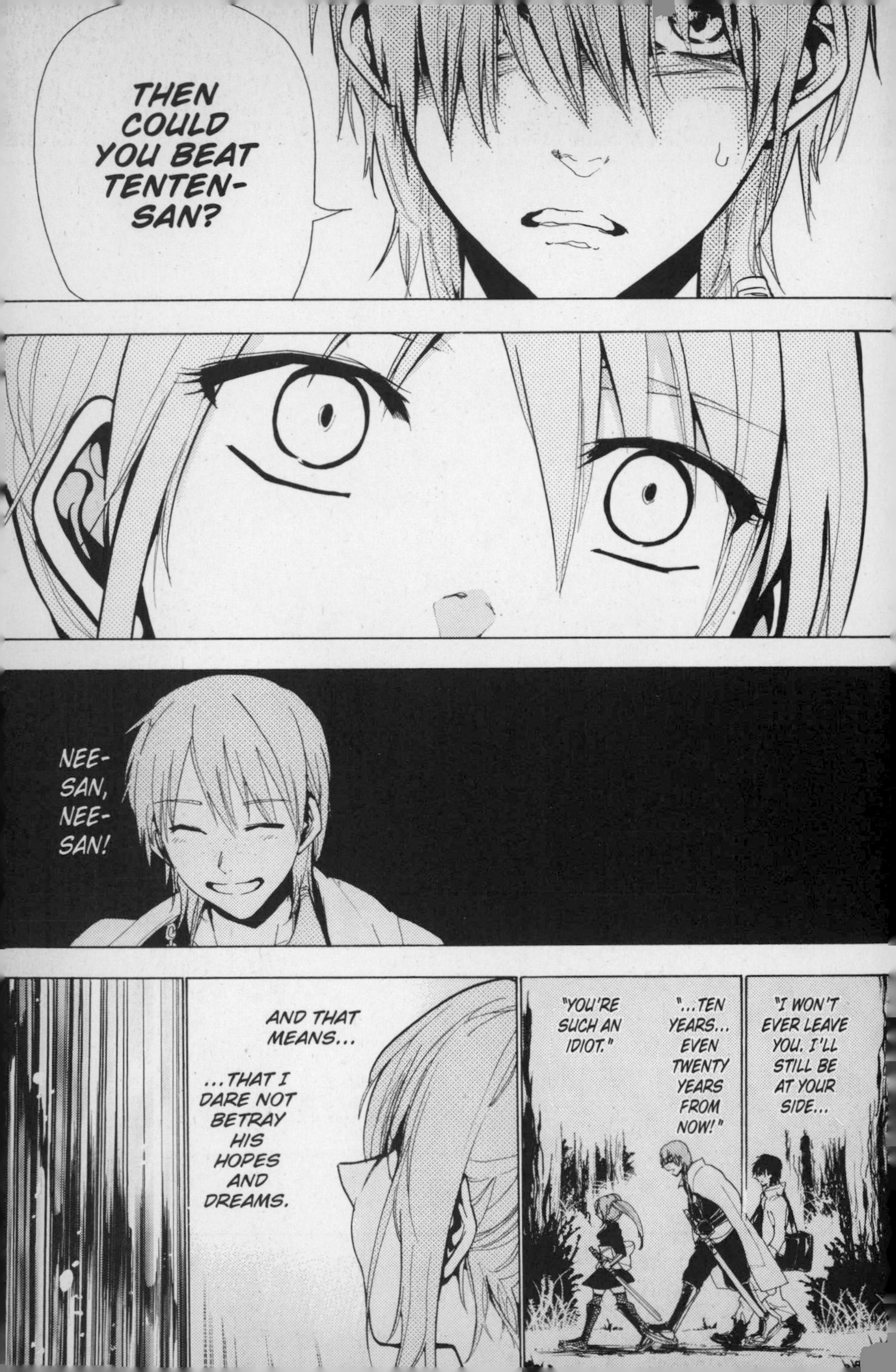
THEN COULD YOU BEAT TENTEN-SAN?
NEE-SAN, NEE-SAN!
"I WON'T EVER LEAVE YOU. I'LL STILL BE AT YOUR SIDE...
"...TEN YEARS... EVEN TWENTY YEARS FROM NOW!"
"YOU'RE SUCH AN IDIOT."
AND THAT MEANS...
...THAT I DARE NOT BETRAY HIS HOPES AND DREAMS.

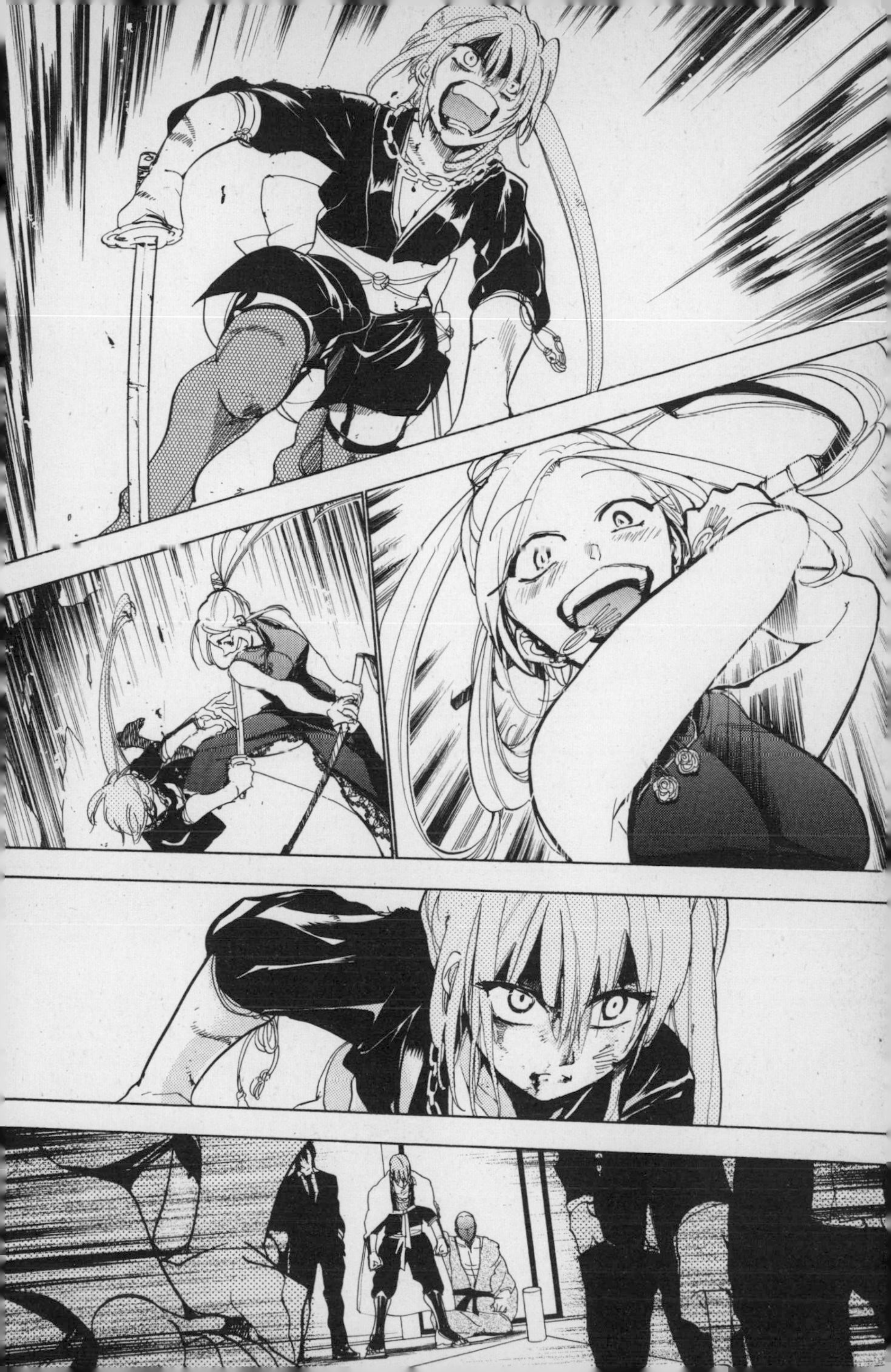

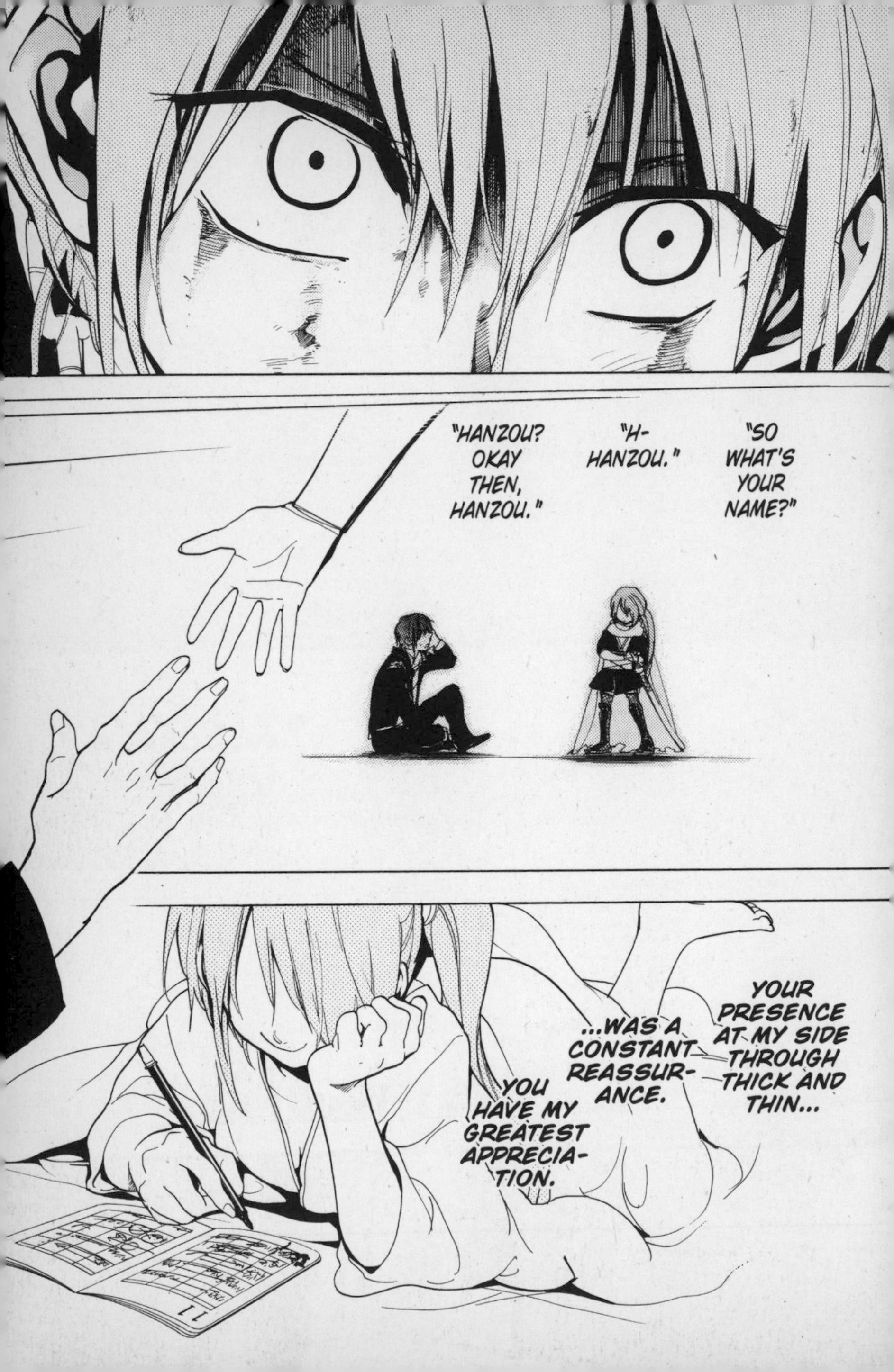
"SO WHAT'S YOUR NAME?"
"H-HANZOU."
"HANZOU? OKAY THEN, HANZOU."
YOUR PRESENCE AT MY SIDE THROUGH THICK AND THIN...
...WAS A CONSTANT REASSURANCE.
YOU HAVE MY GREATEST APPRECIATION.

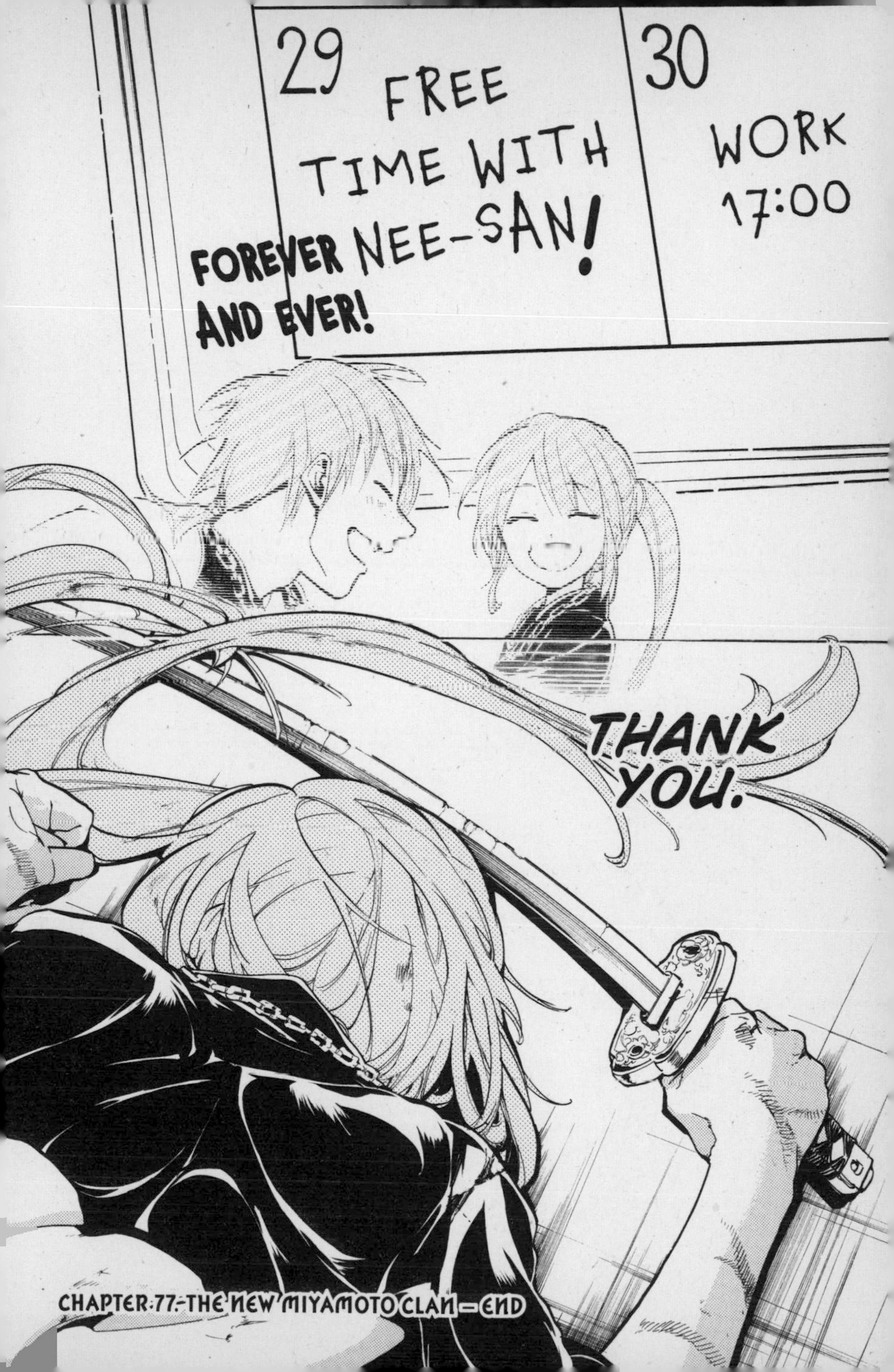
29
FREE TIME WITH NEE-SAN!
30
WORK 17:00
FOREVER AND EVER!
THANK YOU.
CHAPTER 77: THE NEW MIYAMOTO CLAN - END

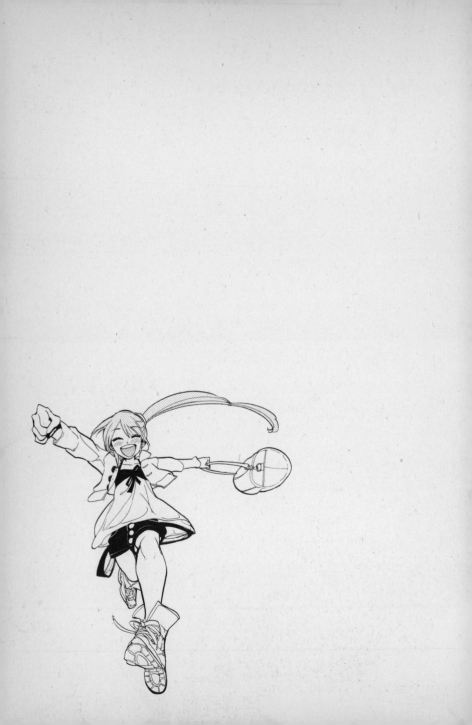

SUMOMOMO, MOMOMO

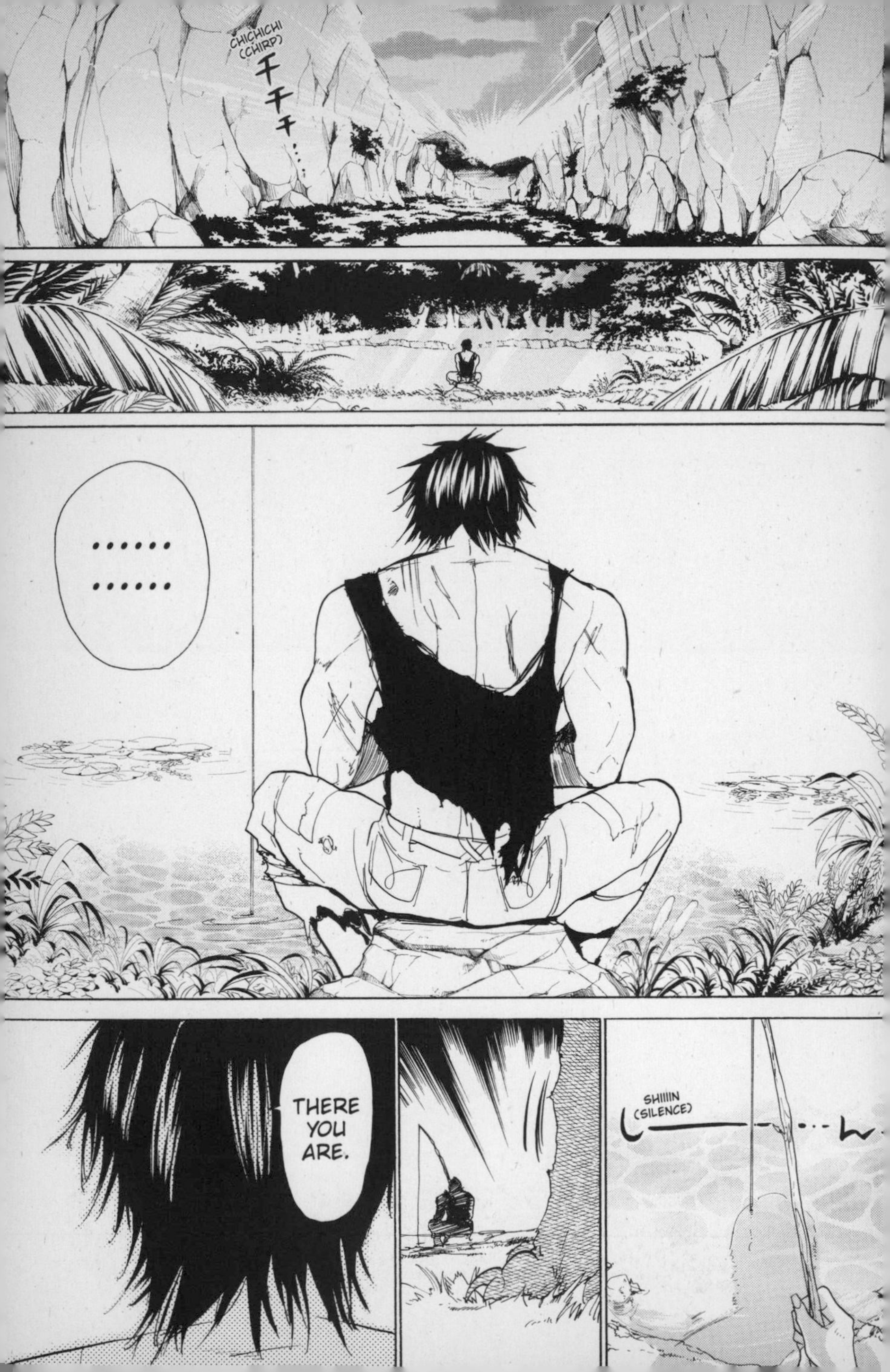
CHICHICHI (CHIRP)
チチチ…
……
……
SHIIIIN (SILENCE)
THERE YOU ARE.

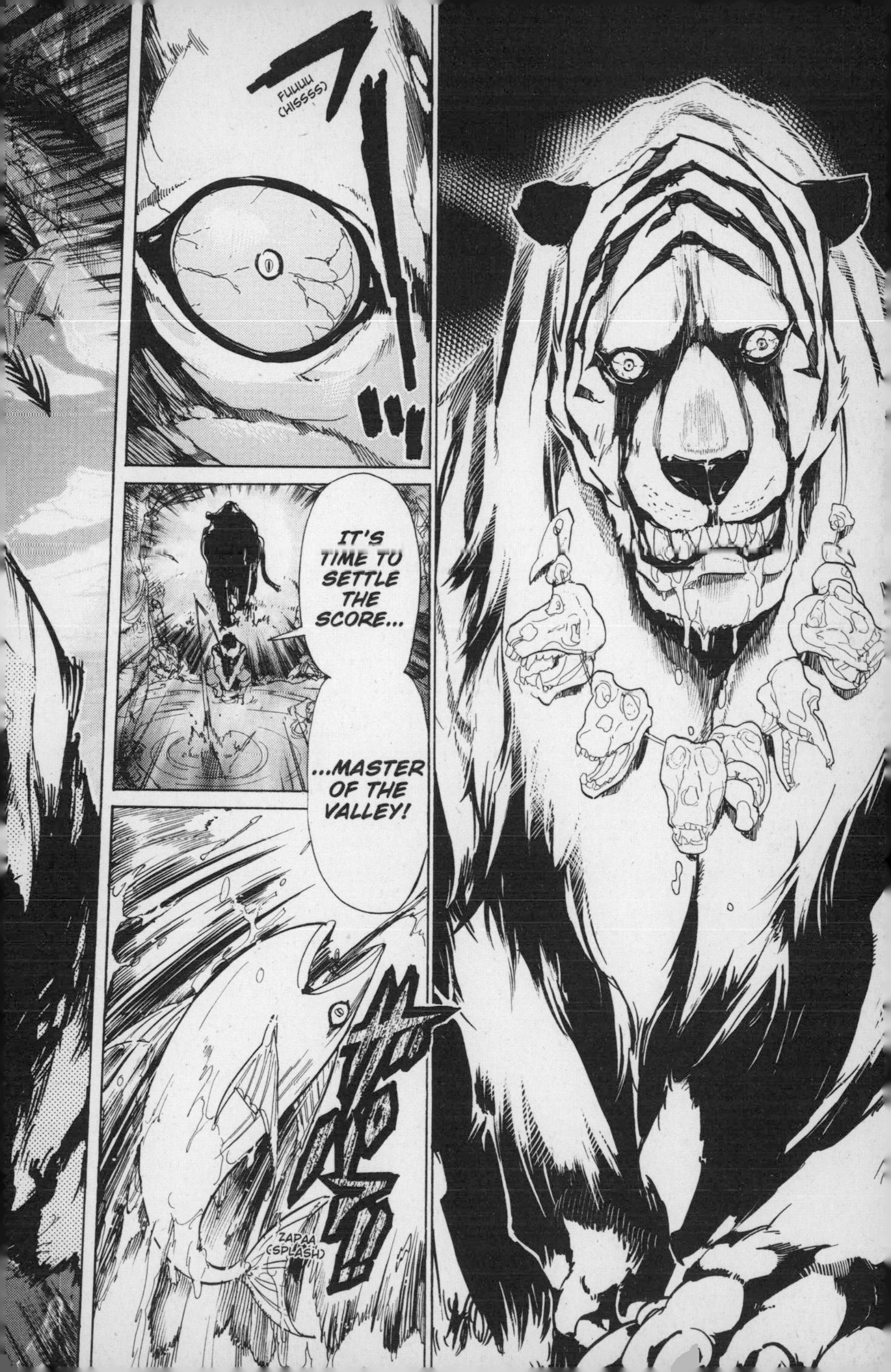
FUUUUU (HISSSS)
IT'S TIME TO SETTLE THE SCORE...
...MASTER OF THE VALLEY!
ZAPAA (SPLASH)

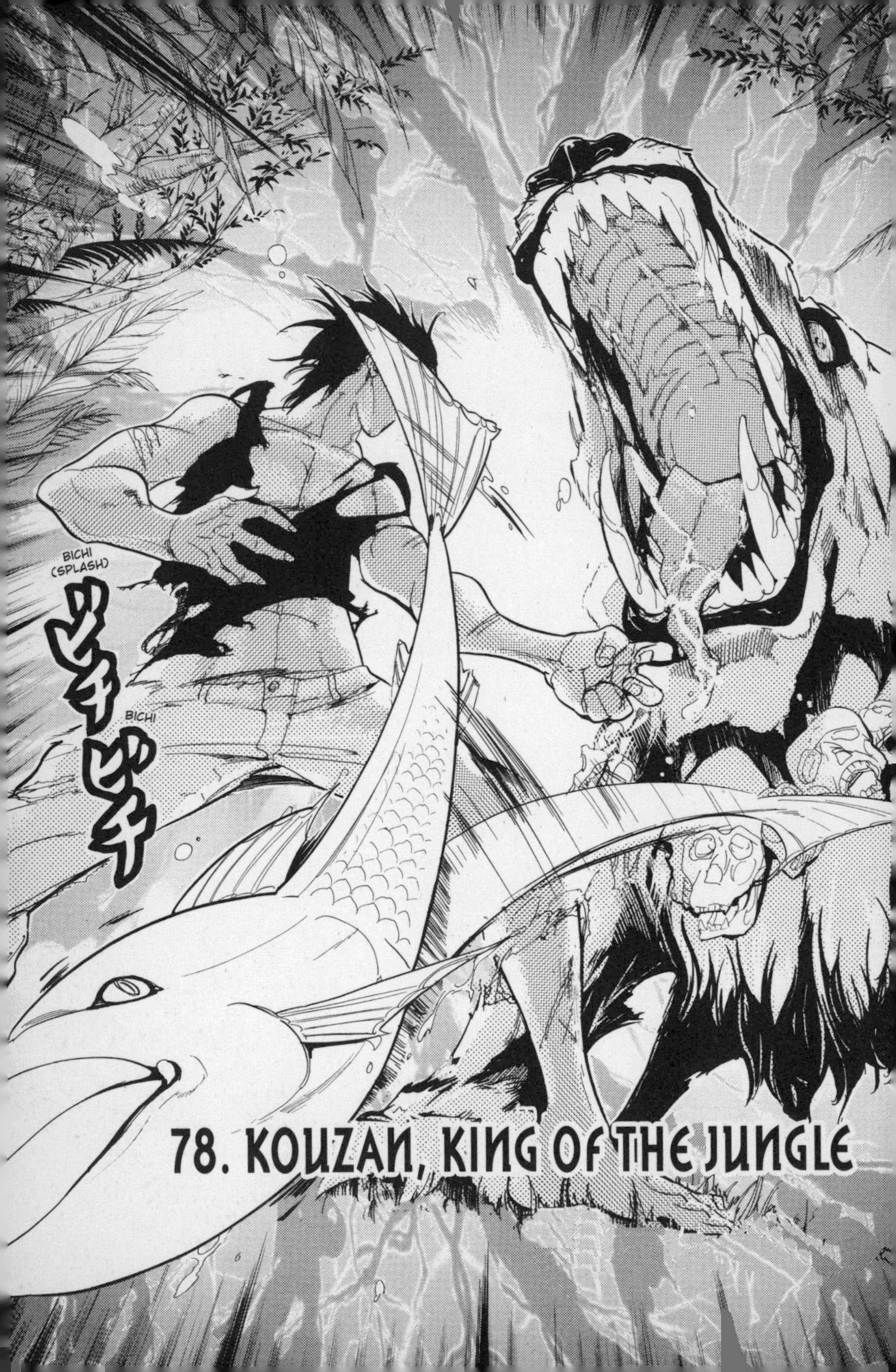
BICHI (SPLASH)
ビチビチ
BICHI
78. KOUZAN, KING OF THE JUNGLE

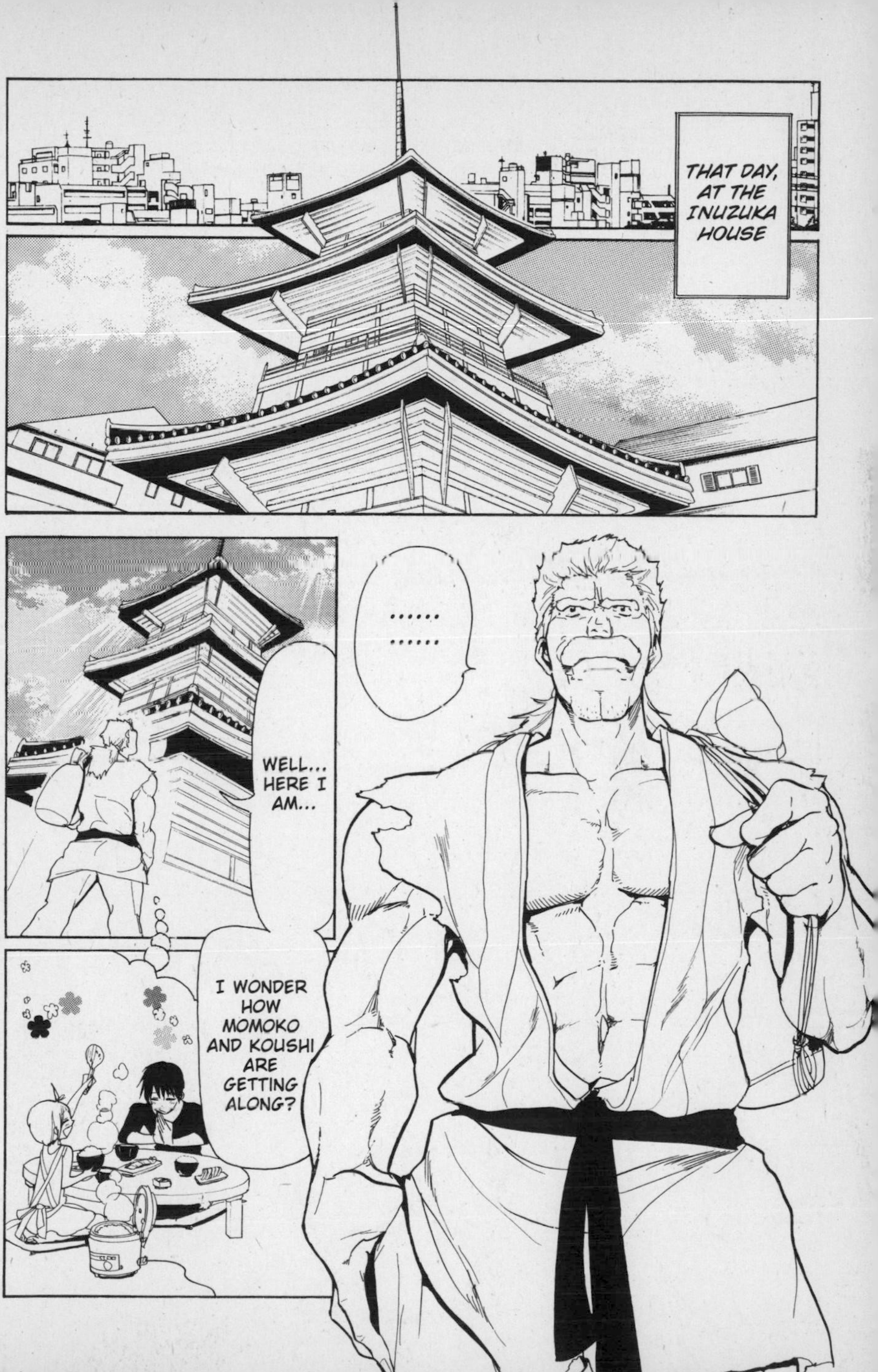
THAT DAY, AT THE INUZUKA HOUSE
....
WELL... HERE I AM...
I WONDER HOW MOMOKO AND KOUSHI ARE GETTING ALONG?

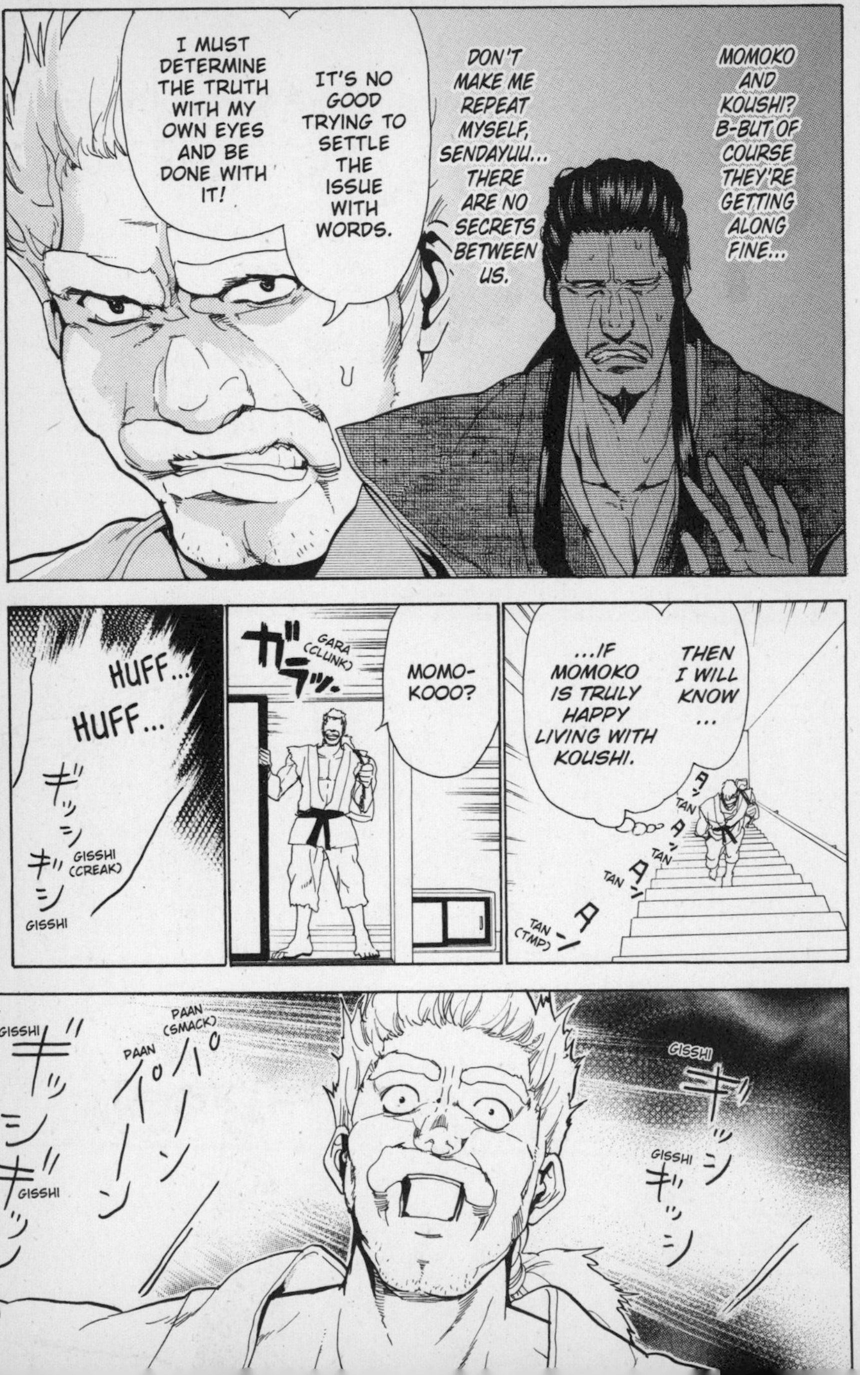
MOMOKO AND KOUSHI? B-BUT OF COURSE THEY'RE GETTING ALONG FINE...
DON'T MAKE ME REPEAT MYSELF, SENDAYUU... THERE ARE NO SECRETS BETWEEN US.
IT'S NO GOOD TRYING TO SETTLE THE ISSUE WITH WORDS.
I MUST DETERMINE THE TRUTH WITH MY OWN EYES AND BE DONE WITH IT!
THEN I WILL KNOW ...
...IF MOMOKO IS TRULY HAPPY LIVING WITH KOUSHI.
TAN
TAN
TAN
TAN (TMP)
MOMO-KOOO?
GARA (CLUNK)
HUFF...
HUFF...
GISSHI (CREAK)
GISSHI
GISSHI
GISSHI
PAAN (SMACK)
PAAN
GISSHI
GISSHI

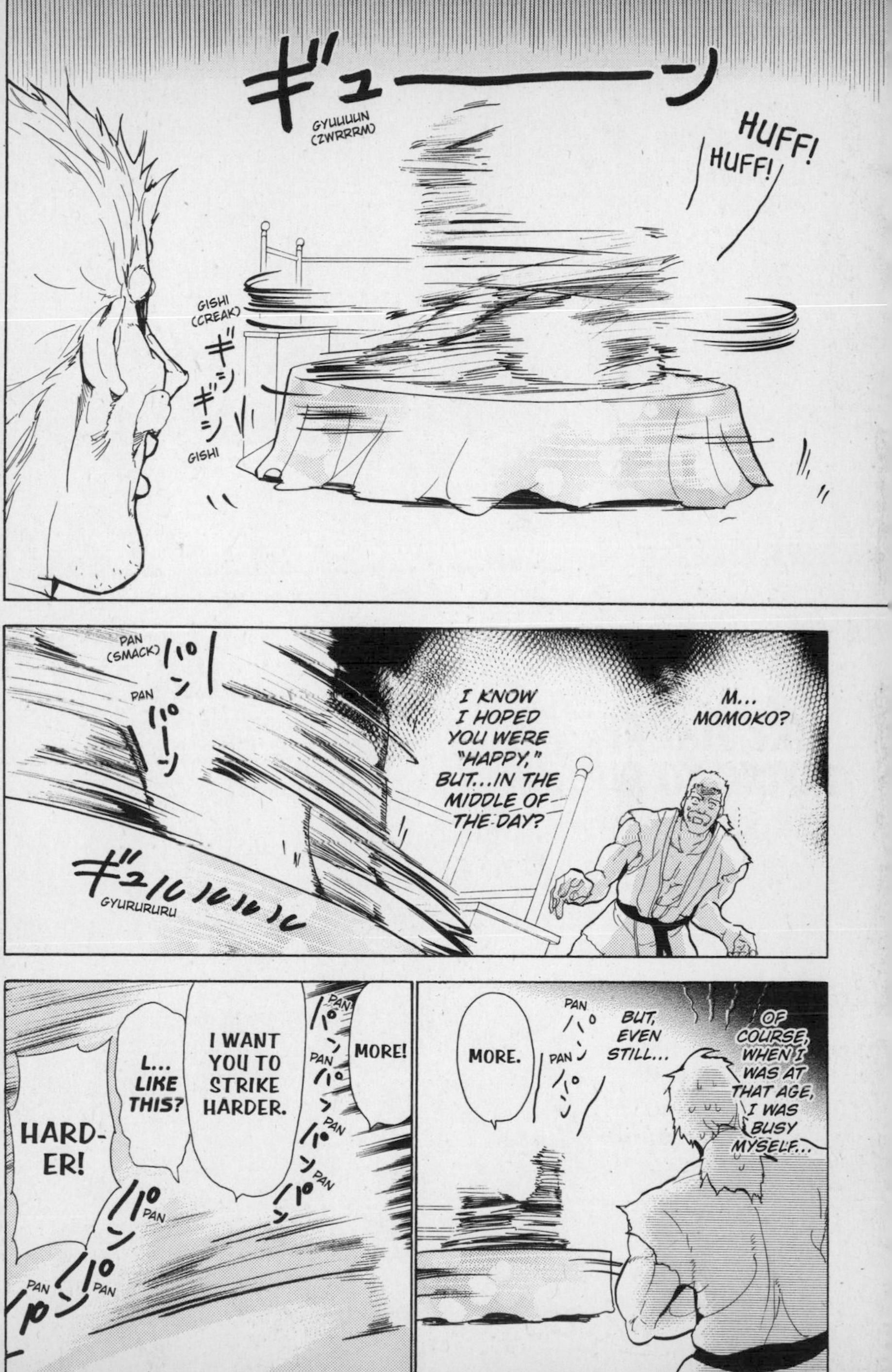
ギューーーン
GYUUUUN (ZWRRRM)
HUFF! HUFF!
GISHI (CREAK)
ギシギシ
GISHI
M... MOMOKO?
I KNOW I HOPED YOU WERE "HAPPY," BUT...IN THE MIDDLE OF THE DAY?
PAN (SMACK)
PAN
GYURURURU
OF COURSE, WHEN I WAS AT THAT AGE, I WAS BUSY MYSELF...
BUT, EVEN STILL...
PAN
PAN
MORE.
MORE!
PAN
PAN
PAN
PAN
I WANT YOU TO STRIKE HARDER.
L... LIKE THIS?
HARDER!
PAN
PAN
PAN

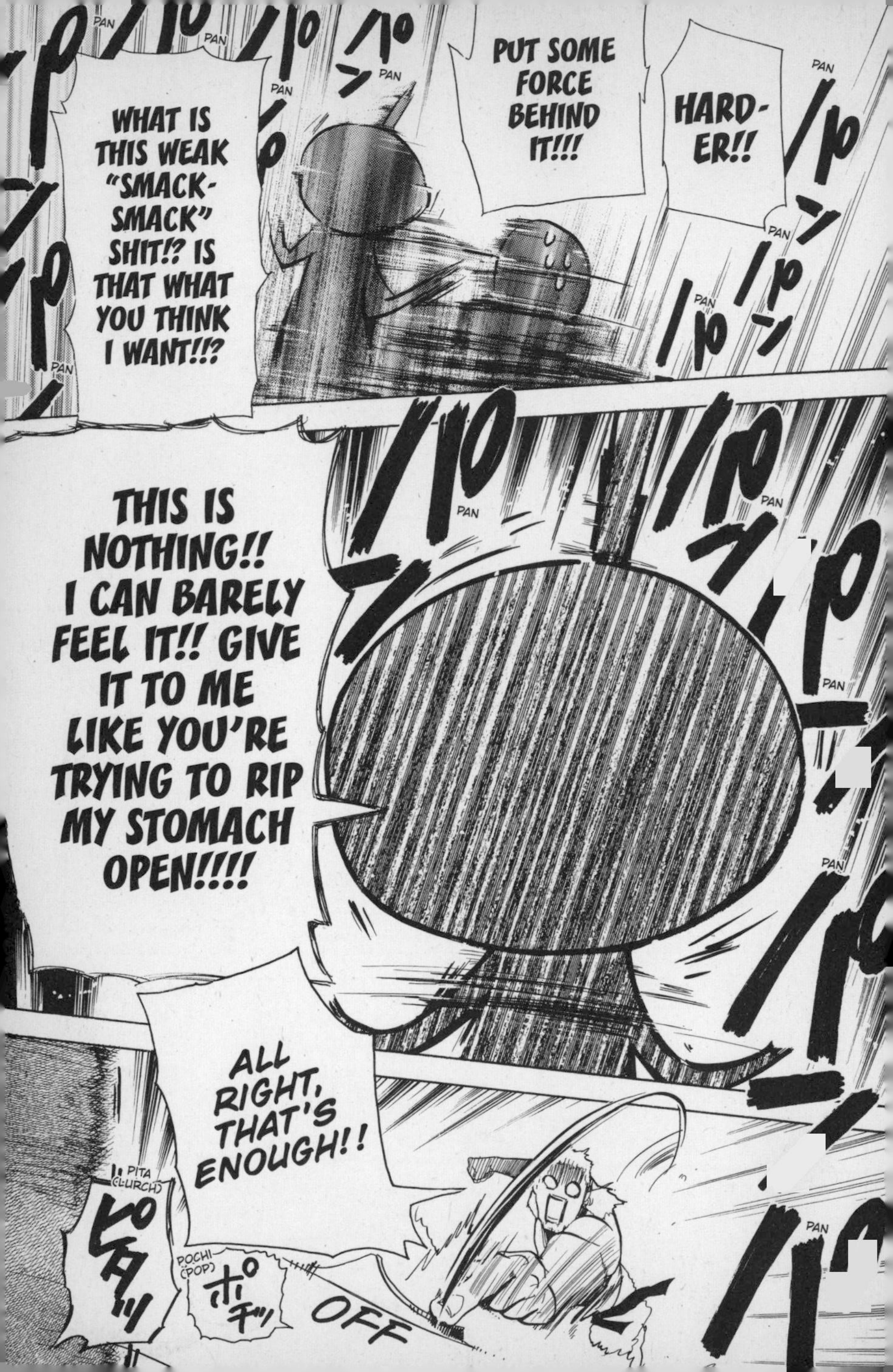
PAN
HARD-ER!!
PUT SOME FORCE BEHIND IT!!!
PAN
WHAT IS THIS WEAK "SMACK-SMACK" SHIT!? IS THAT WHAT YOU THINK I WANT!!?
PAN
THIS IS NOTHING!! I CAN BARELY FEEL IT!! GIVE IT TO ME LIKE YOU'RE TRYING TO RIP MY STOMACH OPEN!!!!
PAN
ALL RIGHT, THAT'S ENOUGH!!
POCHI (POP)
OFF
PITA (CLURCH)

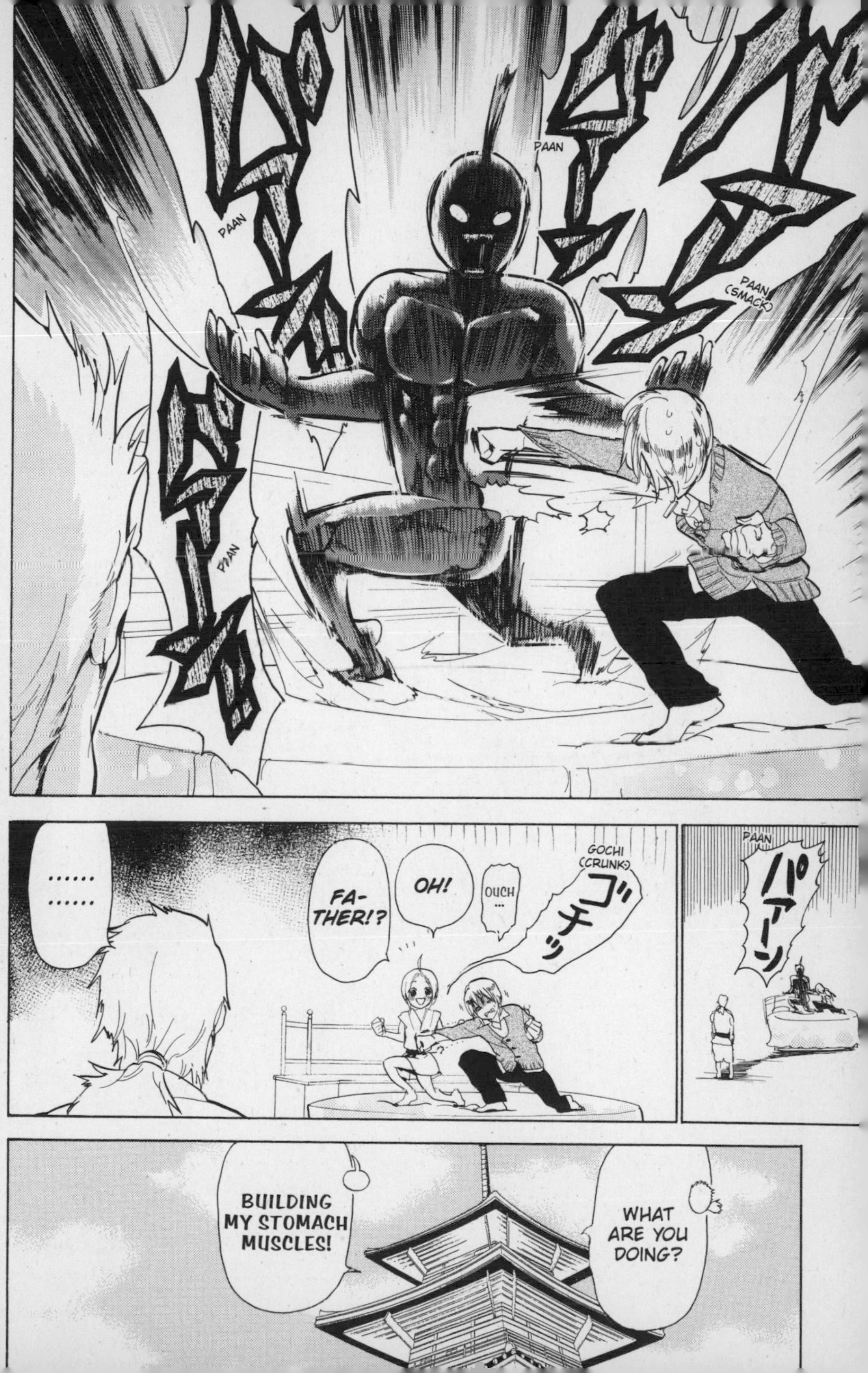
PAAN (SMACK)
PAAN
PAAN
PAAN
PAAN
パアーン
GOCHI (CRUNK)
ゴチッ
OUCH ...
OH!
FA-THER!?
......
......
WHAT ARE YOU DOING?
BUILDING MY STOMACH MUSCLES!

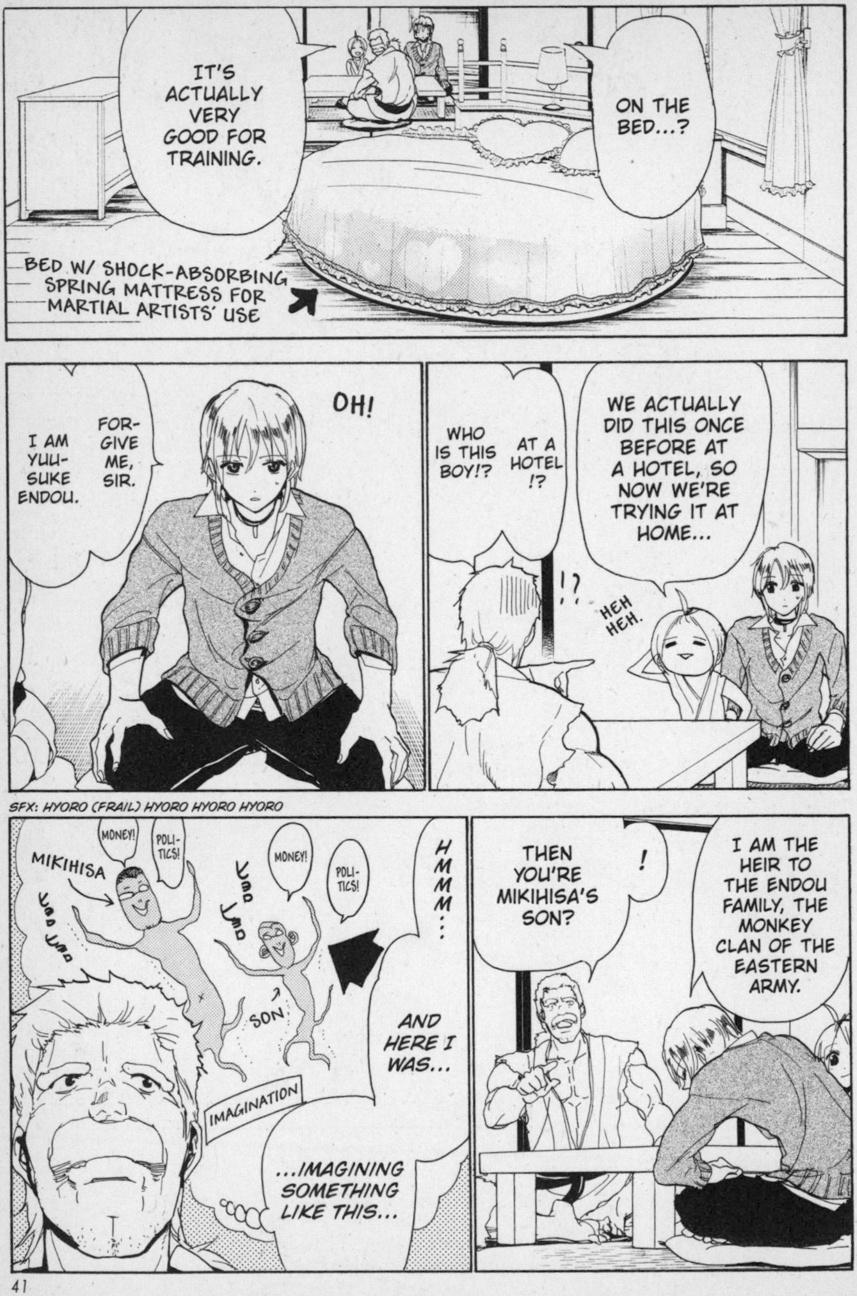

ON THE BED...?
IT'S ACTUALLY VERY GOOD FOR TRAINING.
BED W/ SHOCK-ABSORBING SPRING MATTRESS FOR MARTIAL ARTISTS' USE
WE ACTUALLY DID THIS ONCE BEFORE AT A HOTEL, SO NOW WE'RE TRYING IT AT HOME...
AT A HOTEL !?
WHO IS THIS BOY!?
!?
HEH HEH.
OH!
FORGIVE ME, SIR.
I AM YUUSUKE ENDOU.
SFX: HYORO (FRAIL) HYORO HYORO HYORO
I AM THE HEIR TO THE ENDOU FAMILY, THE MONKEY CLAN OF THE EASTERN ARMY.
!
THEN YOU'RE MIKIHISA'S SON?
HMMM...
AND HERE I WAS...
POLITICS!
MONEY!
POLITICS!
MONEY!
MIKIHISA
SON
IMAGINATION
...IMAGINING SOMETHING LIKE THIS...

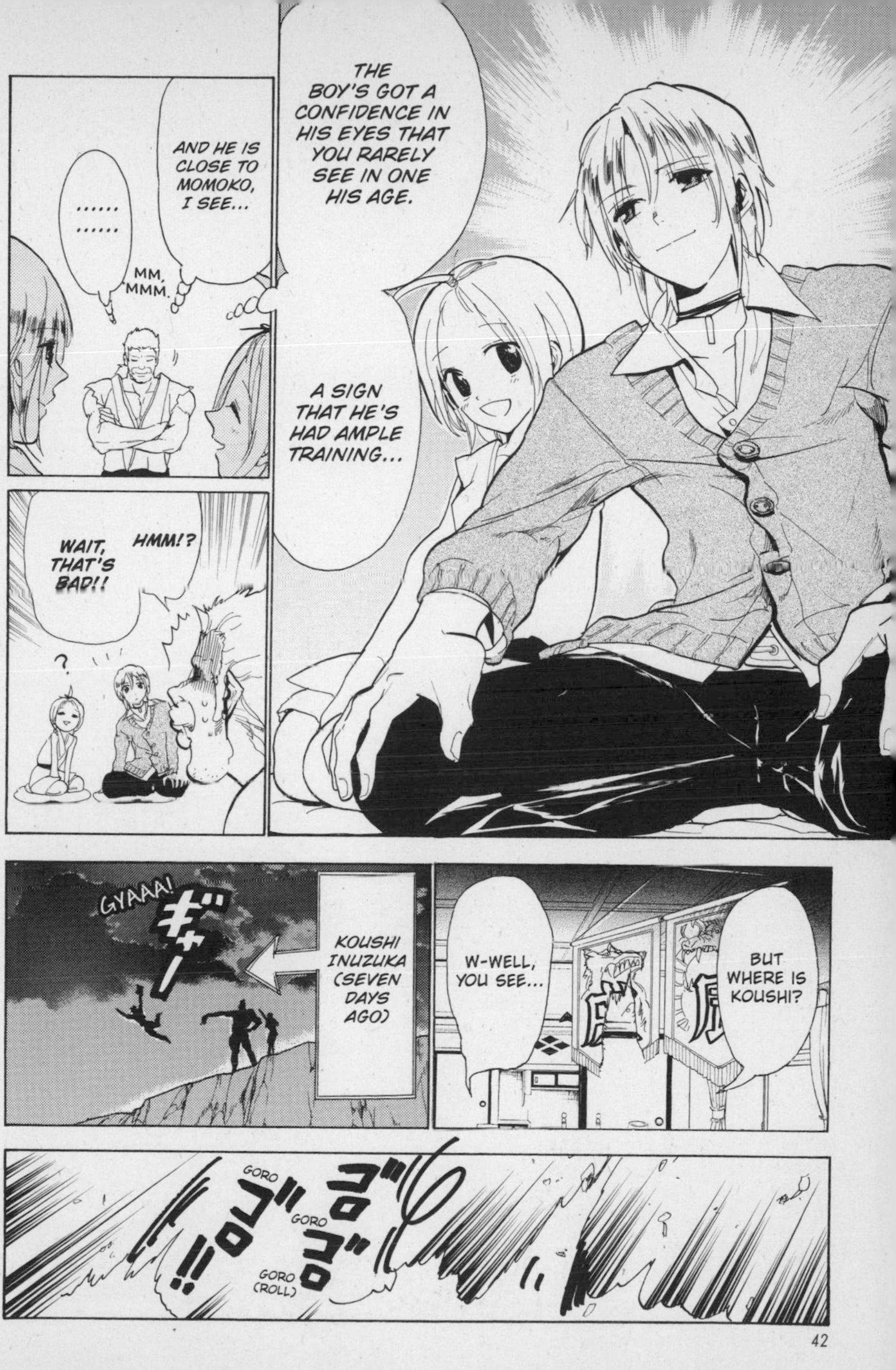
THE BOY'S GOT A CONFIDENCE IN HIS EYES THAT YOU RARELY SEE IN ONE HIS AGE.
A SIGN THAT HE'S HAD AMPLE TRAINING...
AND HE IS CLOSE TO MOMOKO, I SEE...
......
......
MM, MMM.
HMM!?
WAIT, THAT'S BAD!!
?
BUT WHERE IS KOUSHI?
W-WELL, YOU SEE...
KOUSHI INUZUKA (SEVEN DAYS AGO)
GYAAA!
ギャー
GORO
GORO
GORO (ROLL)
ゴロゴロゴロ!!

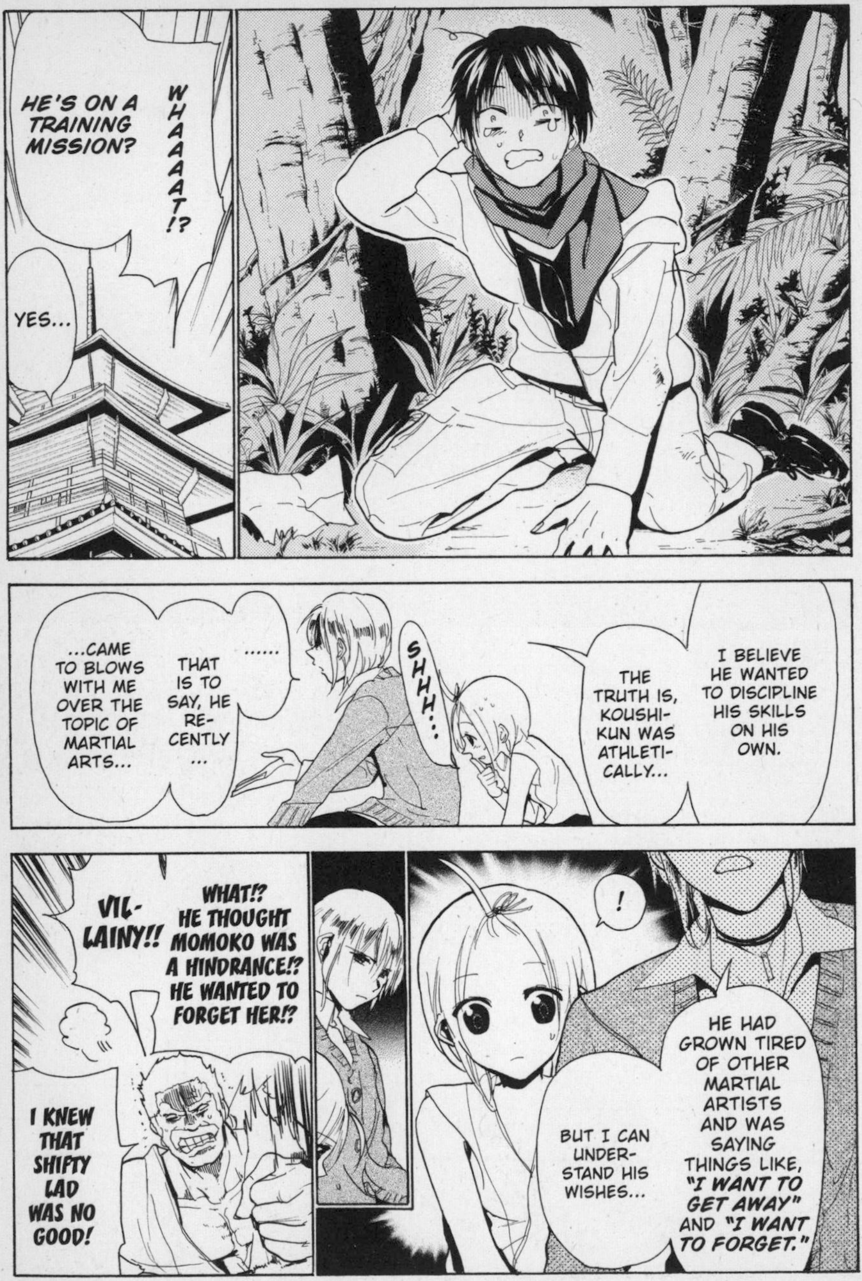
WHAAAAAT!?
HE'S ON A TRAINING MISSION?
YES...
I BELIEVE HE WANTED TO DISCIPLINE HIS SKILLS ON HIS OWN.
THE TRUTH IS, KOUSHI-KUN WAS ATHLETI-CALLY...
SHHH...
......
THAT IS TO SAY, HE RE-CENTLY ...
...CAME TO BLOWS WITH ME OVER THE TOPIC OF MARTIAL ARTS...
!
HE HAD GROWN TIRED OF OTHER MARTIAL ARTISTS AND WAS SAYING THINGS LIKE, "I WANT TO GET AWAY" AND "I WANT TO FORGET."
BUT I CAN UNDER-STAND HIS WISHES...
WHAT!? HE THOUGHT MOMOKO WAS A HINDRANCE!? HE WANTED TO FORGET HER!?
VIL-LAINY!!
I KNEW THAT SHIFTY LAD WAS NO GOOD!

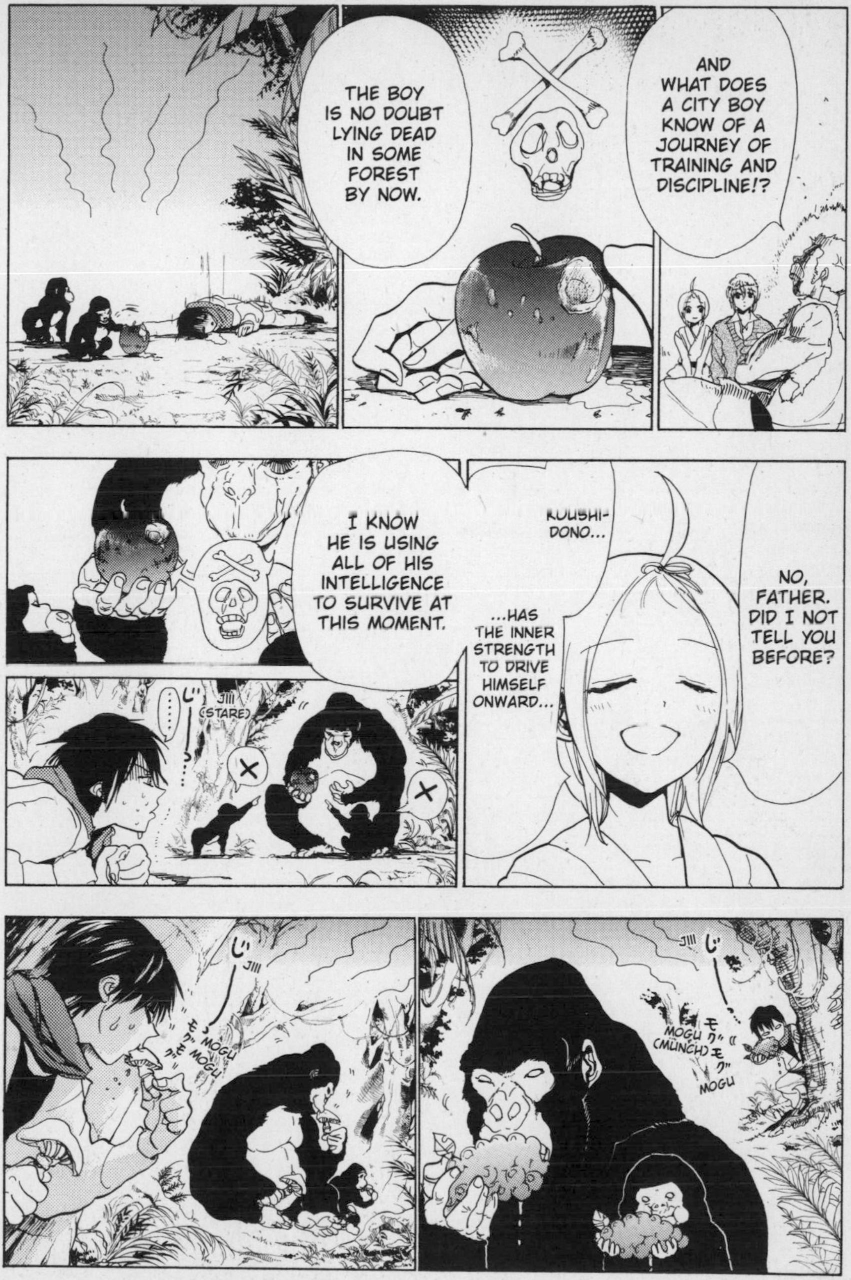
AND WHAT DOES A CITY BOY KNOW OF A JOURNEY OF TRAINING AND DISCIPLINE!?
THE BOY IS NO DOUBT LYING DEAD IN SOME FOREST BY NOW.
NO, FATHER. DID I NOT TELL YOU BEFORE?
KOUSHI-DONO...
...HAS THE INNER STRENGTH TO DRIVE HIMSELF ONWARD...
I KNOW HE IS USING ALL OF HIS INTELLIGENCE TO SURVIVE AT THIS MOMENT.
......
JIII (STARE)
JIII
MOGU (MUNCH) MOGU
JIII
MOGU MOGU

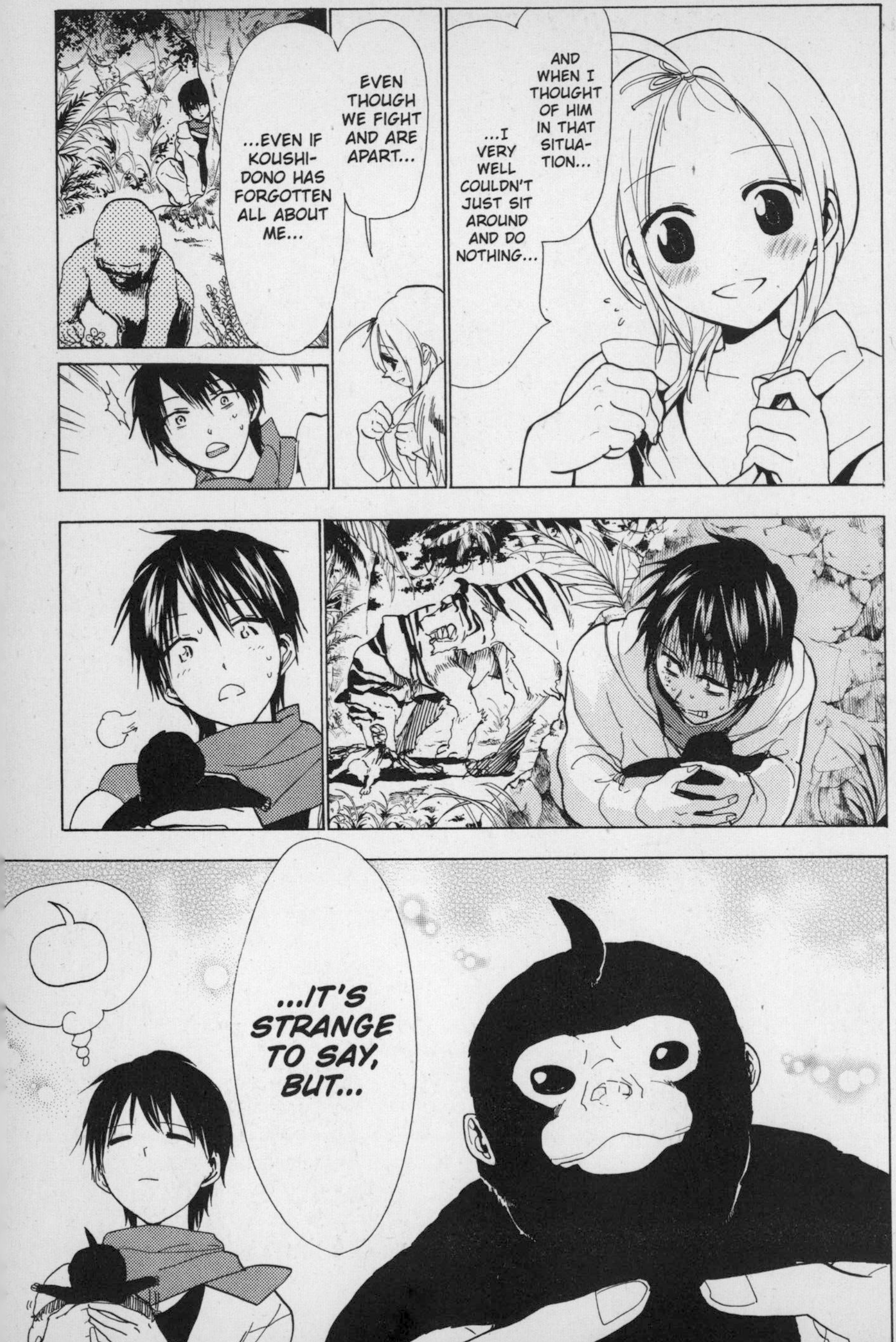
AND WHEN I THOUGHT OF HIM IN THAT SITUA-TION...
...I VERY WELL COULDN'T JUST SIT AROUND AND DO NOTHING...
EVEN THOUGH WE FIGHT AND ARE APART...
...EVEN IF KOUSHI-DONO HAS FORGOTTEN ALL ABOUT ME...
...IT'S STRANGE TO SAY, BUT...

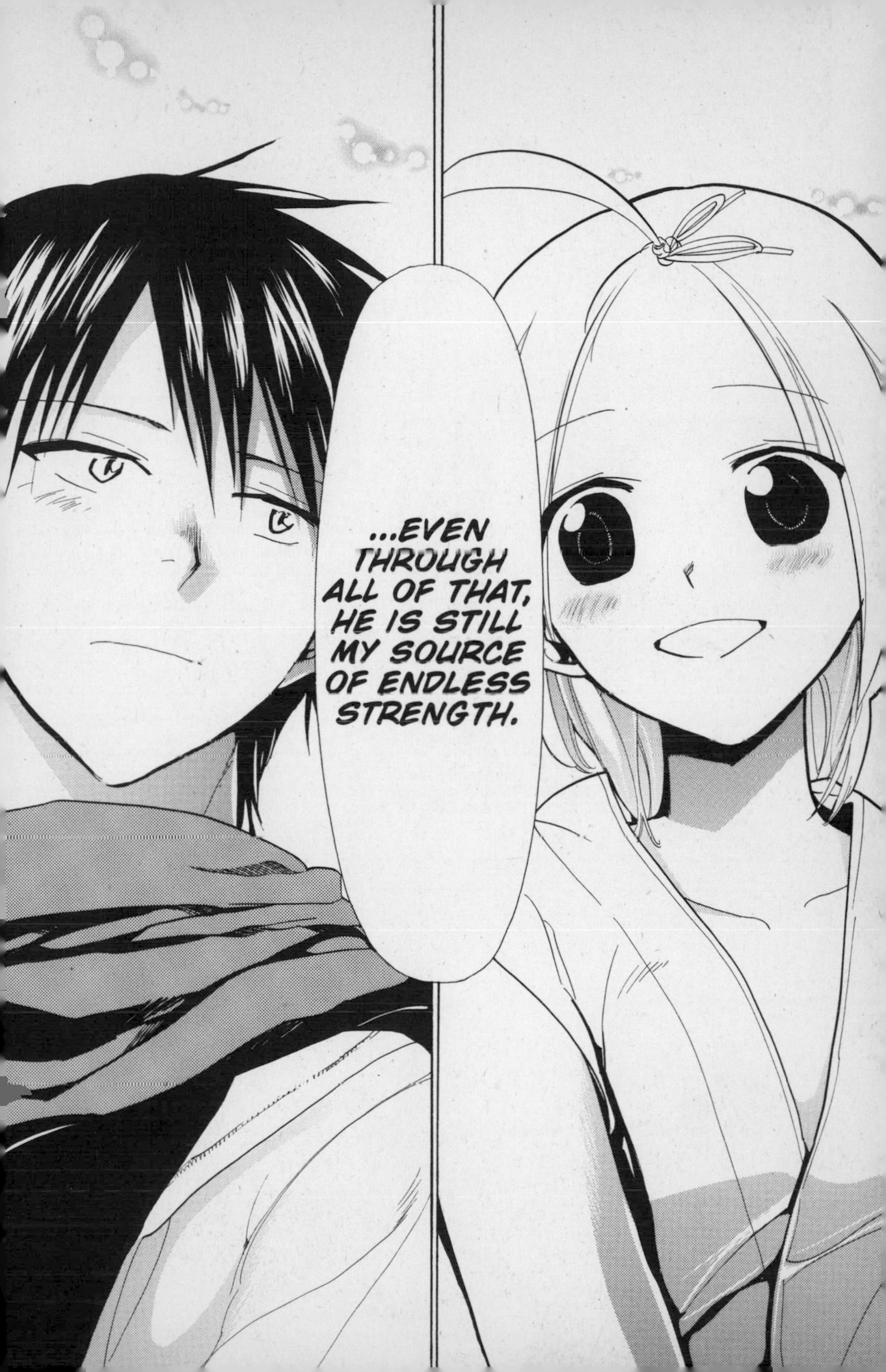
...EVEN THROUGH ALL OF THAT, HE IS STILL MY SOURCE OF ENDLESS STRENGTH.

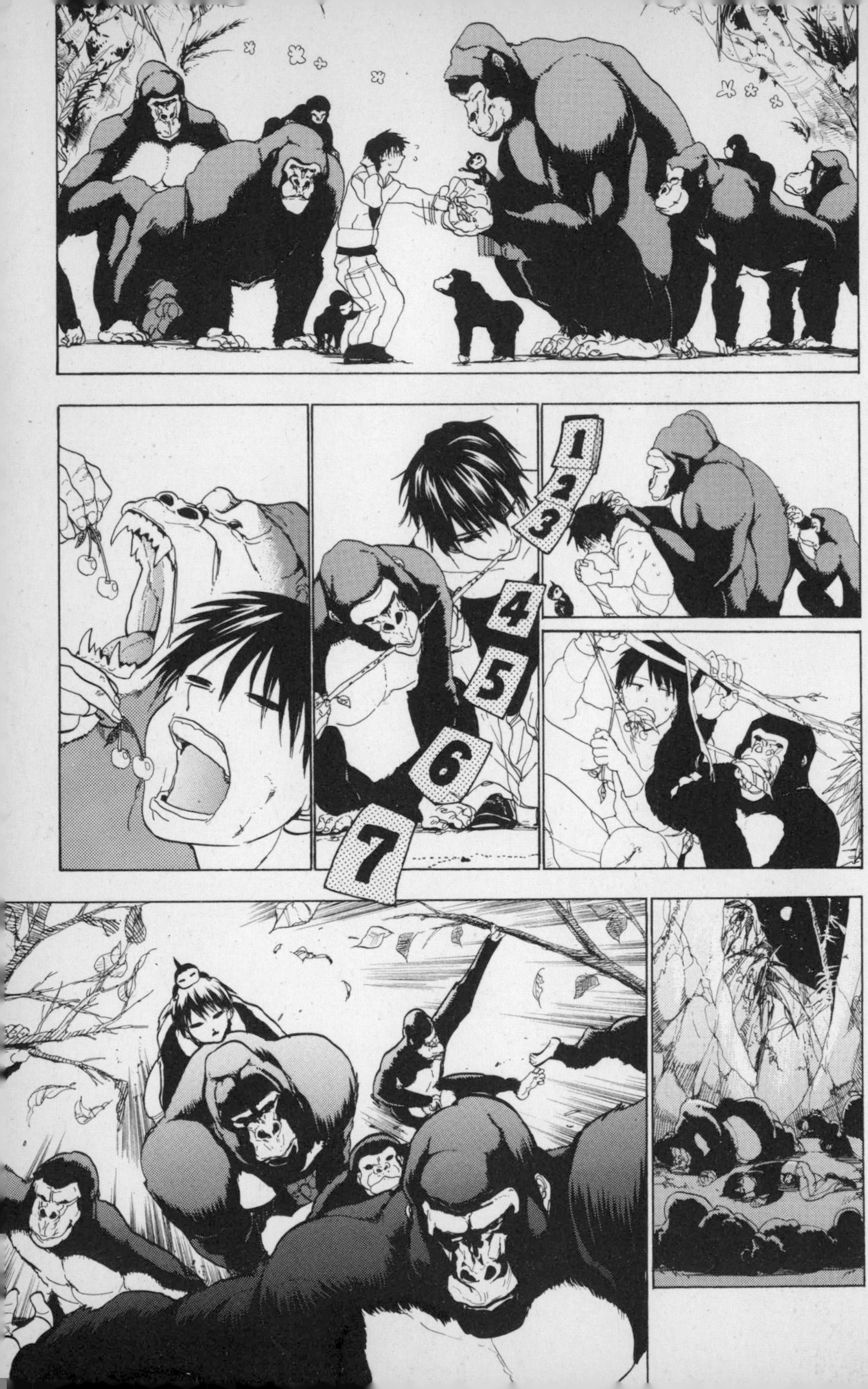
1
2
3
4
5
6
7

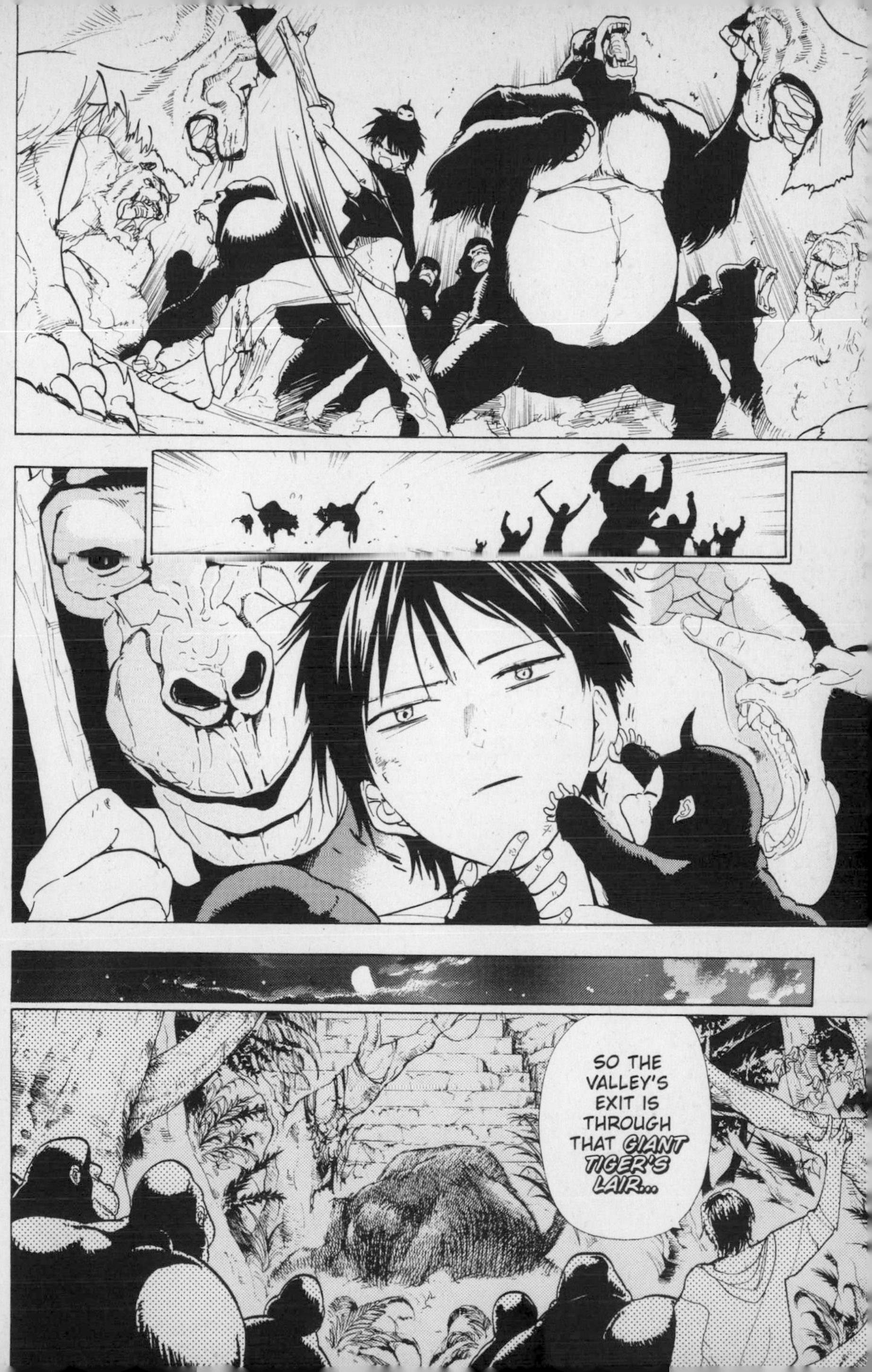
SO THE VALLEY'S EXIT IS THROUGH THAT GIANT TIGER'S LAIR...

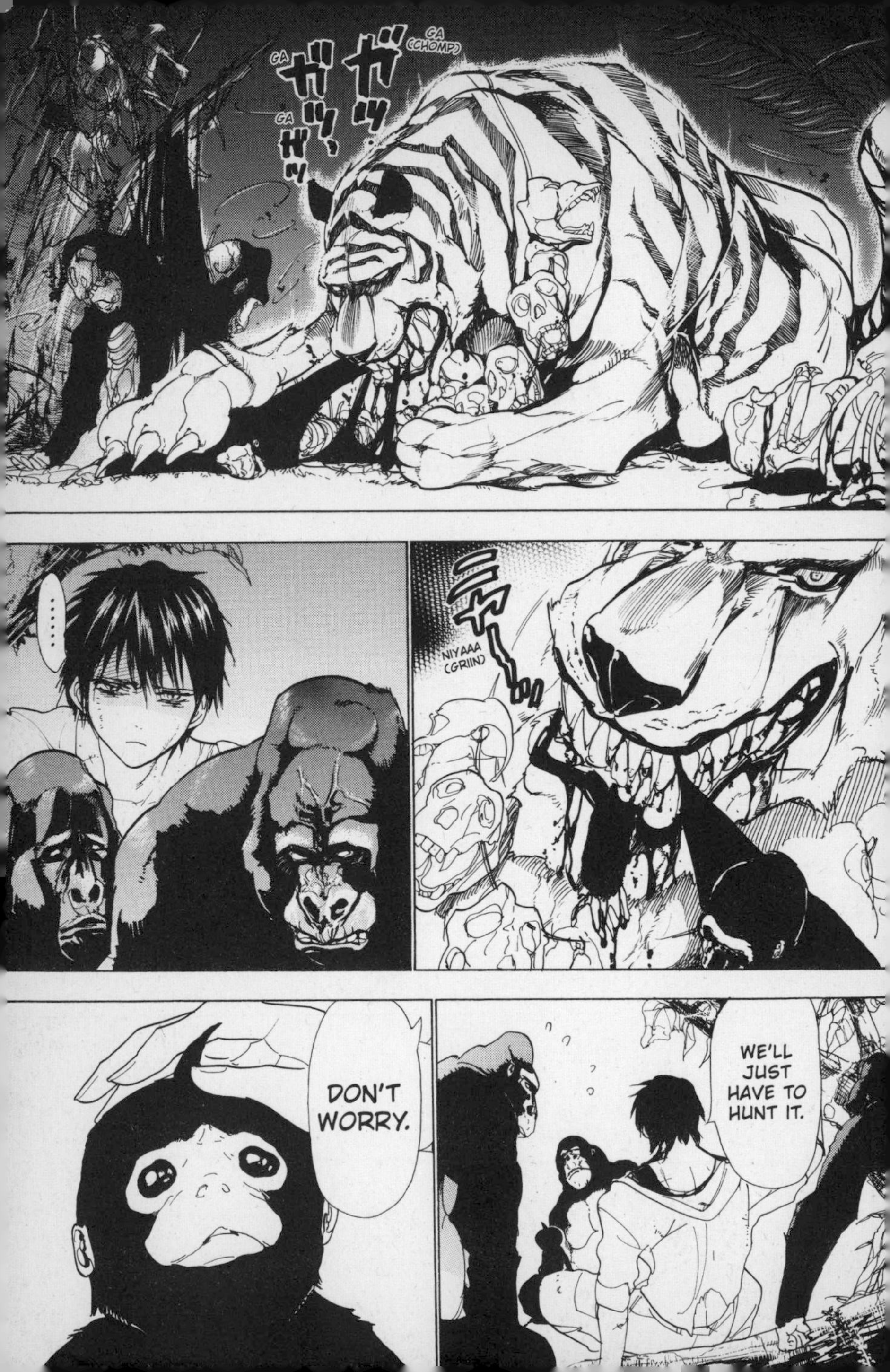
GA (CHOMP)
GA
GA
NIYAAA (GRIIN)
......
WE'LL JUST HAVE TO HUNT IT.
DON'T WORRY.

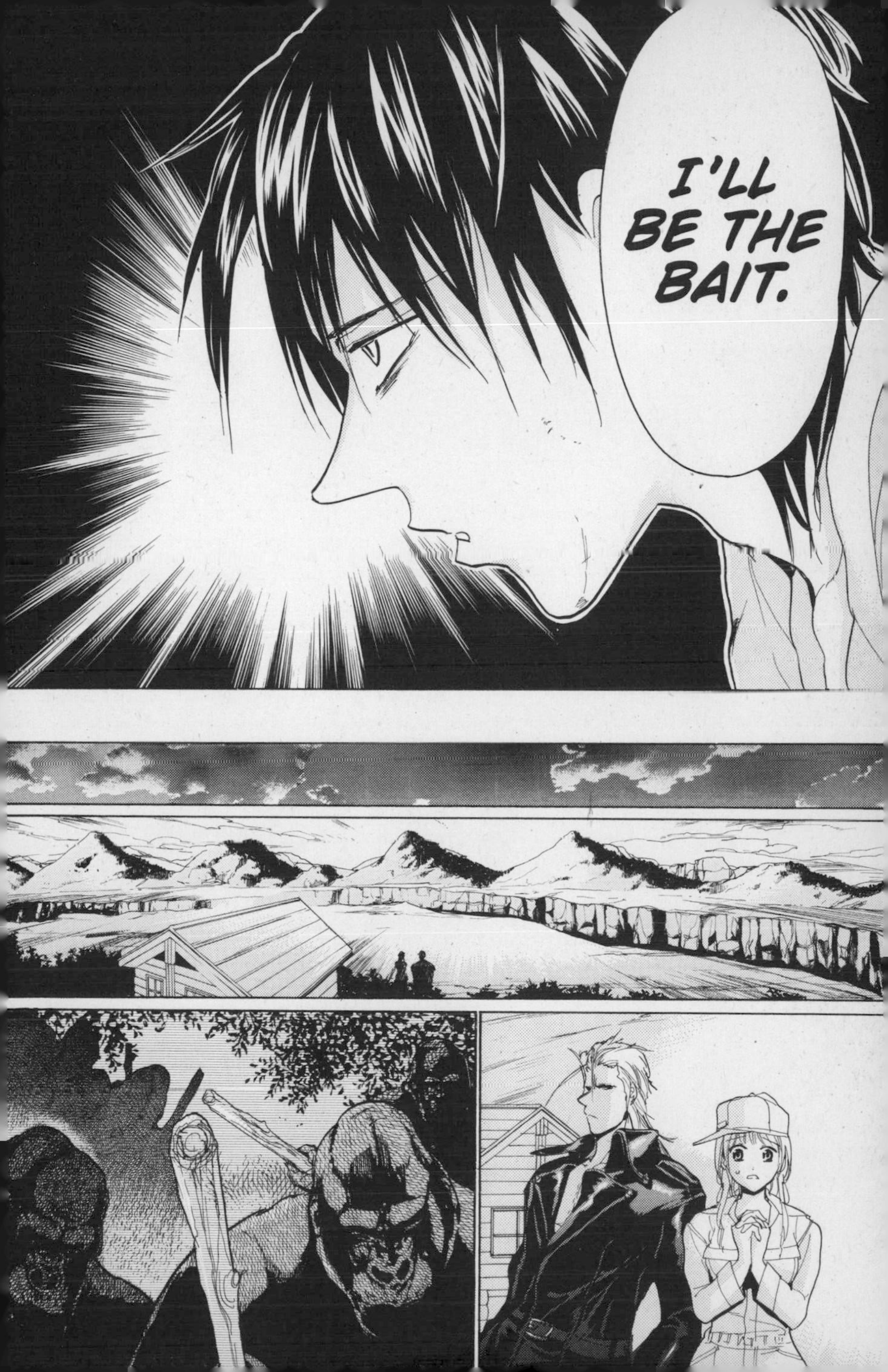
I'LL BE THE BAIT.

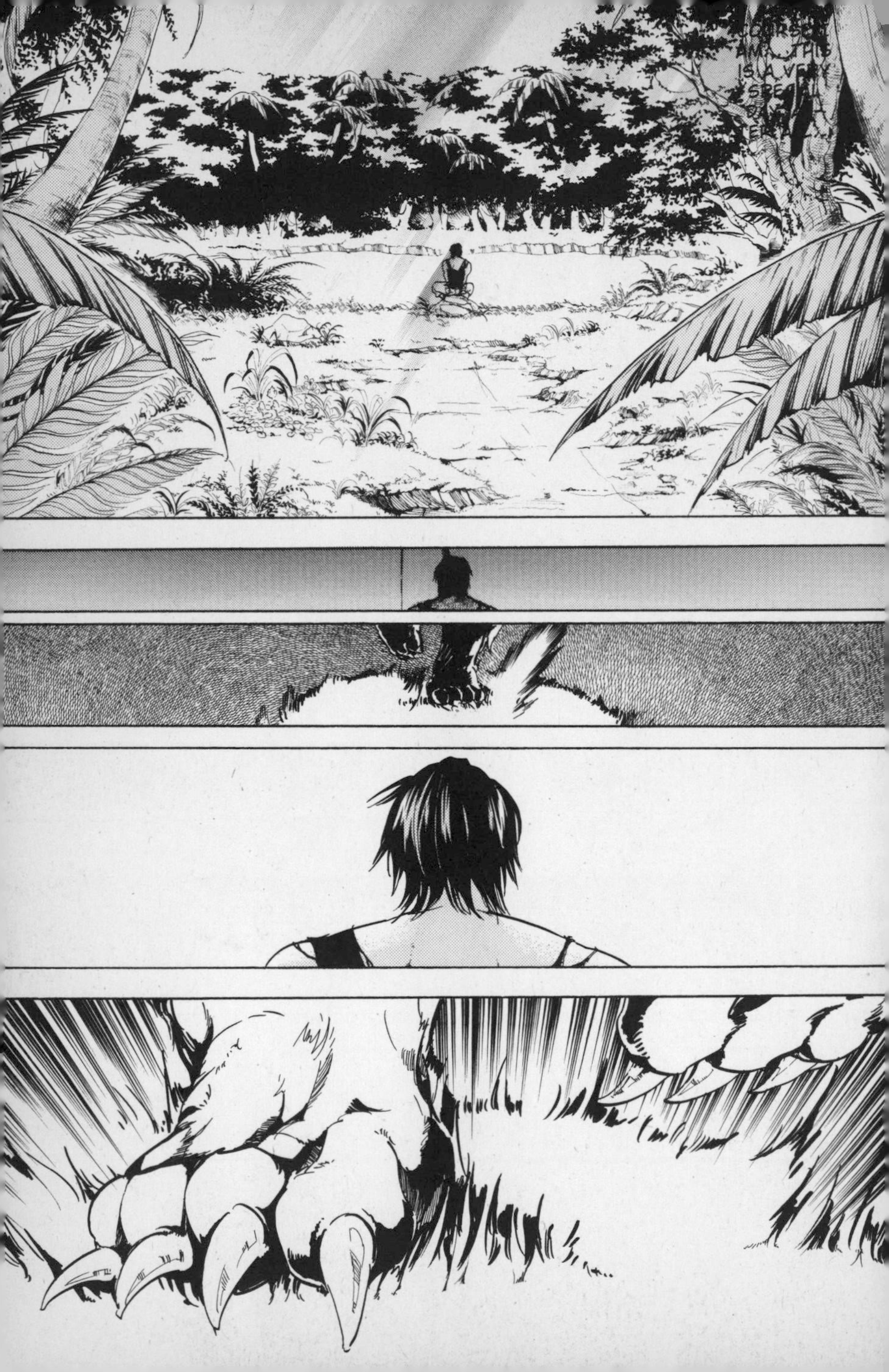
COURSE I AM. THIS IS A

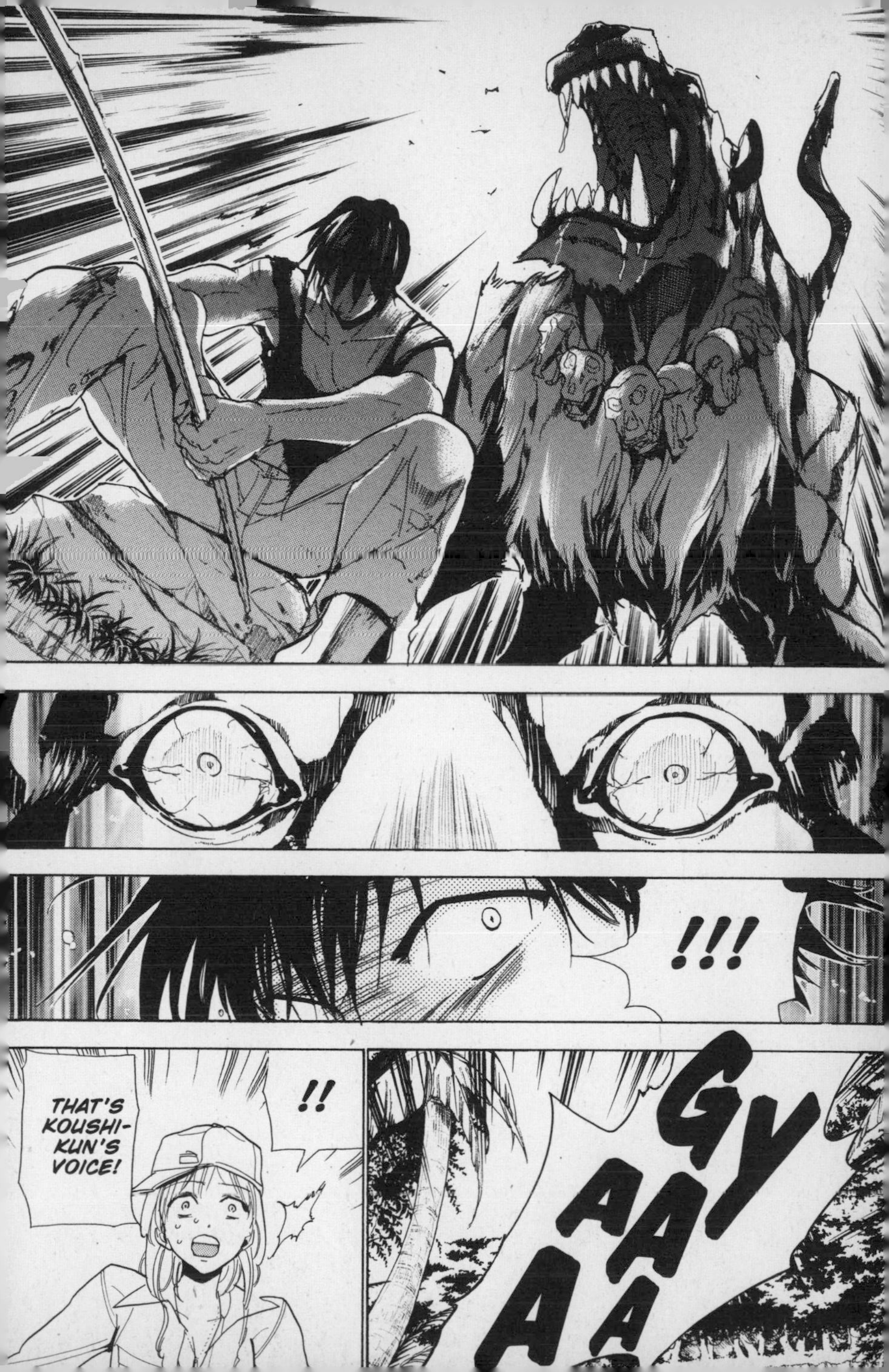
!!!
GYAAAAAA!
!!
THAT'S KOUSHI-KUN'S VOICE!

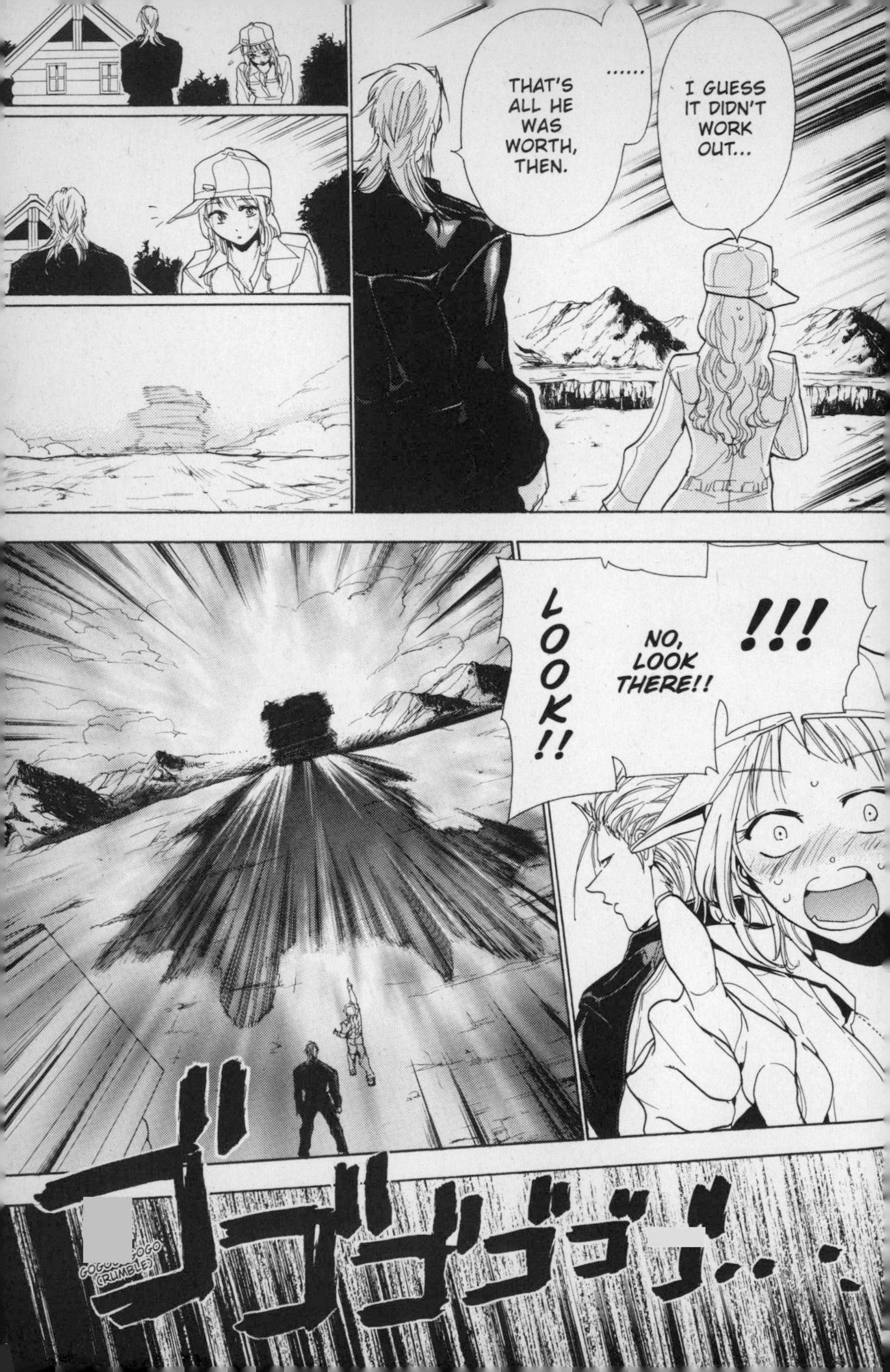

I GUESS IT DIDN'T WORK OUT...
......
THAT'S ALL HE WAS WORTH, THEN.
!!!
NO, LOOK THERE!!
LOOK!!
(RUMBLE)

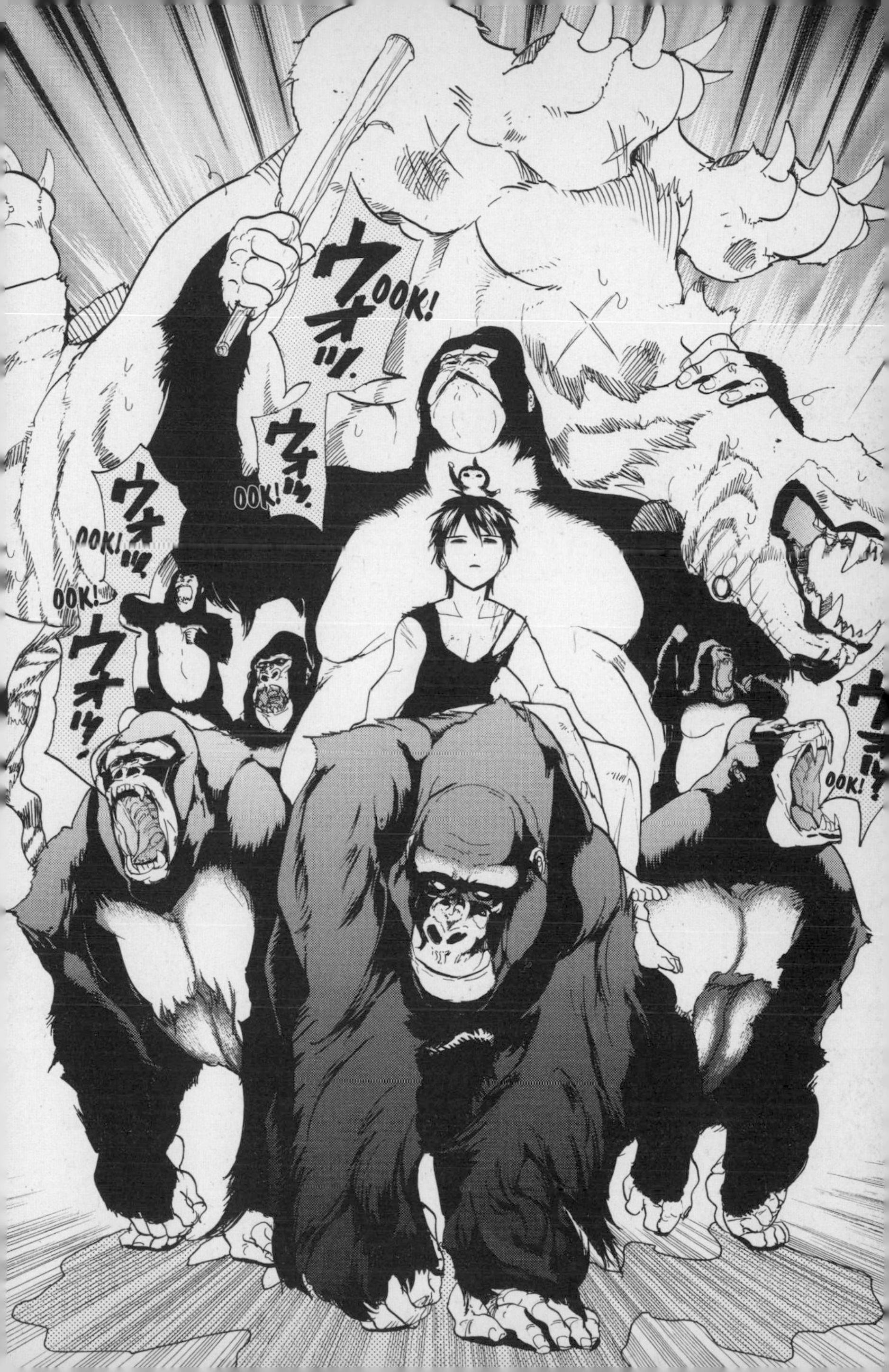

OOK!
ウォォッ!
OOOK!
ウォォッ!
OOK!
ウォォッ!
OOK!
ウォォッ!
OOK!

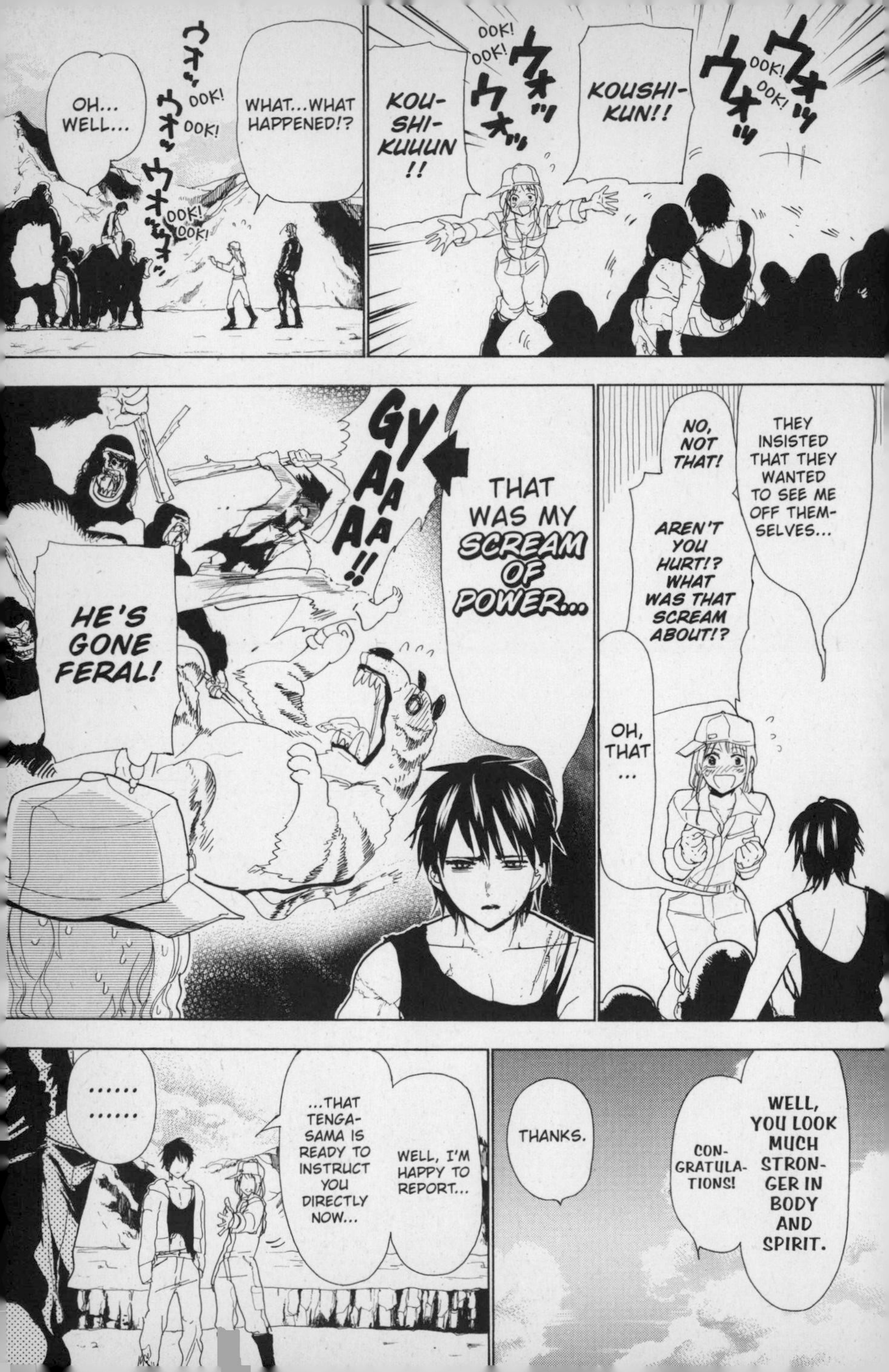
ウォッ ウォッ
OOK! OOK!
KOUSHI-KUN!!
OOK! OOK!
ウォッ ウォッ
KOU-SHI-KUUUN!!
WHAT...WHAT HAPPENED!?
ウォッ ウォッ ウォオ
OOK! OOK!
OOK! OOK!
OH... WELL...
THEY INSISTED THAT THEY WANTED TO SEE ME OFF THEMSELVES...
NO, NOT THAT!
AREN'T YOU HURT!? WHAT WAS THAT SCREAM ABOUT!?
OH, THAT ...
THAT WAS MY SCREAM OF POWER...
GYAAAAA!!
HE'S GONE FERAL!
WELL, YOU LOOK MUCH STRONGER IN BODY AND SPIRIT.
CONGRATULATIONS!
THANKS.
WELL, I'M HAPPY TO REPORT...
...THAT TENGA-SAMA IS READY TO INSTRUCT YOU DIRECTLY NOW...
....

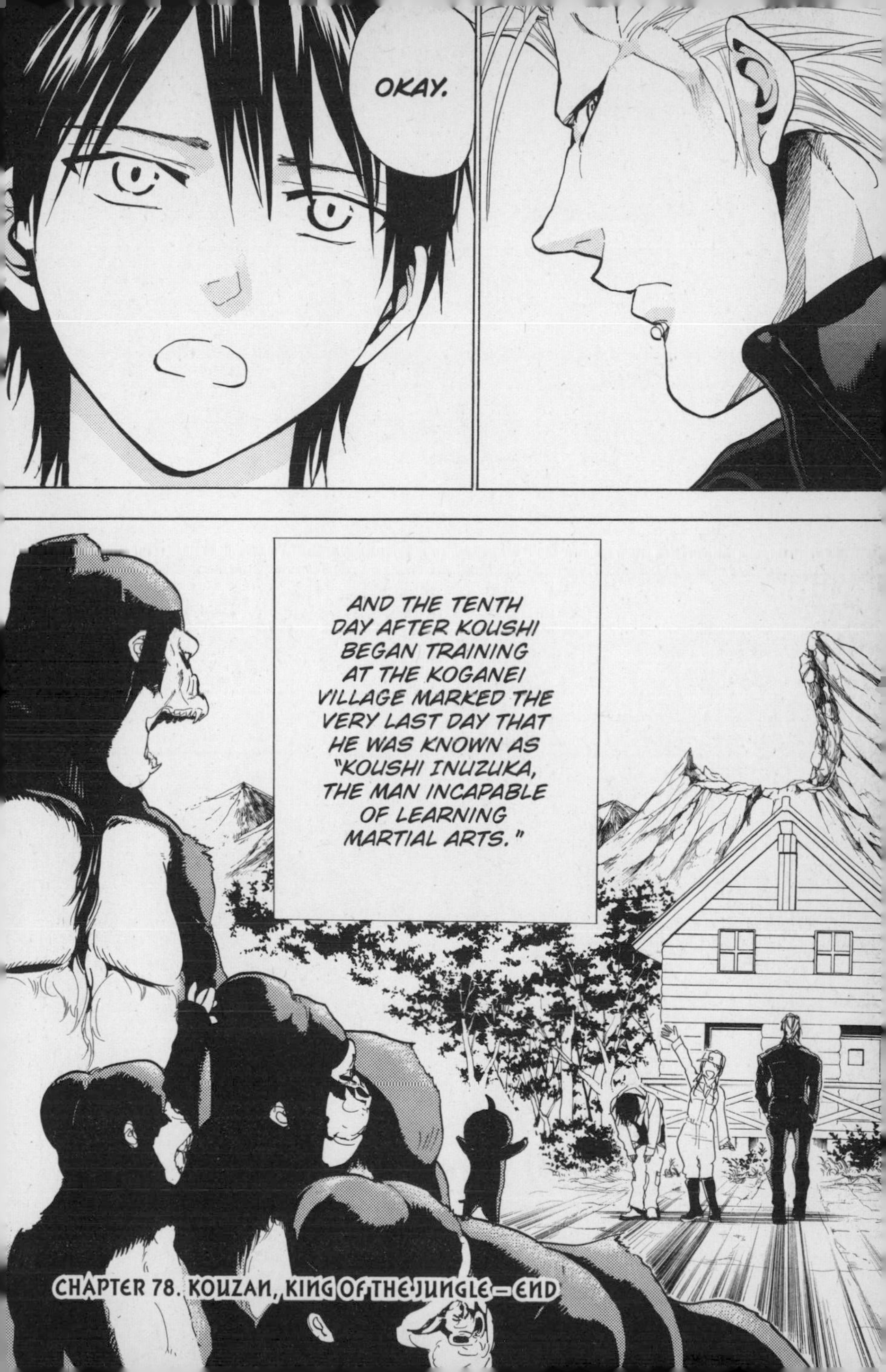
OKAY.
AND THE TENTH DAY AFTER KOUSHI BEGAN TRAINING AT THE KOGANEI VILLAGE MARKED THE VERY LAST DAY THAT HE WAS KNOWN AS "KOUSHI INUZUKA, THE MAN INCAPABLE OF LEARNING MARTIAL ARTS."
CHAPTER 78. KOUZAN, KING OF THE JUNGLE – END

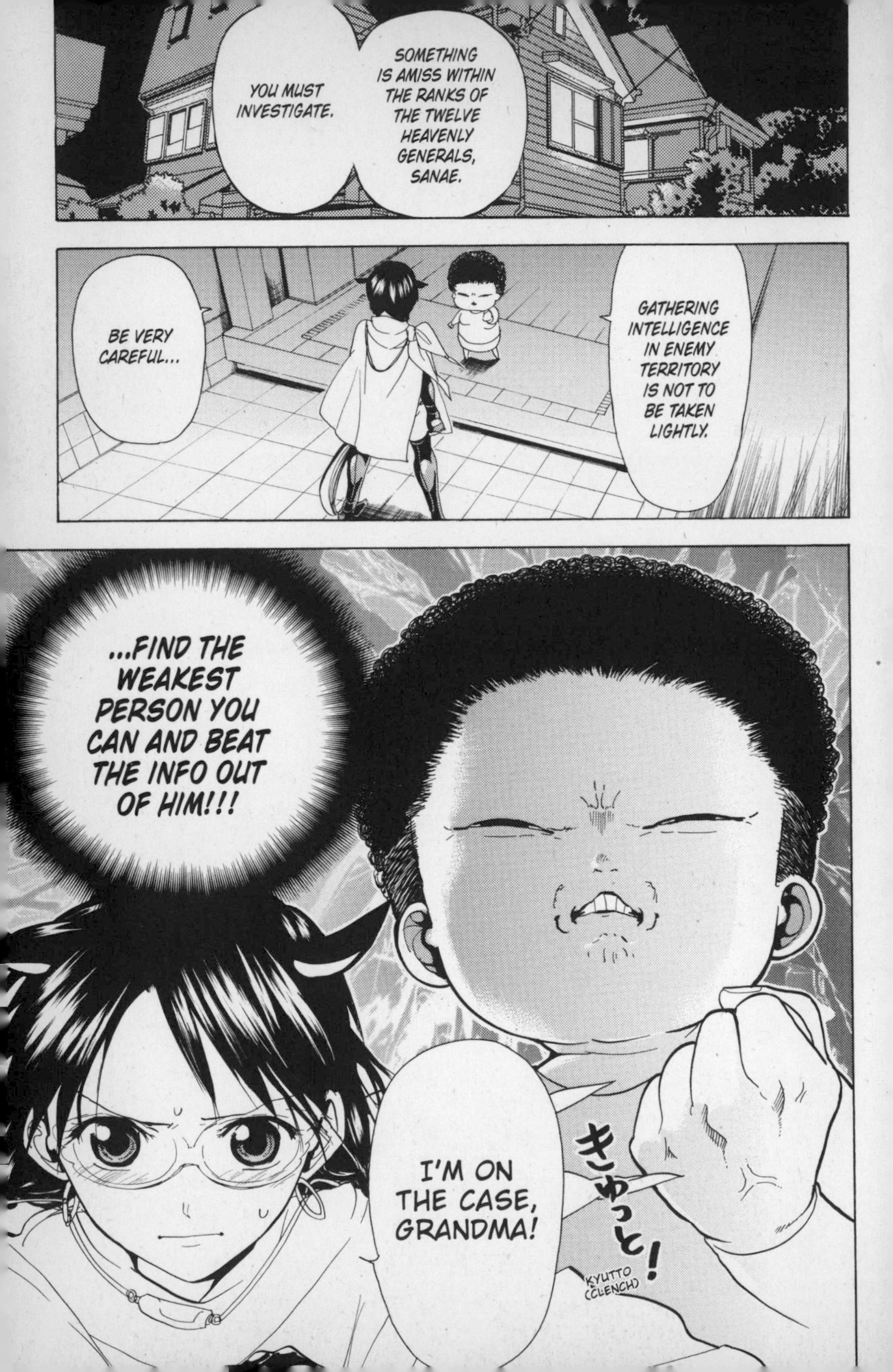
SOMETHING IS AMISS WITHIN THE RANKS OF THE TWELVE HEAVENLY GENERALS, SANAE.
YOU MUST INVESTIGATE.
GATHERING INTELLIGENCE IN ENEMY TERRITORY IS NOT TO BE TAKEN LIGHTLY.
BE VERY CAREFUL...
...FIND THE WEAKEST PERSON YOU CAN AND BEAT THE INFO OUT OF HIM!!!
I'M ON THE CASE, GRANDMA!
きゅっと!
KYUTTO (CLENCH)

79. YOU ARE VERY RUDE FOR A HANZOU

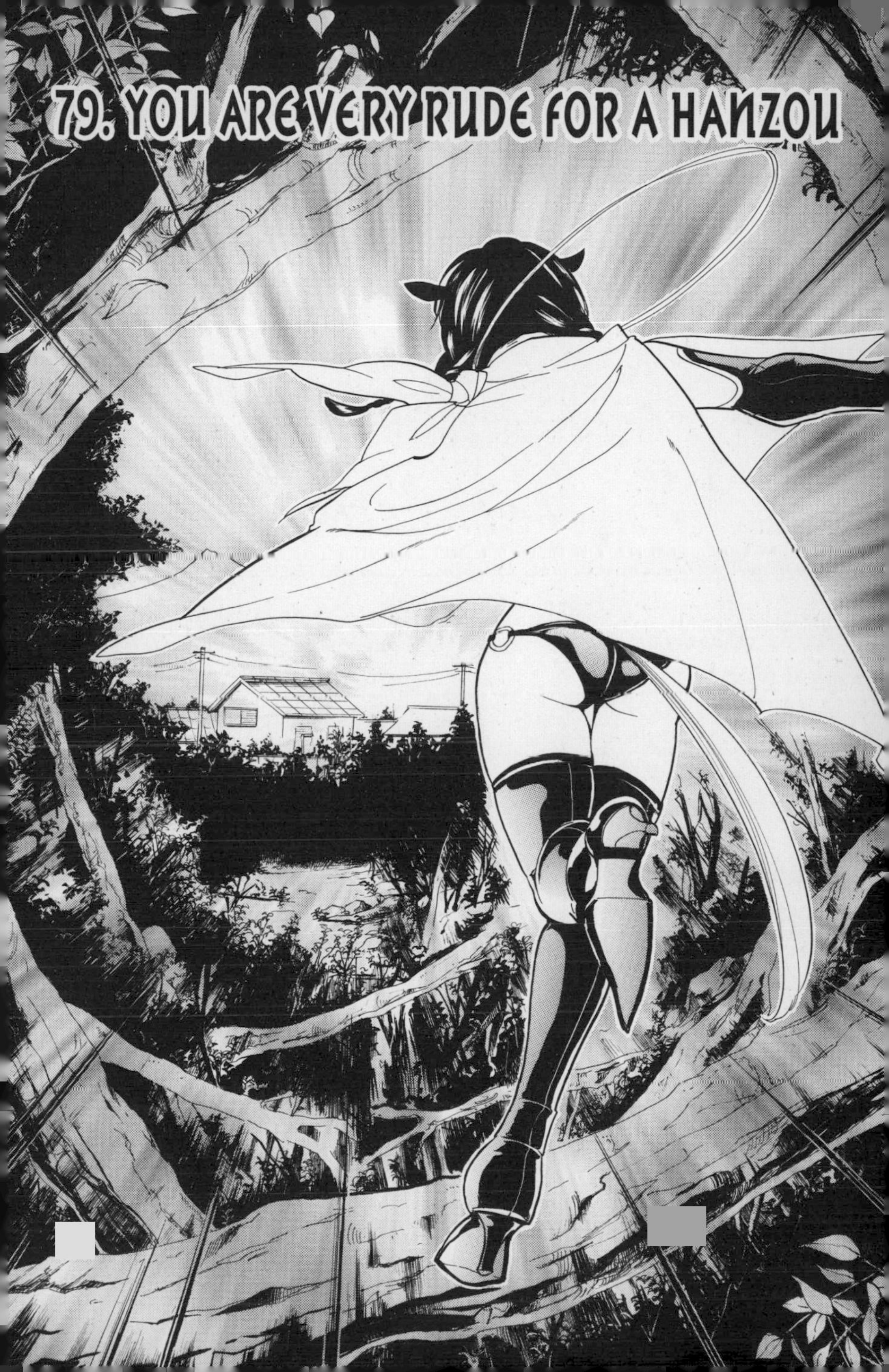

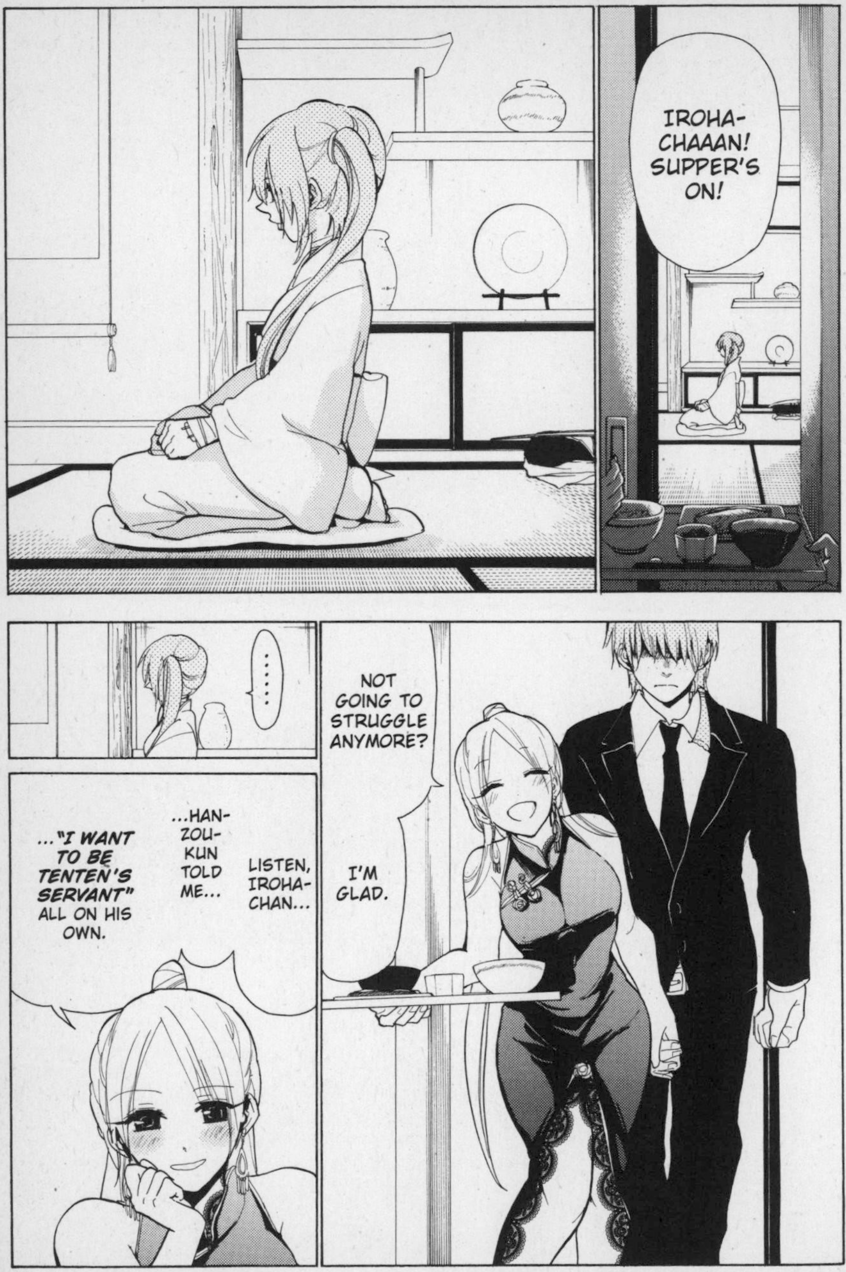
IROHA-CHAAAN! SUPPER'S ON!
NOT GOING TO STRUGGLE ANYMORE?
I'M GLAD.
......
LISTEN, IROHA-CHAN...
...HANZOU-KUN TOLD ME...
..."I WANT TO BE TENTEN'S SERVANT" ALL ON HIS OWN.

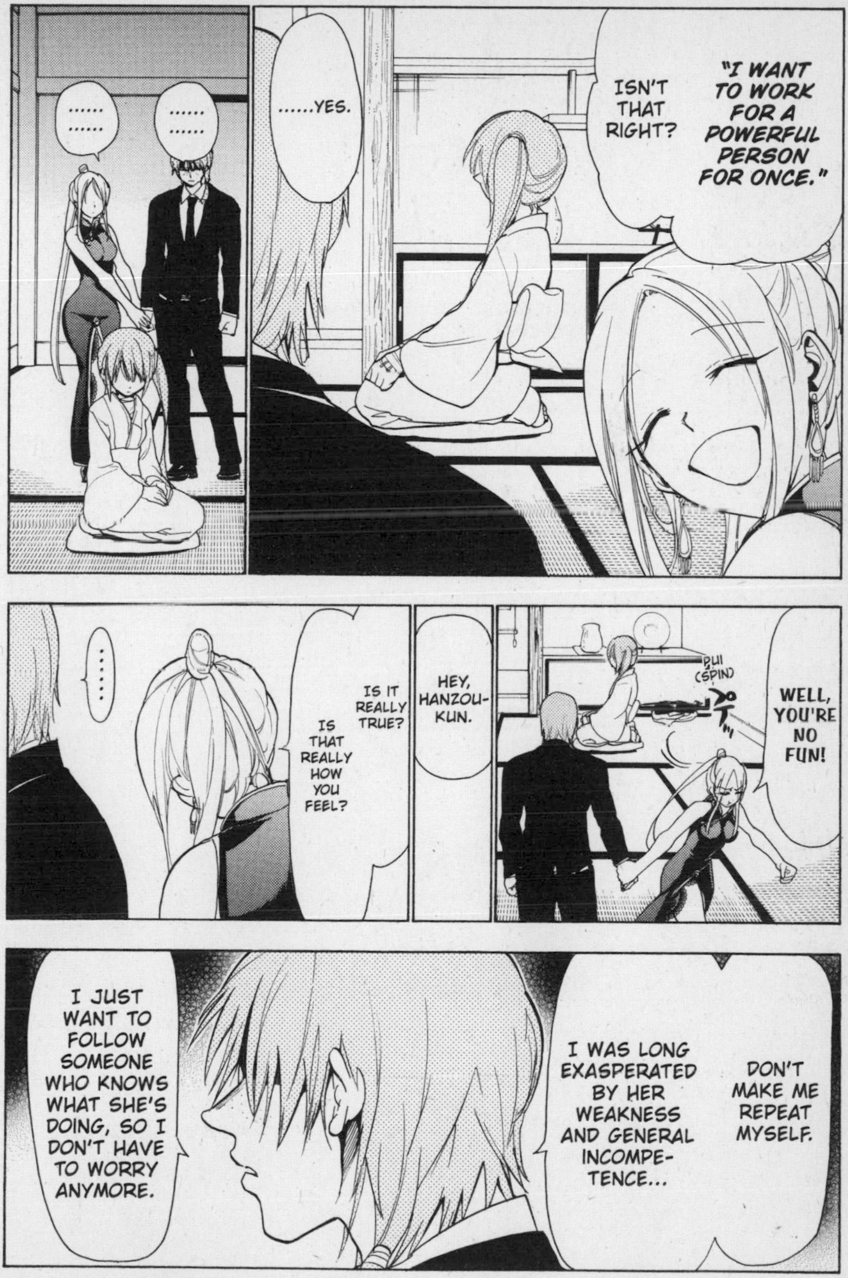
"I WANT TO WORK FOR A POWERFUL PERSON FOR ONCE."
ISN'T THAT RIGHT?
......YES.
....
....
WELL, YOU'RE NO FUN!
PUI (SPIN)
HEY, HANZOU-KUN.
IS IT REALLY TRUE?
IS THAT REALLY HOW YOU FEEL?
......
DON'T MAKE ME REPEAT MYSELF.
I WAS LONG EXASPERATED BY HER WEAKNESS AND GENERAL INCOMPETENCE...
I JUST WANT TO FOLLOW SOMEONE WHO KNOWS WHAT SHE'S DOING, SO I DON'T HAVE TO WORRY ANYMORE.

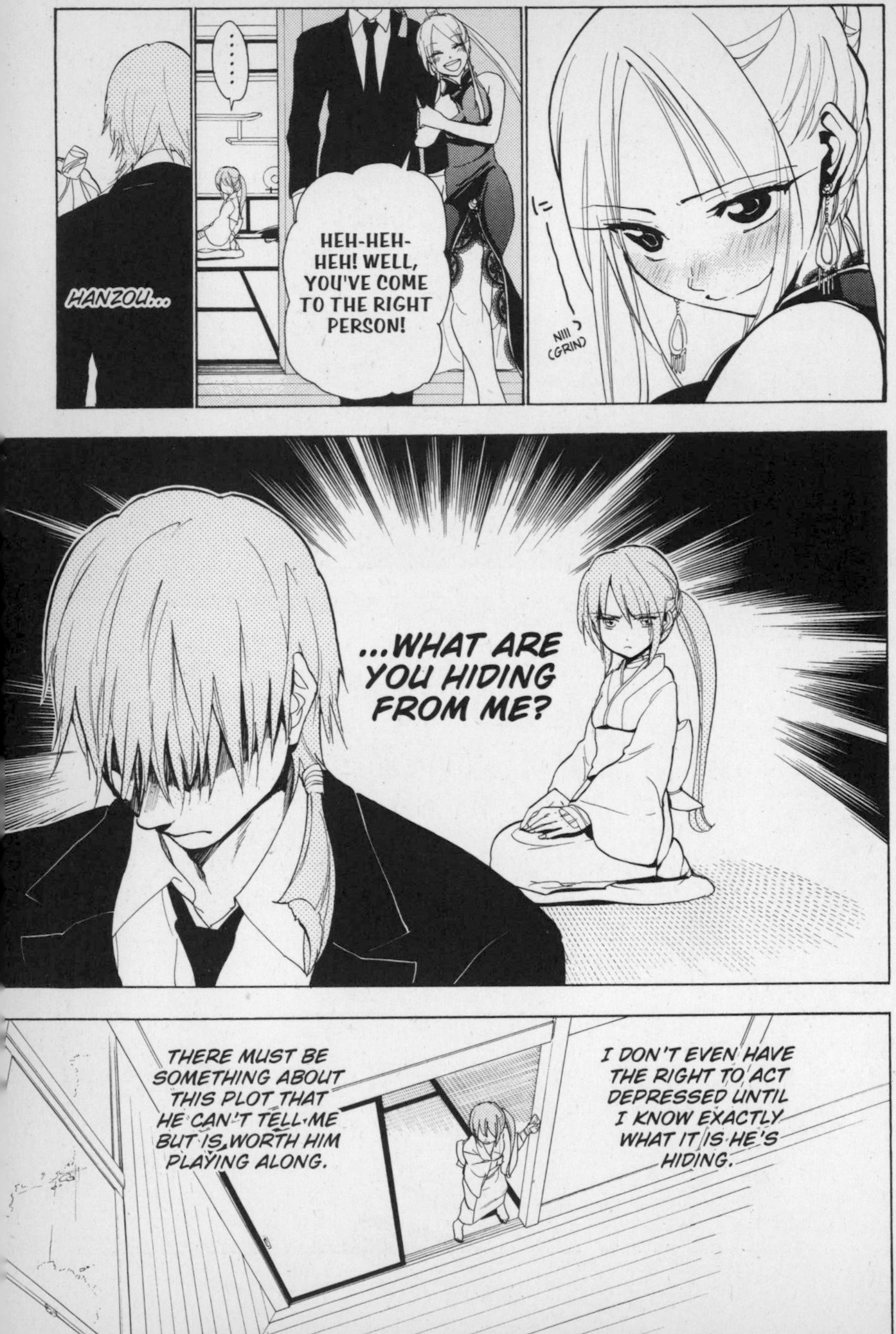

NIII (GRIN)
......
HEH-HEH-HEH! WELL, YOU'VE COME TO THE RIGHT PERSON!
HANZOU...
...WHAT ARE YOU HIDING FROM ME?
I DON'T EVEN HAVE THE RIGHT TO ACT DEPRESSED UNTIL I KNOW EXACTLY WHAT IT IS HE'S HIDING.
THERE MUST BE SOMETHING ABOUT THIS PLOT THAT HE CAN'T TELL ME BUT IS WORTH HIM PLAYING ALONG.

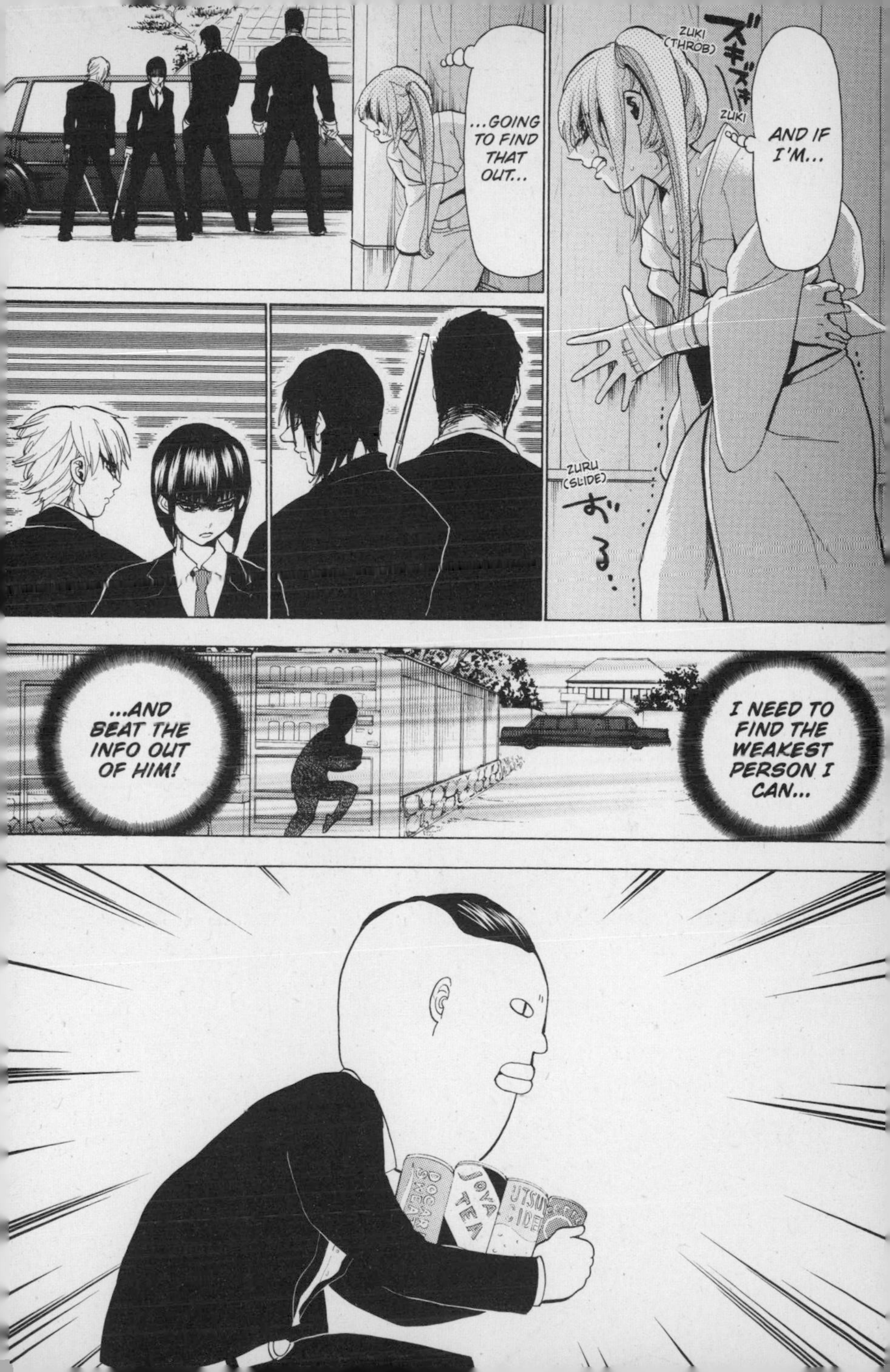
ZUKI (THROB)
ZUKI
AND IF I'M...
ZURU (SLIDE)
...GOING TO FIND THAT OUT...
I NEED TO FIND THE WEAKEST PERSON I CAN...
...AND BEAT THE INFO OUT OF HIM!
JOYA TEA
UTSU CIDE

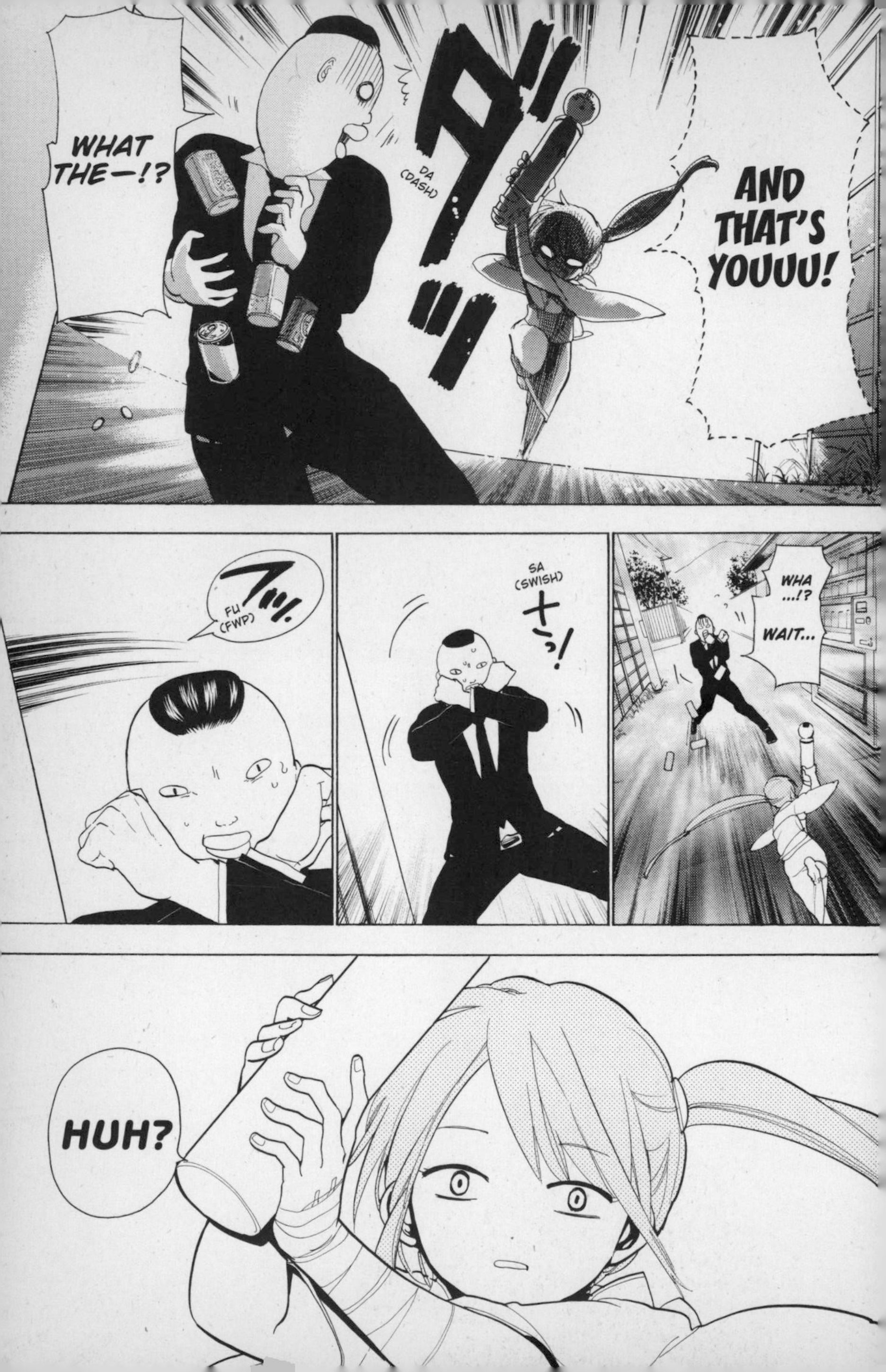
AND THAT'S YOUUU!
DA (DASH)
WHAT THE—!?
WHA ...!?
WAIT...
SA (SWISH)
FU (FWP)
HUH?

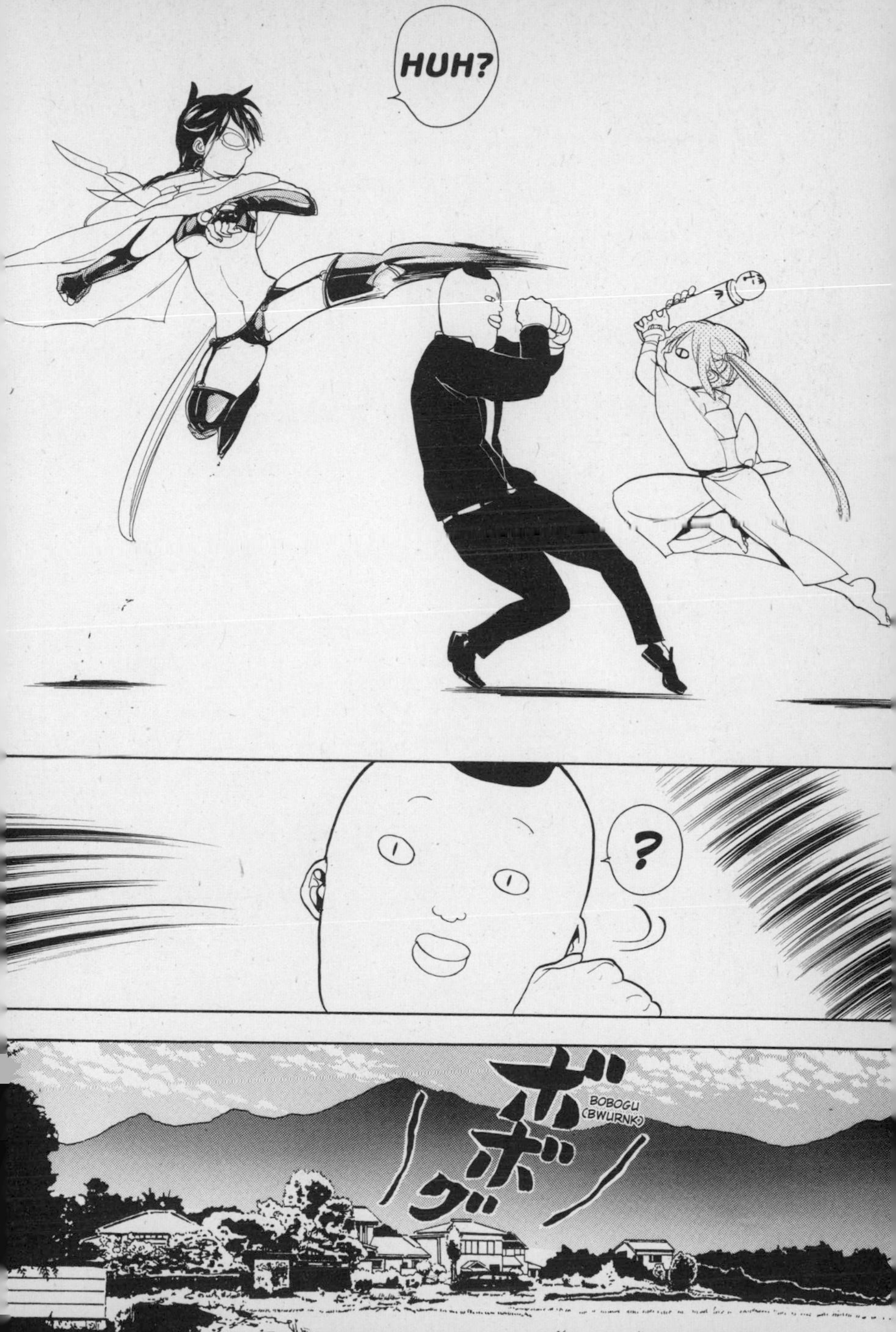
HUH?
?
ボボグ
BOBOGU (BWURNK)

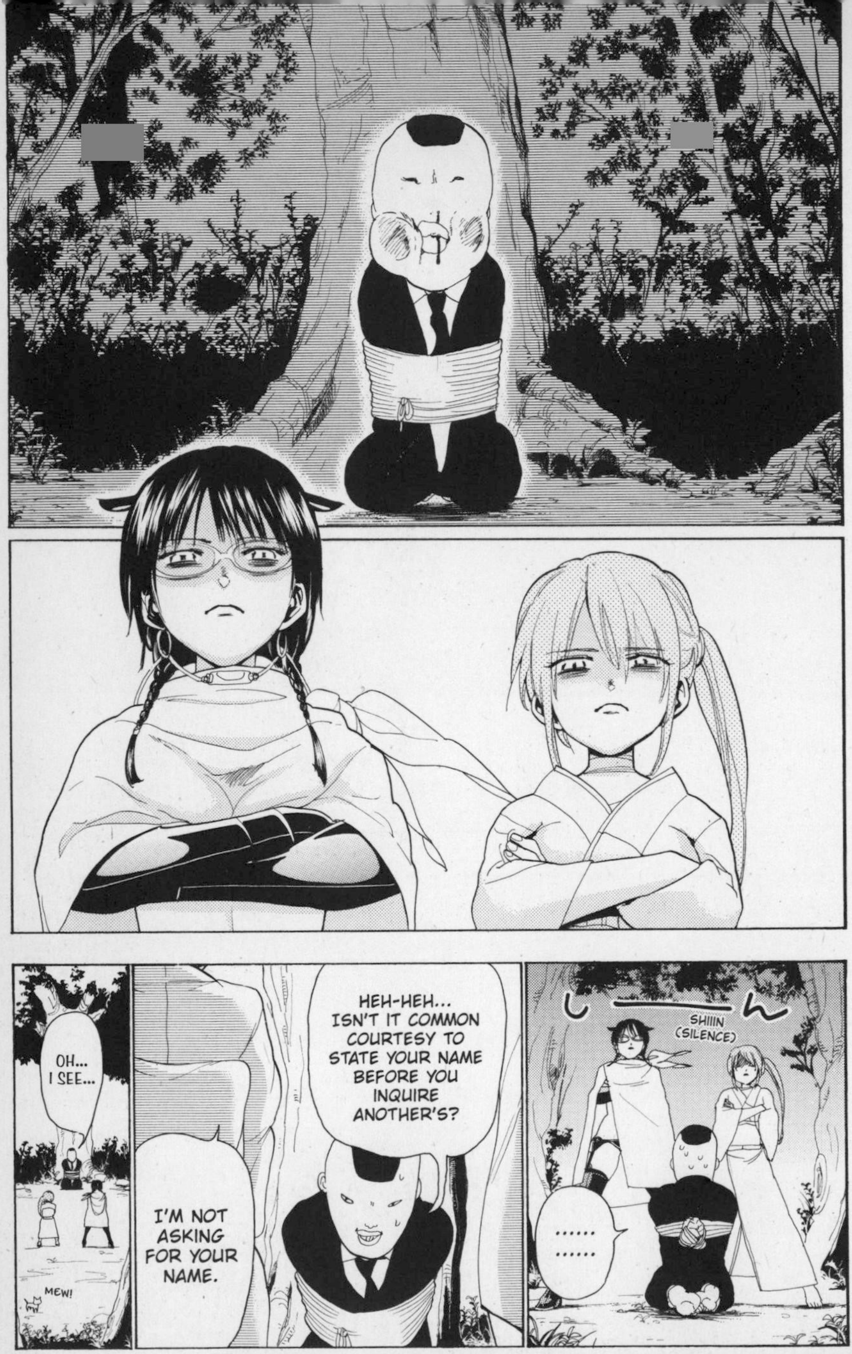

し——ん
SHIIIN (SILENCE)
......
......
HEH-HEH... ISN'T IT COMMON COURTESY TO STATE YOUR NAME BEFORE YOU INQUIRE ANOTHER'S?
I'M NOT ASKING FOR YOUR NAME.
OH... I SEE...
MEW!

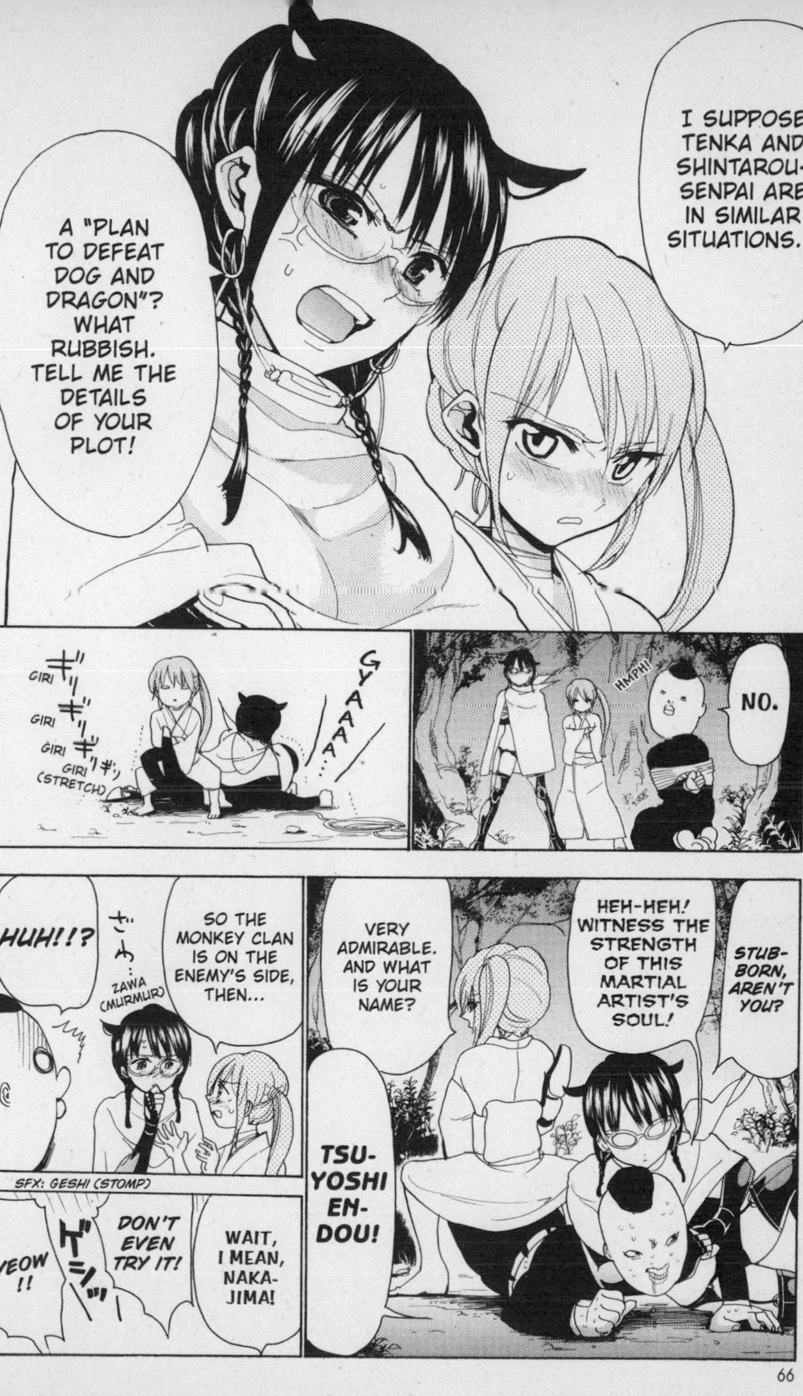
I SUPPOSE TENKA AND SHINTAROU-SENPAI ARE IN SIMILAR SITUATIONS...
A "PLAN TO DEFEAT DOG AND DRAGON"? WHAT RUBBISH. TELL ME THE DETAILS OF YOUR PLOT!
HMPH!
NO.
GIRI
GIRI
GIRI
GIRI (STRETCH)
GYAAAA...
STUB-BORN, AREN'T YOU?
HEH-HEH! WITNESS THE STRENGTH OF THIS MARTIAL ARTIST'S SOUL!
VERY ADMIRABLE. AND WHAT IS YOUR NAME?
TSU-YOSHI EN-DOU!
SO THE MONKEY CLAN IS ON THE ENEMY'S SIDE, THEN...
ZAWA (MURMUR)
HUH!!?
SFX: GESHI (STOMP)
WAIT, I MEAN, NAKA-JIMA!
DON'T EVEN TRY IT!
YEOW!!

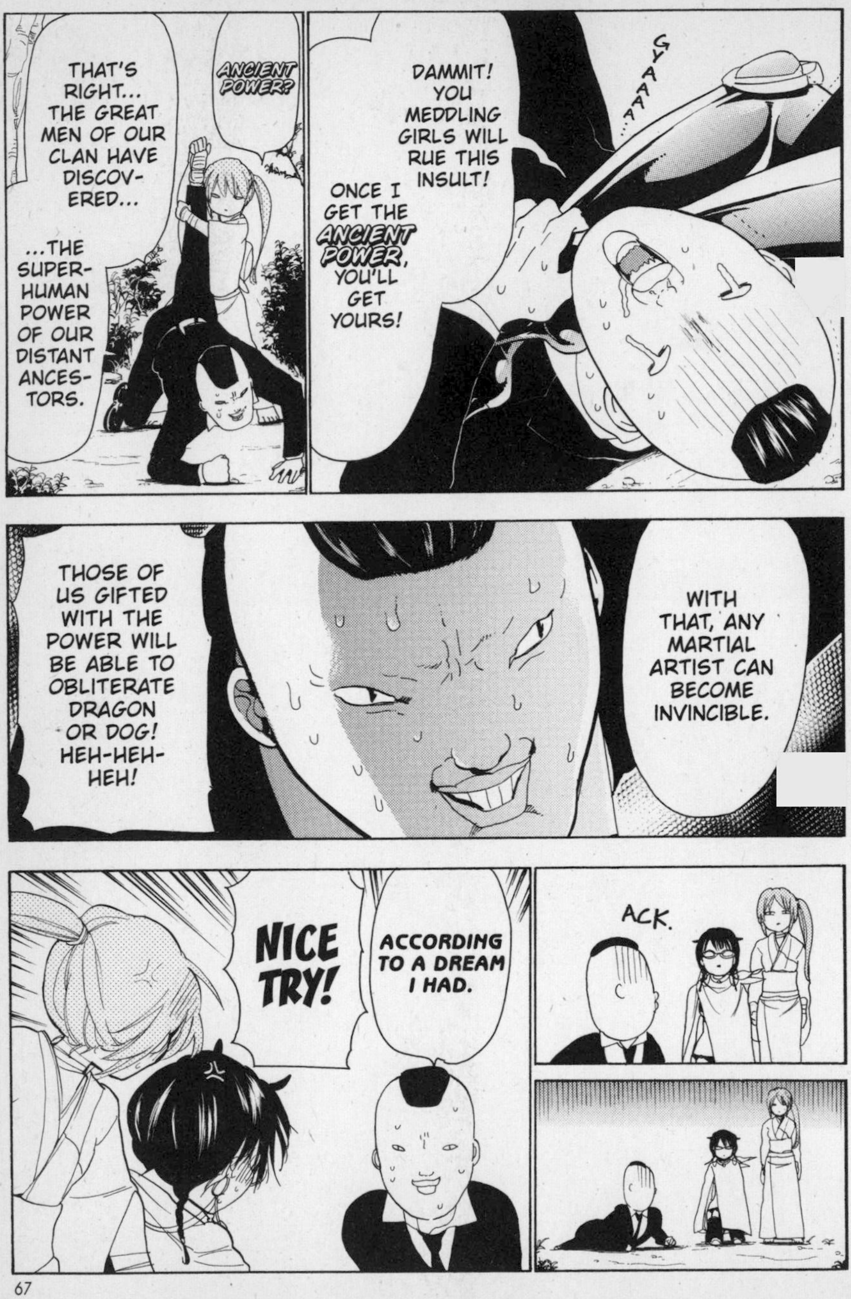
GYAAAA...
DAMMIT! YOU MEDDLING GIRLS WILL RUE THIS INSULT!
ONCE I GET THE ANCIENT POWER, YOU'LL GET YOURS!
ANCIENT POWER?
THAT'S RIGHT... THE GREAT MEN OF OUR CLAN HAVE DISCOVERED...
...THE SUPERHUMAN POWER OF OUR DISTANT ANCESTORS.
WITH THAT, ANY MARTIAL ARTIST CAN BECOME INVINCIBLE.
THOSE OF US GIFTED WITH THE POWER WILL BE ABLE TO OBLITERATE DRAGON OR DOG! HEH-HEH-HEH!
ACK.
ACCORDING TO A DREAM I HAD.
NICE TRY!

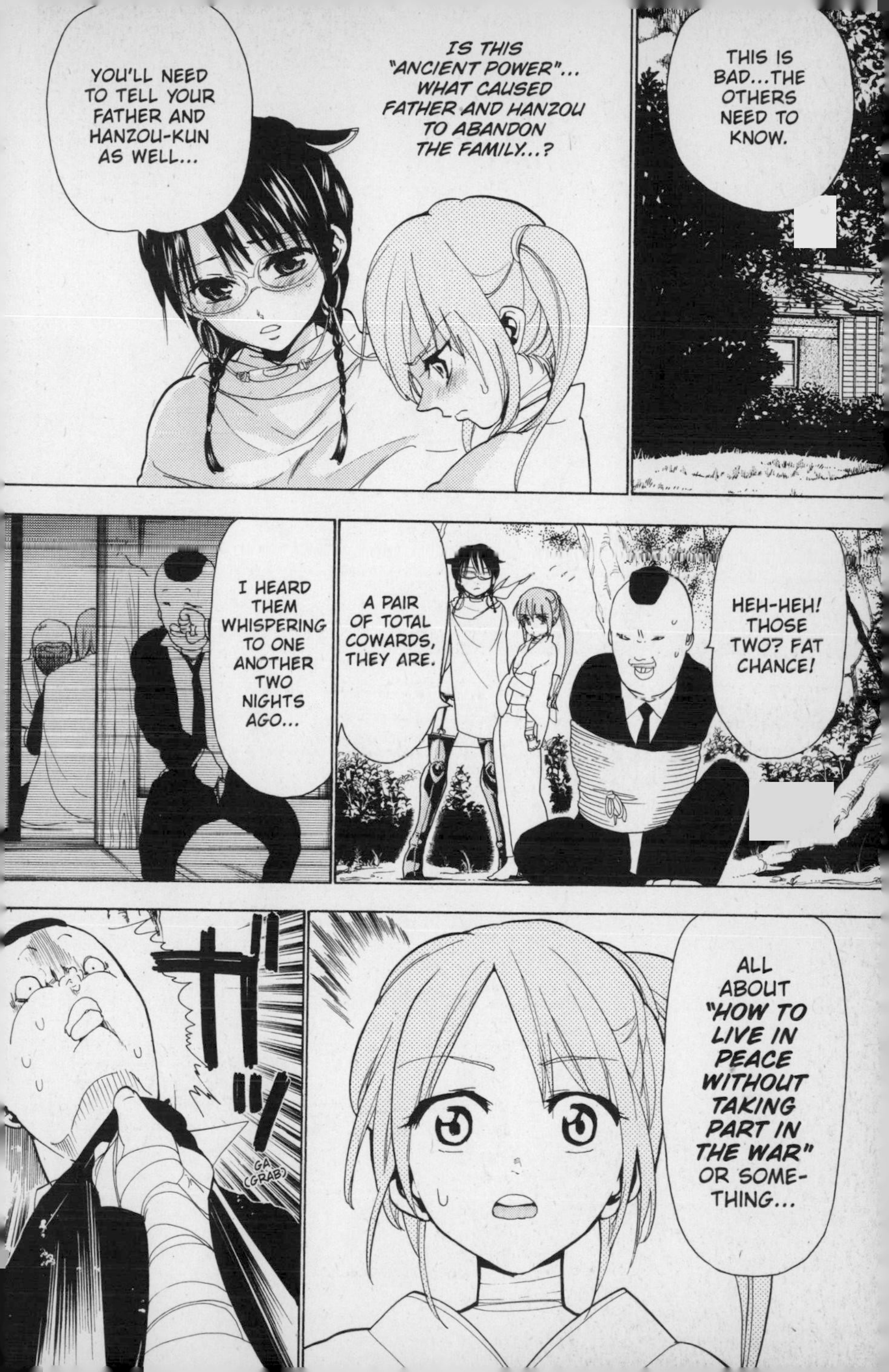
THIS IS BAD...THE OTHERS NEED TO KNOW.
IS THIS "ANCIENT POWER"... WHAT CAUSED FATHER AND HANZOU TO ABANDON THE FAMILY...?
YOU'LL NEED TO TELL YOUR FATHER AND HANZOU-KUN AS WELL...
HEH-HEH! THOSE TWO? FAT CHANCE!
A PAIR OF TOTAL COWARDS, THEY ARE.
I HEARD THEM WHISPERING TO ONE ANOTHER TWO NIGHTS AGO...
ALL ABOUT "HOW TO LIVE IN PEACE WITHOUT TAKING PART IN THE WAR" OR SOMETHING...
GA (GRAB)

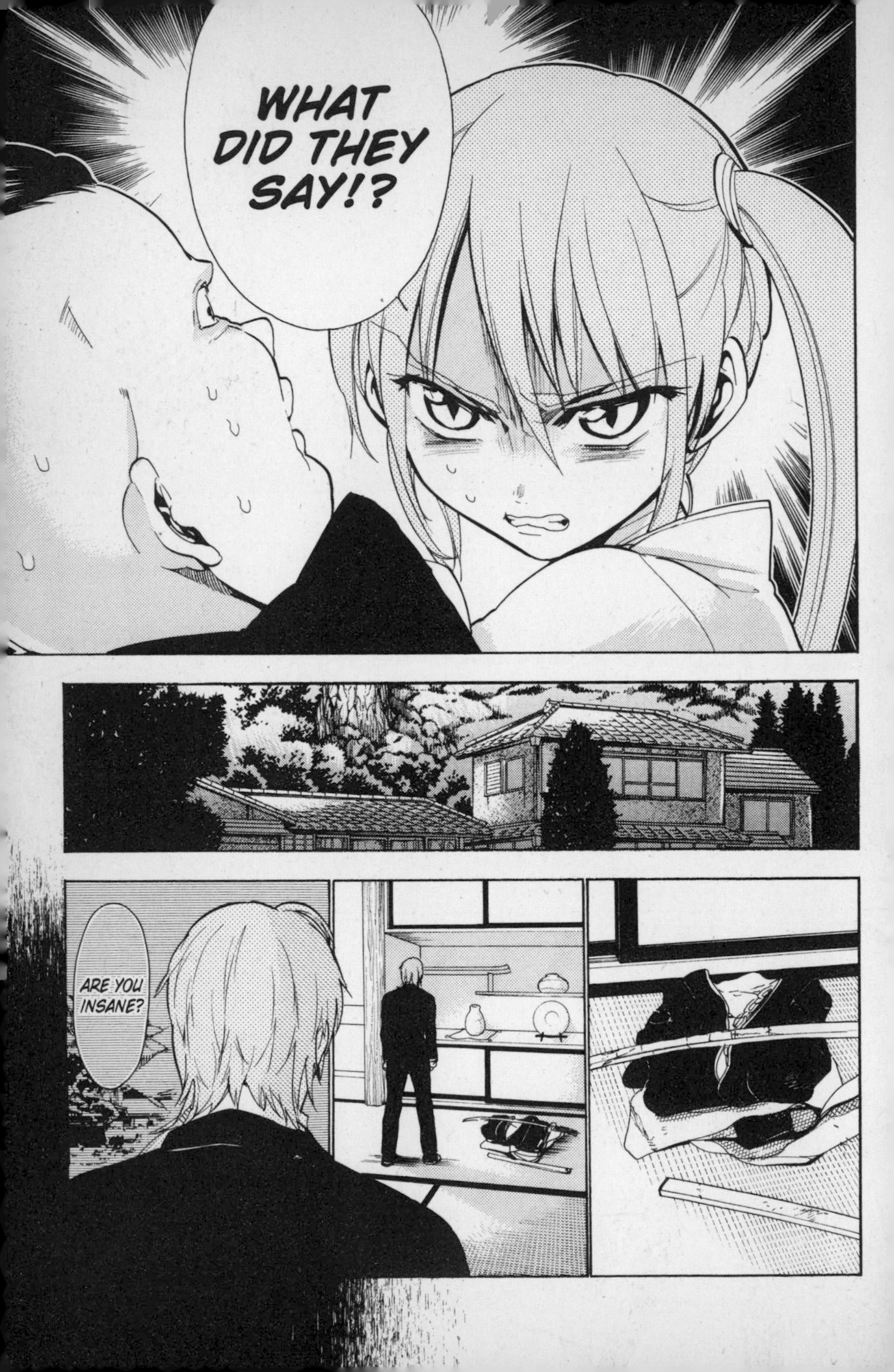
WHAT DID THEY SAY!?
ARE YOU INSANE?

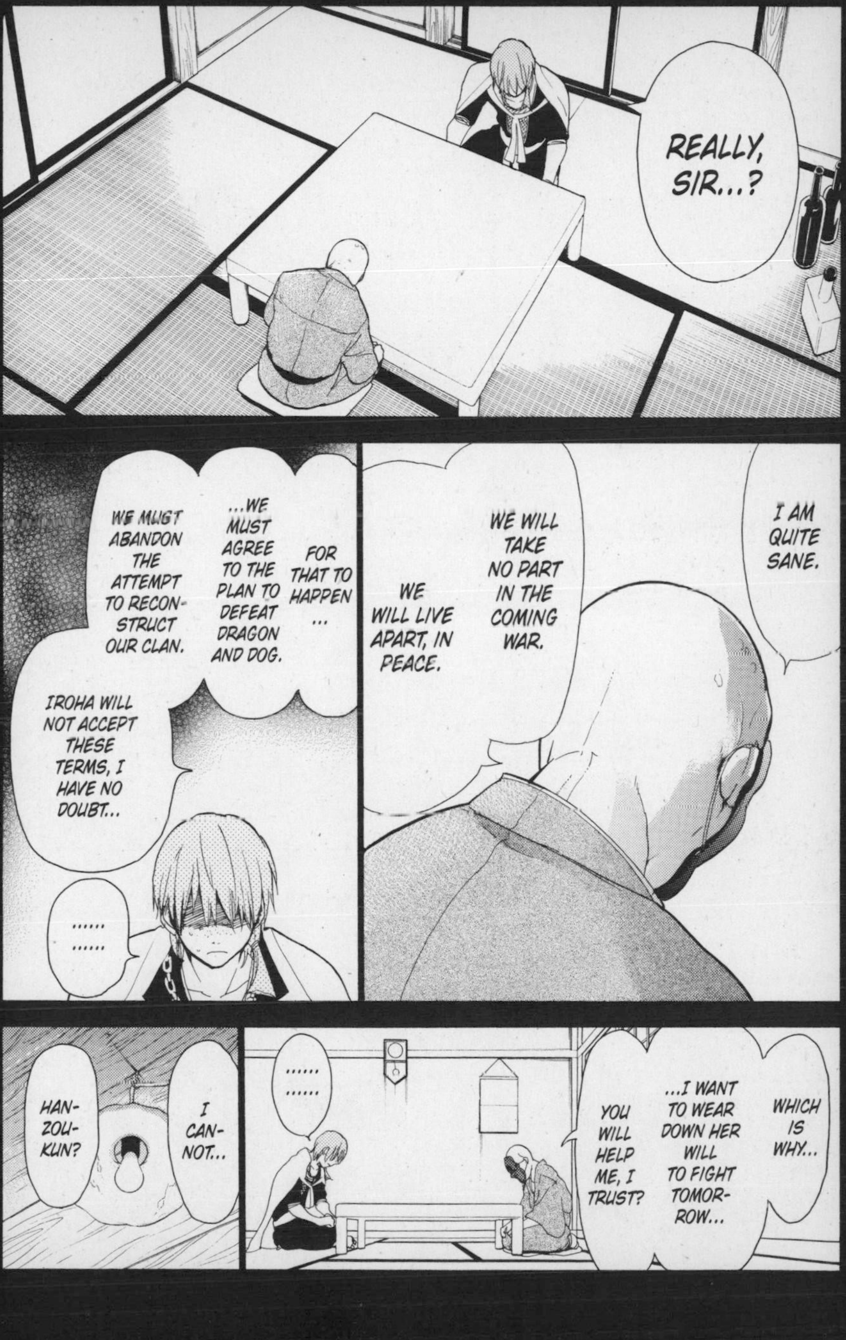
REALLY, SIR...?
I AM QUITE SANE.
WE WILL TAKE NO PART IN THE COMING WAR.
WE WILL LIVE APART, IN PEACE.
FOR THAT TO HAPPEN ...
...WE MUST AGREE TO THE PLAN TO DEFEAT DRAGON AND DOG.
WE MUST ABANDON THE ATTEMPT TO RECON-STRUCT OUR CLAN.
IROHA WILL NOT ACCEPT THESE TERMS, I HAVE NO DOUBT...
....
WHICH IS WHY...
...I WANT TO WEAR DOWN HER WILL TO FIGHT TOMOR-ROW...
YOU WILL HELP ME, I TRUST?
....
I CAN-NOT...
HAN-ZOU-KUN?

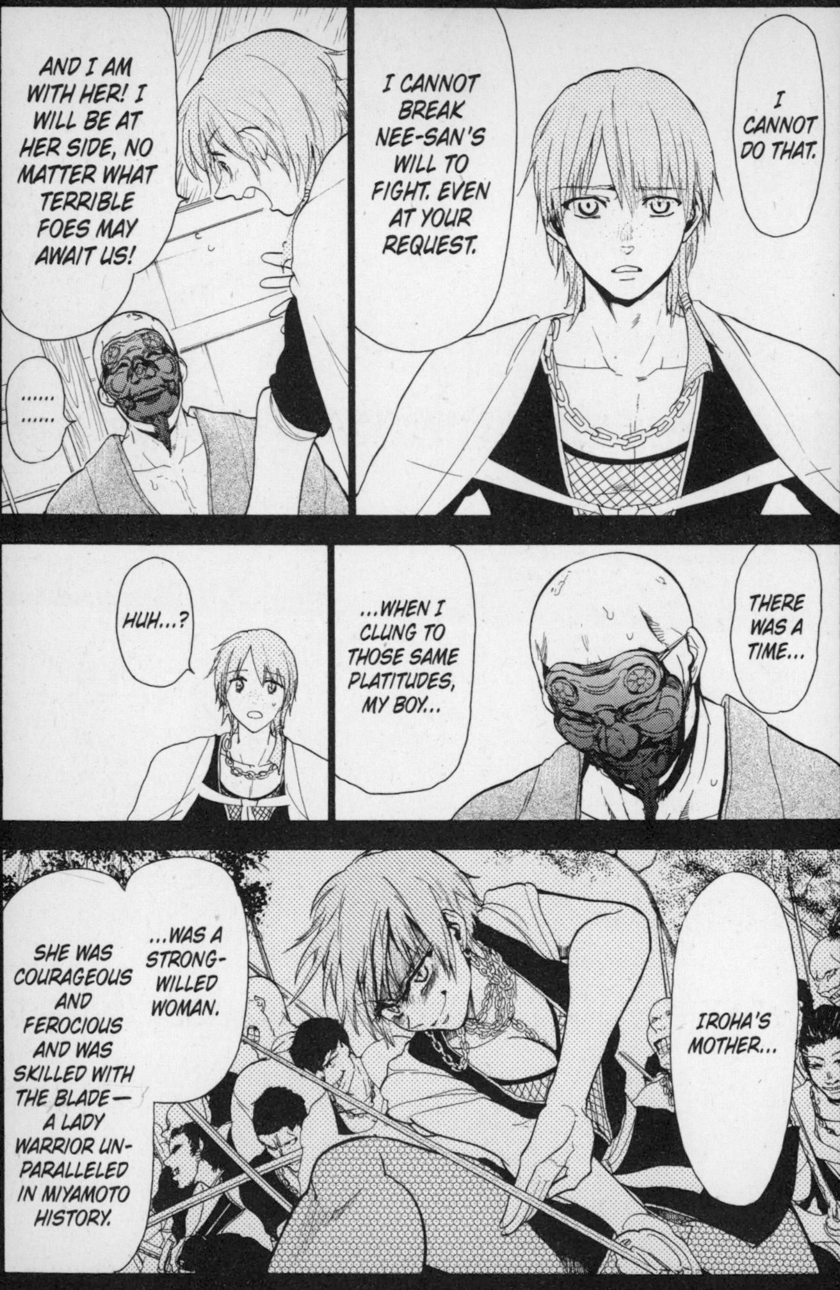
I CANNOT DO THAT.
I CANNOT BREAK NEE-SAN'S WILL TO FIGHT. EVEN AT YOUR REQUEST.
AND I AM WITH HER! I WILL BE AT HER SIDE, NO MATTER WHAT TERRIBLE FOES MAY AWAIT US!
....
THERE WAS A TIME...
...WHEN I CLUNG TO THOSE SAME PLATITUDES, MY BOY...
HUH...?
IROHA'S MOTHER...
...WAS A STRONG-WILLED WOMAN.
SHE WAS COURAGEOUS AND FEROCIOUS AND WAS SKILLED WITH THE BLADE— A LADY WARRIOR UN-PARALLELED IN MIYAMOTO HISTORY.

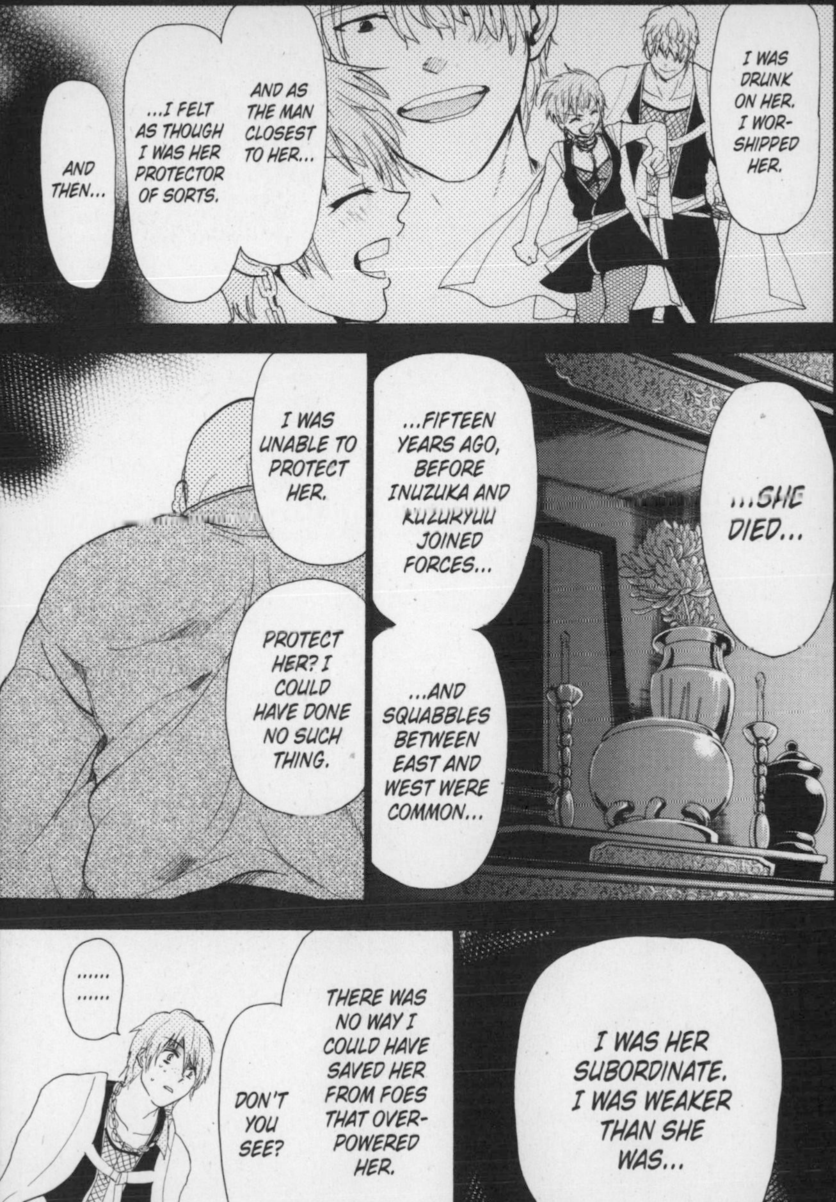
I WAS DRUNK ON HER. I WOR-SHIPPED HER.
AND AS THE MAN CLOSEST TO HER...
...I FELT AS THOUGH I WAS HER PROTECTOR OF SORTS.
AND THEN...
...SHE DIED...
...FIFTEEN YEARS AGO, BEFORE INUZUKA AND KUZURYUU JOINED FORCES...
...AND SQUABBLES BETWEEN EAST AND WEST WERE COMMON...
I WAS UNABLE TO PROTECT HER.
PROTECT HER? I COULD HAVE DONE NO SUCH THING.
I WAS HER SUBORDINATE. I WAS WEAKER THAN SHE WAS...
THERE WAS NO WAY I COULD HAVE SAVED HER FROM FOES THAT OVER-POWERED HER.
DON'T YOU SEE?
......
......

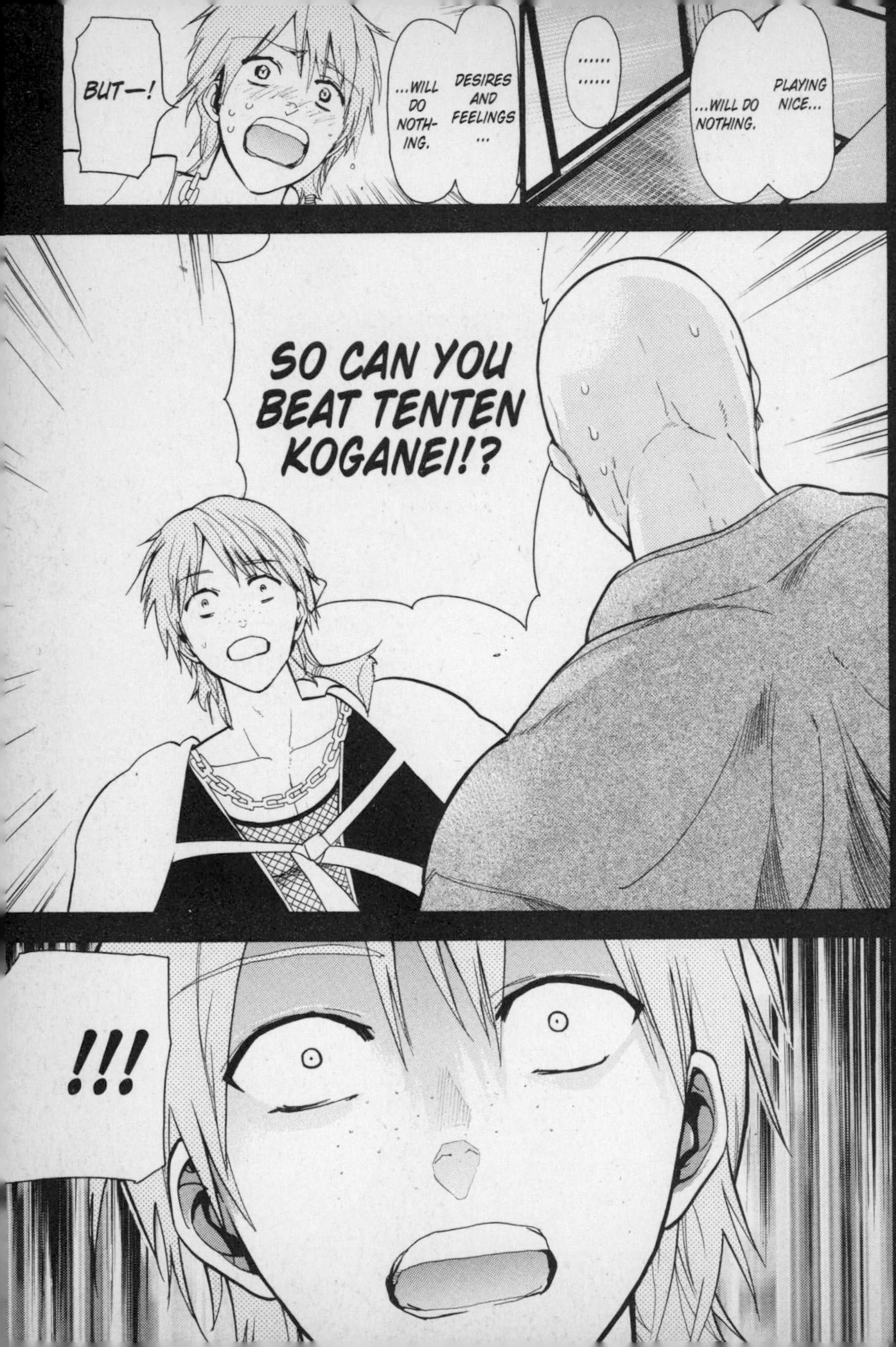
PLAYING NICE...
...WILL DO NOTHING.
......
......
DESIRES AND FEELINGS...
...WILL DO NOTHING.
BUT—!
SO CAN YOU BEAT TENTEN KOGANEI!?
!!!

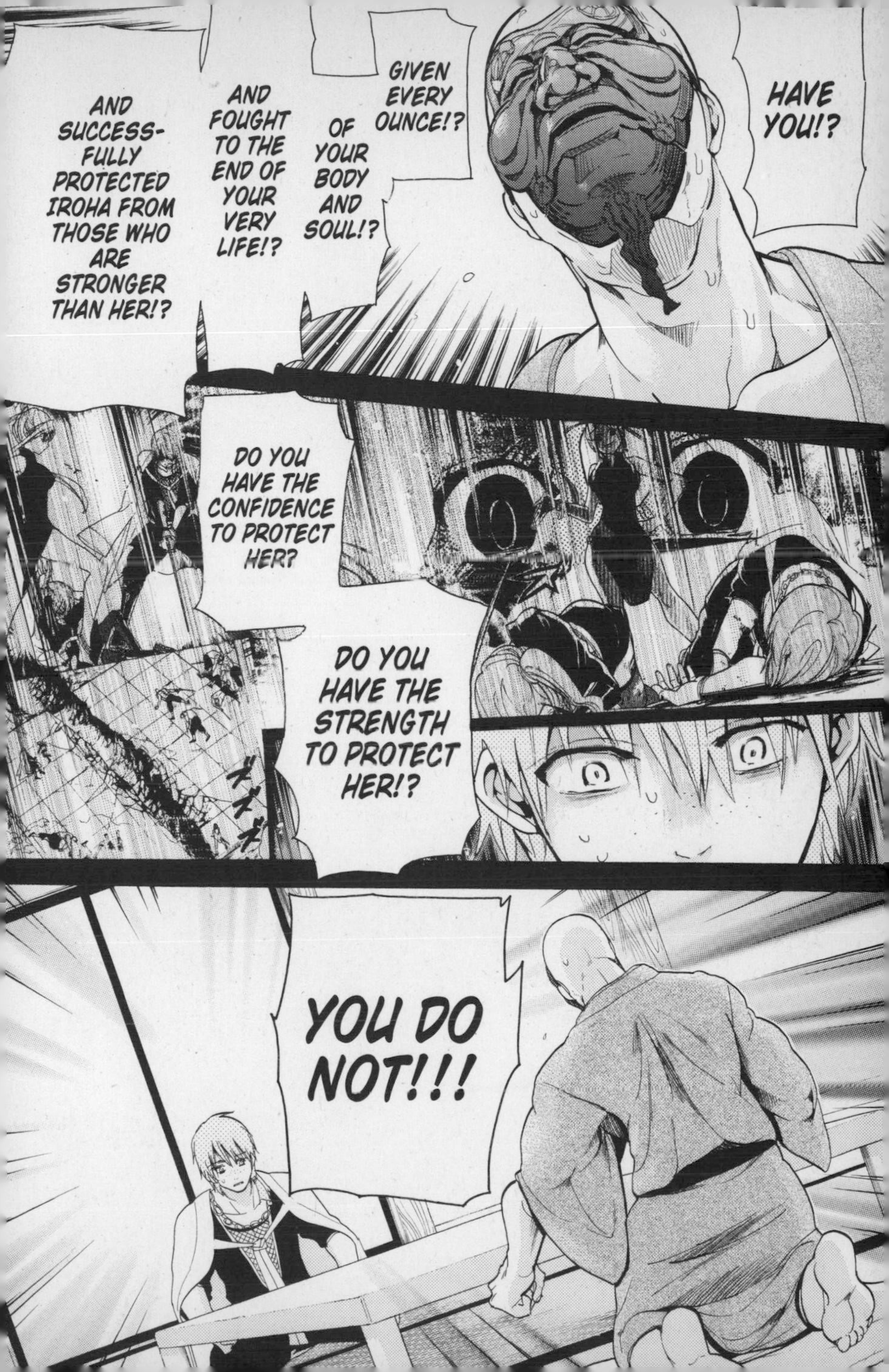
HAVE YOU!?
GIVEN EVERY OUNCE!?
OF YOUR BODY AND SOUL!?
AND FOUGHT TO THE END OF YOUR VERY LIFE!?
AND SUCCESS-FULLY PROTECTED IROHA FROM THOSE WHO ARE STRONGER THAN HER!?
DO YOU HAVE THE CONFIDENCE TO PROTECT HER?
DO YOU HAVE THE STRENGTH TO PROTECT HER!?
ズズズ
YOU DO NOT!!!

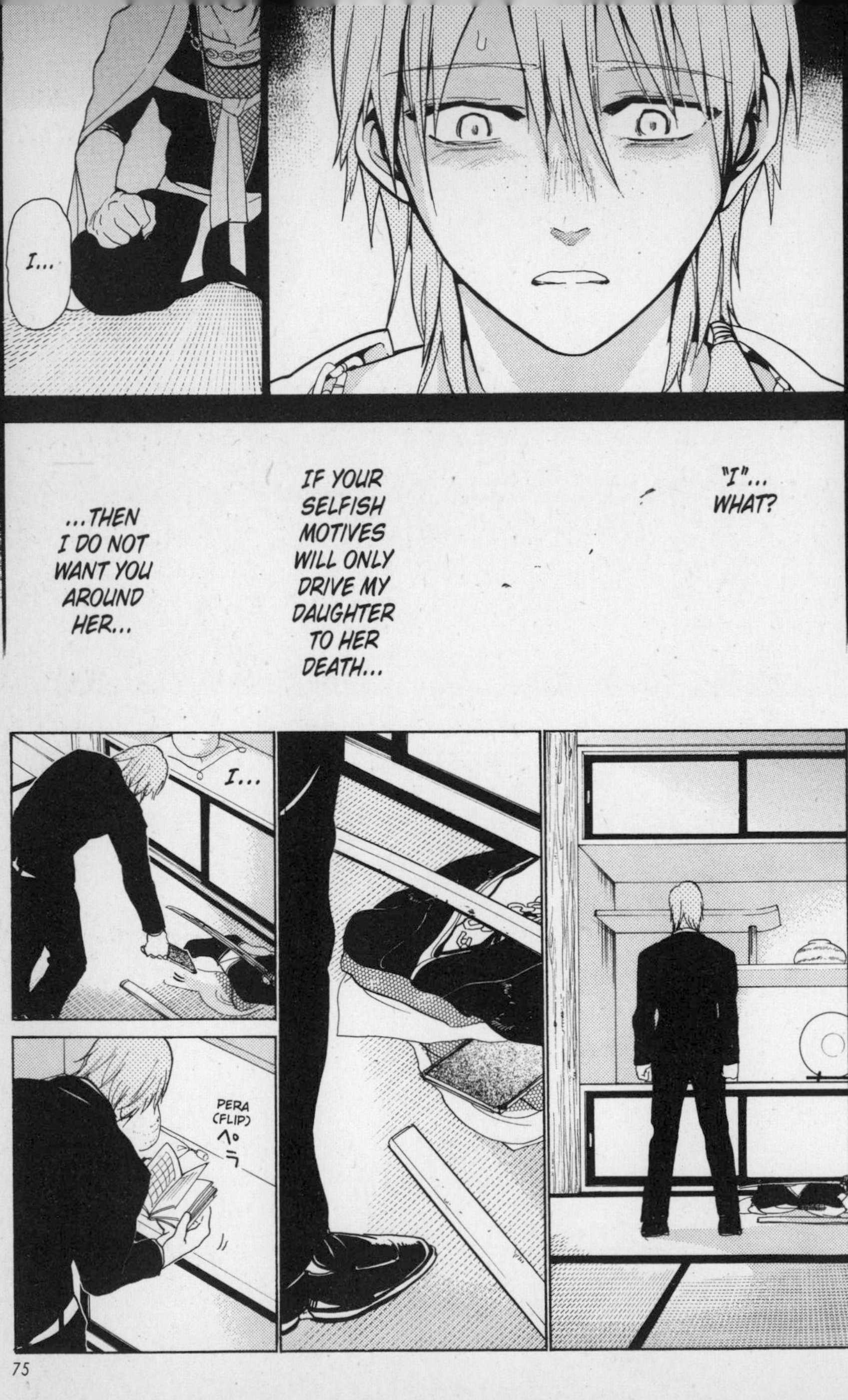
I...
"I"... WHAT?
IF YOUR SELFISH MOTIVES WILL ONLY DRIVE MY DAUGHTER TO HER DEATH...
...THEN I DO NOT WANT YOU AROUND HER...
I...
PERA (FLIP)
ペラ

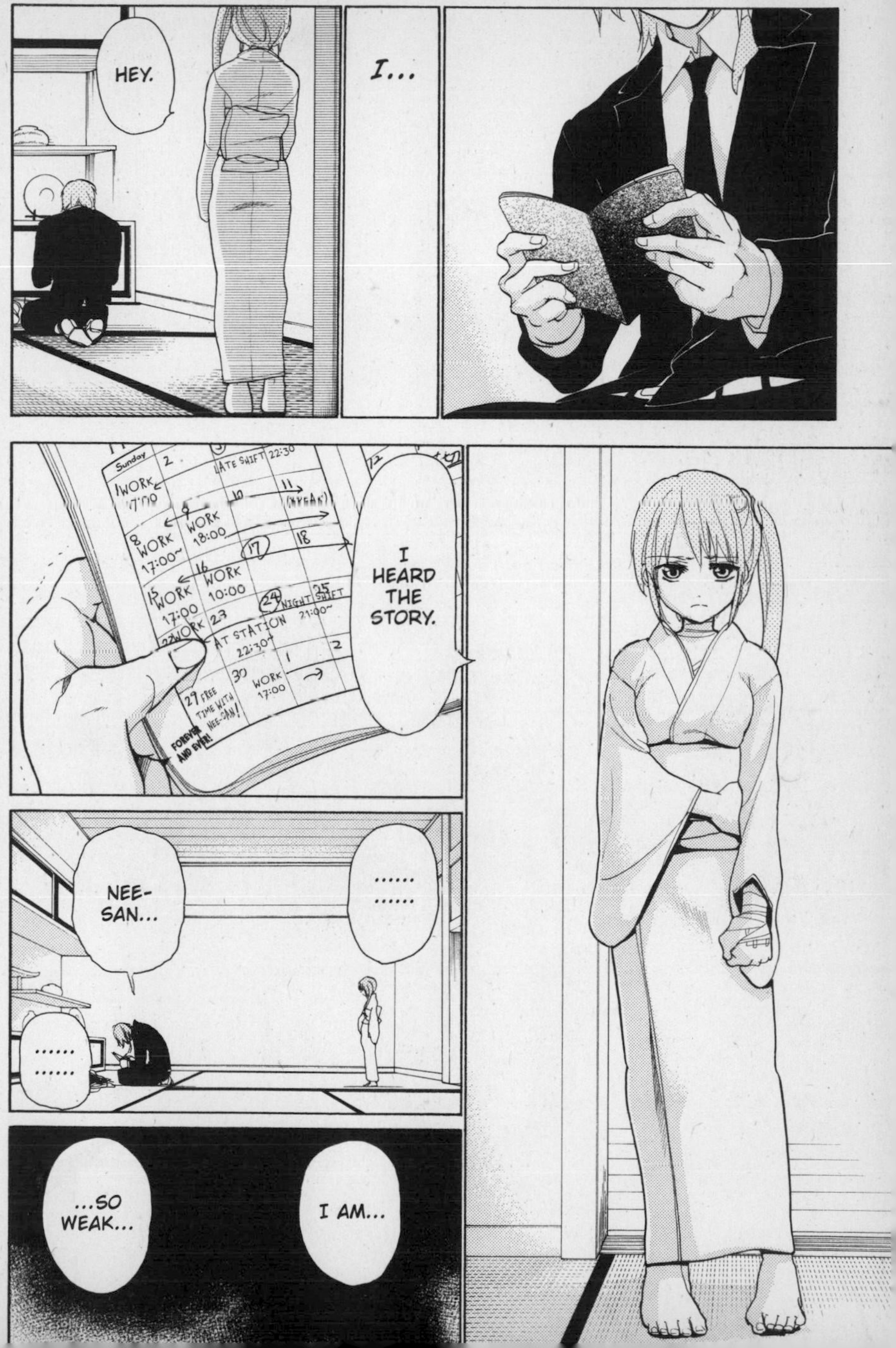
I...
HEY.
I HEARD THE STORY.
Sunday
LATE SHIFT 22:30
WORK 17:00
WORK 18:00
WORK 17:00~
WORK 10:00
WORK 17:00
NIGHT SHIFT 21:00~
AT STATION 22:30~
WORK 17:00
FREE TIME WITH NEE-SAN!
FOREVER AND EVER!
....
NEE-SAN...
....
I AM...
...SO WEAK...

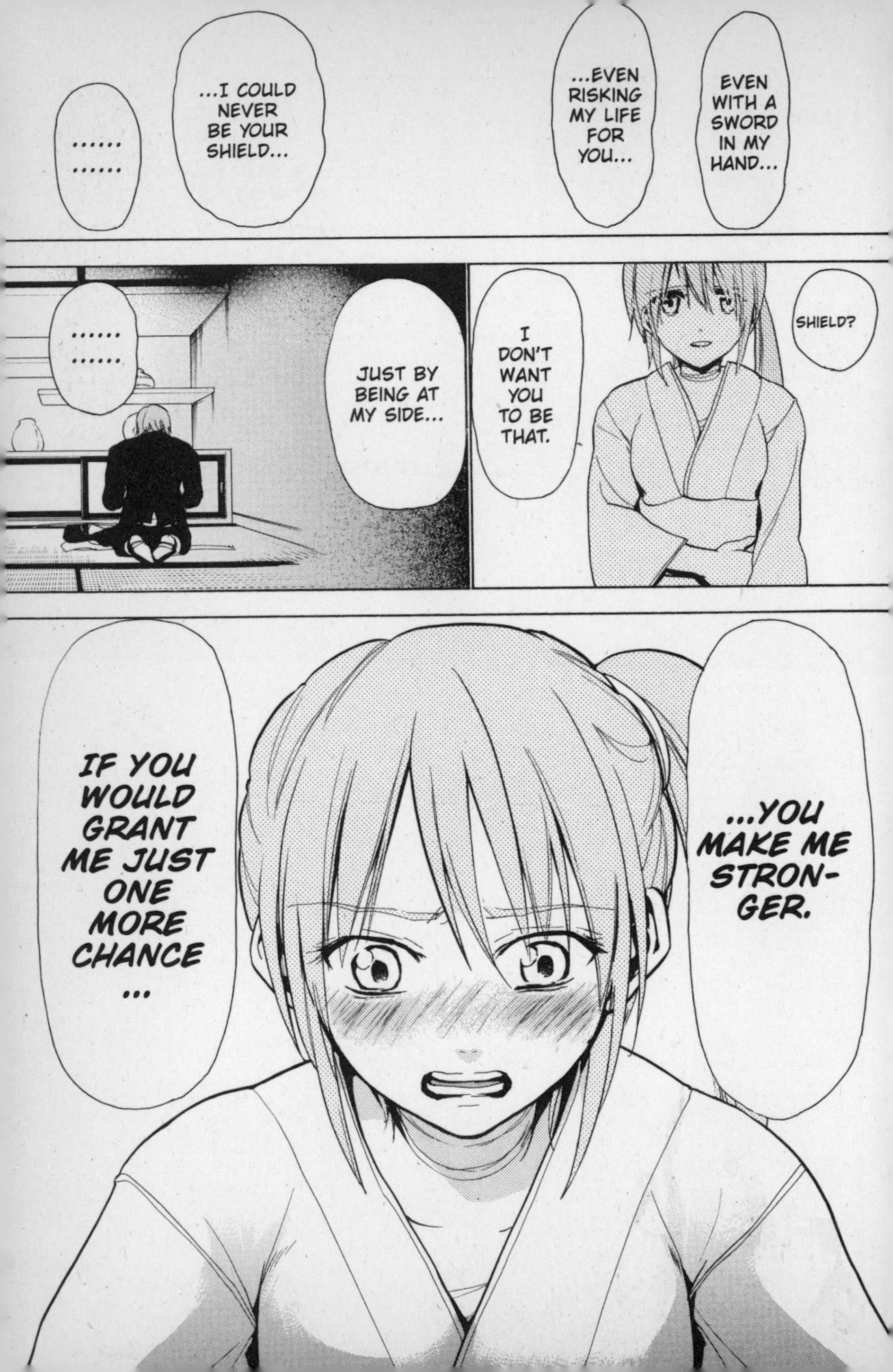
EVEN WITH A SWORD IN MY HAND...
...EVEN RISKING MY LIFE FOR YOU...
...I COULD NEVER BE YOUR SHIELD...
....
SHIELD?
I DON'T WANT YOU TO BE THAT.
JUST BY BEING AT MY SIDE...
....
...YOU MAKE ME STRONGER.
IF YOU WOULD GRANT ME JUST ONE MORE CHANCE...

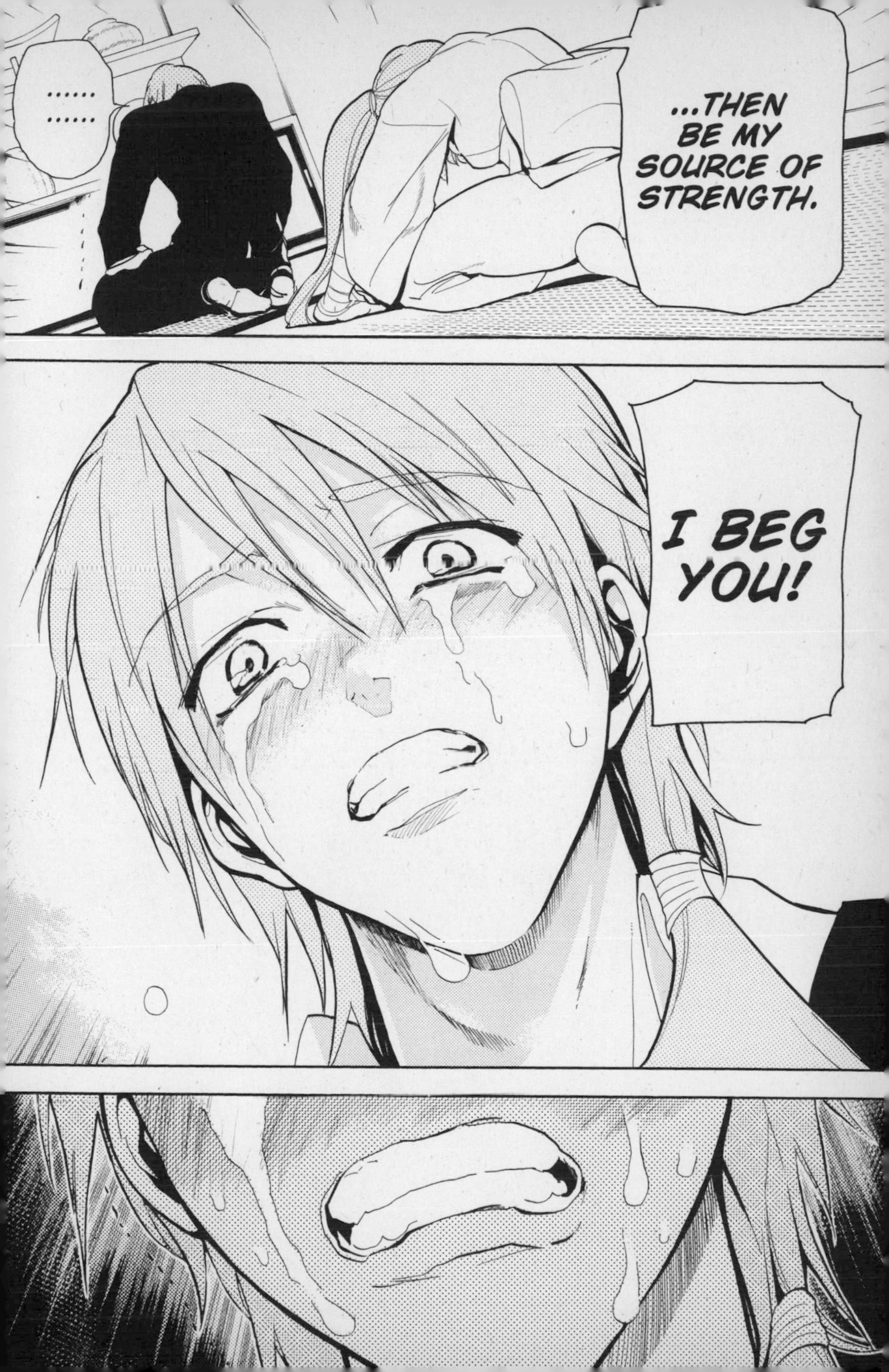
...THEN BE MY SOURCE OF STRENGTH.
....
I BEG YOU!

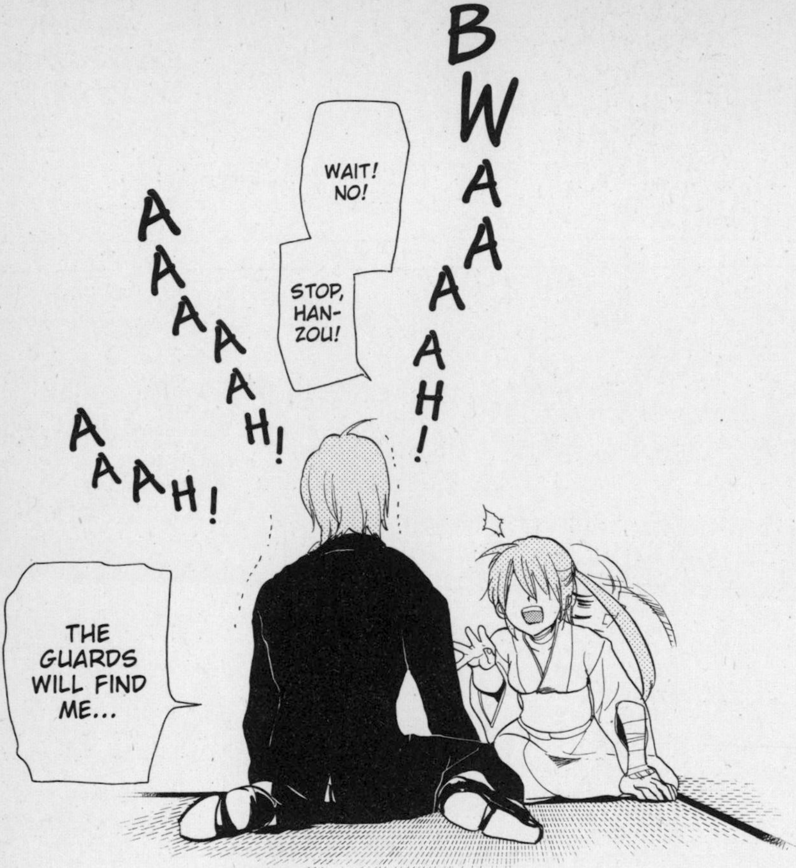
BWAAAAH!
WAIT! NO!
STOP, HAN-ZOU!
AAAAAH!
AAAH!
THE GUARDS WILL FIND ME...

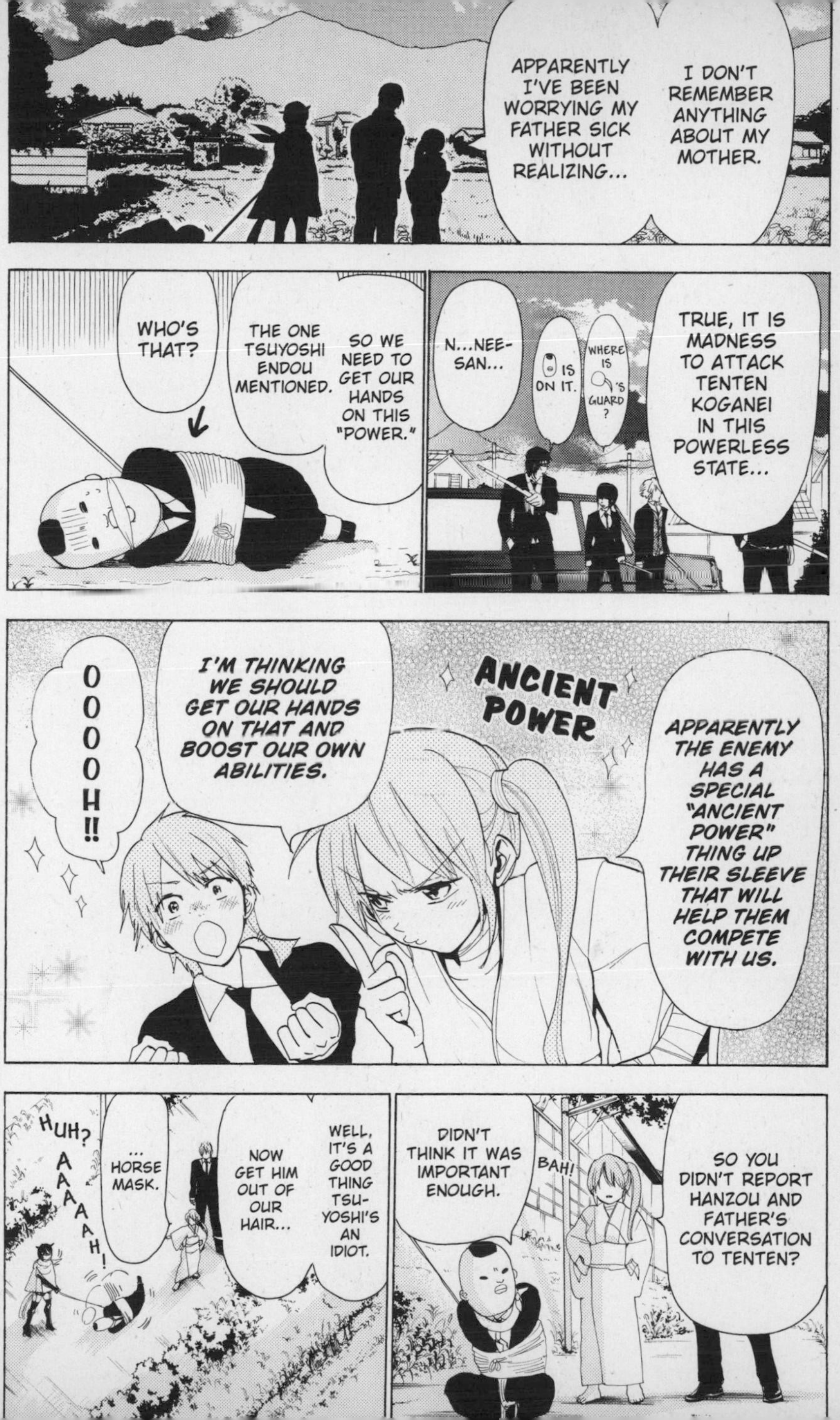
I DON'T REMEMBER ANYTHING ABOUT MY MOTHER.
APPARENTLY I'VE BEEN WORRYING MY FATHER SICK WITHOUT REALIZING...
TRUE, IT IS MADNESS TO ATTACK TENTEN KOGANEI IN THIS POWERLESS STATE...
WHERE IS 'S GUARD?
IS ON IT.
N...NEE-SAN...
SO WE NEED TO GET OUR HANDS ON THIS "POWER."
THE ONE TSUYOSHI ENDOU MENTIONED.
WHO'S THAT?
APPARENTLY THE ENEMY HAS A SPECIAL "ANCIENT POWER" THING UP THEIR SLEEVE THAT WILL HELP THEM COMPETE WITH US.
ANCIENT POWER
I'M THINKING WE SHOULD GET OUR HANDS ON THAT AND BOOST OUR OWN ABILITIES.
OOOOOH!!
SO YOU DIDN'T REPORT HANZOU AND FATHER'S CONVERSATION TO TENTEN?
BAH!
DIDN'T THINK IT WAS IMPORTANT ENOUGH.
WELL, IT'S A GOOD THING TSUYOSHI'S AN IDIOT.
NOW GET HIM OUT OF OUR HAIR...
...HORSE MASK.
HUH?
AAAAAAH!

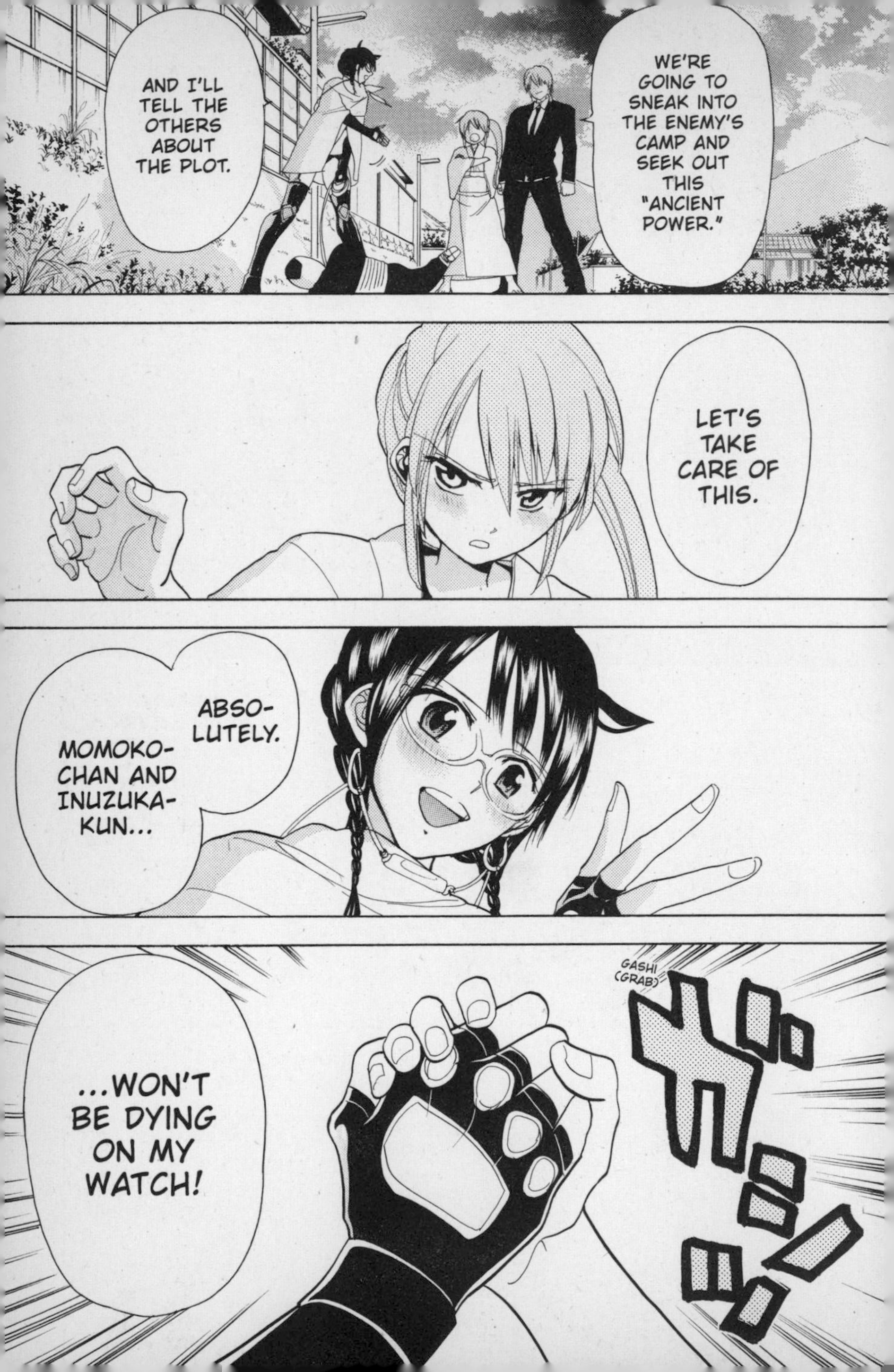
WE'RE GOING TO SNEAK INTO THE ENEMY'S CAMP AND SEEK OUT THIS "ANCIENT POWER."
AND I'LL TELL THE OTHERS ABOUT THE PLOT.
LET'S TAKE CARE OF THIS.
ABSO-LUTELY.
MOMOKO-CHAN AND INUZUKA-KUN...
GASHI (GRAB)
...WON'T BE DYING ON MY WATCH!

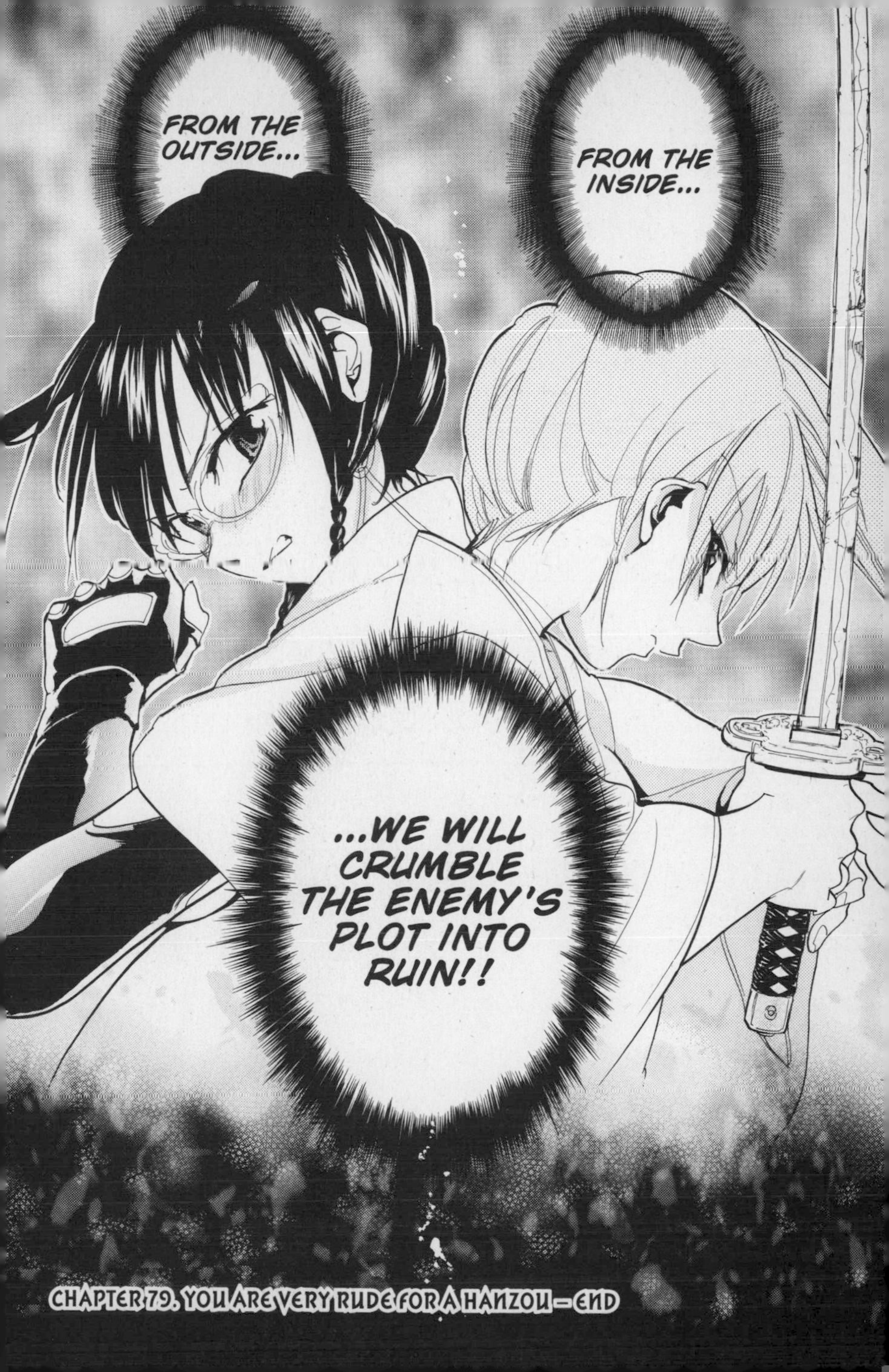
FROM THE INSIDE...
FROM THE OUTSIDE...
...WE WILL CRUMBLE THE ENEMY'S PLOT INTO RUIN!!
CHAPTER 79. YOU ARE VERY RUDE FOR A HANZOU — END

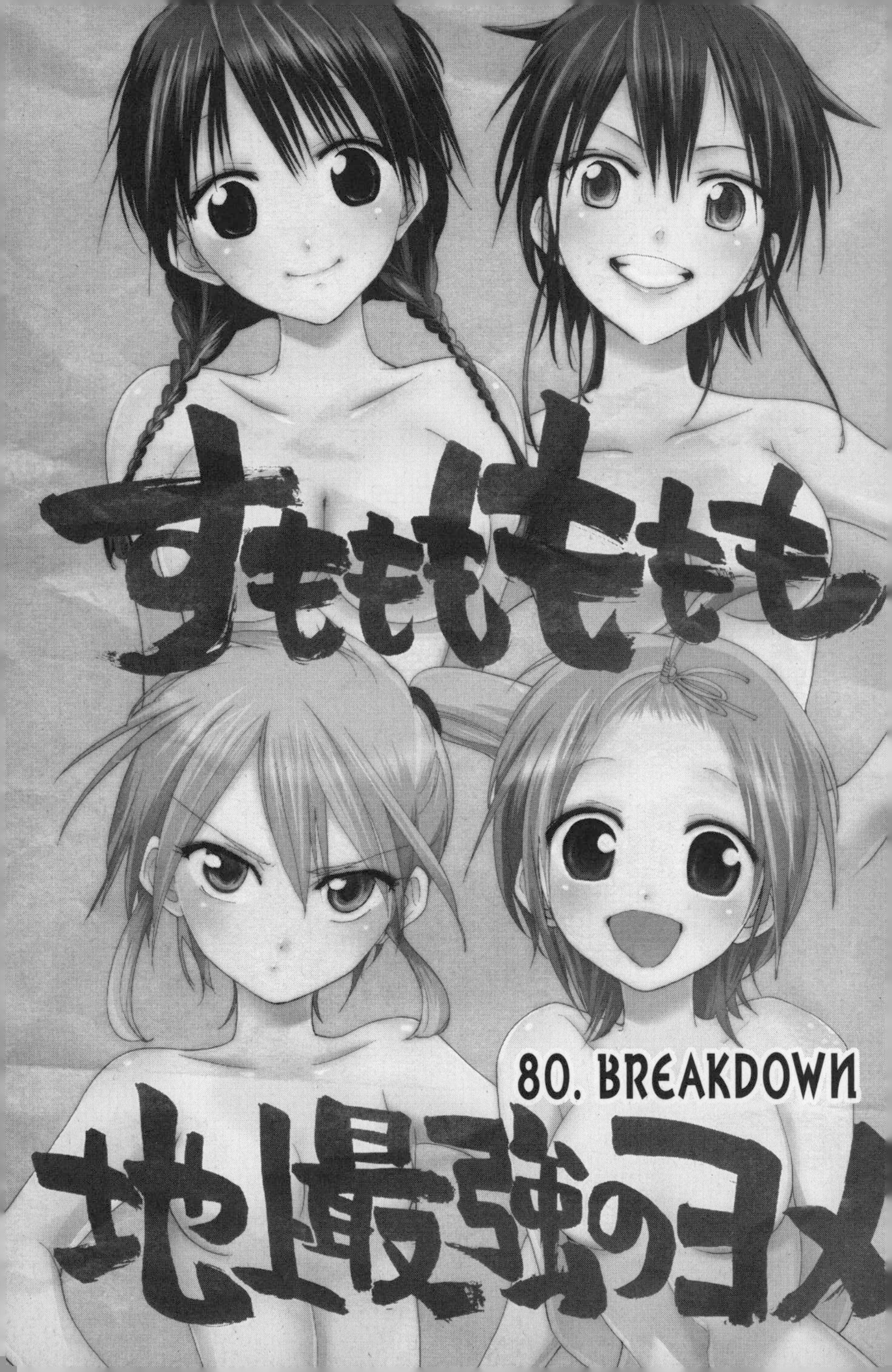
すもももももも
80. BREAKDOWN
地上最強のヨメ

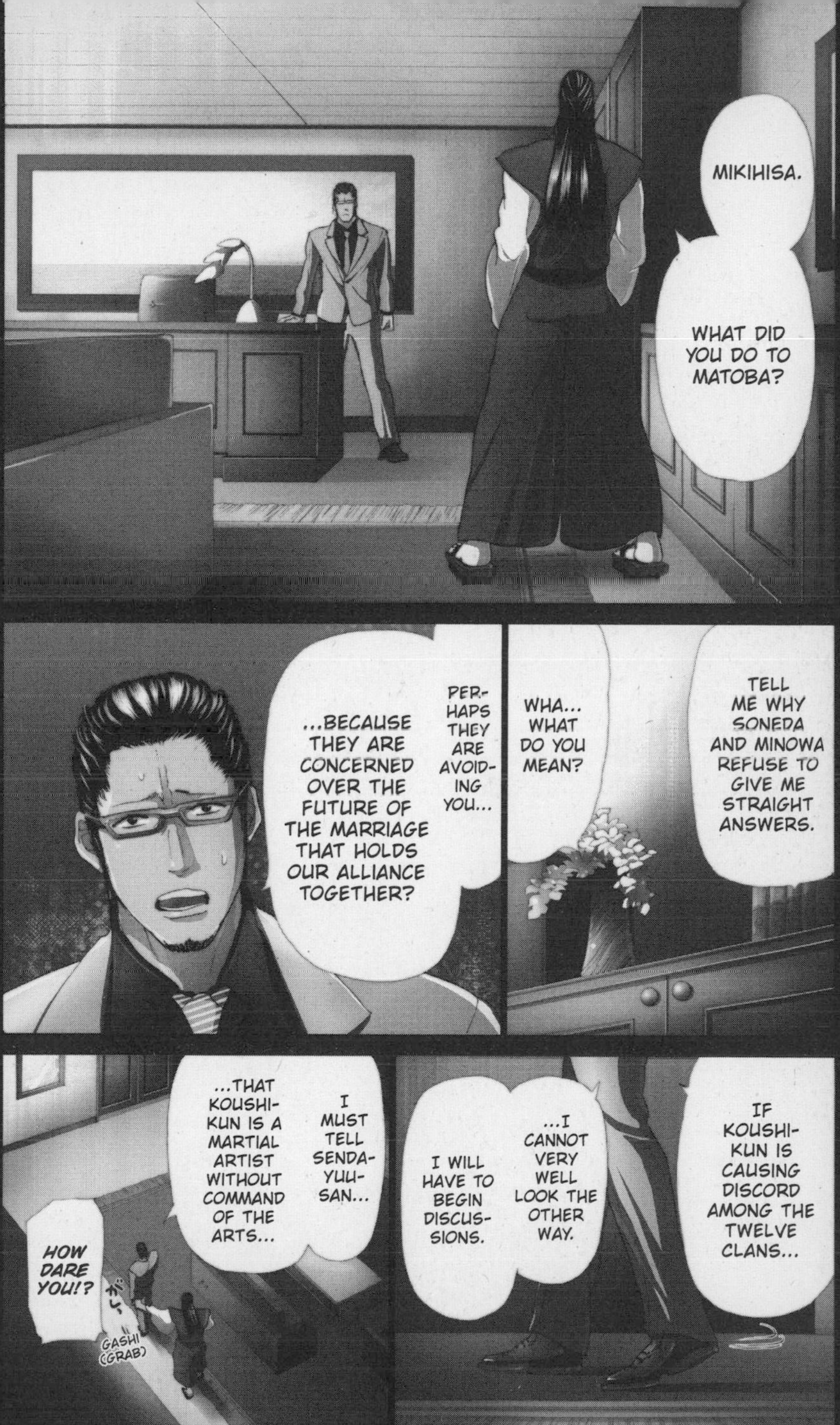
MIKIHISA.
WHAT DID YOU DO TO MATOBA?
TELL ME WHY SONEDA AND MINOWA REFUSE TO GIVE ME STRAIGHT ANSWERS.
WHA... WHAT DO YOU MEAN?
PERHAPS THEY ARE AVOIDING YOU...
...BECAUSE THEY ARE CONCERNED OVER THE FUTURE OF THE MARRIAGE THAT HOLDS OUR ALLIANCE TOGETHER?
IF KOUSHI-KUN IS CAUSING DISCORD AMONG THE TWELVE CLANS...
...I CANNOT VERY WELL LOOK THE OTHER WAY.
I WILL HAVE TO BEGIN DISCUSSIONS.
I MUST TELL SENDA-YUU-SAN...
...THAT KOUSHI-KUN IS A MARTIAL ARTIST WITHOUT COMMAND OF THE ARTS...
HOW DARE YOU!?
GASHI (GRAB)

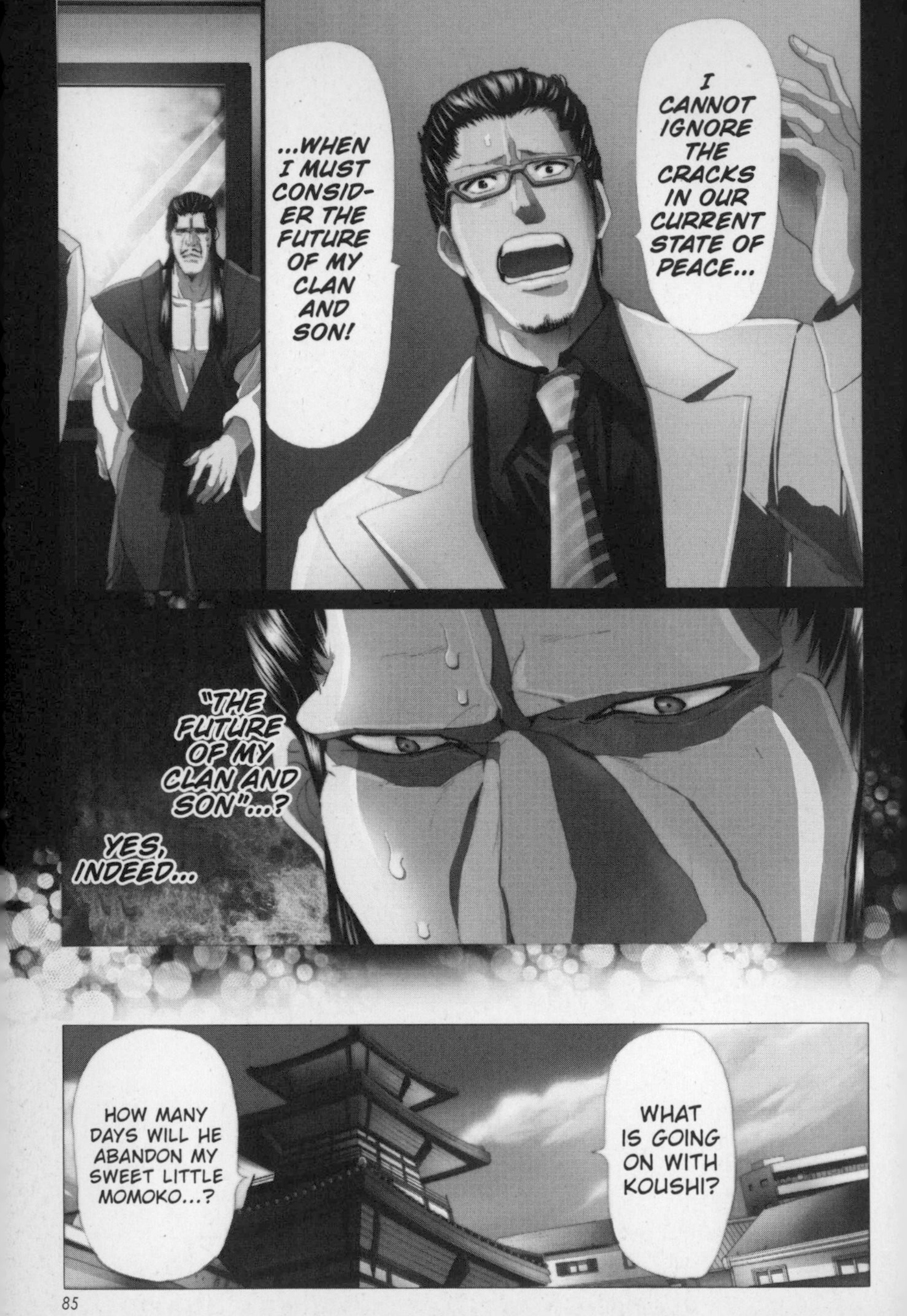
I CANNOT IGNORE THE CRACKS IN OUR CURRENT STATE OF PEACE...
...WHEN I MUST CONSIDER THE FUTURE OF MY CLAN AND SON!
"THE FUTURE OF MY CLAN AND SON"...?
YES, INDEED...
WHAT IS GOING ON WITH KOUSHI?
HOW MANY DAYS WILL HE ABANDON MY SWEET LITTLE MOMOKO...?

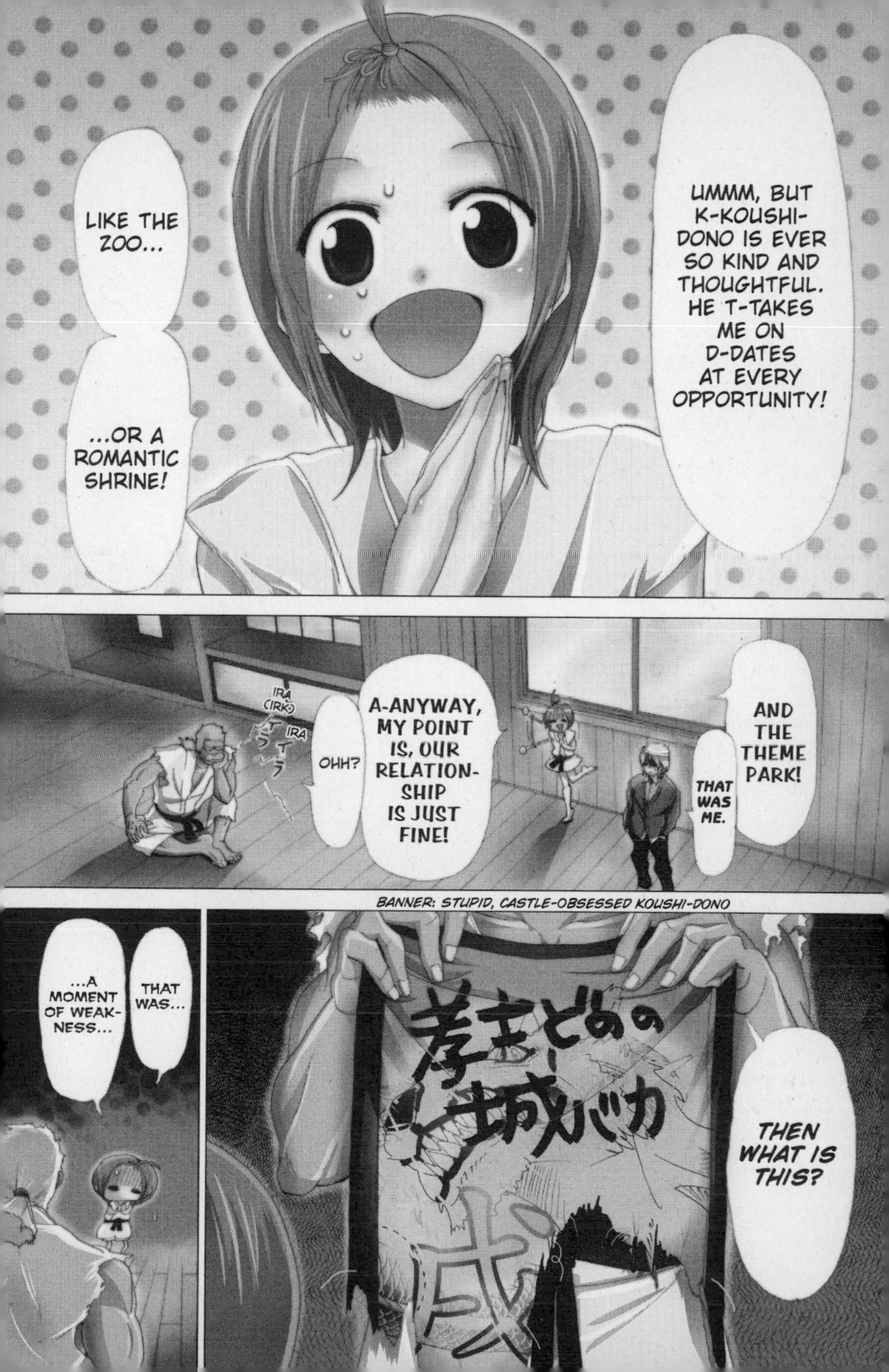
UMMM, BUT K-KOUSHI-DONO IS EVER SO KIND AND THOUGHTFUL. HE T-TAKES ME ON D-DATES AT EVERY OPPORTUNITY!
LIKE THE ZOO...
...OR A ROMANTIC SHRINE!
AND THE THEME PARK!
THAT WAS ME.
A-ANYWAY, MY POINT IS, OUR RELATIONSHIP IS JUST FINE!
OHH?
IRA (IRK) IRA
BANNER: STUPID, CASTLE-OBSESSED KOUSHI-DONO
孝士どのの城バカ
THEN WHAT IS THIS?
THAT WAS...
...A MOMENT OF WEAKNESS...

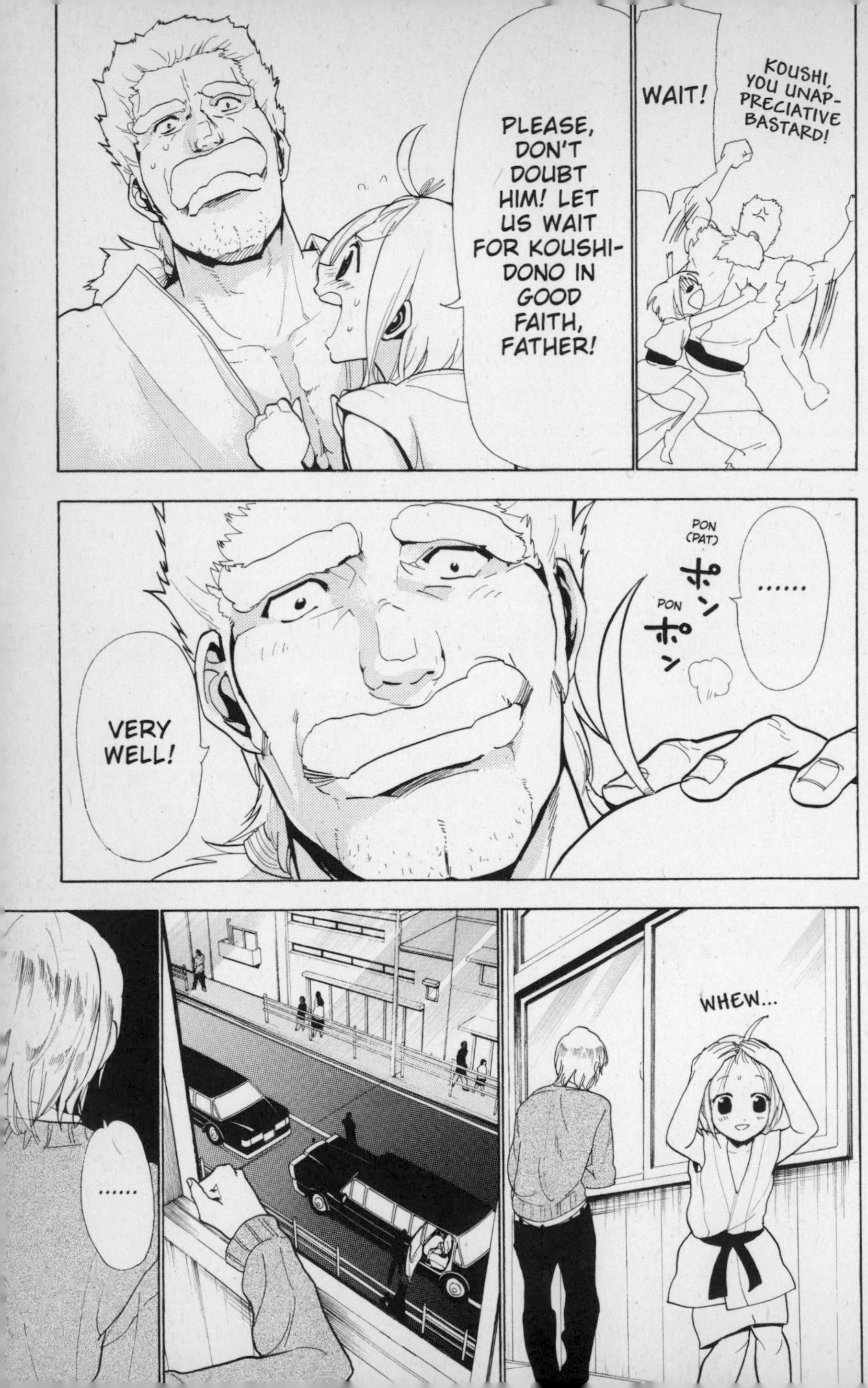
KOUSHI, YOU UNAPPRECIATIVE BASTARD!
WAIT!
PLEASE, DON'T DOUBT HIM! LET US WAIT FOR KOUSHI-DONO IN GOOD FAITH, FATHER!
......
PON (PAT)
ポン
PON
ポン
VERY WELL!
WHEW...
......

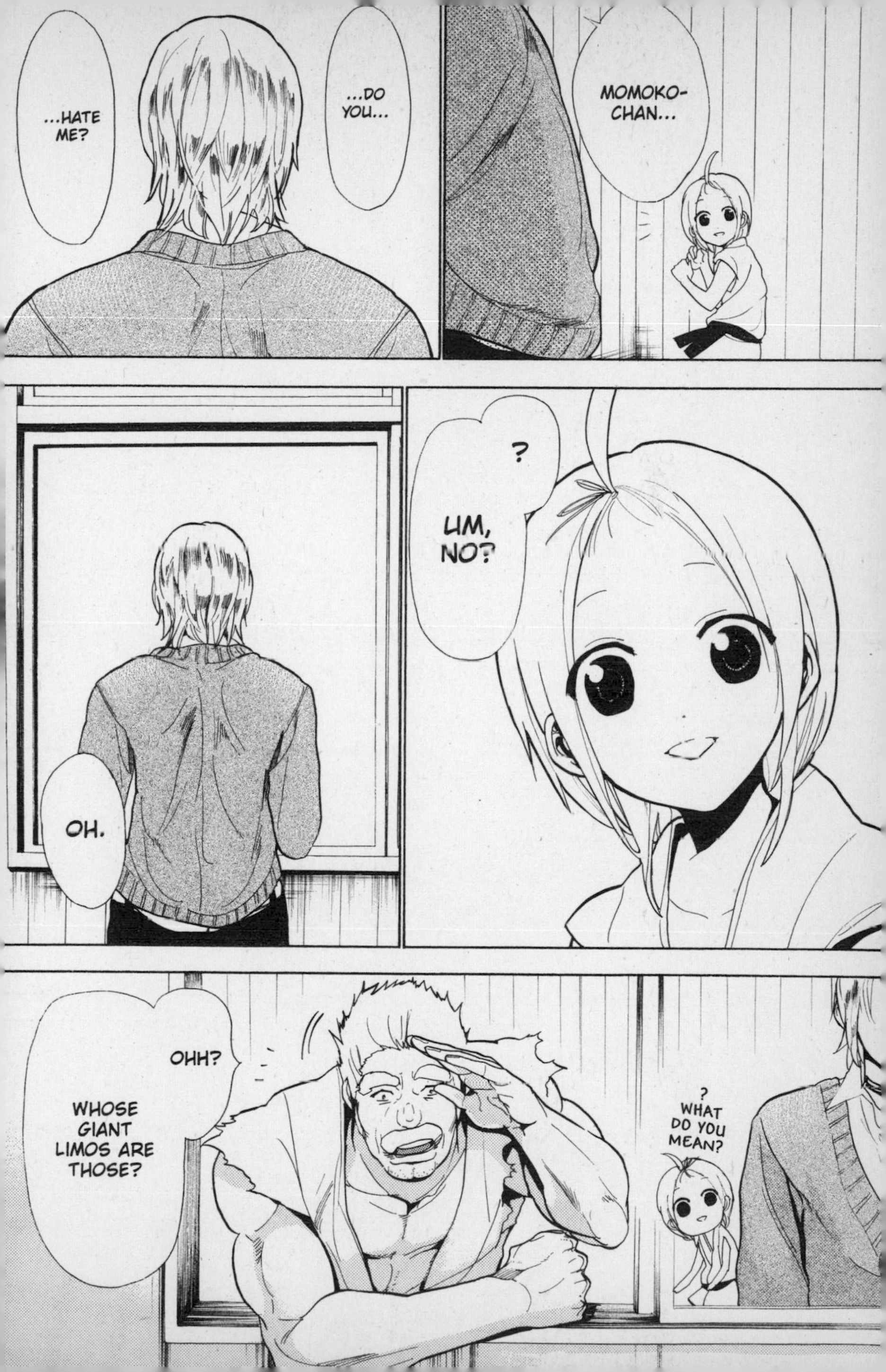
MOMOKO-CHAN...
...DO YOU...
...HATE ME?
?
UM, NO?
OH.
? WHAT DO YOU MEAN?
OHH?
WHOSE GIANT LIMOS ARE THOSE?

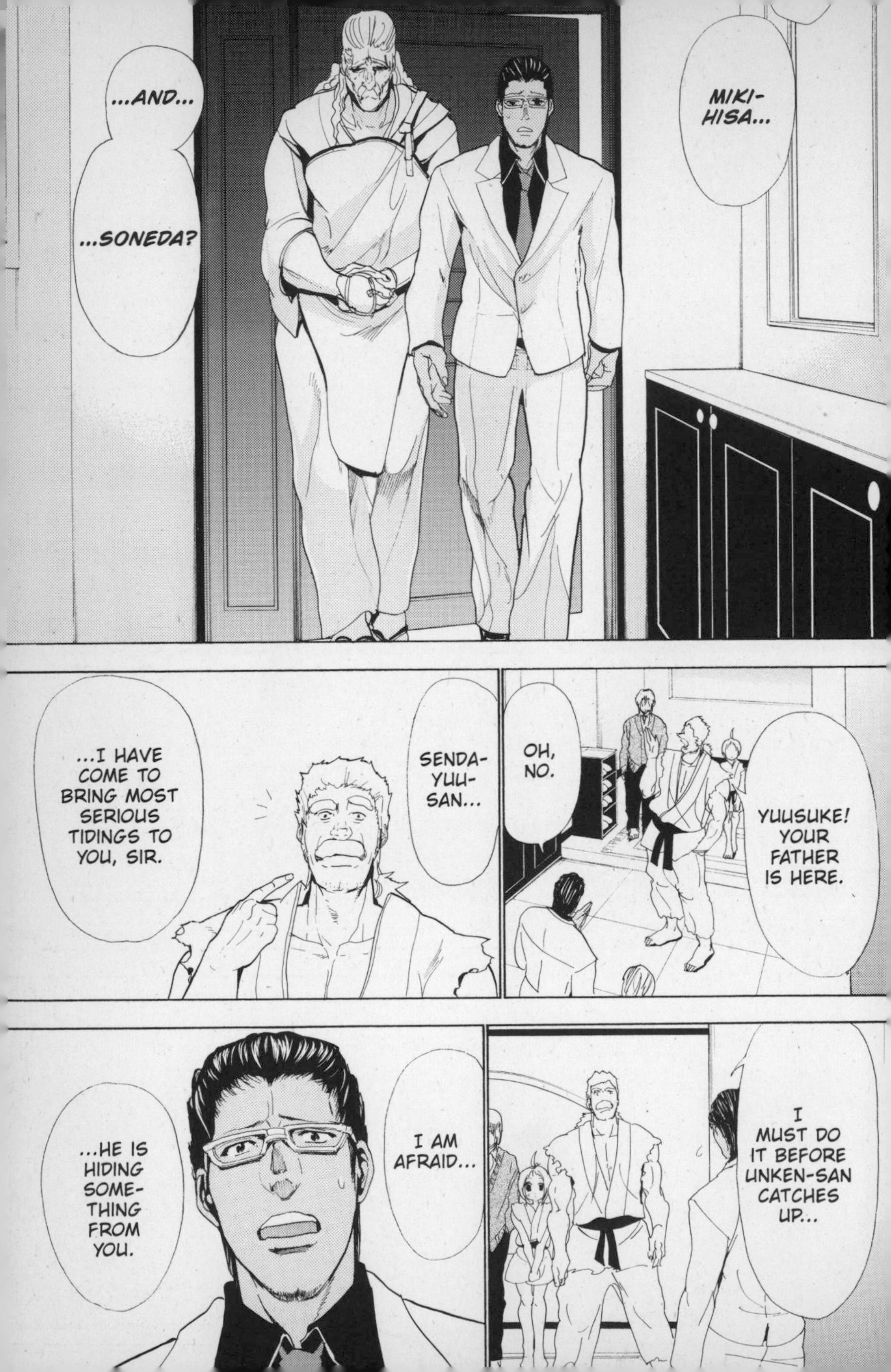
MIKI-HISA...
...AND...
...SONEDA?
YUUSUKE! YOUR FATHER IS HERE.
OH, NO.
SENDA-YUU-SAN...
...I HAVE COME TO BRING MOST SERIOUS TIDINGS TO YOU, SIR.
I MUST DO IT BEFORE UNKEN-SAN CATCHES UP...
I AM AFRAID...
...HE IS HIDING SOME-THING FROM YOU.

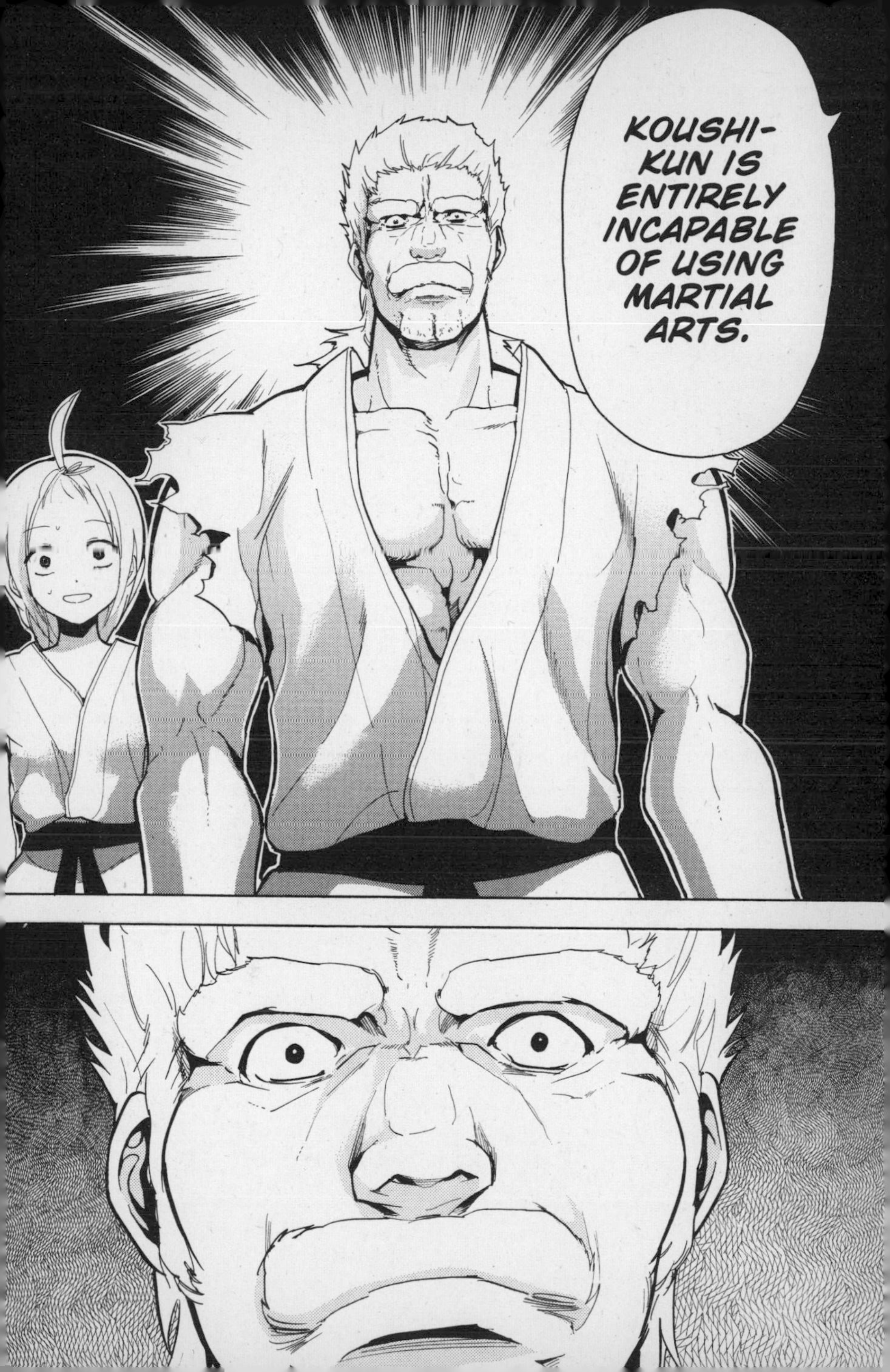
KOUSHI-KUN IS ENTIRELY INCAPABLE OF USING MARTIAL ARTS.

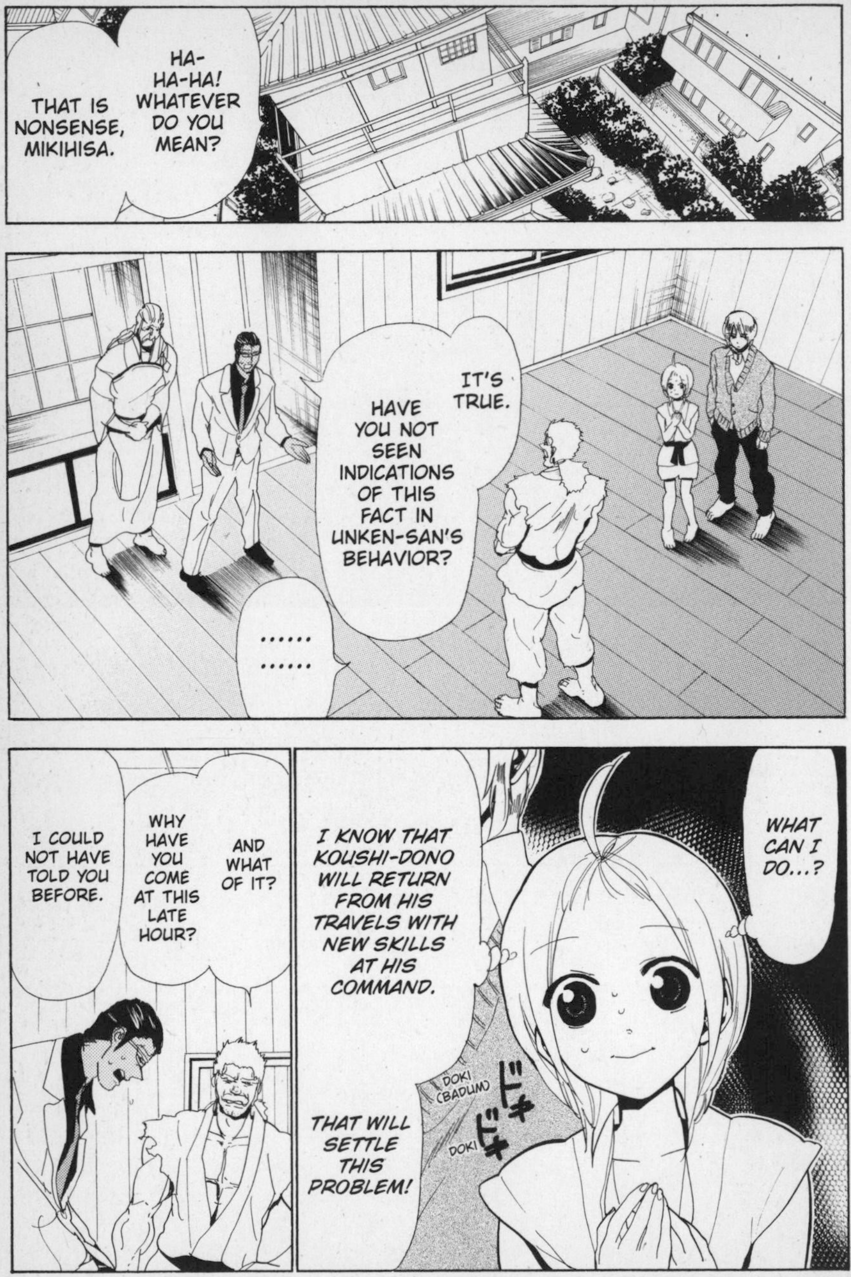
HA-HA-HA! WHATEVER DO YOU MEAN?
THAT IS NONSENSE, MIKIHISA.
IT'S TRUE.
HAVE YOU NOT SEEN INDICATIONS OF THIS FACT IN UNKEN-SAN'S BEHAVIOR?
....
WHAT CAN I DO...?
I KNOW THAT KOUSHI-DONO WILL RETURN FROM HIS TRAVELS WITH NEW SKILLS AT HIS COMMAND.
DOKI (BADUM)
DOKI
THAT WILL SETTLE THIS PROBLEM!
AND WHAT OF IT?
WHY HAVE YOU COME AT THIS LATE HOUR?
I COULD NOT HAVE TOLD YOU BEFORE.

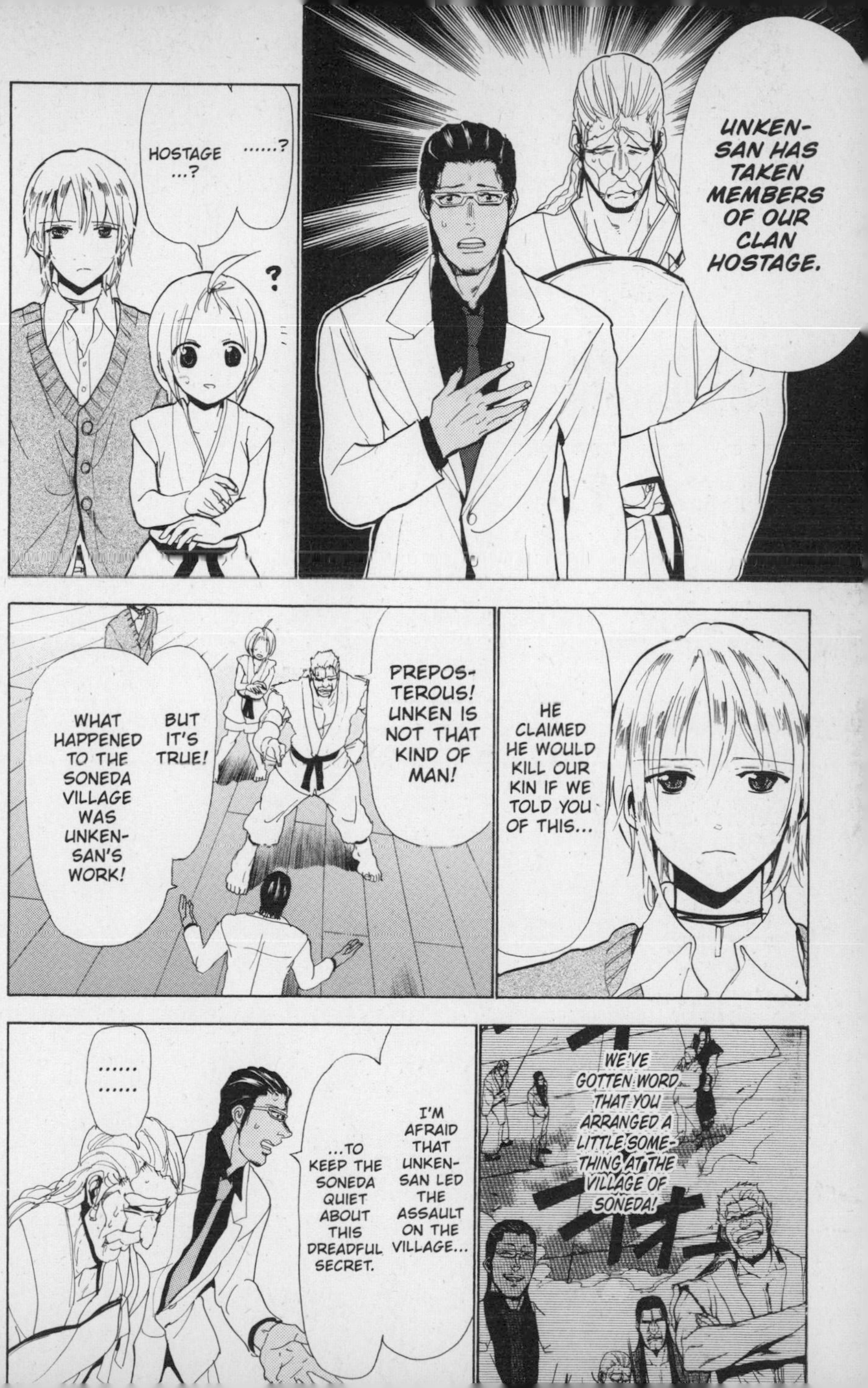
UNKEN-SAN HAS TAKEN MEMBERS OF OUR CLAN HOSTAGE.
......?
HOSTAGE ...?
?
HE CLAIMED HE WOULD KILL OUR KIN IF WE TOLD YOU OF THIS...
PREPOSTEROUS! UNKEN IS NOT THAT KIND OF MAN!
BUT IT'S TRUE!
WHAT HAPPENED TO THE SONEDA VILLAGE WAS UNKEN-SAN'S WORK!
WE'VE GOTTEN WORD THAT YOU ARRANGED A LITTLE SOMETHING AT THE VILLAGE OF SONEDA!
I'M AFRAID THAT UNKEN-SAN LED THE ASSAULT ON THE VILLAGE...
...TO KEEP THE SONEDA QUIET ABOUT THIS DREADFUL SECRET.
....

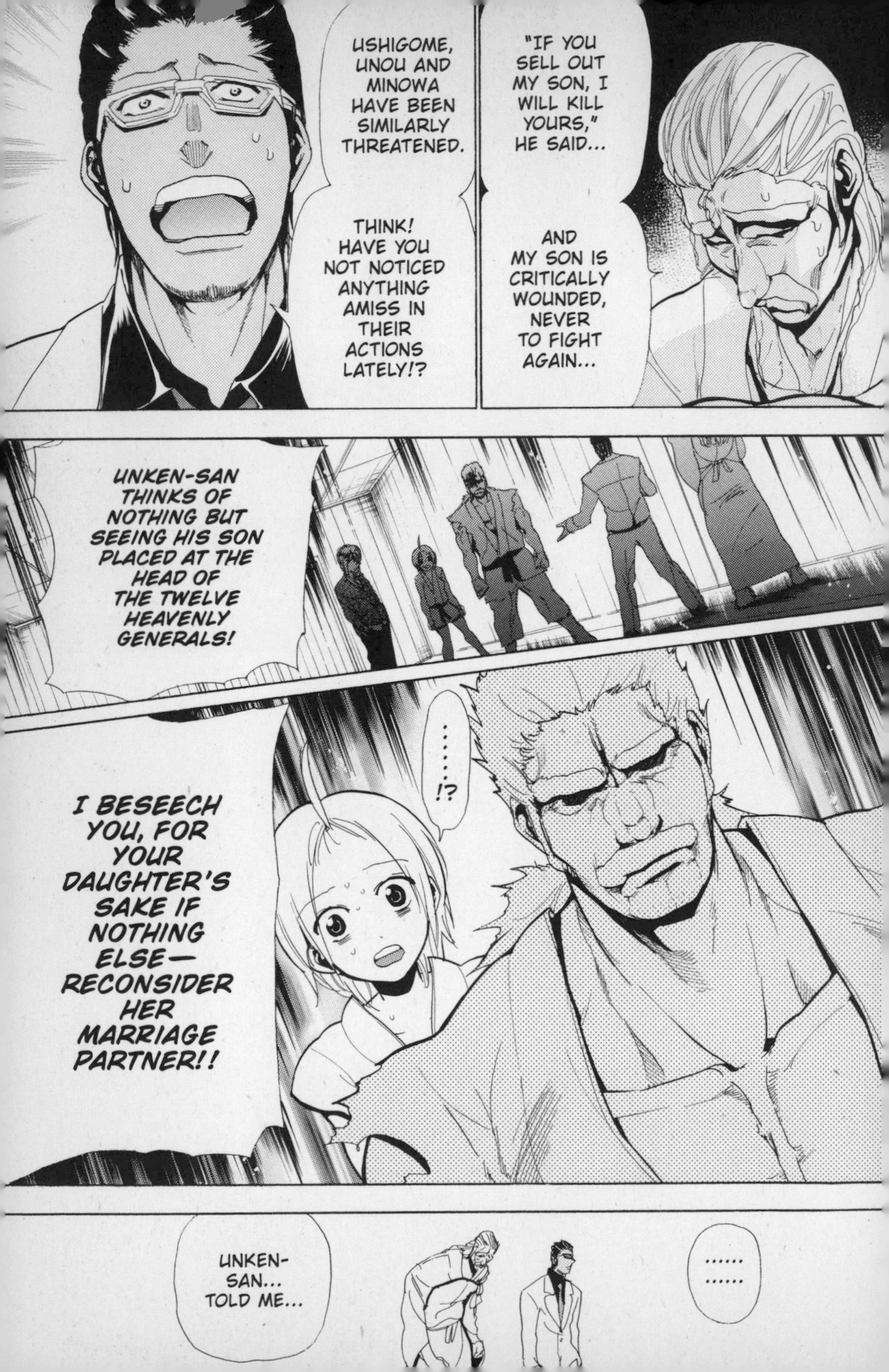
"IF YOU SELL OUT MY SON, I WILL KILL YOURS," HE SAID...
AND MY SON IS CRITICALLY WOUNDED, NEVER TO FIGHT AGAIN...
USHIGOME, UNOU AND MINOWA HAVE BEEN SIMILARLY THREATENED.
THINK! HAVE YOU NOT NOTICED ANYTHING AMISS IN THEIR ACTIONS LATELY!?
UNKEN-SAN THINKS OF NOTHING BUT SEEING HIS SON PLACED AT THE HEAD OF THE TWELVE HEAVENLY GENERALS!
......!?
I BESEECH YOU, FOR YOUR DAUGHTER'S SAKE IF NOTHING ELSE—RECONSIDER HER MARRIAGE PARTNER!!
....
UNKEN-SAN... TOLD ME...

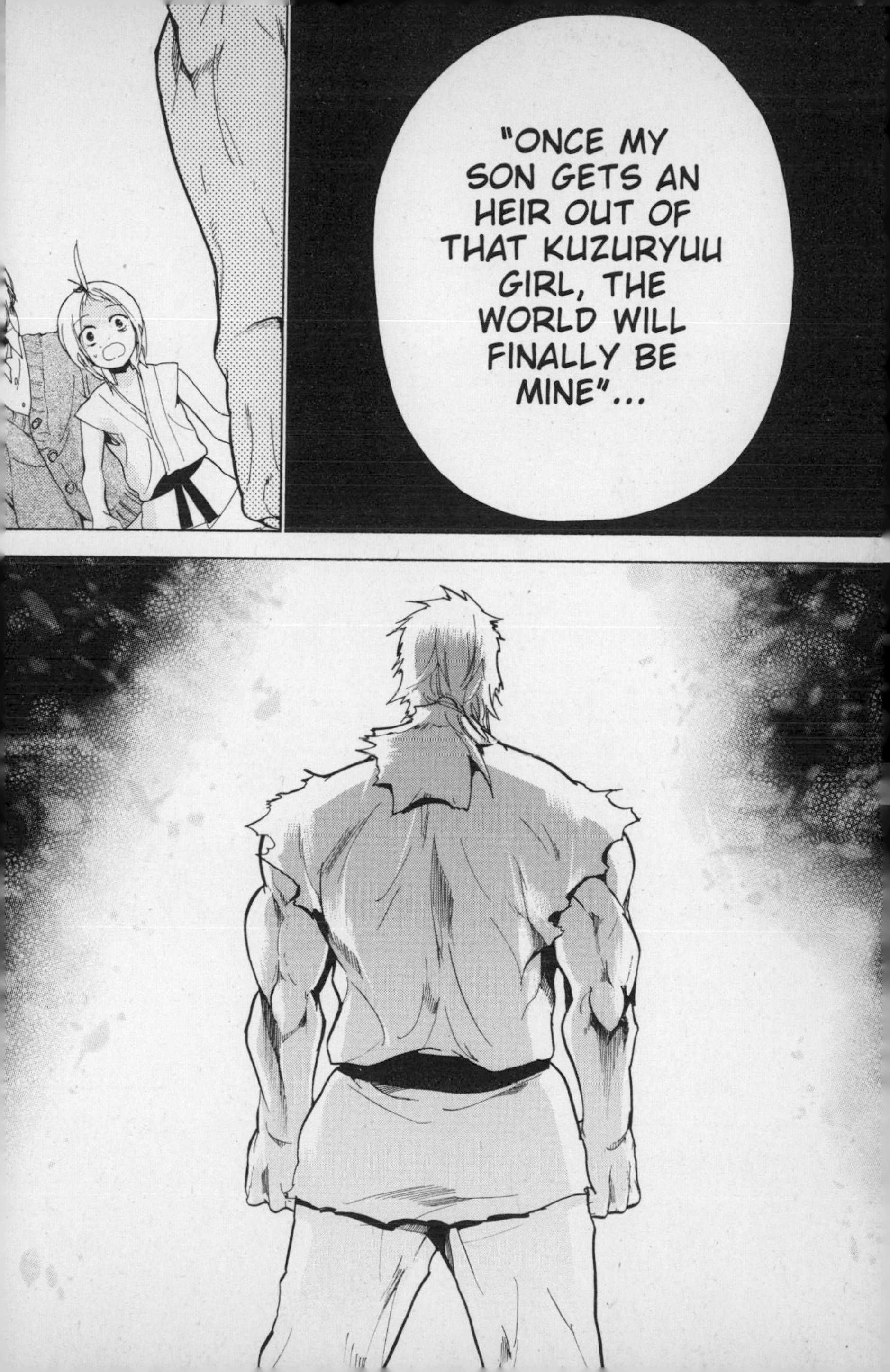
"ONCE MY SON GETS AN HEIR OUT OF THAT KUZURYUU GIRL, THE WORLD WILL FINALLY BE MINE"...

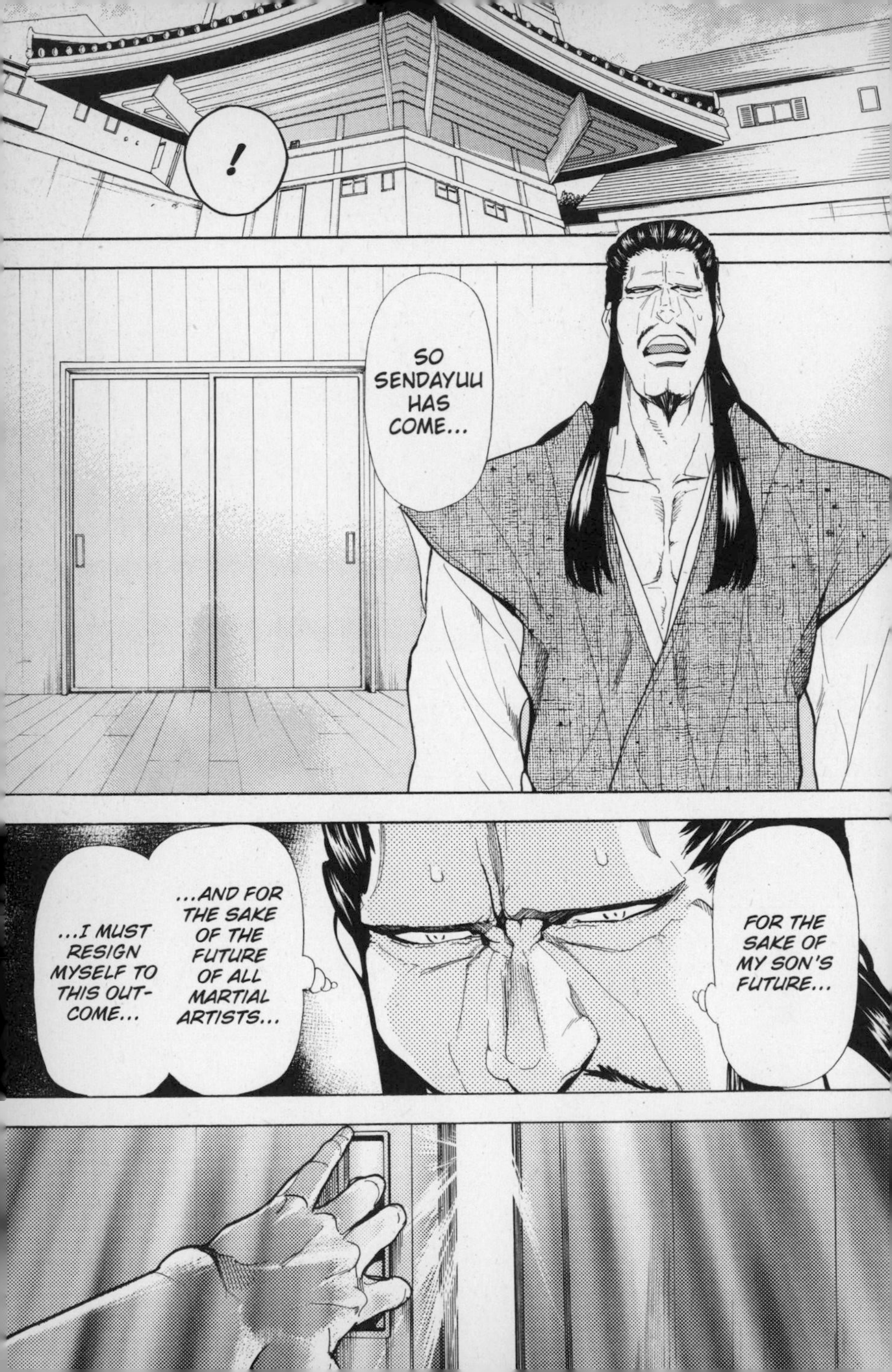
!
SO SENDAYUU HAS COME...
FOR THE SAKE OF MY SON'S FUTURE...
...AND FOR THE SAKE OF THE FUTURE OF ALL MARTIAL ARTISTS...
...I MUST RESIGN MYSELF TO THIS OUT-COME...

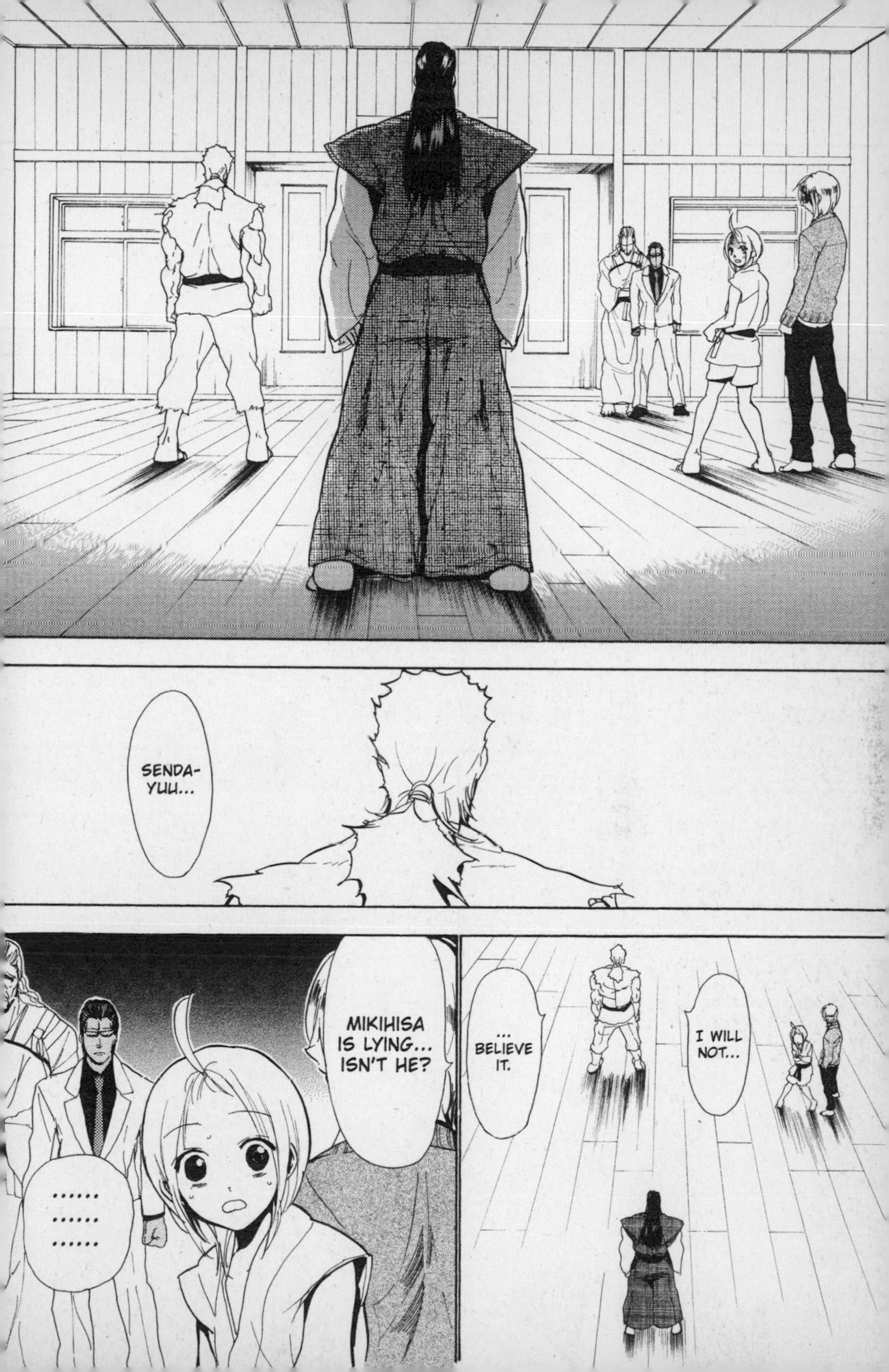
SENDA-YUU...
I WILL NOT...
... BELIEVE IT.
MIKIHISA IS LYING... ISN'T HE?
......
......
......

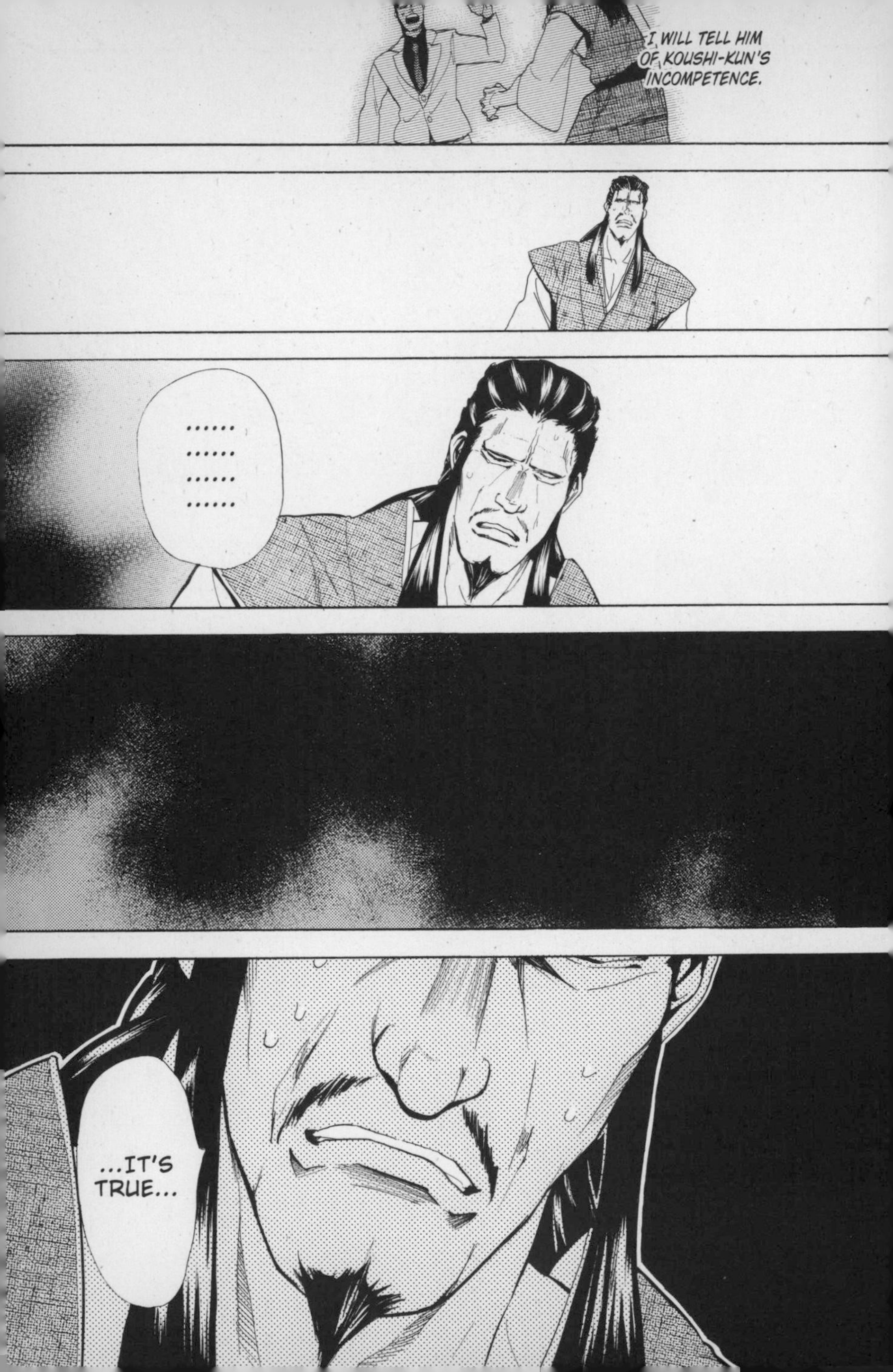
I WILL TELL HIM OF KOUSHI-KUN'S INCOMPETENCE.
......
......
......
......
...IT'S TRUE...

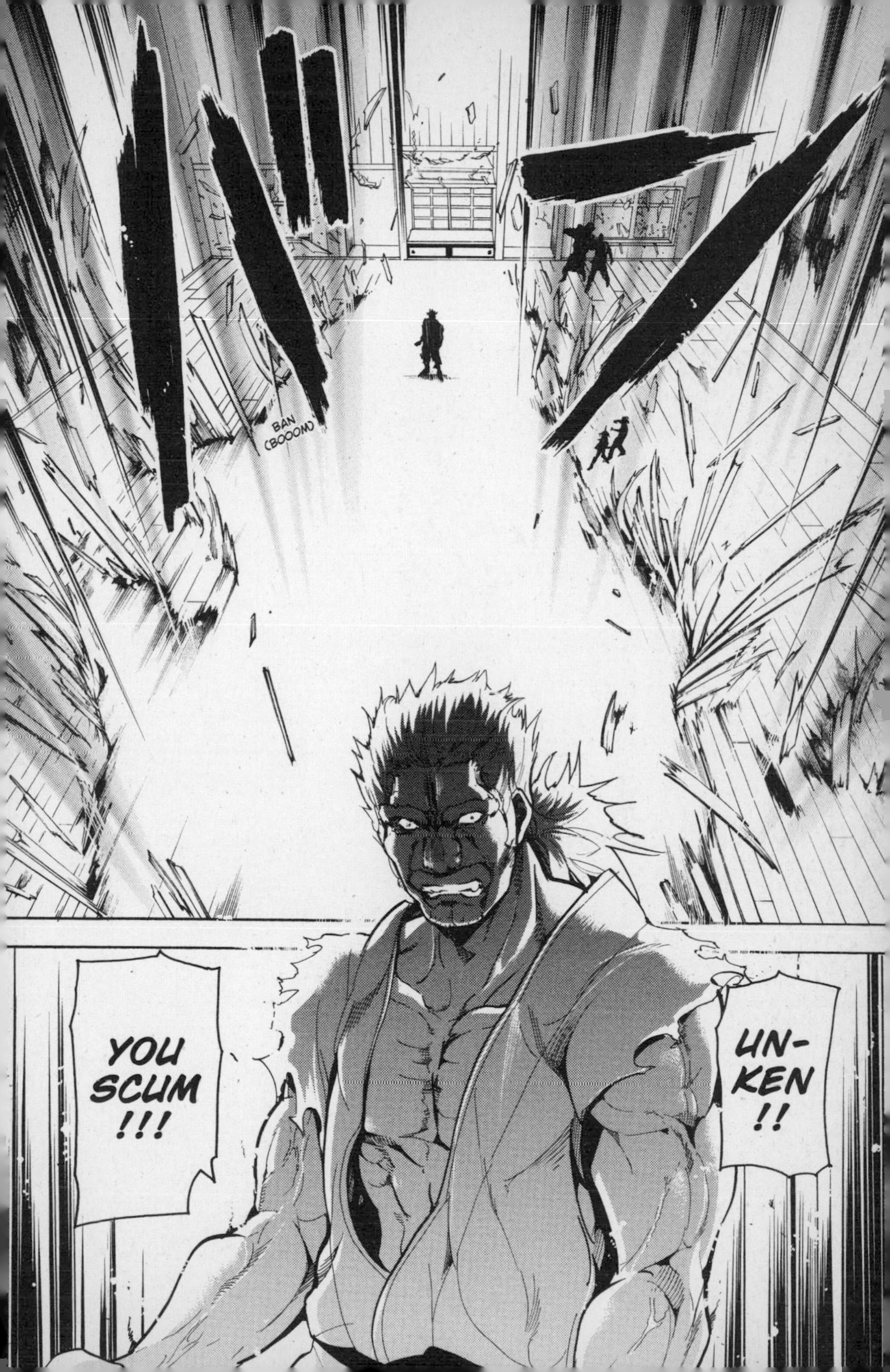
BAN (BOOOM)
UN-KEN!!
YOU SCUM!!!

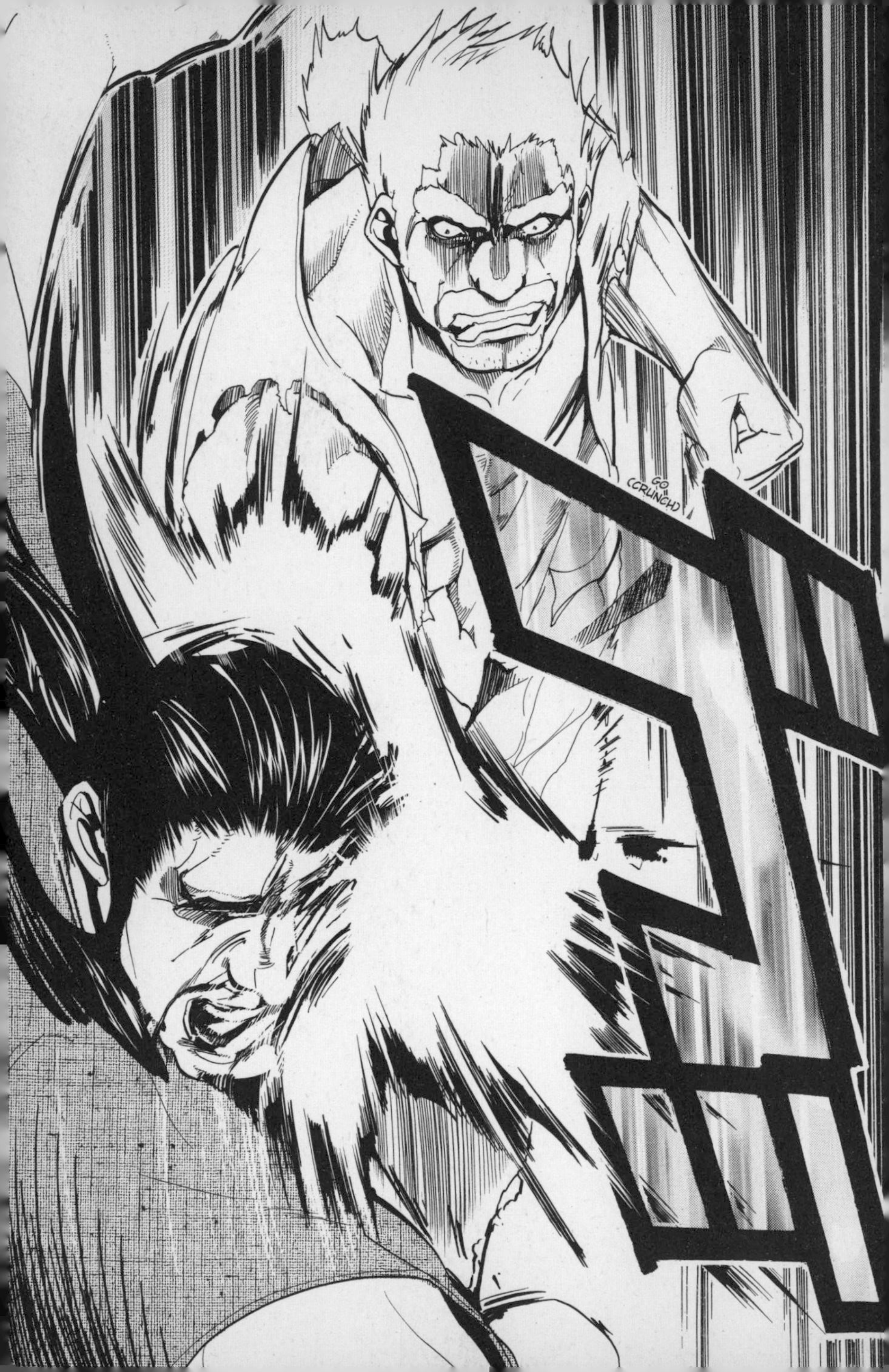
GO
(CRUNCH)

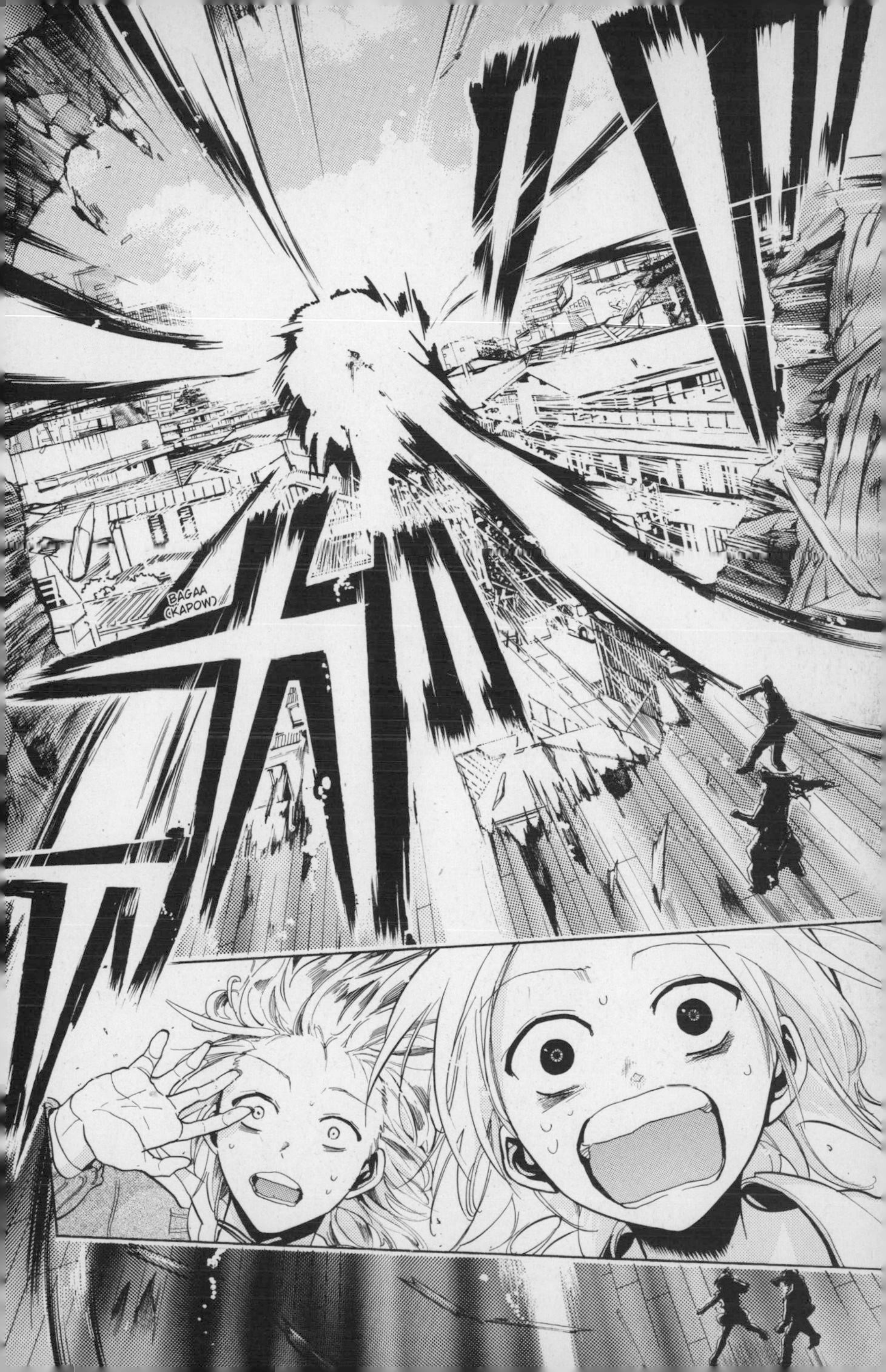
BAGAA
(KAPOW)

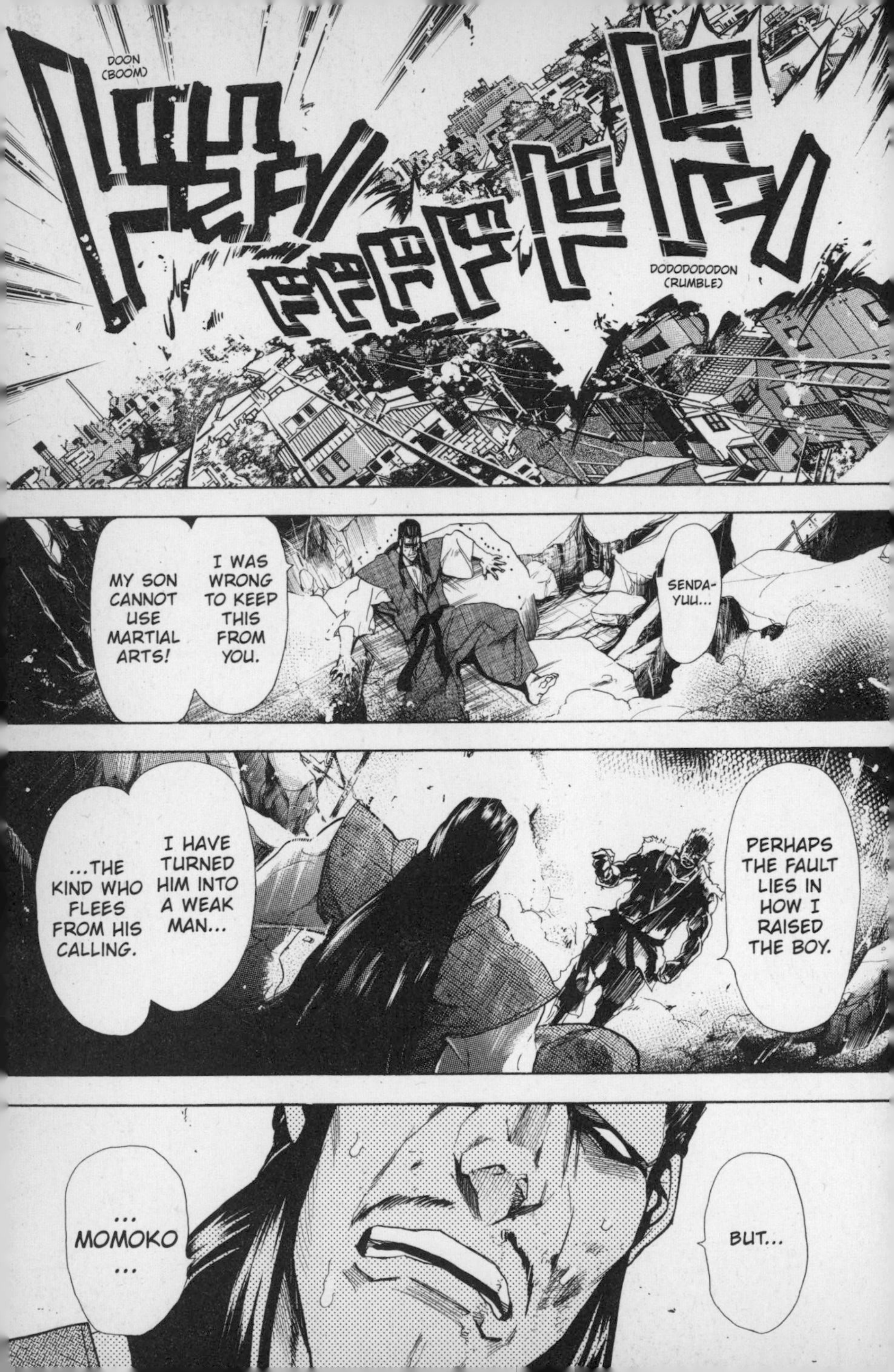
DOON (BOOM)
DODODODODON (RUMBLE)
SENDA-YUU...
I WAS WRONG TO KEEP THIS FROM YOU.
MY SON CANNOT USE MARTIAL ARTS!
PERHAPS THE FAULT LIES IN HOW I RAISED THE BOY.
I HAVE TURNED HIM INTO A WEAK MAN...
...THE KIND WHO FLEES FROM HIS CALLING.
BUT...
... MOMOKO ...

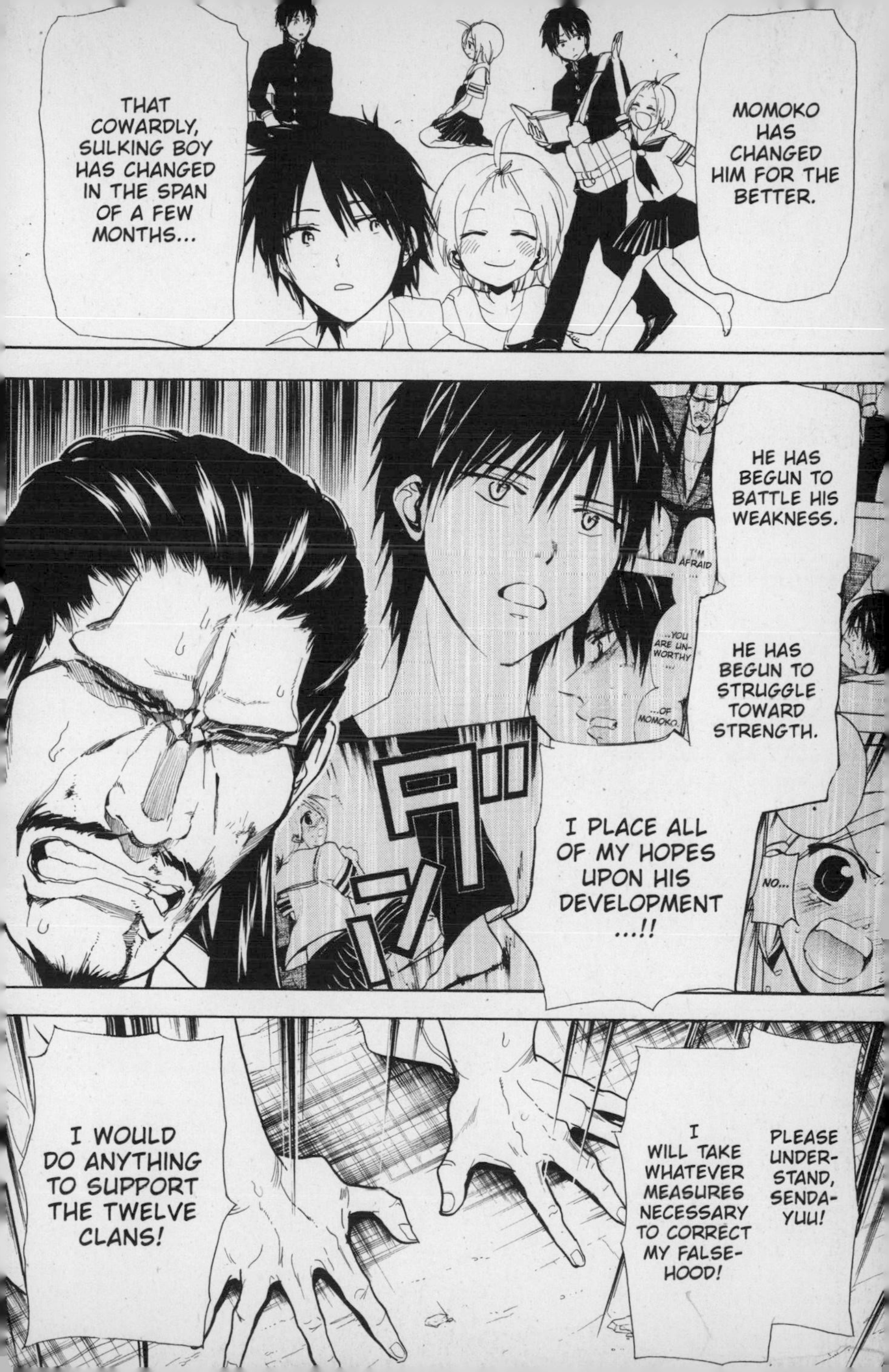
MOMOKO HAS CHANGED HIM FOR THE BETTER.
THAT COWARDLY, SULKING BOY HAS CHANGED IN THE SPAN OF A FEW MONTHS...
HE HAS BEGUN TO BATTLE HIS WEAKNESS.
I'M AFRAID...
...YOU ARE UN-WORTHY...
...OF MOMOKO.
HE HAS BEGUN TO STRUGGLE TOWARD STRENGTH.
NO...
I PLACE ALL OF MY HOPES UPON HIS DEVELOPMENT ...!!
PLEASE UNDER-STAND, SENDA-YUU!
I WILL TAKE WHATEVER MEASURES NECESSARY TO CORRECT MY FALSE-HOOD!
I WOULD DO ANYTHING TO SUPPORT THE TWELVE CLANS!

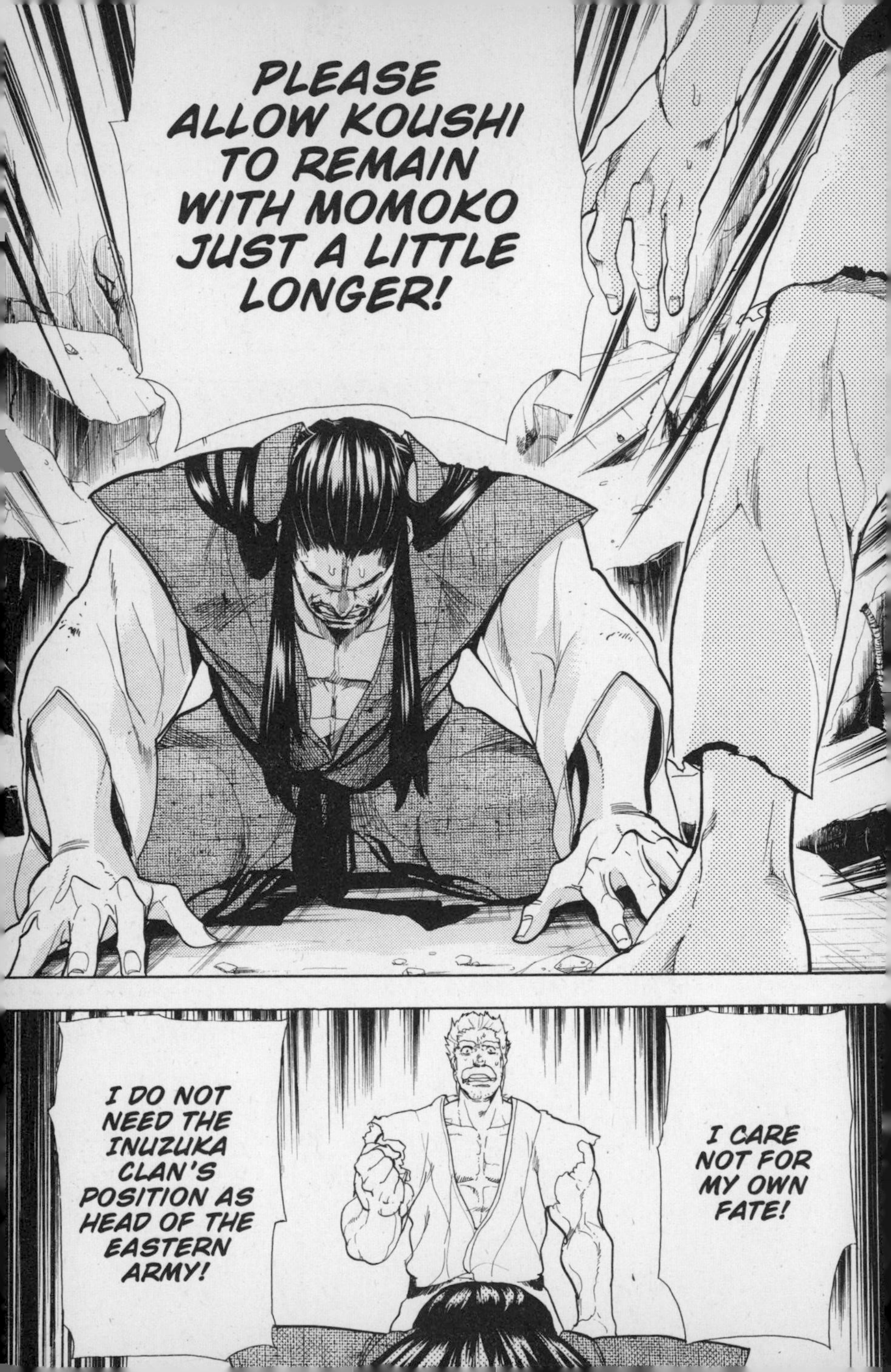
PLEASE ALLOW KOUSHI TO REMAIN WITH MOMOKO JUST A LITTLE LONGER!
I CARE NOT FOR MY OWN FATE!
I DO NOT NEED THE INUZUKA CLAN'S POSITION AS HEAD OF THE EASTERN ARMY!

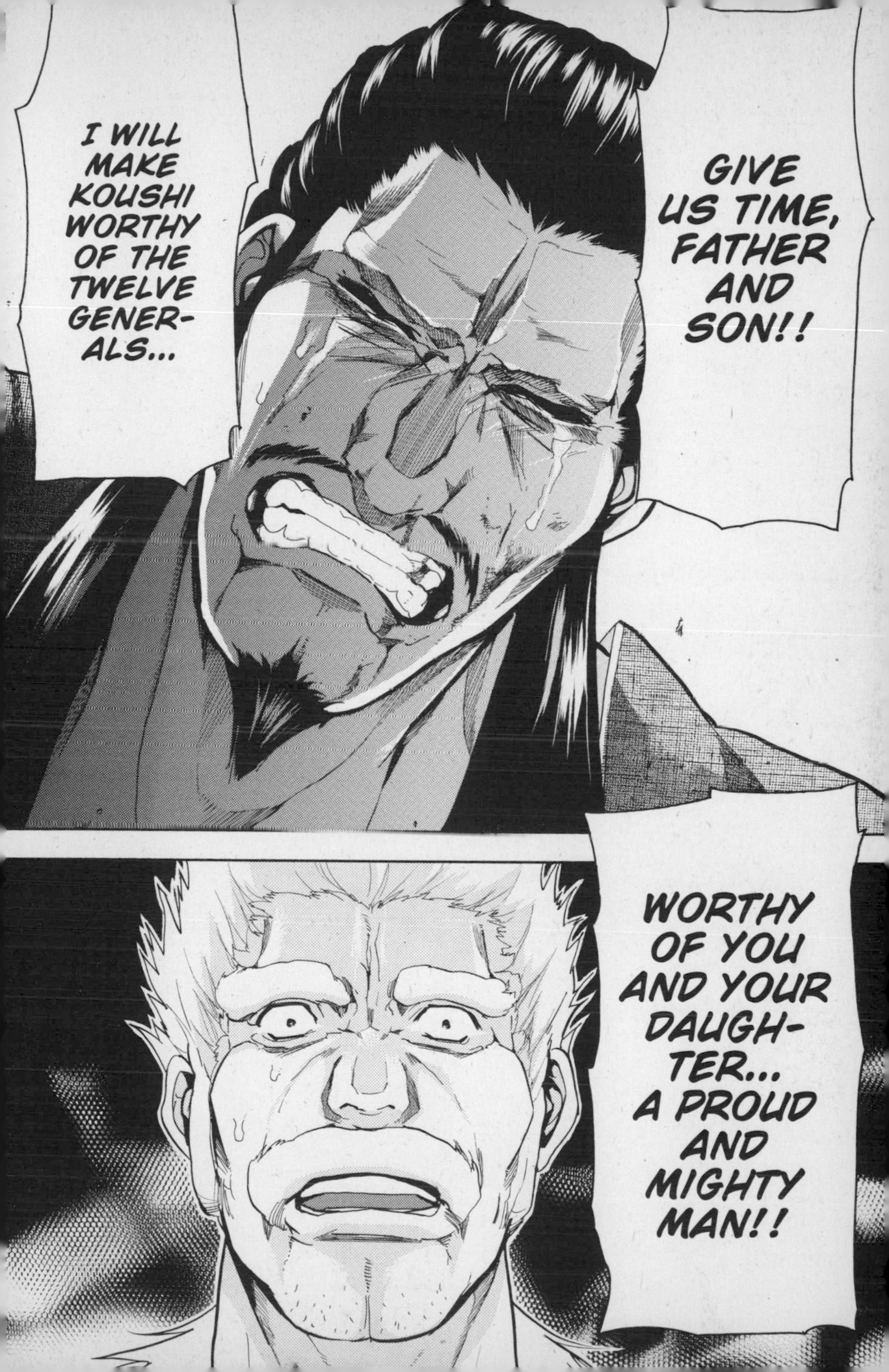
GIVE US TIME, FATHER AND SON!!
I WILL MAKE KOUSHI WORTHY OF THE TWELVE GENER-ALS...
WORTHY OF YOU AND YOUR DAUGH-TER... A PROUD AND MIGHTY MAN!!

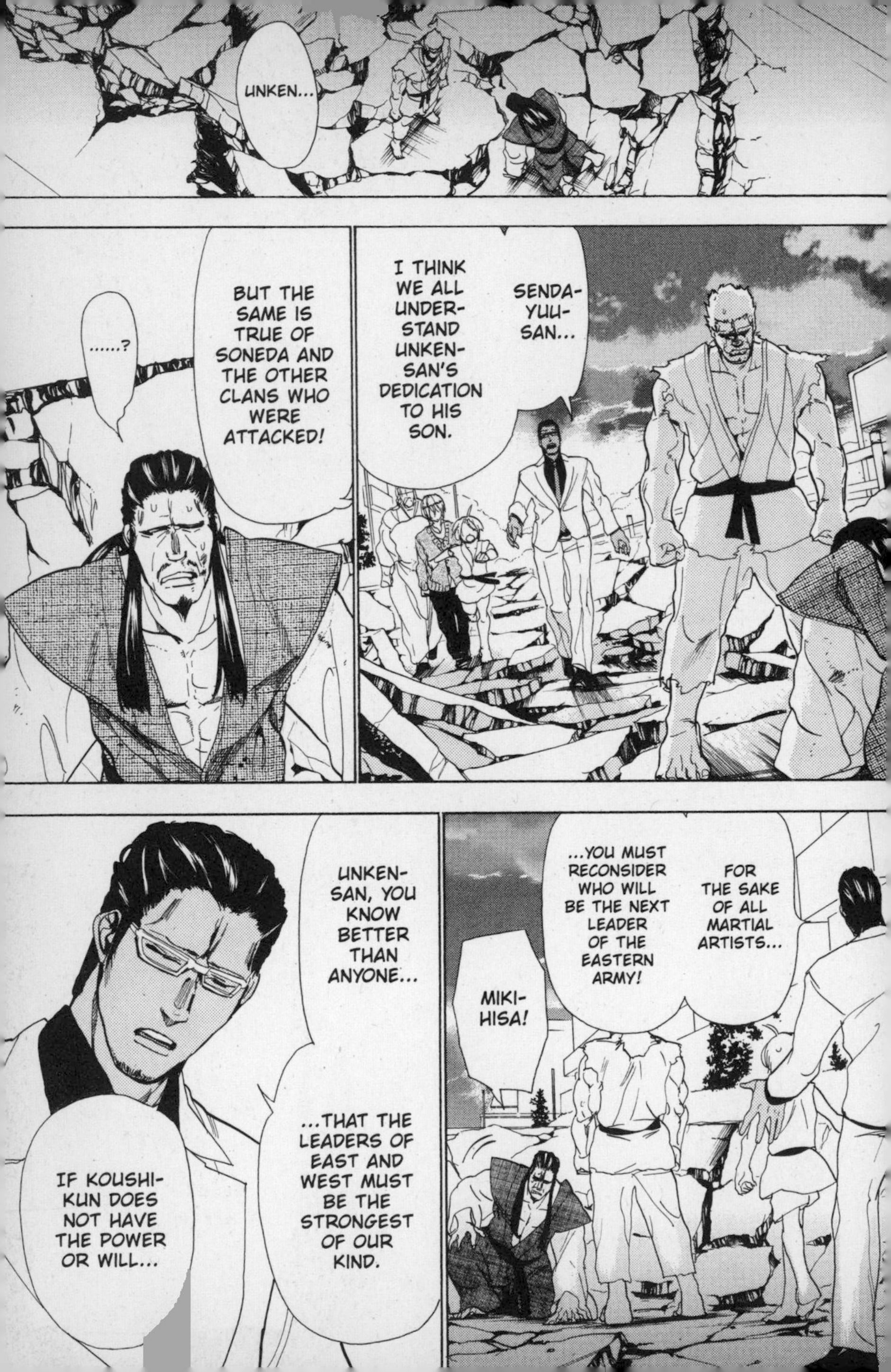
UNKEN...
SENDA-YUU-SAN...
I THINK WE ALL UNDER-STAND UNKEN-SAN'S DEDICATION TO HIS SON.
BUT THE SAME IS TRUE OF SONEDA AND THE OTHER CLANS WHO WERE ATTACKED!
......?
FOR THE SAKE OF ALL MARTIAL ARTISTS...
...YOU MUST RECONSIDER WHO WILL BE THE NEXT LEADER OF THE EASTERN ARMY!
MIKI-HISA!
UNKEN-SAN, YOU KNOW BETTER THAN ANYONE...
...THAT THE LEADERS OF EAST AND WEST MUST BE THE STRONGEST OF OUR KIND.
IF KOUSHI-KUN DOES NOT HAVE THE POWER OR WILL...

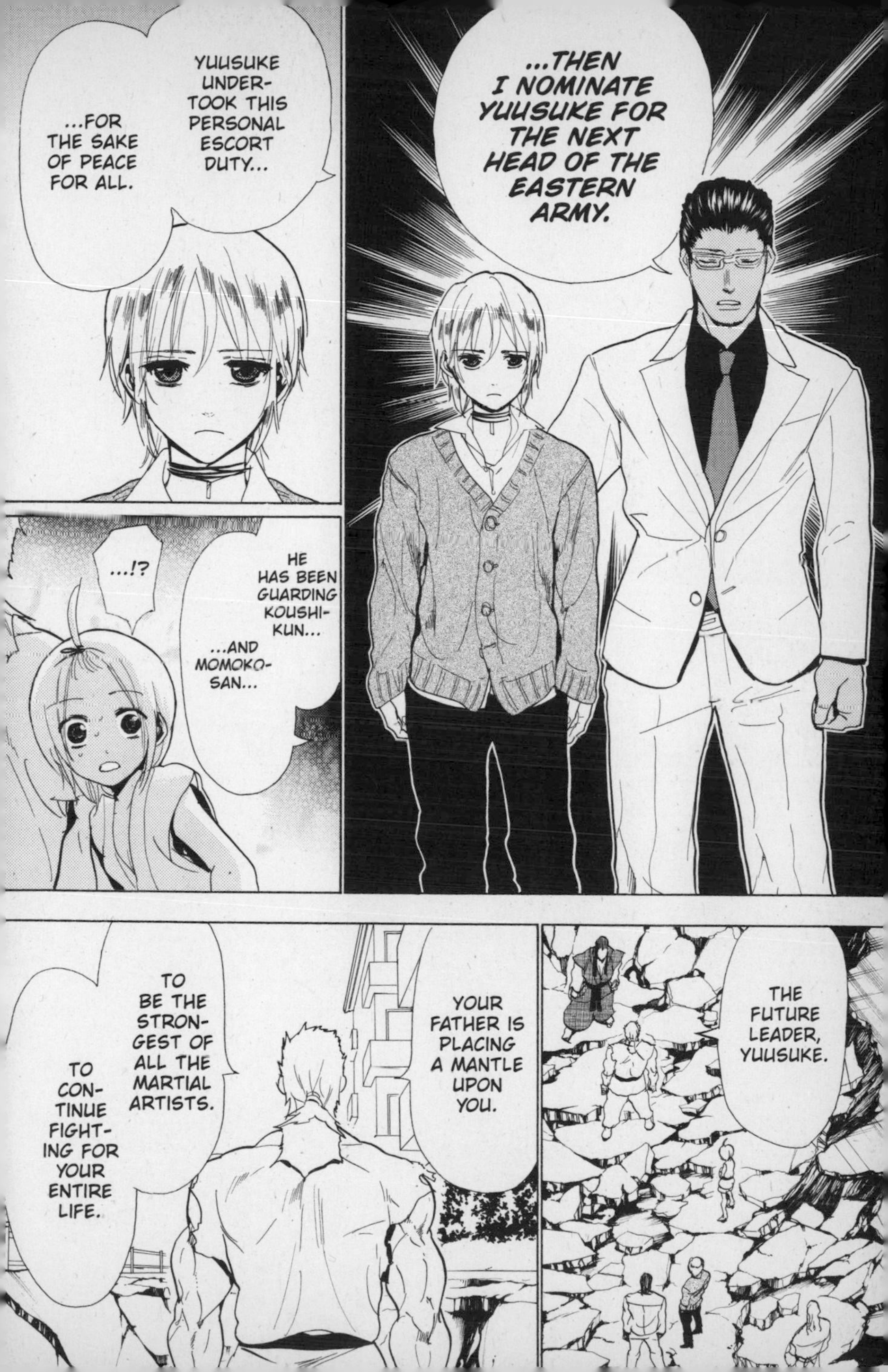
...THEN I NOMINATE YUUSUKE FOR THE NEXT HEAD OF THE EASTERN ARMY.
YUUSUKE UNDERTOOK THIS PERSONAL ESCORT DUTY...
...FOR THE SAKE OF PEACE FOR ALL.
HE HAS BEEN GUARDING KOUSHI-KUN...
...AND MOMOKO-SAN...
...!?
THE FUTURE LEADER, YUUSUKE.
YOUR FATHER IS PLACING A MANTLE UPON YOU.
TO BE THE STRONGEST OF ALL THE MARTIAL ARTISTS.
TO CONTINUE FIGHTING FOR YOUR ENTIRE LIFE.

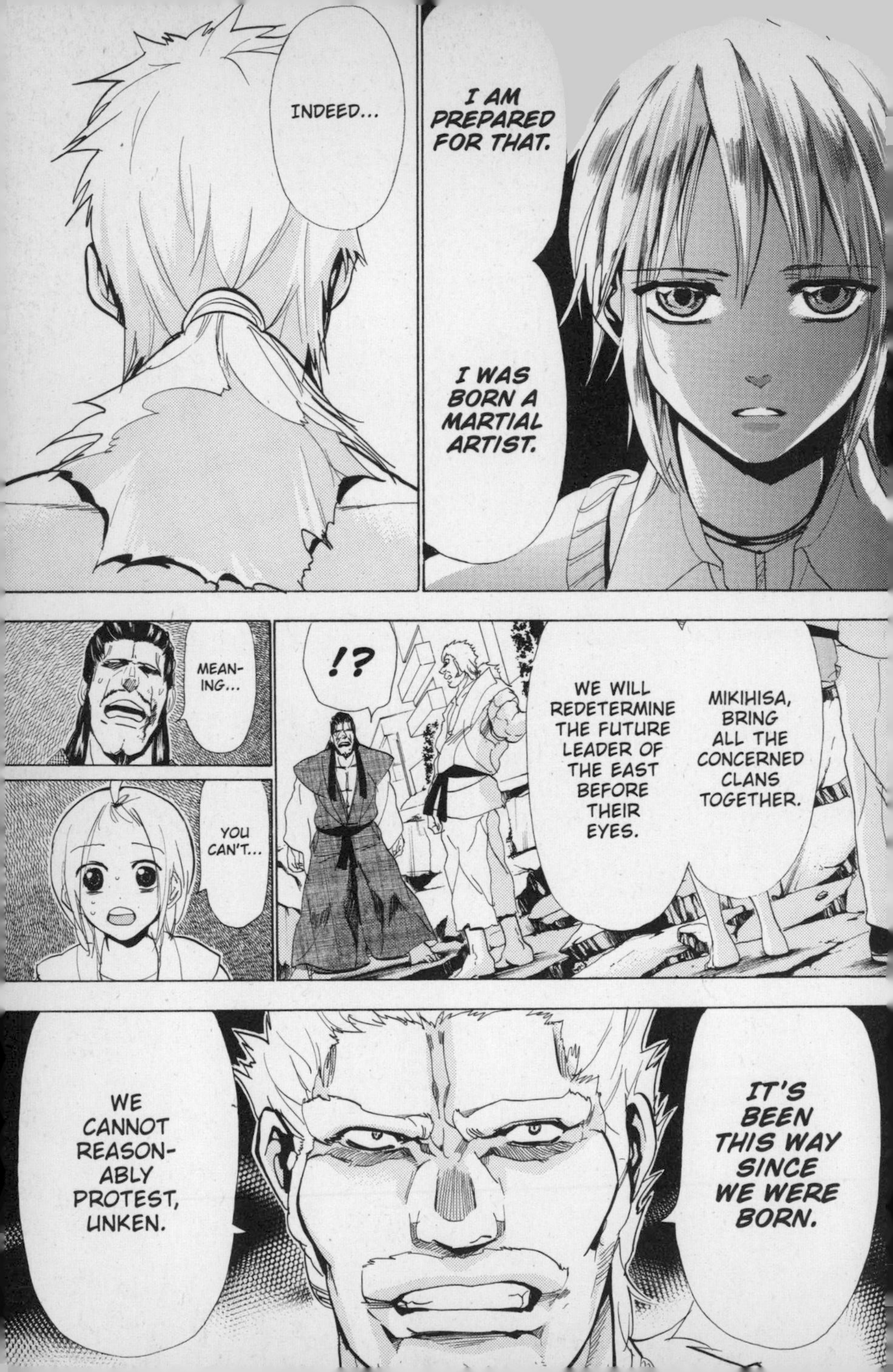
I AM PREPARED FOR THAT.
I WAS BORN A MARTIAL ARTIST.
INDEED...
MIKIHISA, BRING ALL THE CONCERNED CLANS TOGETHER.
WE WILL REDETERMINE THE FUTURE LEADER OF THE EAST BEFORE THEIR EYES.
!?
MEAN-ING...
YOU CAN'T...
IT'S BEEN THIS WAY SINCE WE WERE BORN.
WE CANNOT REASON-ABLY PROTEST, UNKEN.

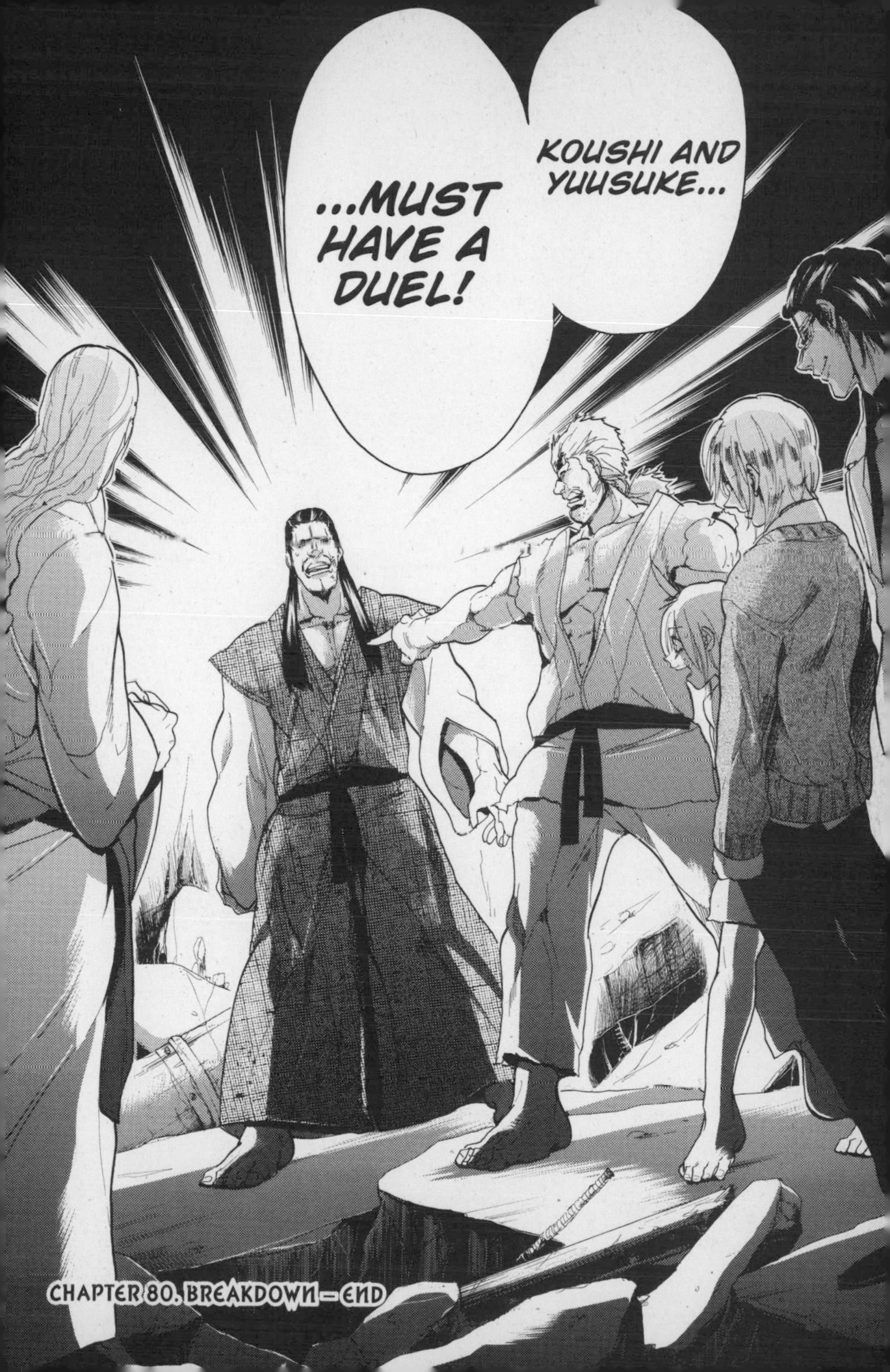
KOUSHI AND YUUSUKE...
...MUST HAVE A DUEL!
CHAPTER 80. BREAKDOWN – END

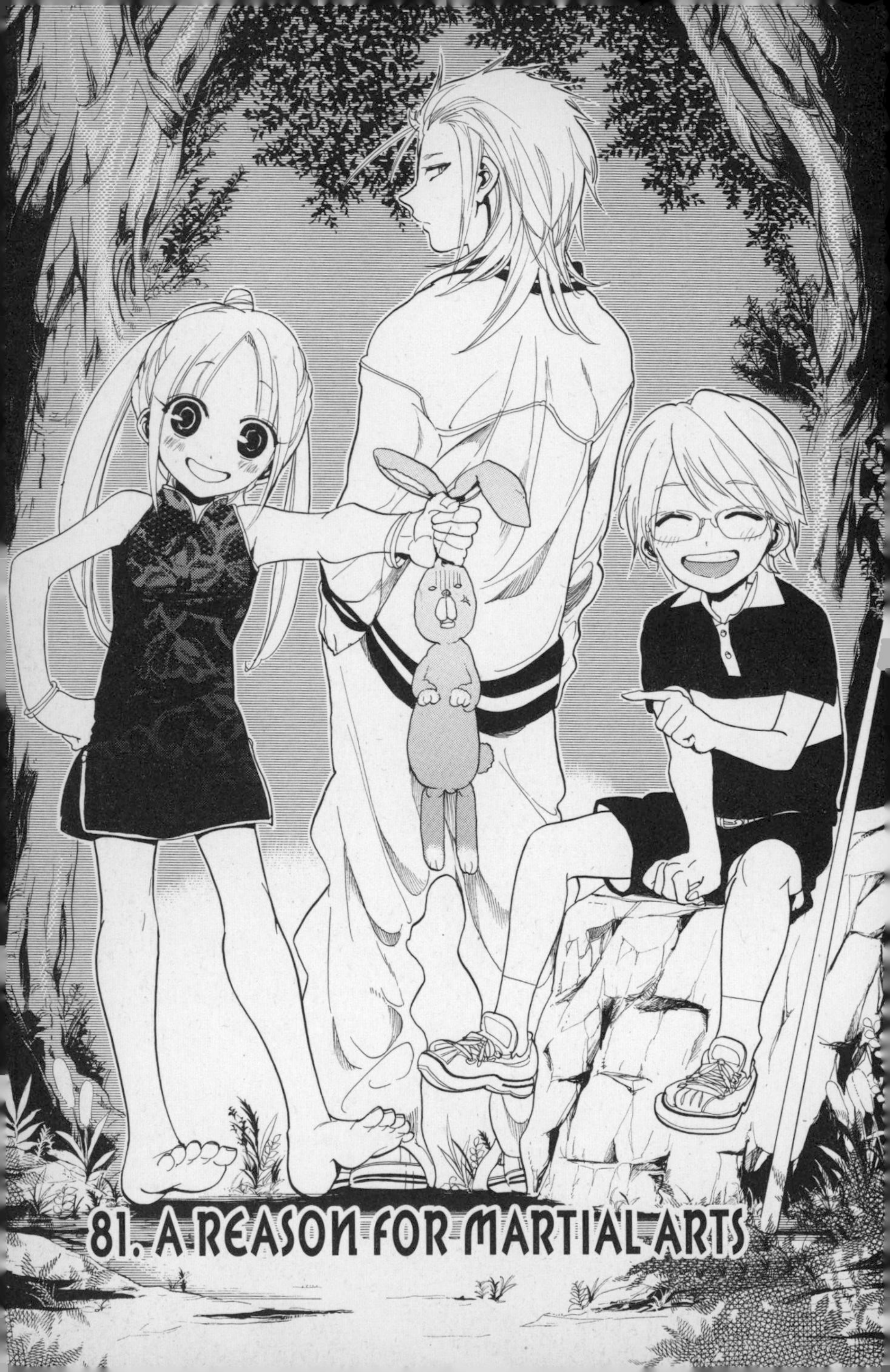
81. A REASON FOR MARTIAL ARTS

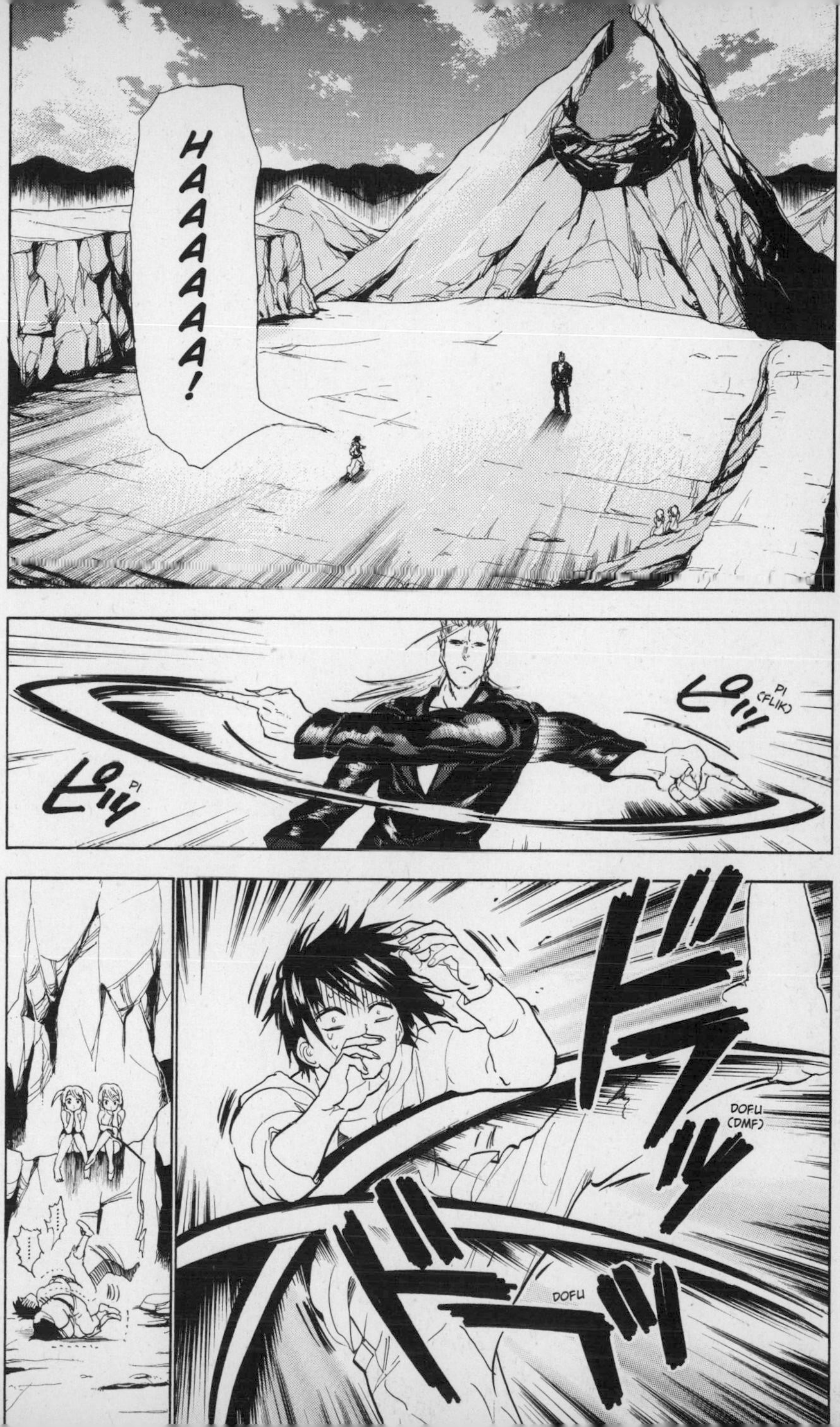
HAAAAAAA!
PI (FLIK)
PI
DOFU (DMF)
DOFU

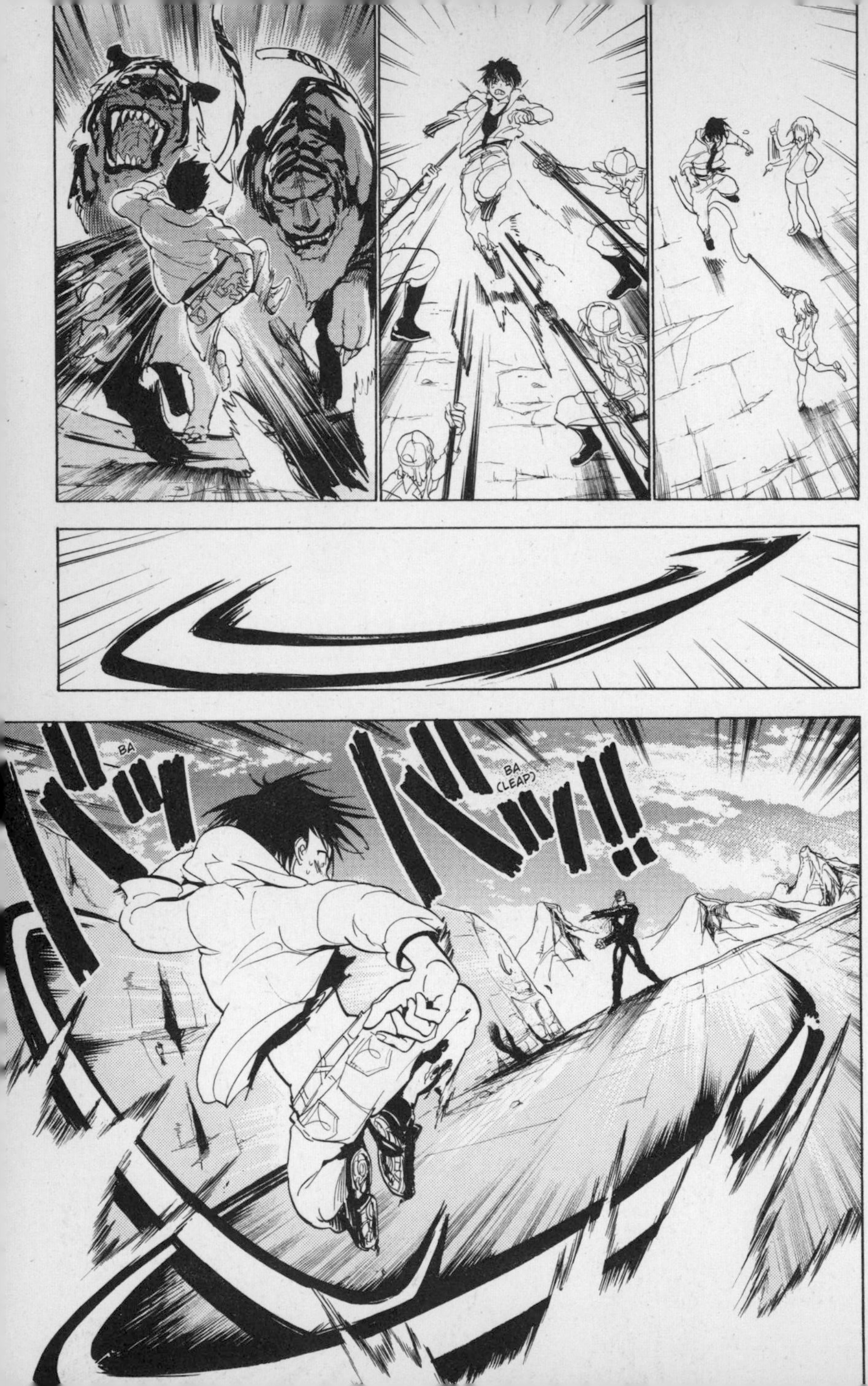
BA
(LEAP)
BA

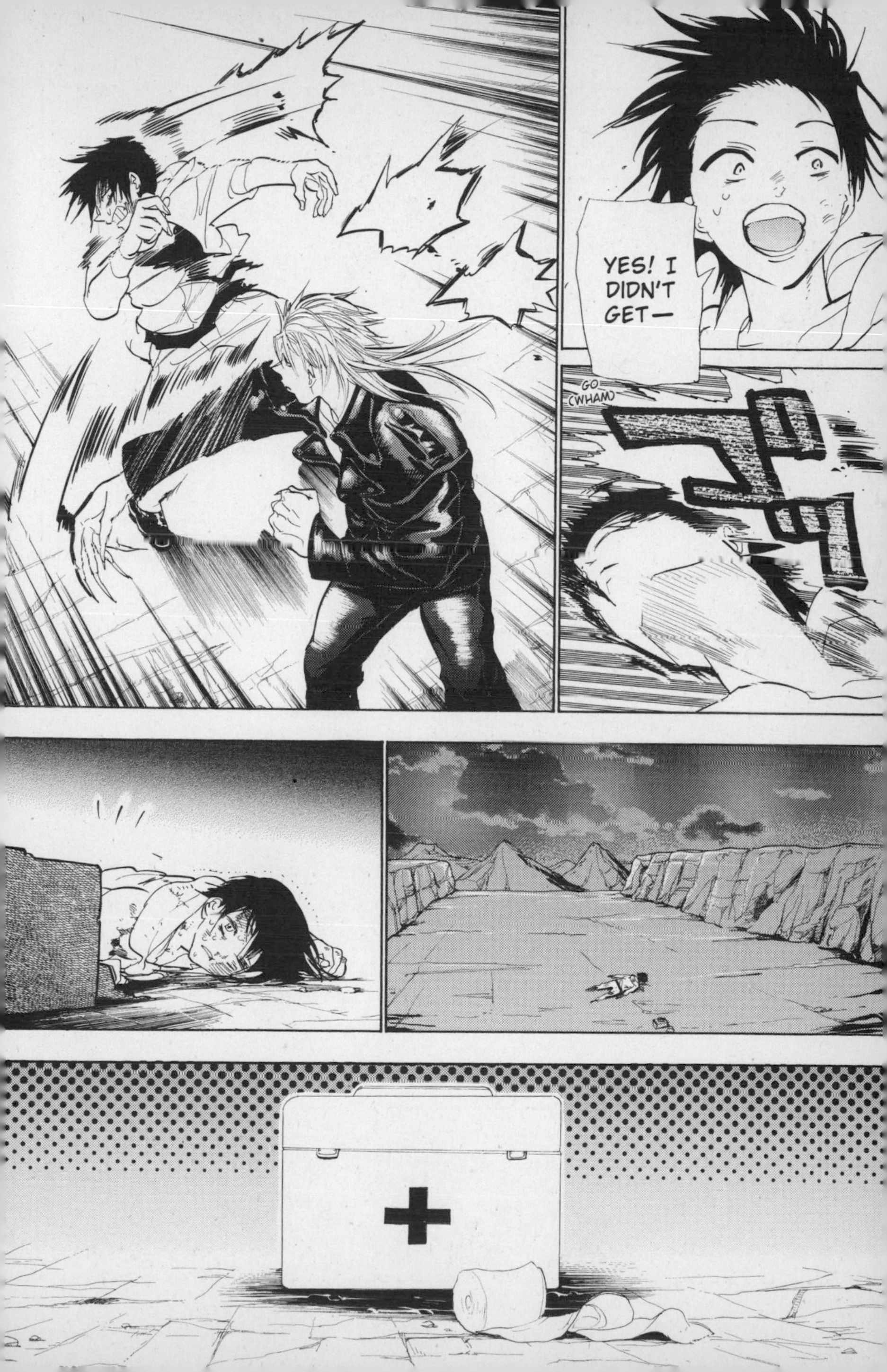
YES! I DIDN'T GET—
GO (WHAM)

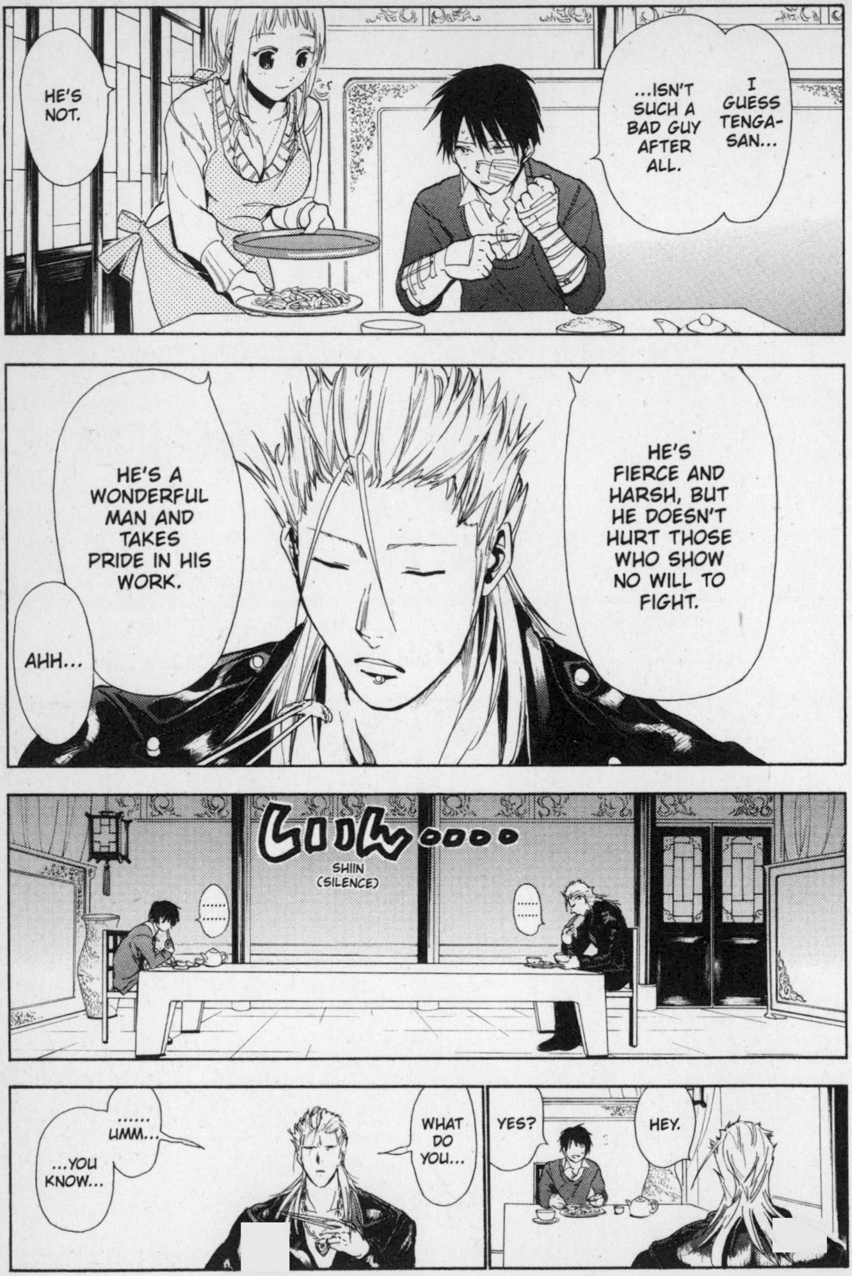
I GUESS TENGA-SAN...
...ISN'T SUCH A BAD GUY AFTER ALL.
HE'S NOT.
HE'S FIERCE AND HARSH, BUT HE DOESN'T HURT THOSE WHO SHOW NO WILL TO FIGHT.
HE'S A WONDERFUL MAN AND TAKES PRIDE IN HIS WORK.
AHH...
SHIIN (SILENCE)
......
......
HEY.
YES?
WHAT DO YOU...
...... UMM...
...YOU KNOW...

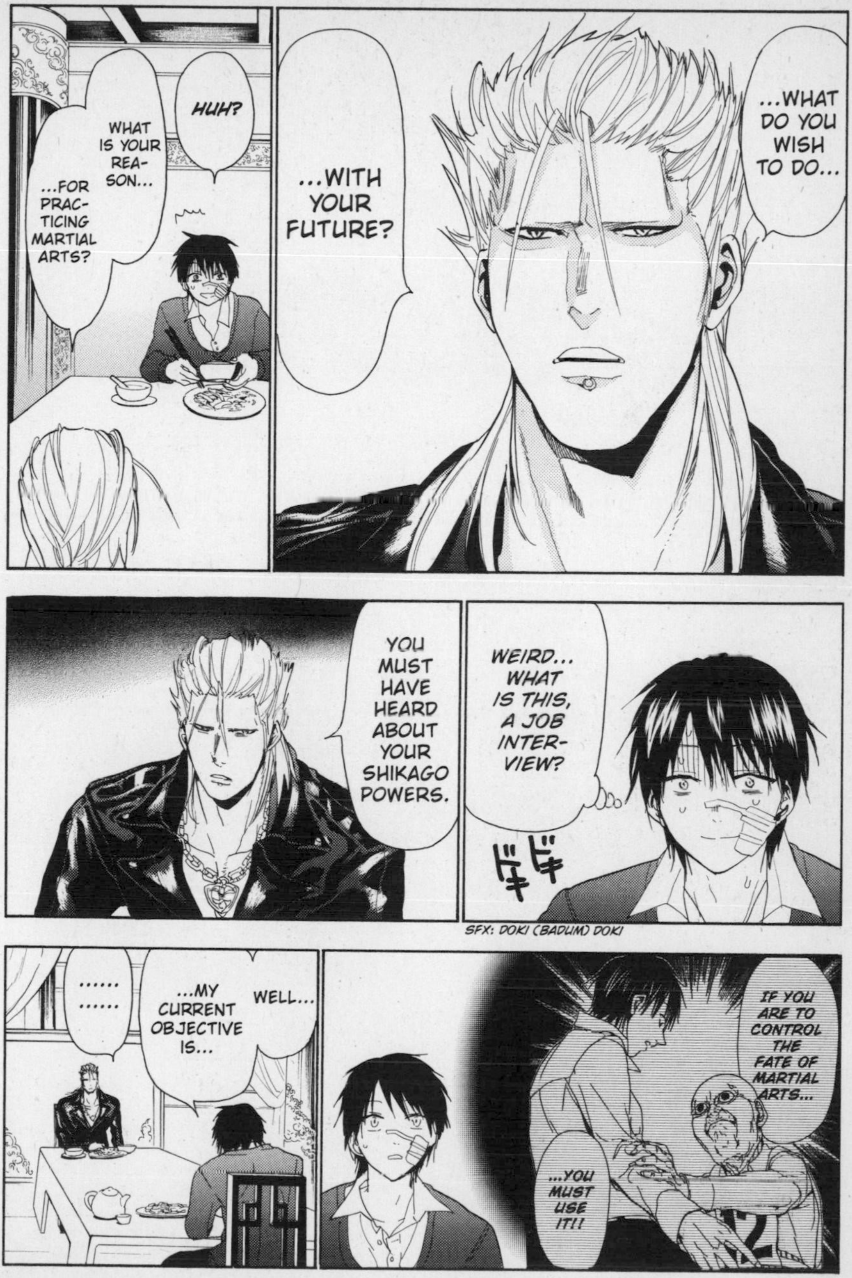
...WHAT DO YOU WISH TO DO...
...WITH YOUR FUTURE?
HUH?
WHAT IS YOUR REASON...
...FOR PRACTICING MARTIAL ARTS?
WEIRD... WHAT IS THIS, A JOB INTERVIEW?
ドキドキ
SFX: DOKI (BADUM) DOKI
YOU MUST HAVE HEARD ABOUT YOUR SHIKAGO POWERS.
IF YOU ARE TO CONTROL THE FATE OF MARTIAL ARTS...
...YOU MUST USE IT!!
WELL...
...MY CURRENT OBJECTIVE IS...
......
......

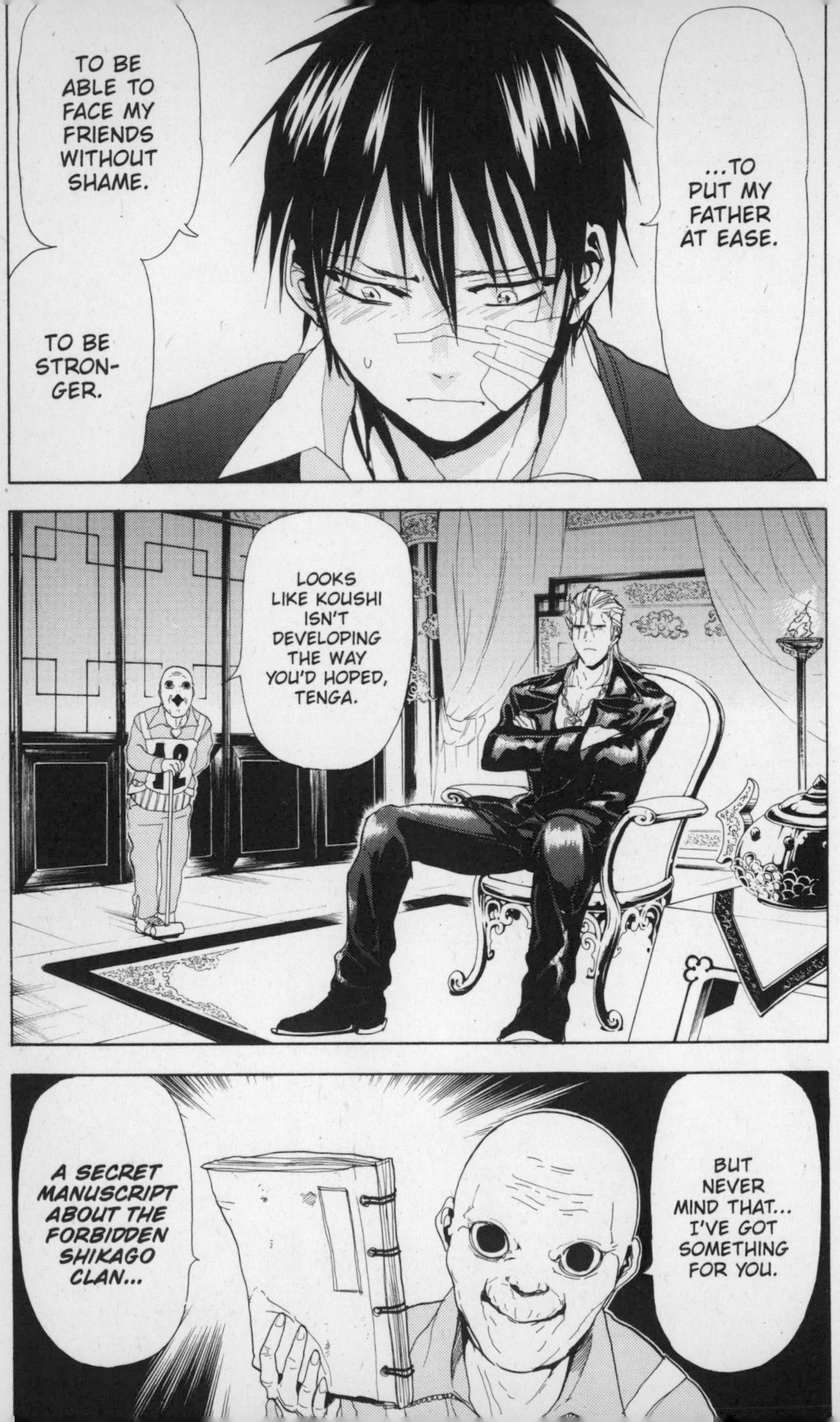
...TO PUT MY FATHER AT EASE.
TO BE ABLE TO FACE MY FRIENDS WITHOUT SHAME.
TO BE STRONGER.
LOOKS LIKE KOUSHI ISN'T DEVELOPING THE WAY YOU'D HOPED, TENGA.
BUT NEVER MIND THAT... I'VE GOT SOMETHING FOR YOU.
A SECRET MANUSCRIPT ABOUT THE FORBIDDEN SHIKAGO CLAN...

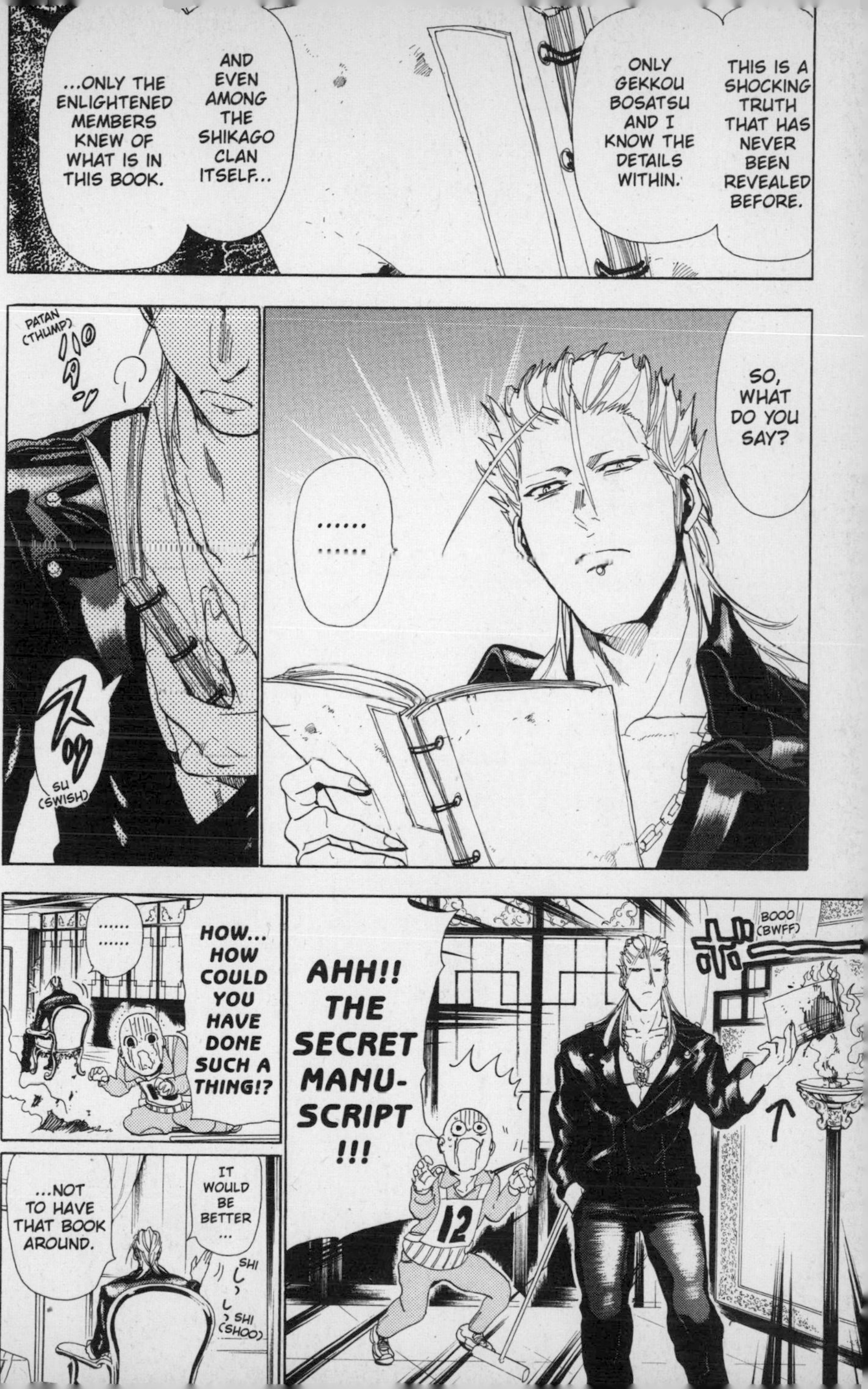
THIS IS A SHOCKING TRUTH THAT HAS NEVER BEEN REVEALED BEFORE.
ONLY GEKKOU BOSATSU AND I KNOW THE DETAILS WITHIN.
AND EVEN AMONG THE SHIKAGO CLAN ITSELF...
...ONLY THE ENLIGHTENED MEMBERS KNEW OF WHAT IS IN THIS BOOK.
SO, WHAT DO YOU SAY?
....
PATAN (THUMP)
SU (SWISH)
BOOO (BWFF)
AHH!! THE SECRET MANU-SCRIPT!!!
HOW... HOW COULD YOU HAVE DONE SUCH A THING!?
....
IT WOULD BE BETTER...
...NOT TO HAVE THAT BOOK AROUND.
SHI SHI (SHOO)

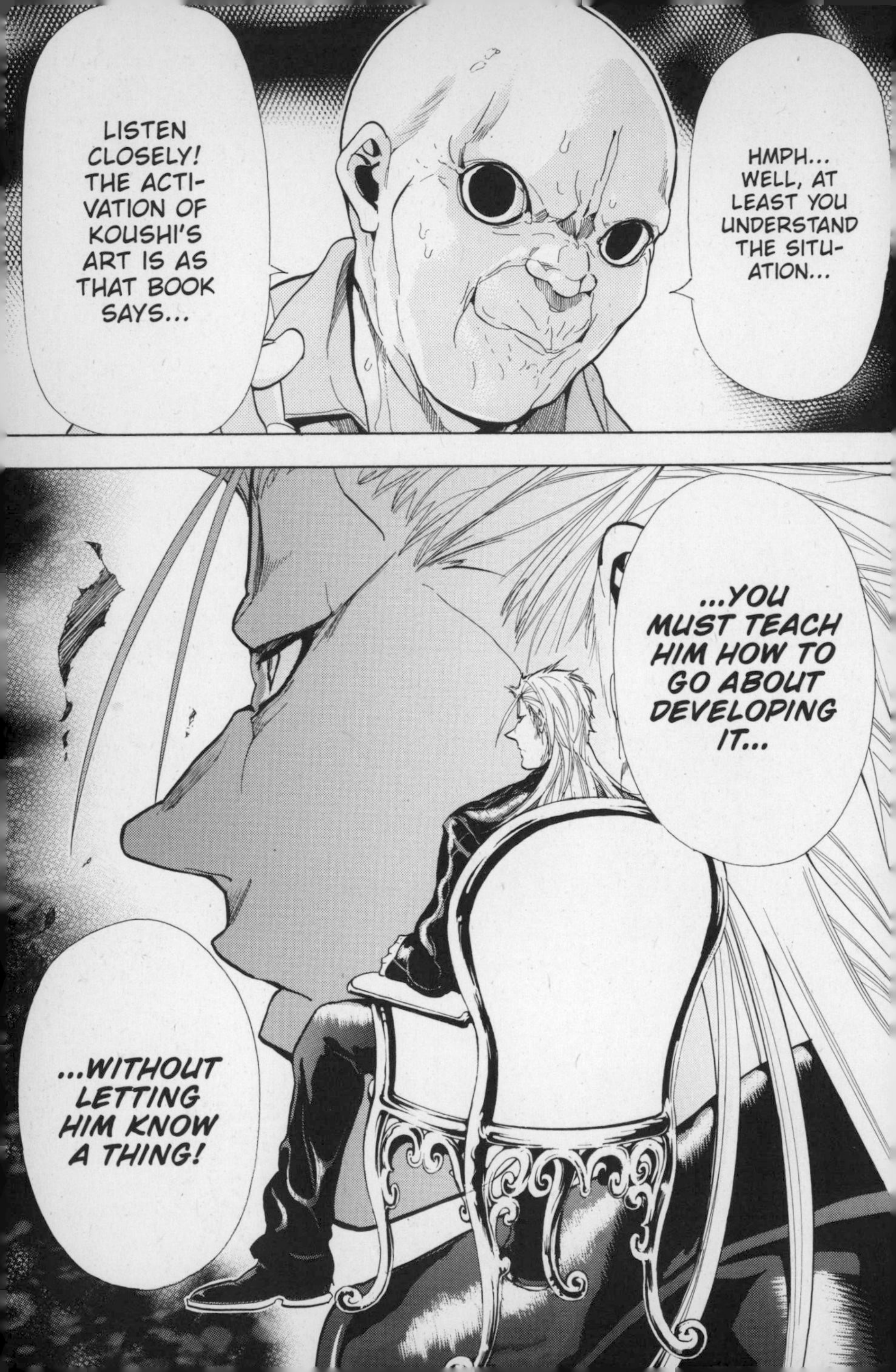
HMPH... WELL, AT LEAST YOU UNDERSTAND THE SITU-ATION...
LISTEN CLOSELY! THE ACTI-VATION OF KOUSHI'S ART IS AS THAT BOOK SAYS...
...YOU MUST TEACH HIM HOW TO GO ABOUT DEVELOPING IT...
...WITHOUT LETTING HIM KNOW A THING!

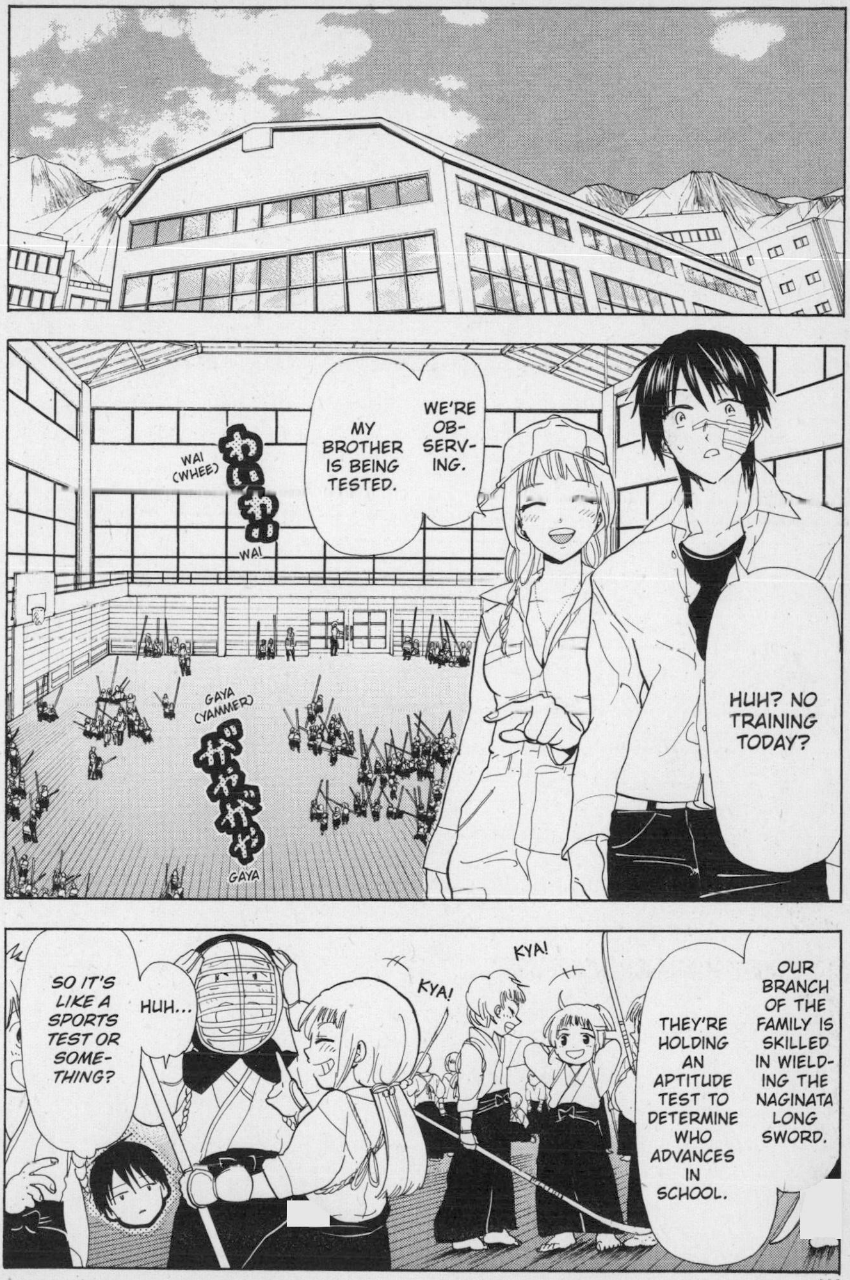
HUH? NO TRAINING TODAY?
WE'RE OB-SERV-ING.
MY BROTHER IS BEING TESTED.
WAI (WHEE)
わいわい
WAI
GAYA (YAMMER)
がやがや
GAYA
OUR BRANCH OF THE FAMILY IS SKILLED IN WIELD-ING THE NAGINATA LONG SWORD.
THEY'RE HOLDING AN APTITUDE TEST TO DETERMINE WHO ADVANCES IN SCHOOL.
KYA!
KYA!
HUH...
SO IT'S LIKE A SPORTS TEST OR SOME-THING?

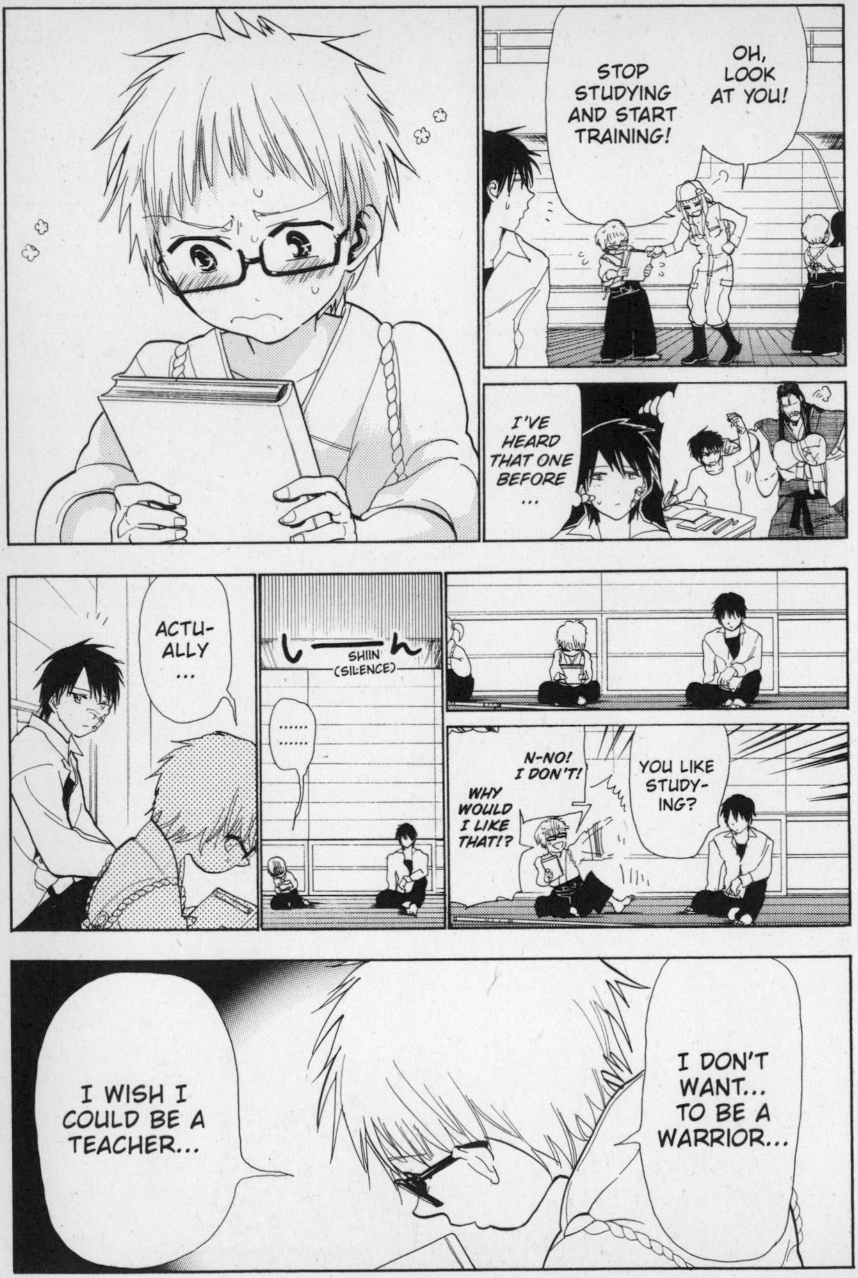
OH, LOOK AT YOU!
STOP STUDYING AND START TRAINING!
I'VE HEARD THAT ONE BEFORE...
YOU LIKE STUDY-ING?
N-NO! I DON'T!
WHY WOULD I LIKE THAT!?
しーん
SHIIN (SILENCE)
......
......
ACTU-ALLY...
I DON'T WANT... TO BE A WARRIOR...
I WISH I COULD BE A TEACHER...

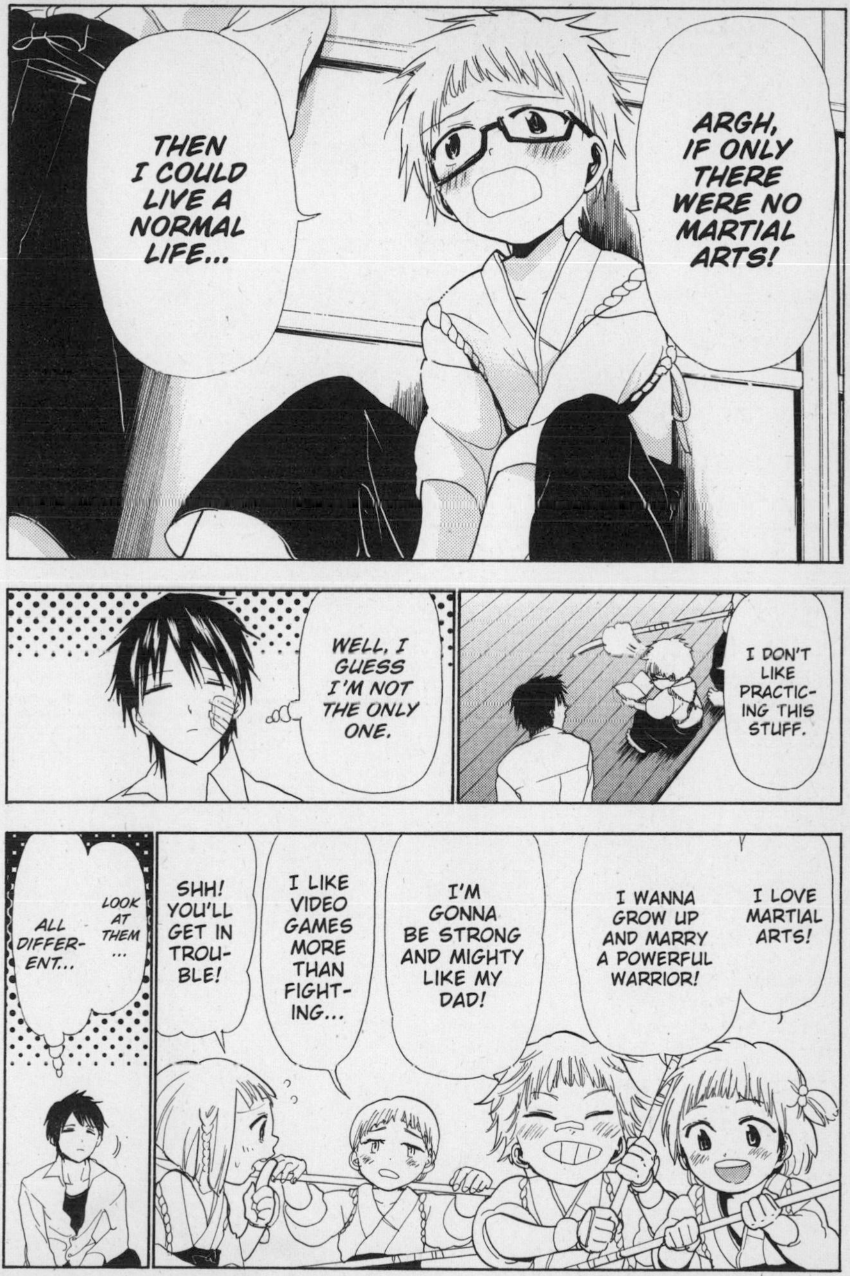
ARGH, IF ONLY THERE WERE NO MARTIAL ARTS!
THEN I COULD LIVE A NORMAL LIFE...
I DON'T LIKE PRACTICING THIS STUFF.
WELL, I GUESS I'M NOT THE ONLY ONE.
I LOVE MARTIAL ARTS!
I WANNA GROW UP AND MARRY A POWERFUL WARRIOR!
I'M GONNA BE STRONG AND MIGHTY LIKE MY DAD!
I LIKE VIDEO GAMES MORE THAN FIGHTING...
SHH! YOU'LL GET IN TROUBLE!
LOOK AT THEM...
ALL DIFFERENT...

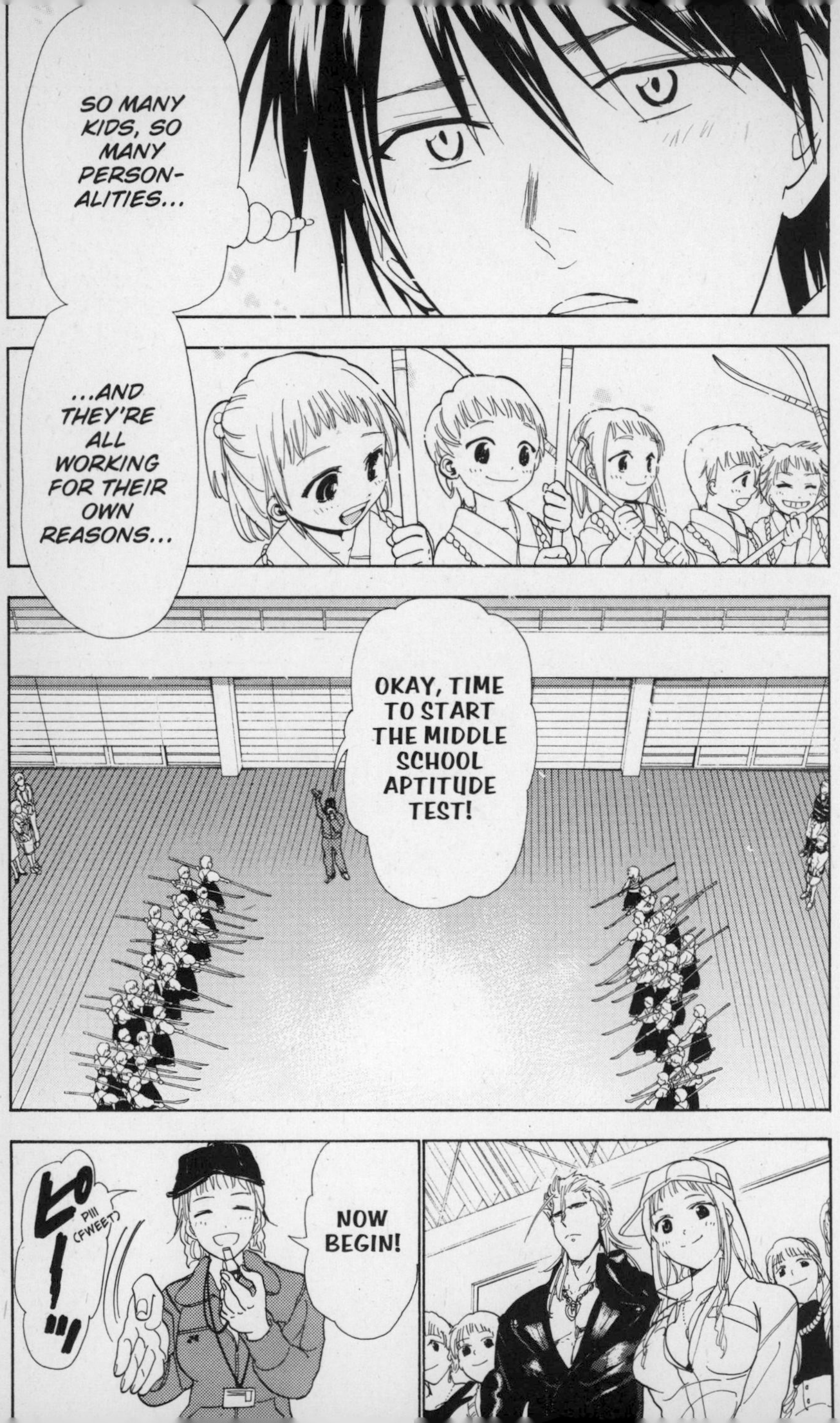
SO MANY KIDS, SO MANY PERSON-ALITIES...
...AND THEY'RE ALL WORKING FOR THEIR OWN REASONS...
OKAY, TIME TO START THE MIDDLE SCHOOL APTITUDE TEST!
NOW BEGIN!
PIII (FWEET)

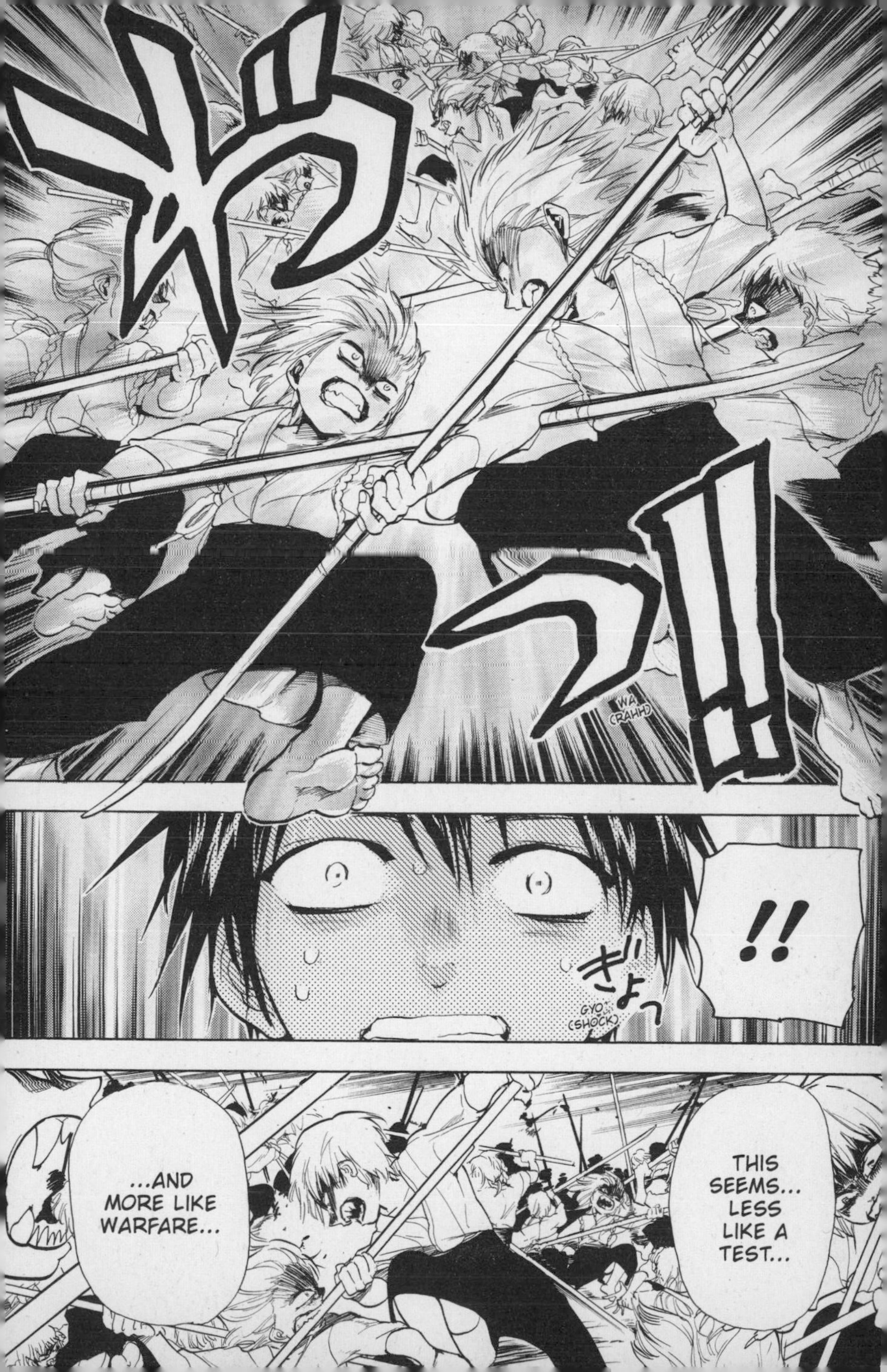

WA (RAHH)
!!
ぎょっ
GYO (SHOCK)
THIS SEEMS... LESS LIKE A TEST...
...AND MORE LIKE WARFARE...

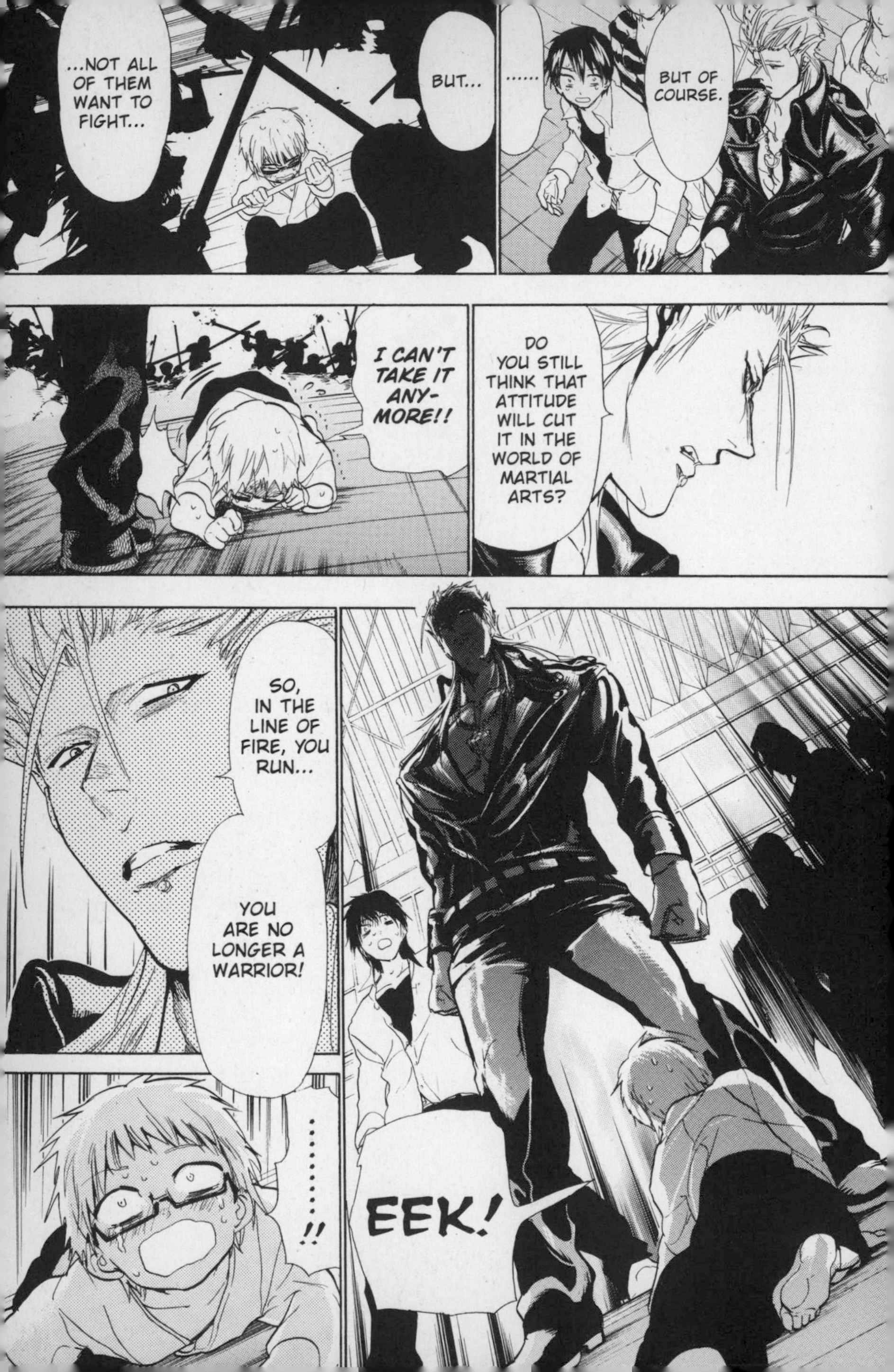
BUT OF COURSE.
......
BUT...
...NOT ALL OF THEM WANT TO FIGHT...
DO YOU STILL THINK THAT ATTITUDE WILL CUT IT IN THE WORLD OF MARTIAL ARTS?
I CAN'T TAKE IT ANY-MORE!!
EEK!
SO, IN THE LINE OF FIRE, YOU RUN...
YOU ARE NO LONGER A WARRIOR!
......!!

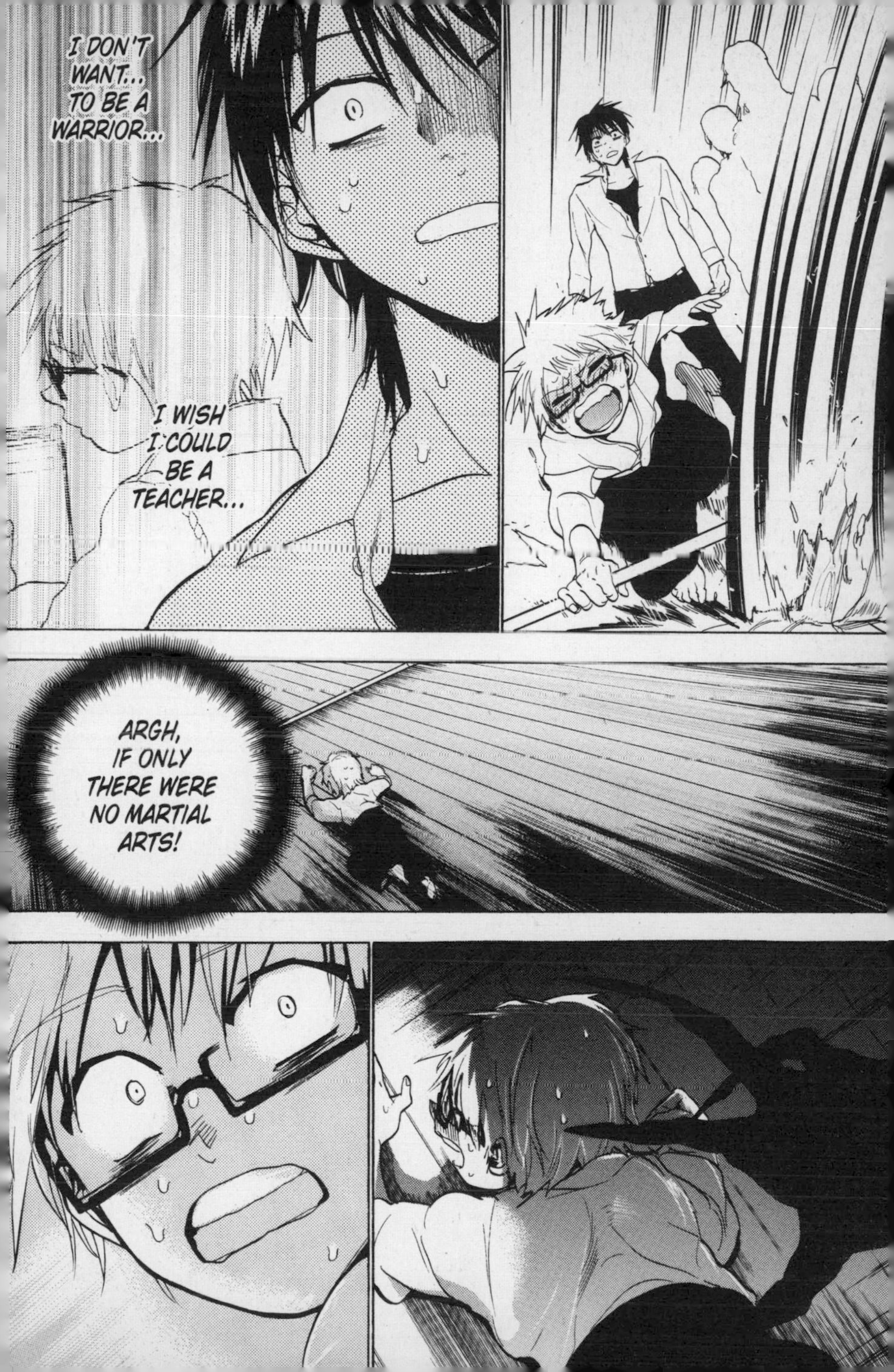
I DON'T WANT... TO BE A WARRIOR...
I WISH I COULD BE A TEACHER...
ARGH, IF ONLY THERE WERE NO MARTIAL ARTS!

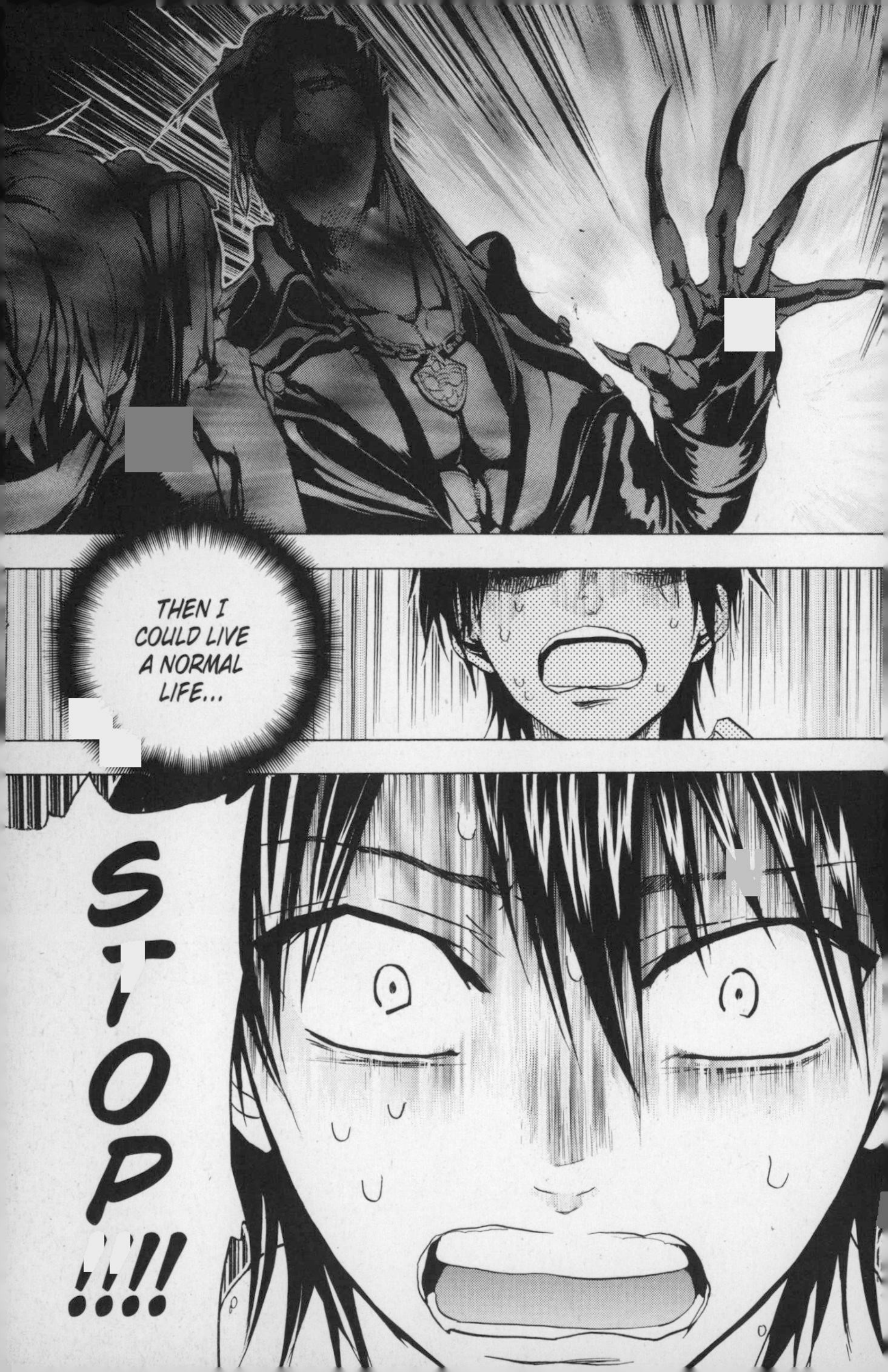
THEN I COULD LIVE A NORMAL LIFE...
STOP!!!!

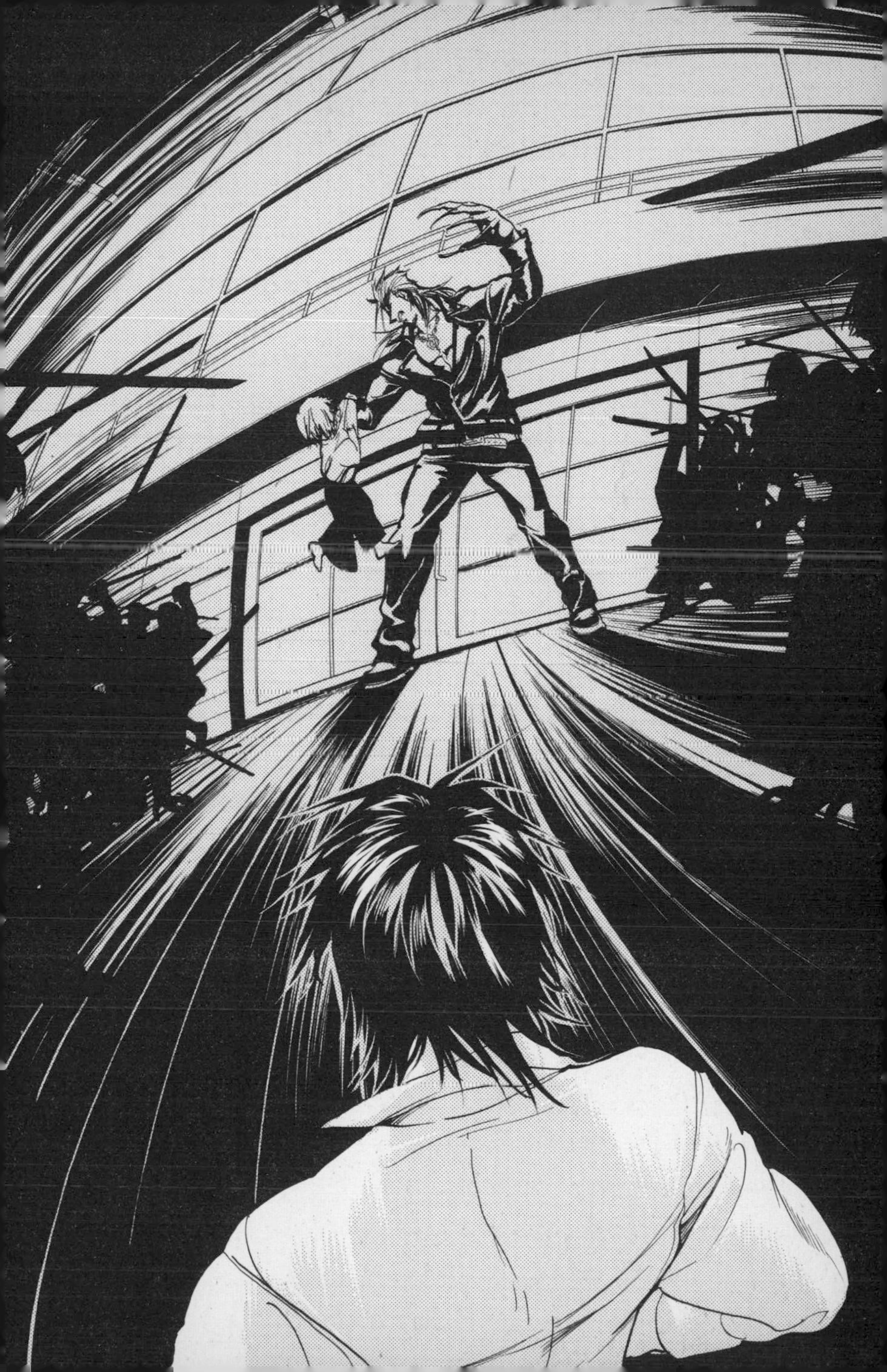

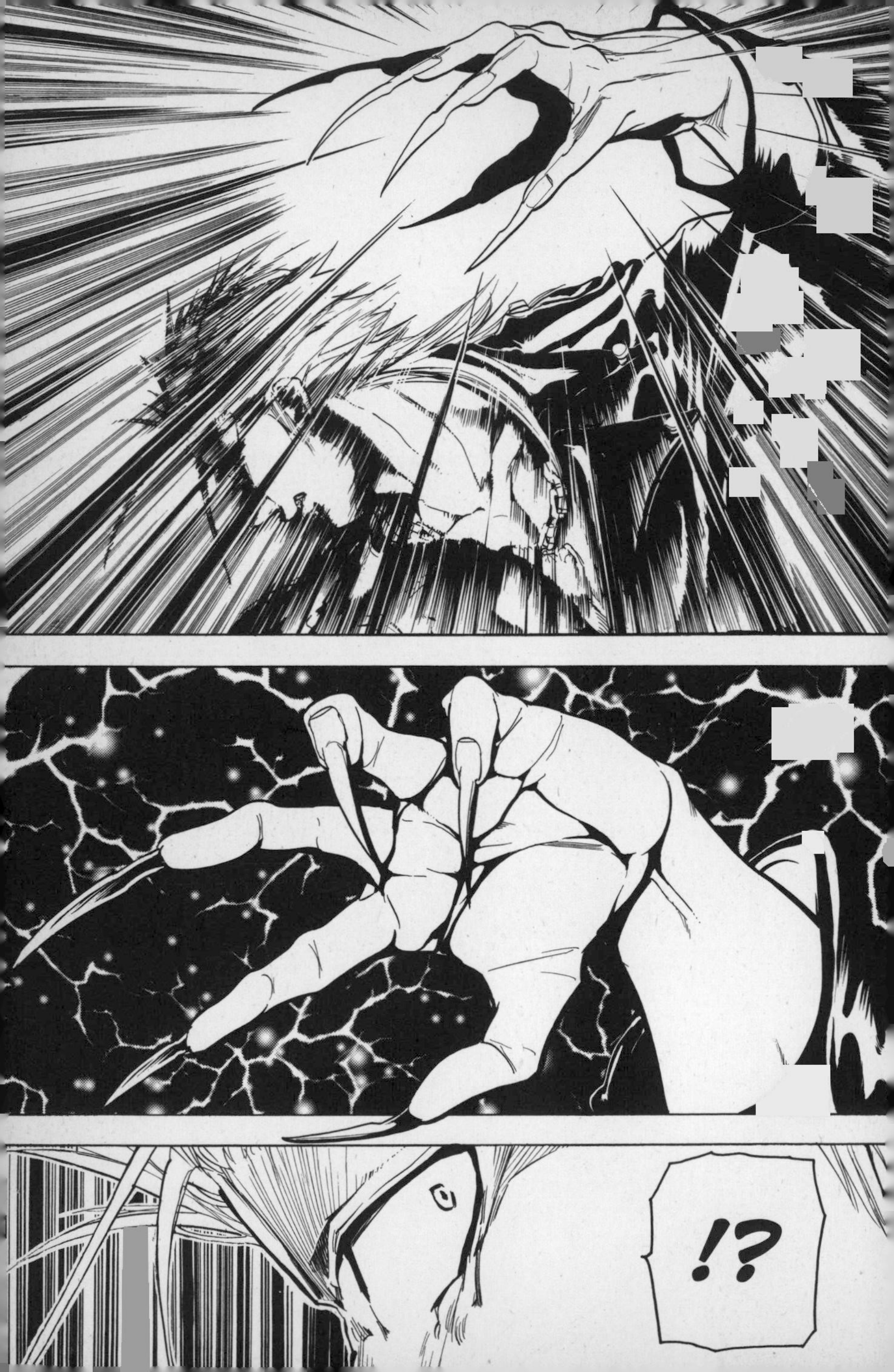
!?

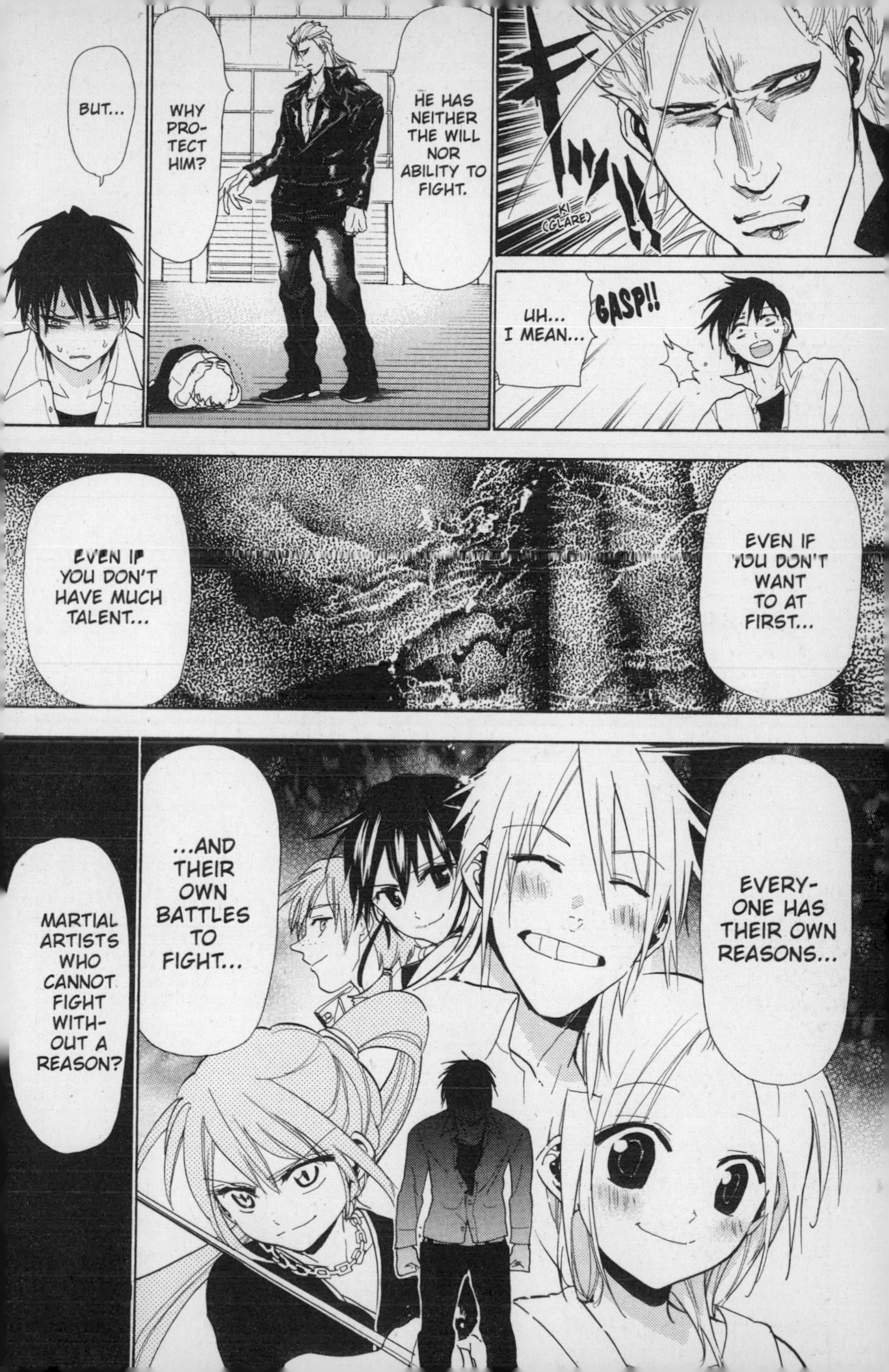
KI (GLARE)
GASP!!
UH... I MEAN...
HE HAS NEITHER THE WILL NOR ABILITY TO FIGHT.
WHY PRO-TECT HIM?
BUT...
EVEN IF YOU DON'T WANT TO AT FIRST...
EVEN IF YOU DON'T HAVE MUCH TALENT...
EVERY-ONE HAS THEIR OWN REASONS...
...AND THEIR OWN BATTLES TO FIGHT...
MARTIAL ARTISTS WHO CANNOT FIGHT WITH-OUT A REASON?

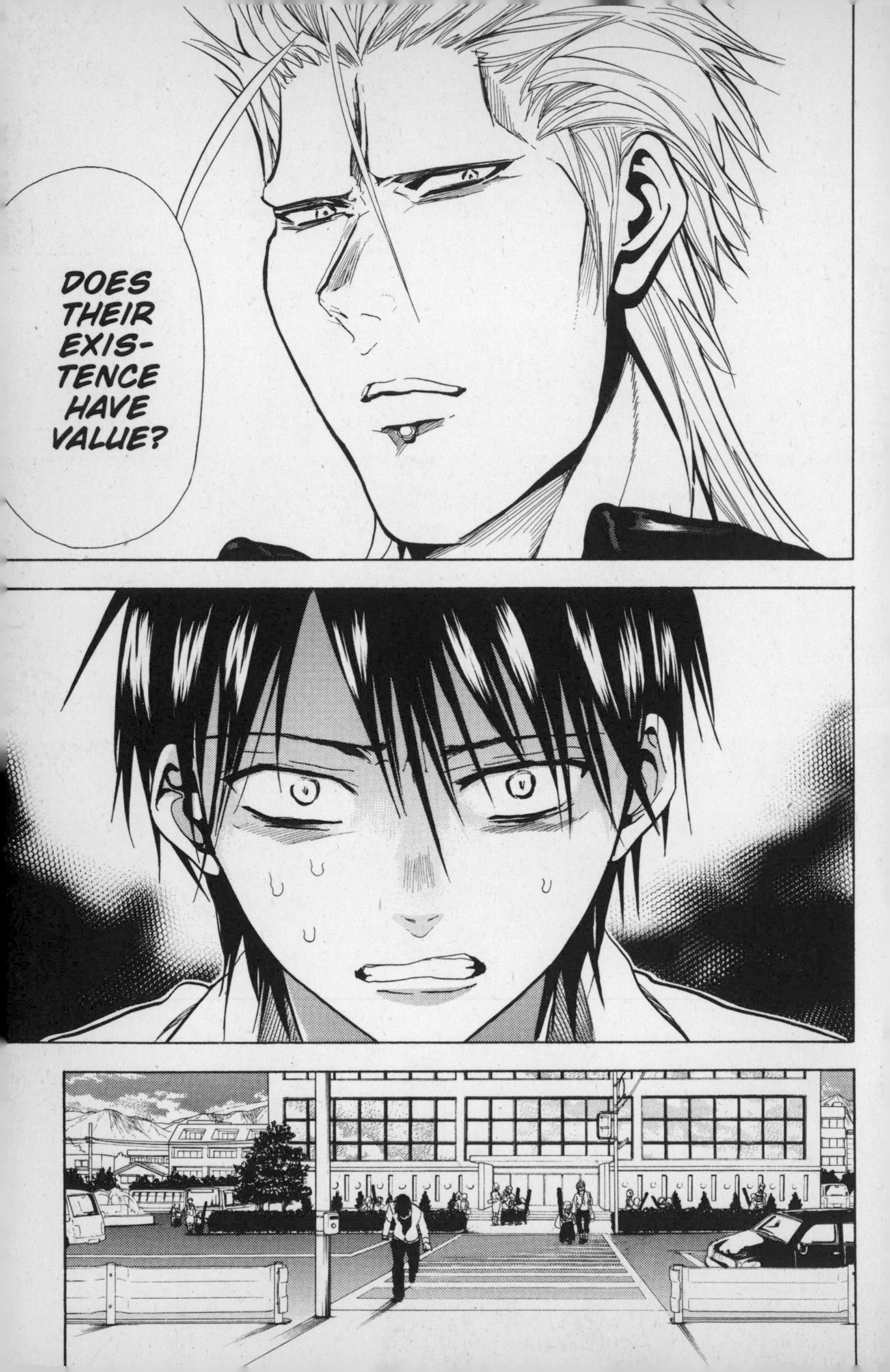
DOES THEIR EXIS-TENCE HAVE VALUE?

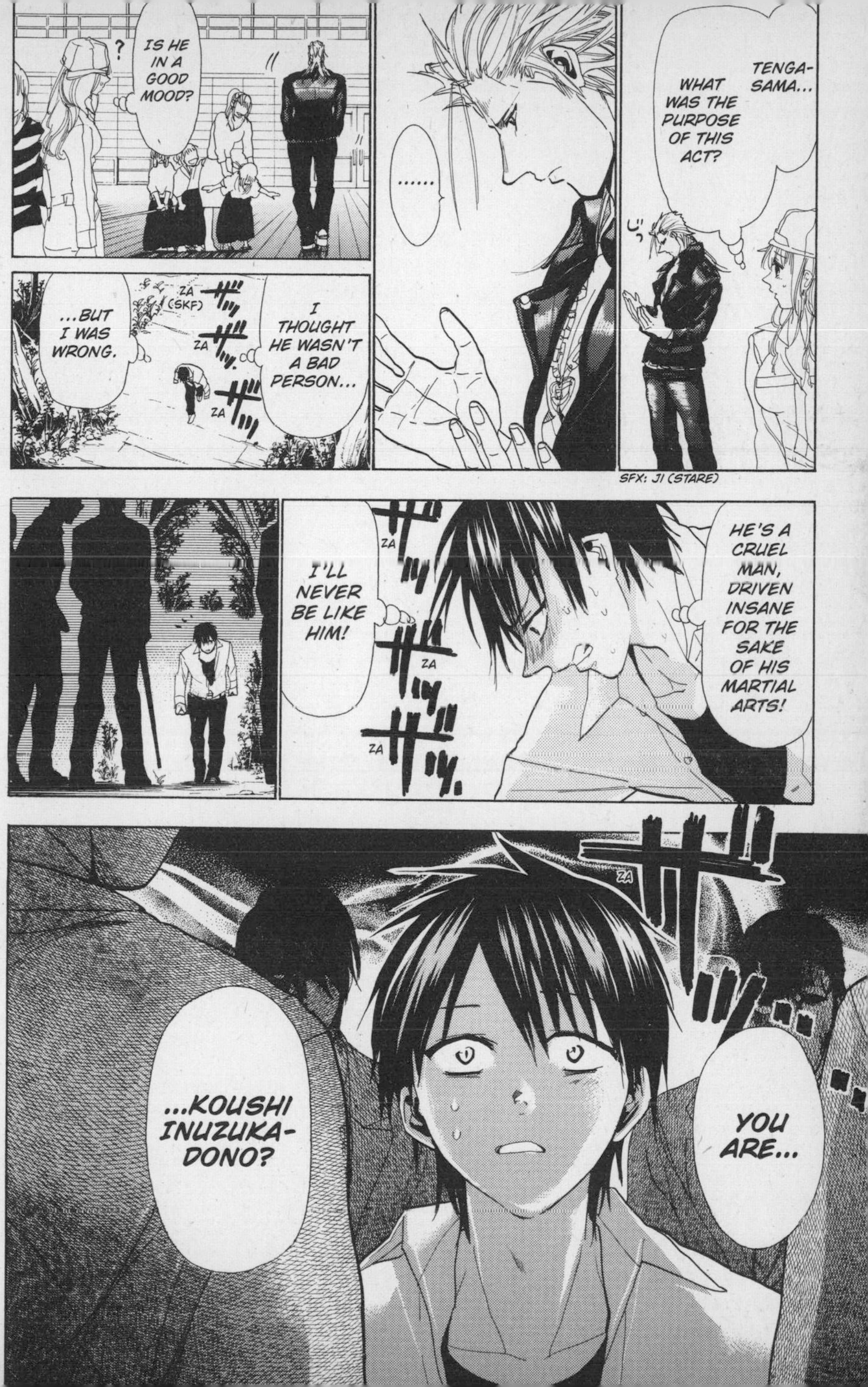
TENGA-SAMA... WHAT WAS THE PURPOSE OF THIS ACT?
SFX: JI (STARE)
......
?
IS HE IN A GOOD MOOD?
ZA (SKF)
ZA
I THOUGHT HE WASN'T A BAD PERSON...
ZA
...BUT I WAS WRONG.
HE'S A CRUEL MAN, DRIVEN INSANE FOR THE SAKE OF HIS MARTIAL ARTS!
ZA
I'LL NEVER BE LIKE HIM!
ZA
ZA
ZA
YOU ARE...
...KOUSHI INUZUKA-DONO?

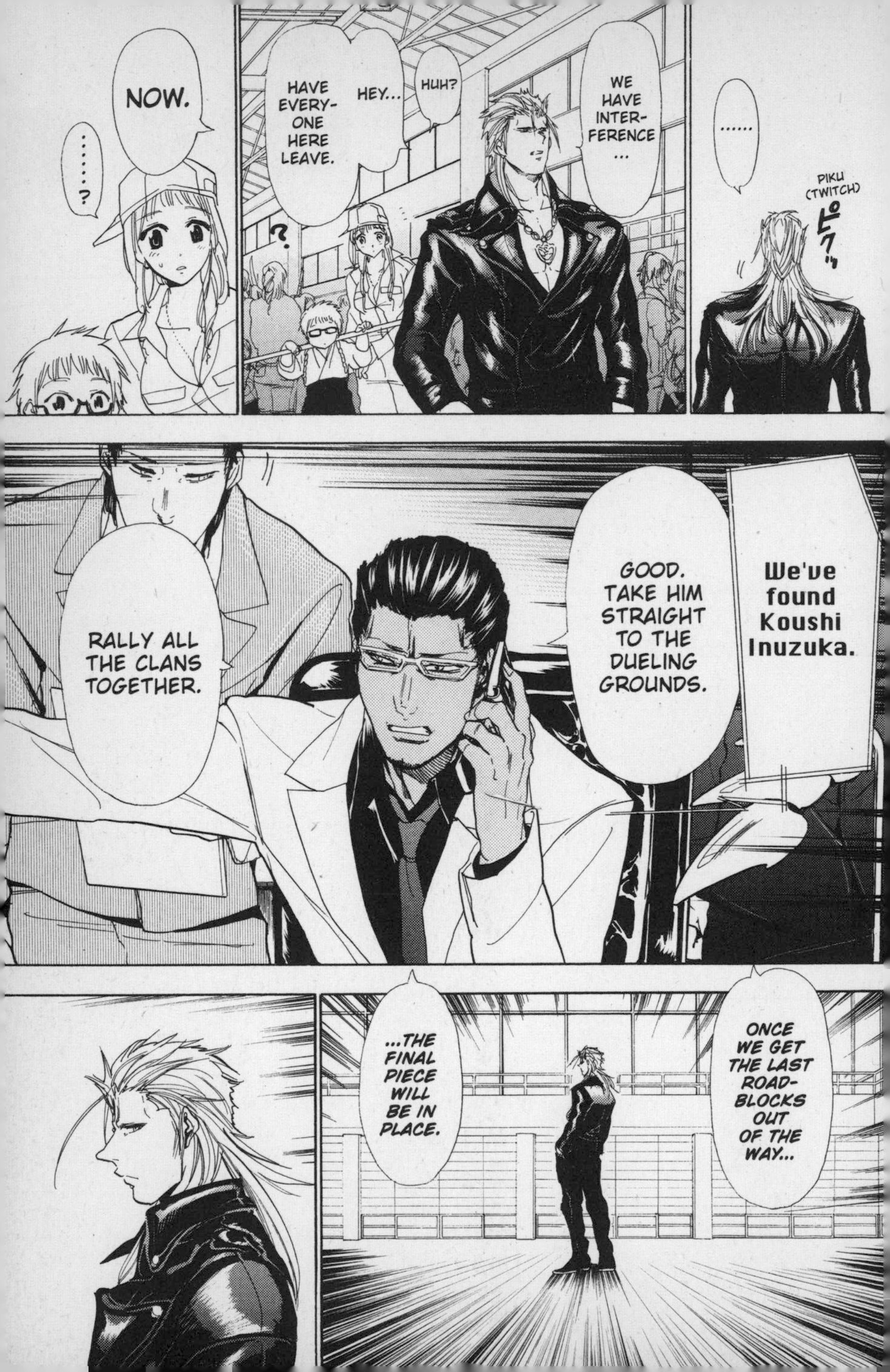
......
PIKU (TWITCH)
WE HAVE INTERFERENCE...
HUH?
HEY...
HAVE EVERYONE HERE LEAVE.
?
NOW.
......?
We've found Koushi Inuzuka.
GOOD. TAKE HIM STRAIGHT TO THE DUELING GROUNDS.
RALLY ALL THE CLANS TOGETHER.
ONCE WE GET THE LAST ROADBLOCKS OUT OF THE WAY...
...THE FINAL PIECE WILL BE IN PLACE.

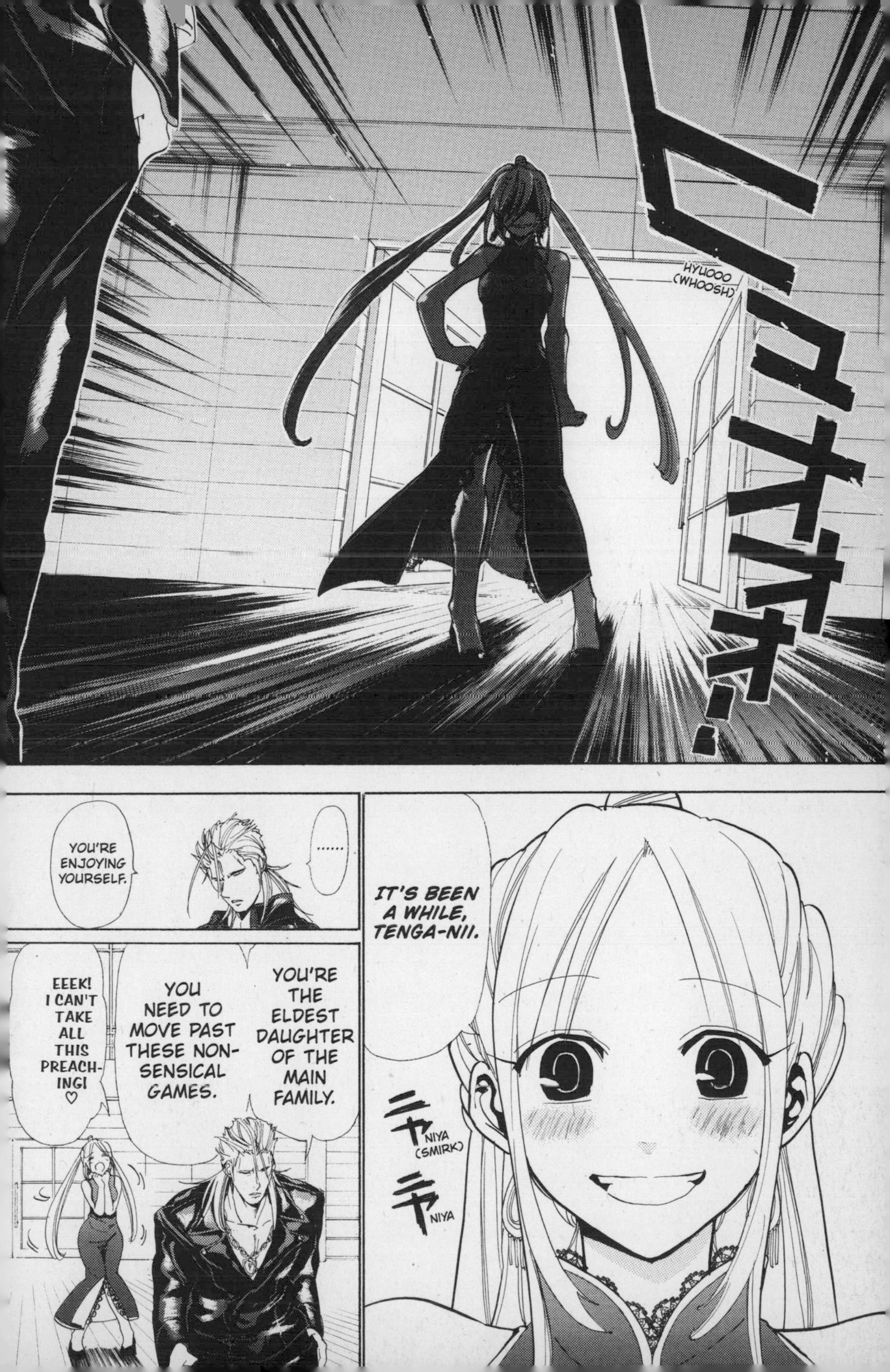
HYUOOO (WHOOSH)
IT'S BEEN A WHILE, TENGA-NII.
ニヤ NIYA (SMIRK)
ニヤ NIYA
......
YOU'RE ENJOYING YOURSELF.
YOU'RE THE ELDEST DAUGHTER OF THE MAIN FAMILY.
YOU NEED TO MOVE PAST THESE NON-SENSICAL GAMES.
EEEK! I CAN'T TAKE ALL THIS PREACHING! ♡

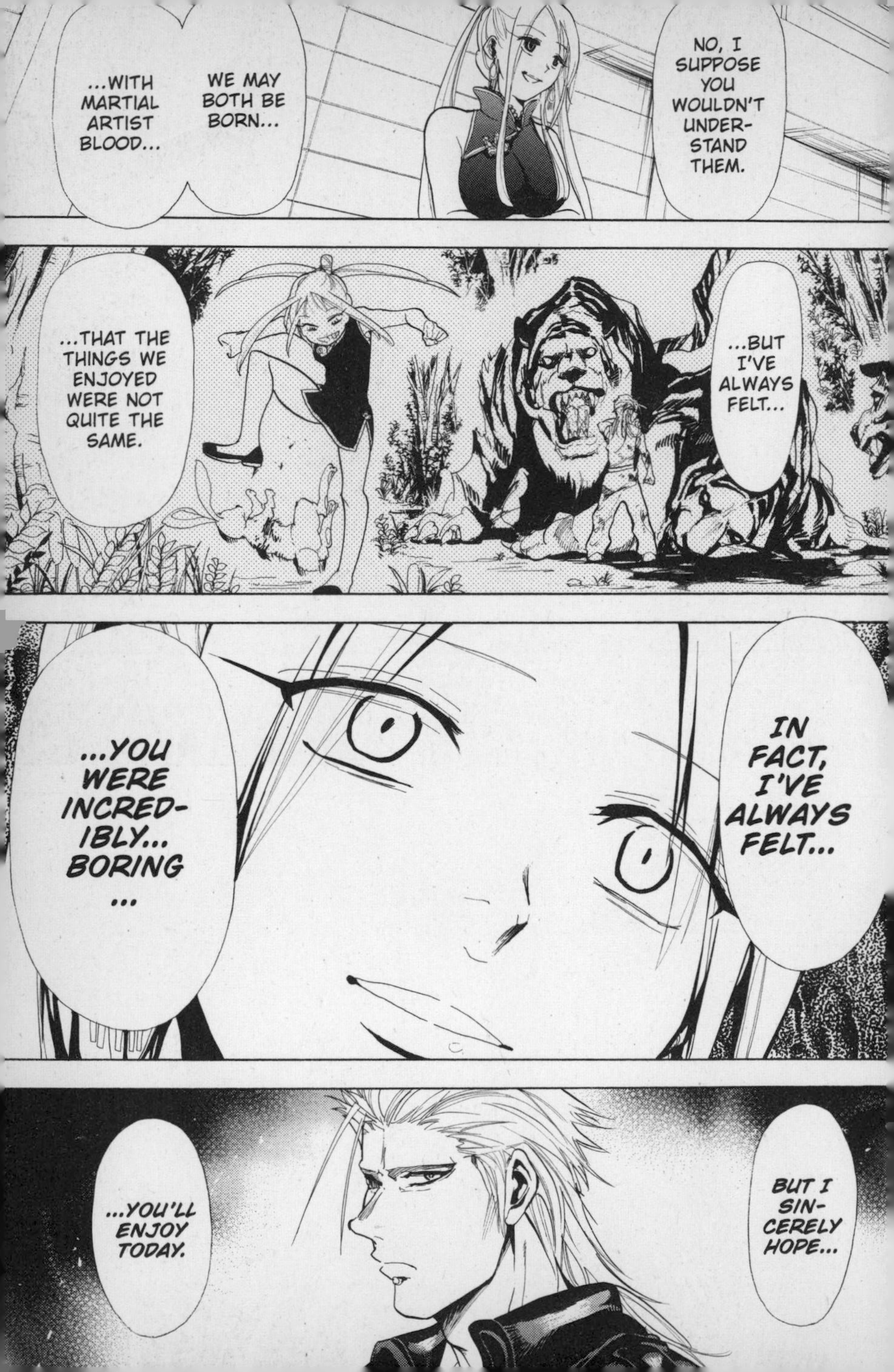
NO, I SUPPOSE YOU WOULDN'T UNDER-STAND THEM.
WE MAY BOTH BE BORN...
...WITH MARTIAL ARTIST BLOOD...
...BUT I'VE ALWAYS FELT...
...THAT THE THINGS WE ENJOYED WERE NOT QUITE THE SAME.
IN FACT, I'VE ALWAYS FELT...
...YOU WERE INCRED-IBLY... BORING ...
BUT I SIN-CERELY HOPE...
...YOU'LL ENJOY TODAY.

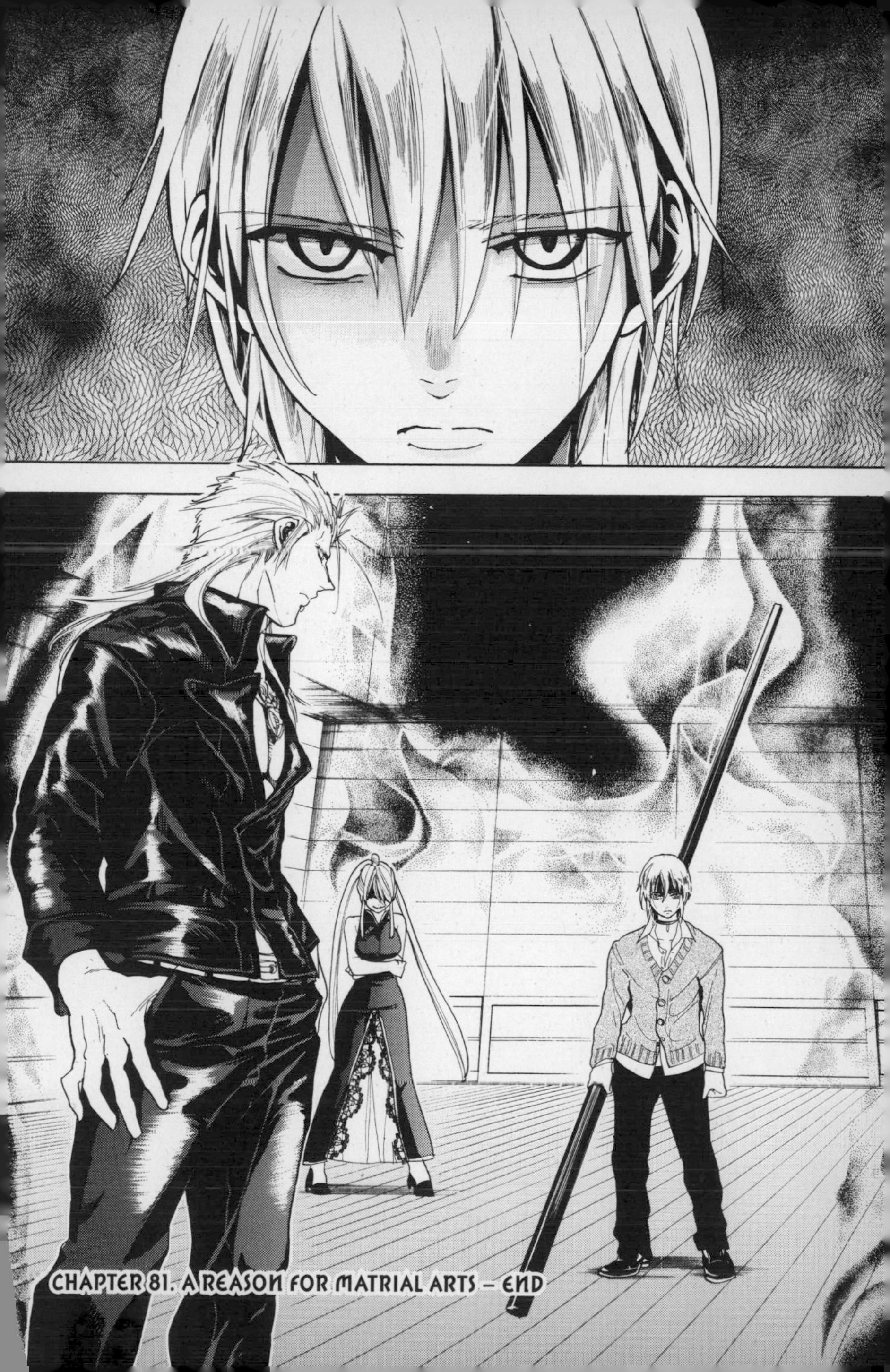
CHAPTER 81. A REASON FOR MATRIAL ARTS – END

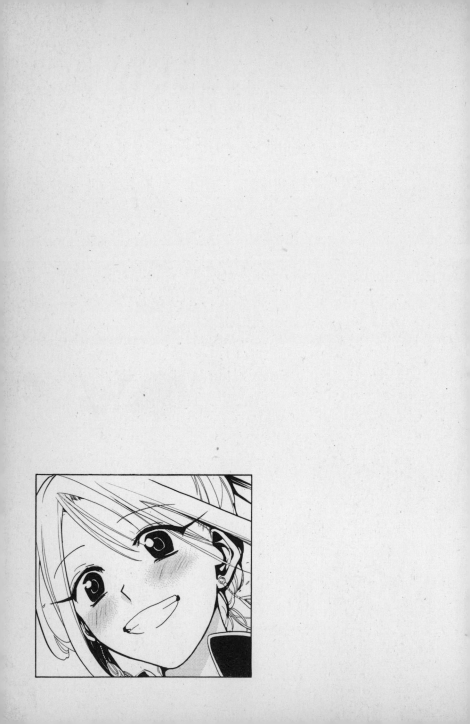

SUMOMOMO, MOMOMO

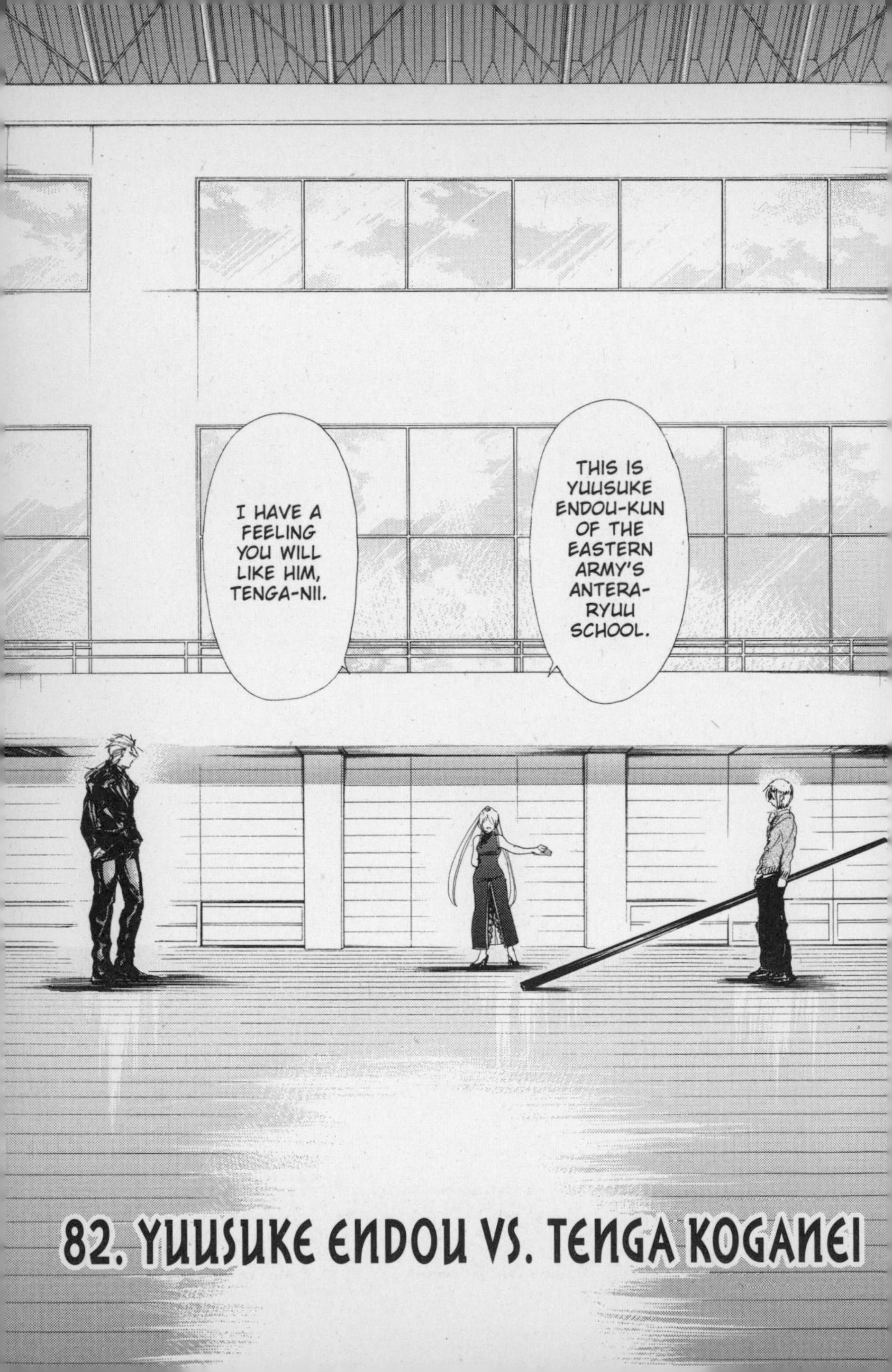
THIS IS YUUSUKE ENDOU-KUN OF THE EASTERN ARMY'S ANTERA-RYUU SCHOOL.
I HAVE A FEELING YOU WILL LIKE HIM, TENGA-NII.

82. YUUSUKE ENDOU VS. TENGA KOGANEI

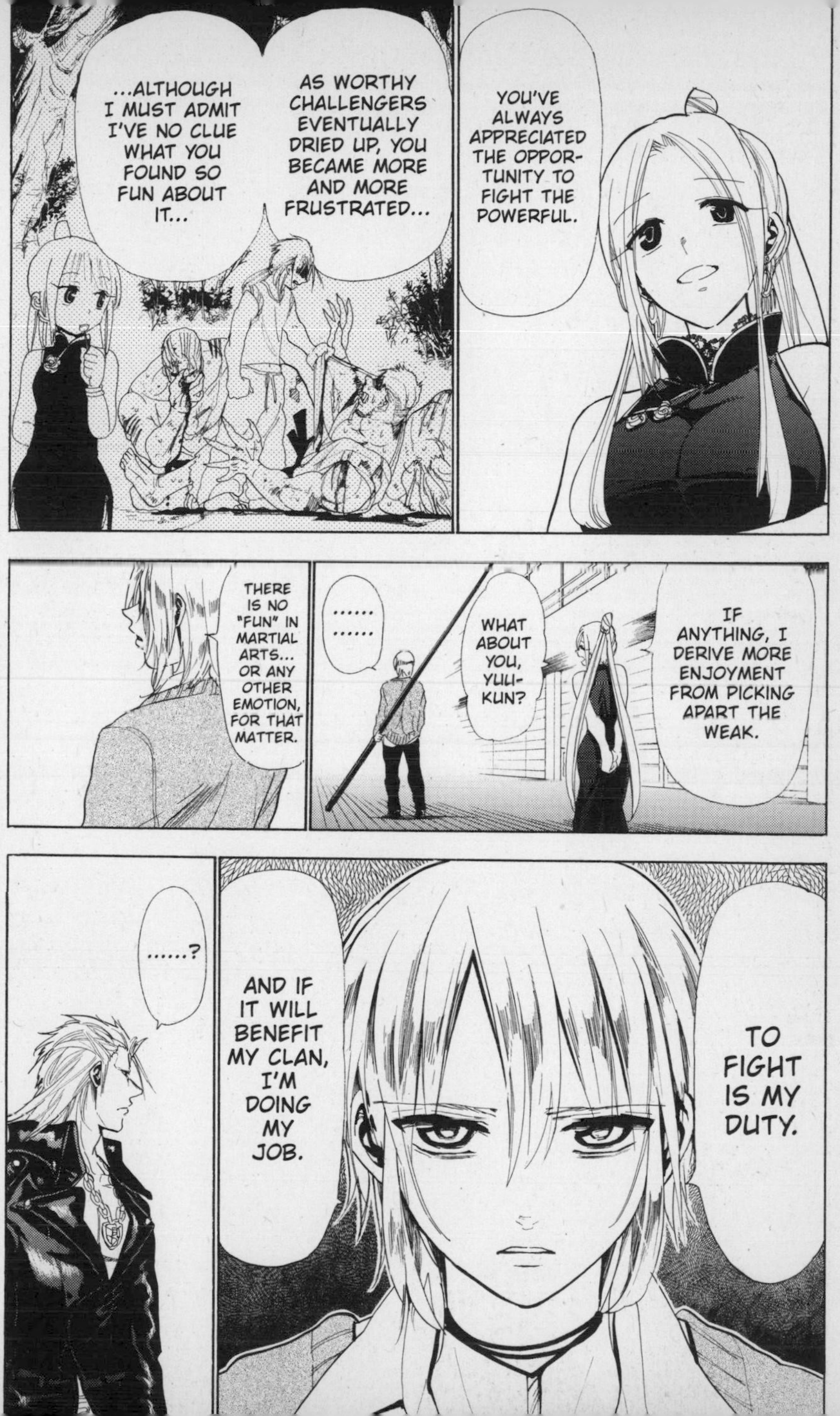
YOU'VE ALWAYS APPRECIATED THE OPPORTUNITY TO FIGHT THE POWERFUL.
AS WORTHY CHALLENGERS EVENTUALLY DRIED UP, YOU BECAME MORE AND MORE FRUSTRATED...
...ALTHOUGH I MUST ADMIT I'VE NO CLUE WHAT YOU FOUND SO FUN ABOUT IT...
IF ANYTHING, I DERIVE MORE ENJOYMENT FROM PICKING APART THE WEAK.
WHAT ABOUT YOU, YUU-KUN?
....
THERE IS NO "FUN" IN MARTIAL ARTS... OR ANY OTHER EMOTION, FOR THAT MATTER.
TO FIGHT IS MY DUTY.
AND IF IT WILL BENEFIT MY CLAN, I'M DOING MY JOB.
......?

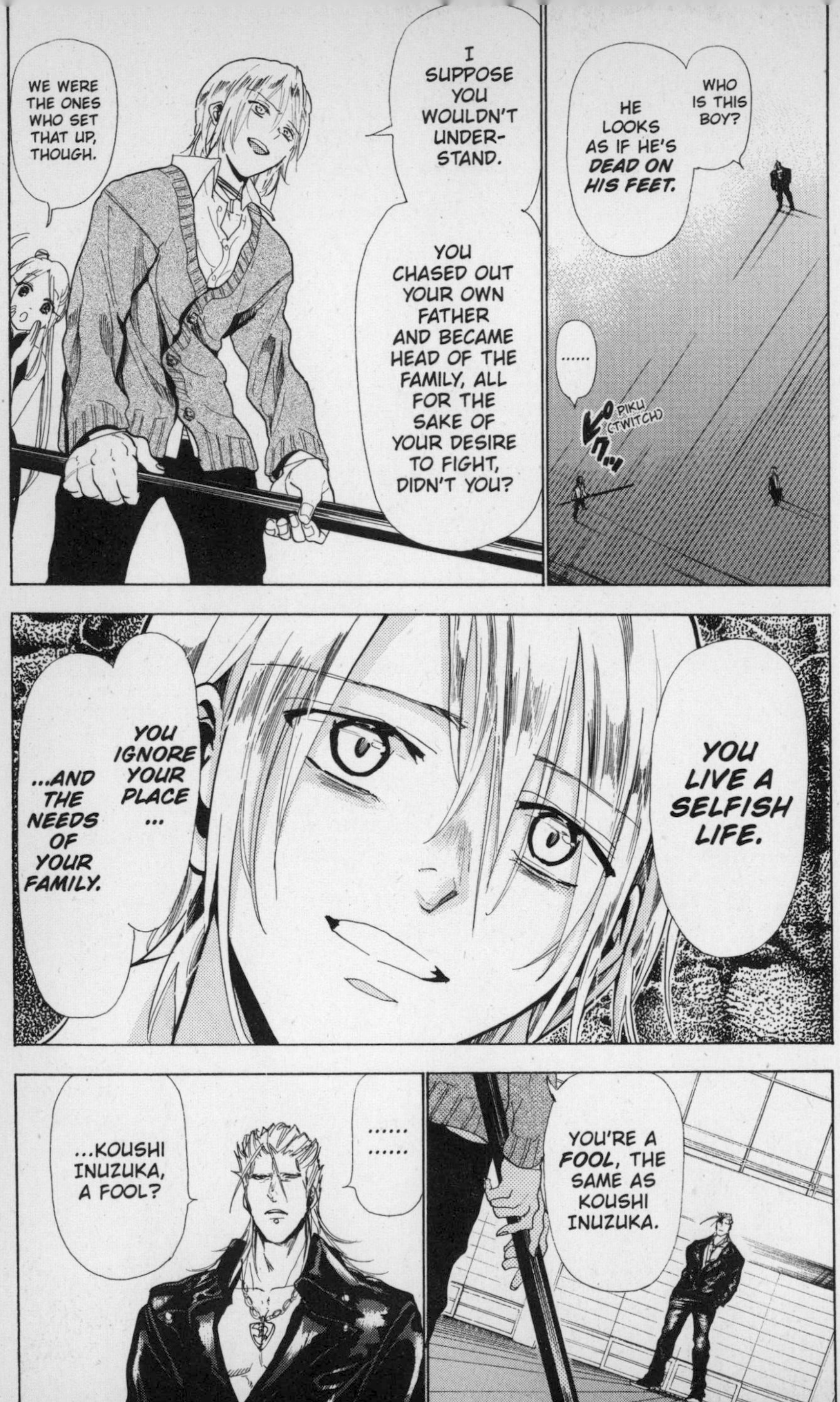
WHO IS THIS BOY?
HE LOOKS AS IF HE'S DEAD ON HIS FEET.
......
PIKU (TWITCH)
I SUPPOSE YOU WOULDN'T UNDER-STAND.
YOU CHASED OUT YOUR OWN FATHER AND BECAME HEAD OF THE FAMILY, ALL FOR THE SAKE OF YOUR DESIRE TO FIGHT, DIDN'T YOU?
WE WERE THE ONES WHO SET THAT UP, THOUGH.
YOU LIVE A SELFISH LIFE.
YOU IGNORE YOUR PLACE ...
...AND THE NEEDS OF YOUR FAMILY.
YOU'RE A FOOL, THE SAME AS KOUSHI INUZUKA.
....
...KOUSHI INUZUKA, A FOOL?

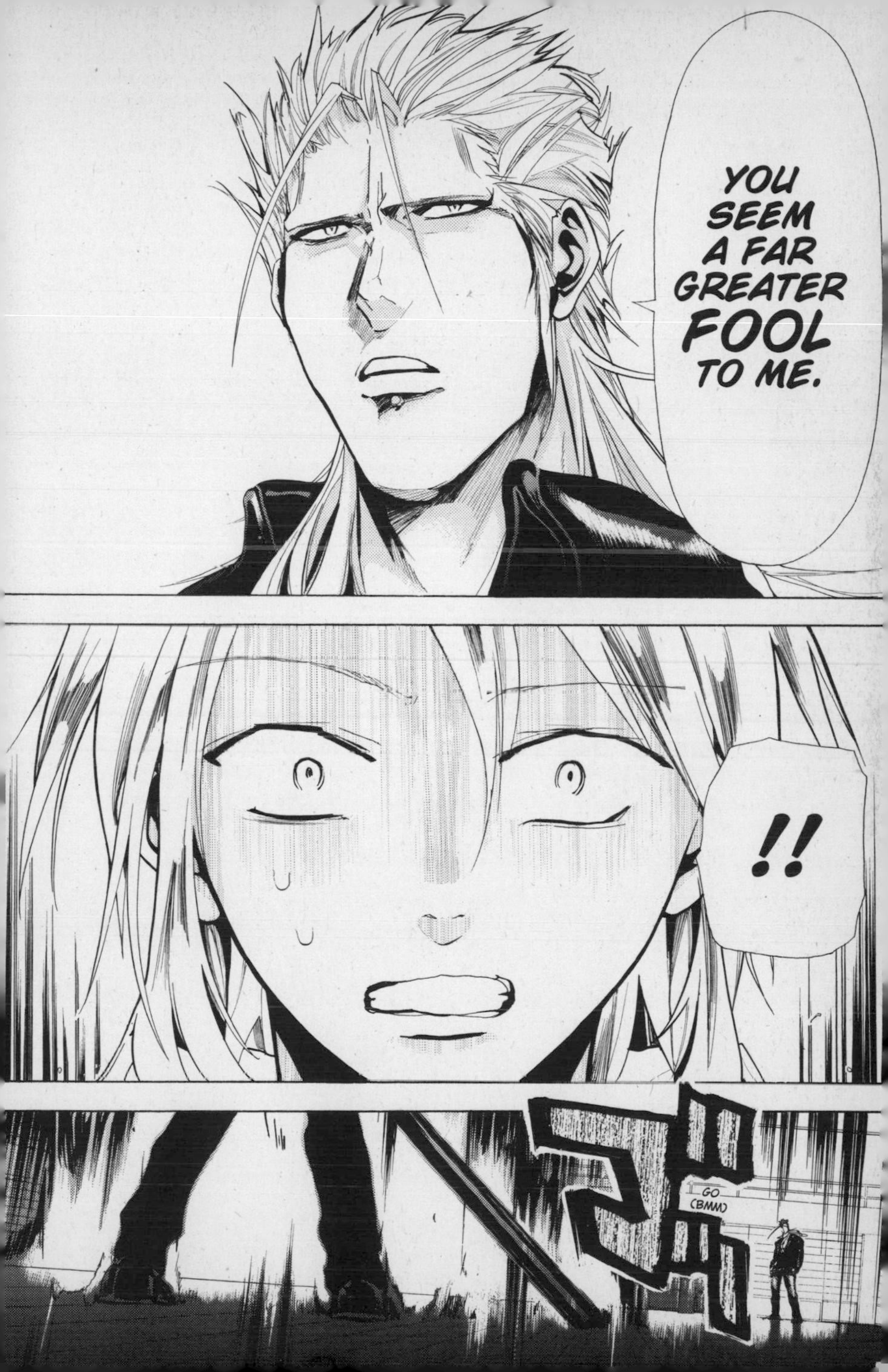
YOU SEEM A FAR GREATER FOOL TO ME.
!!
GO (BMM)

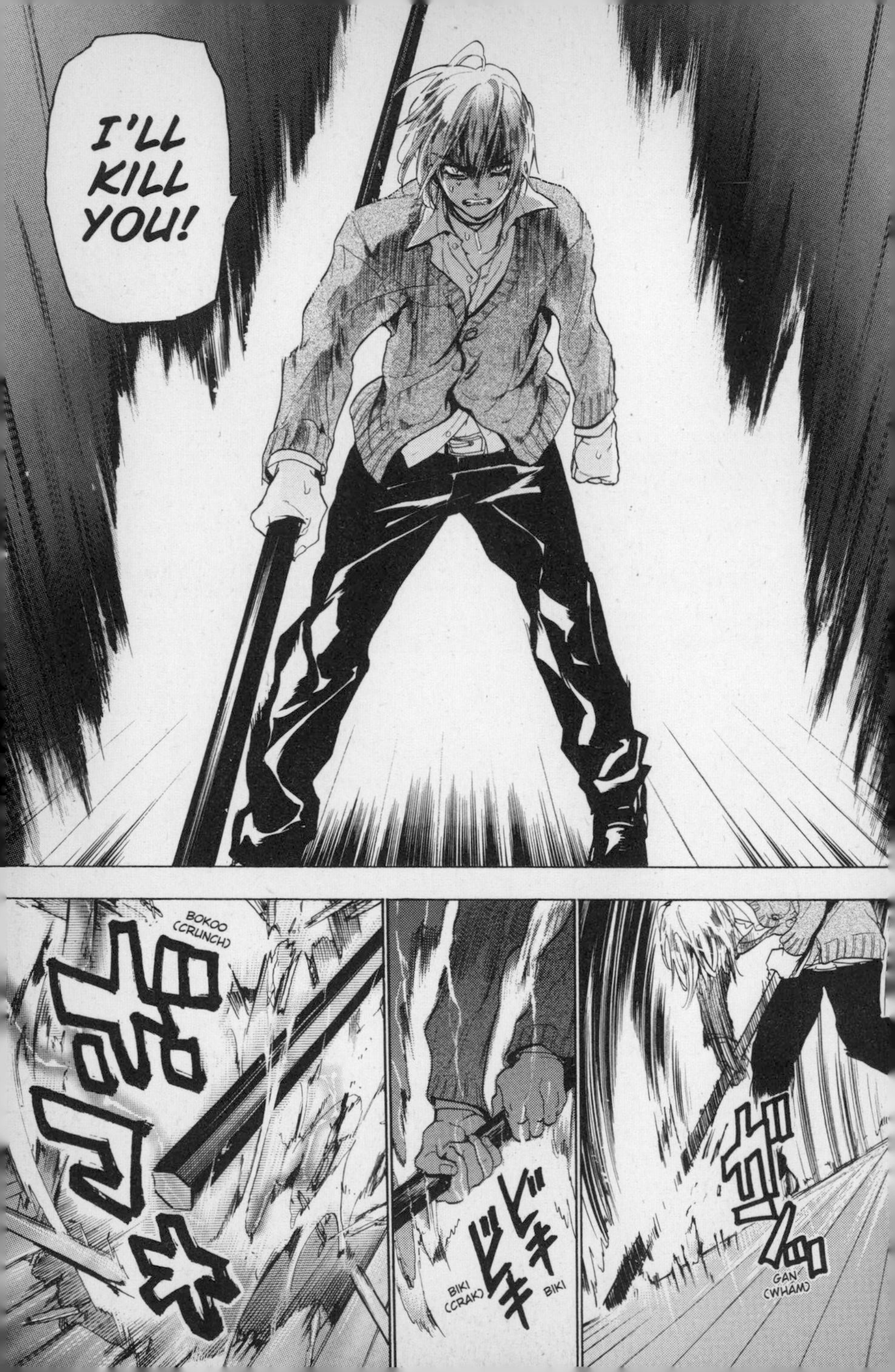
I'LL KILL YOU!
GAN (WHAM)
BIKI (CRAK) BIKI
BOKOO (CRUNCH)

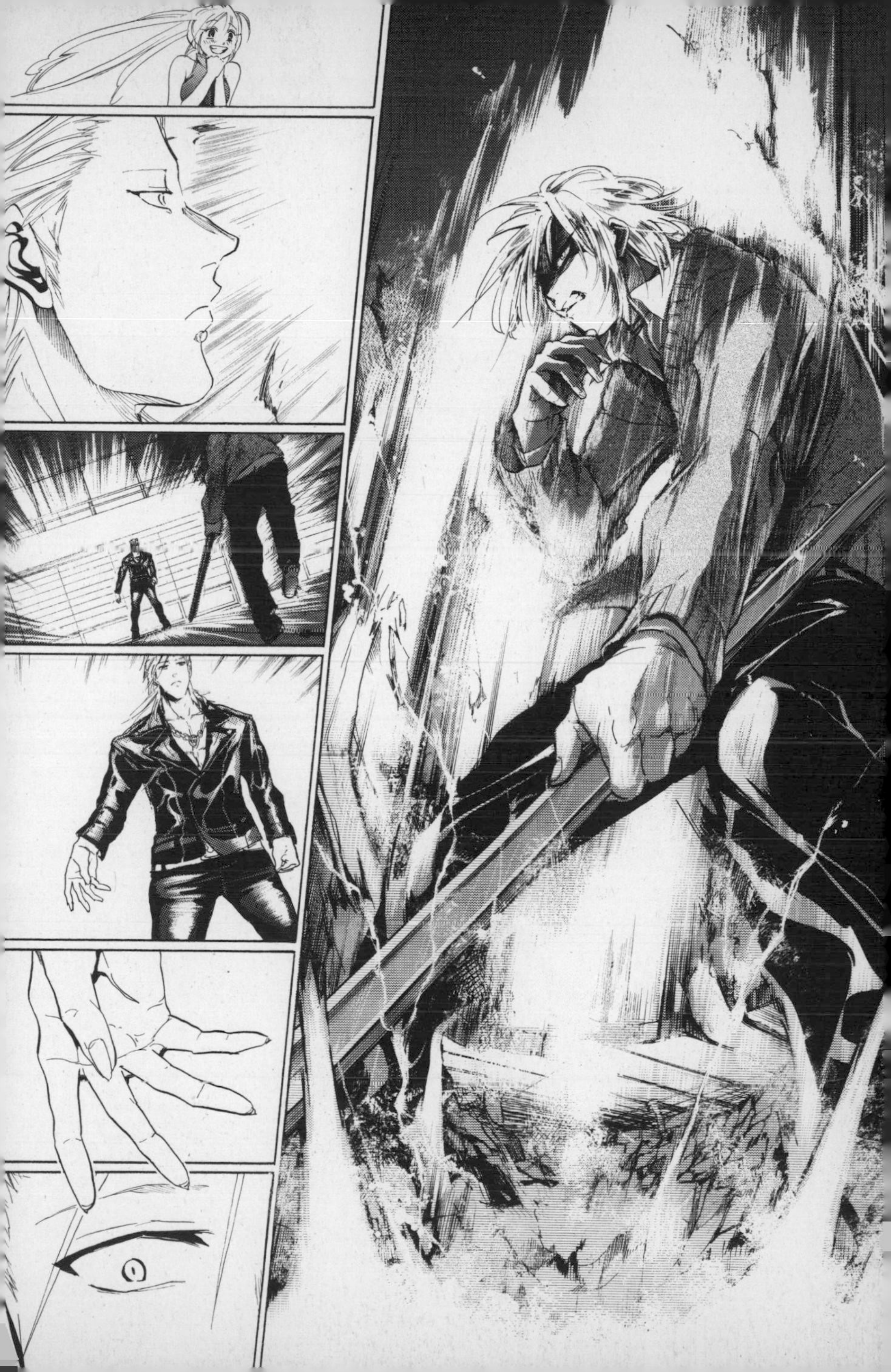

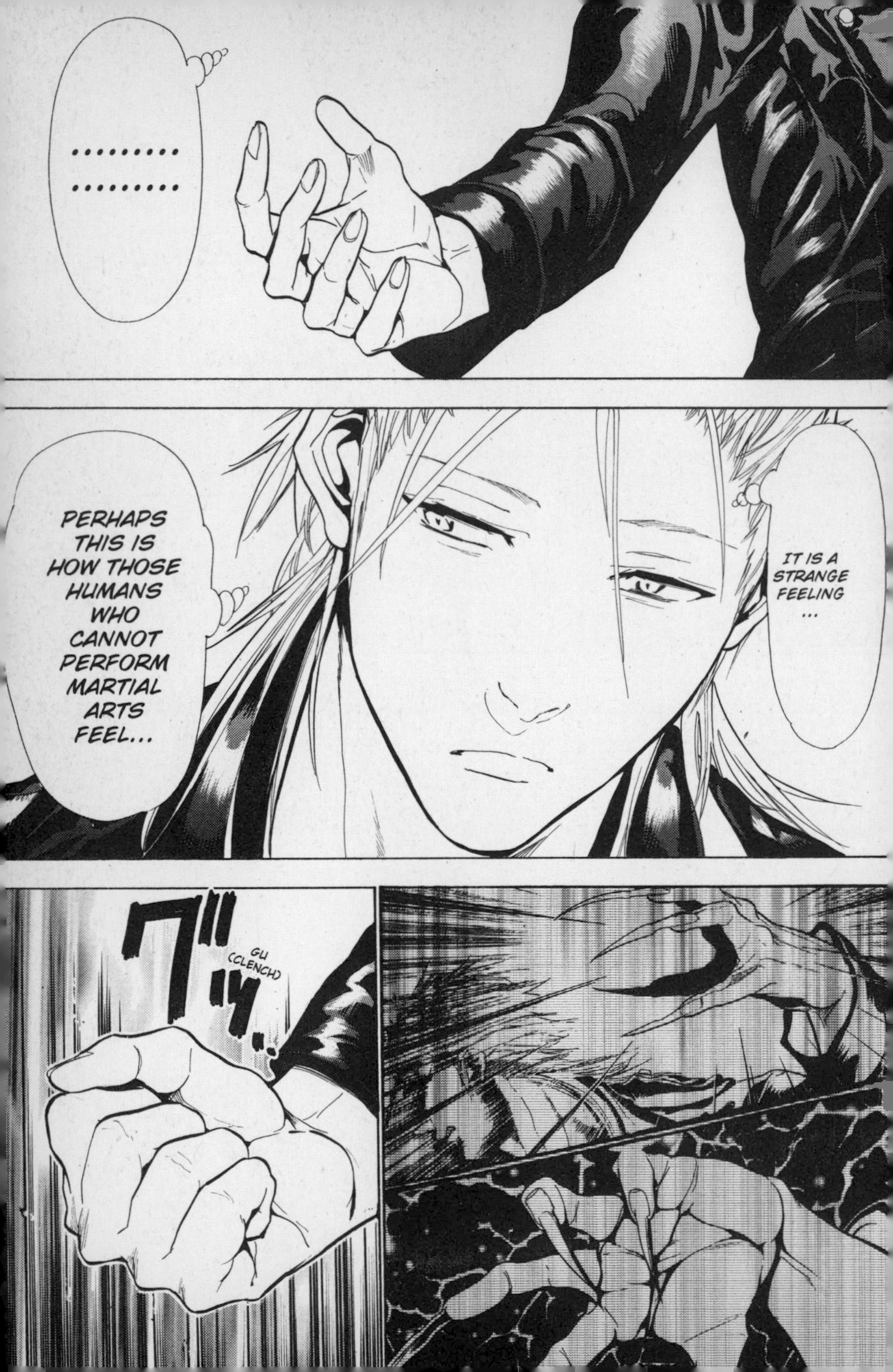
....
....
IT IS A STRANGE FEELING...
PERHAPS THIS IS HOW THOSE HUMANS WHO CANNOT PERFORM MARTIAL ARTS FEEL...
GU (CLENCH)

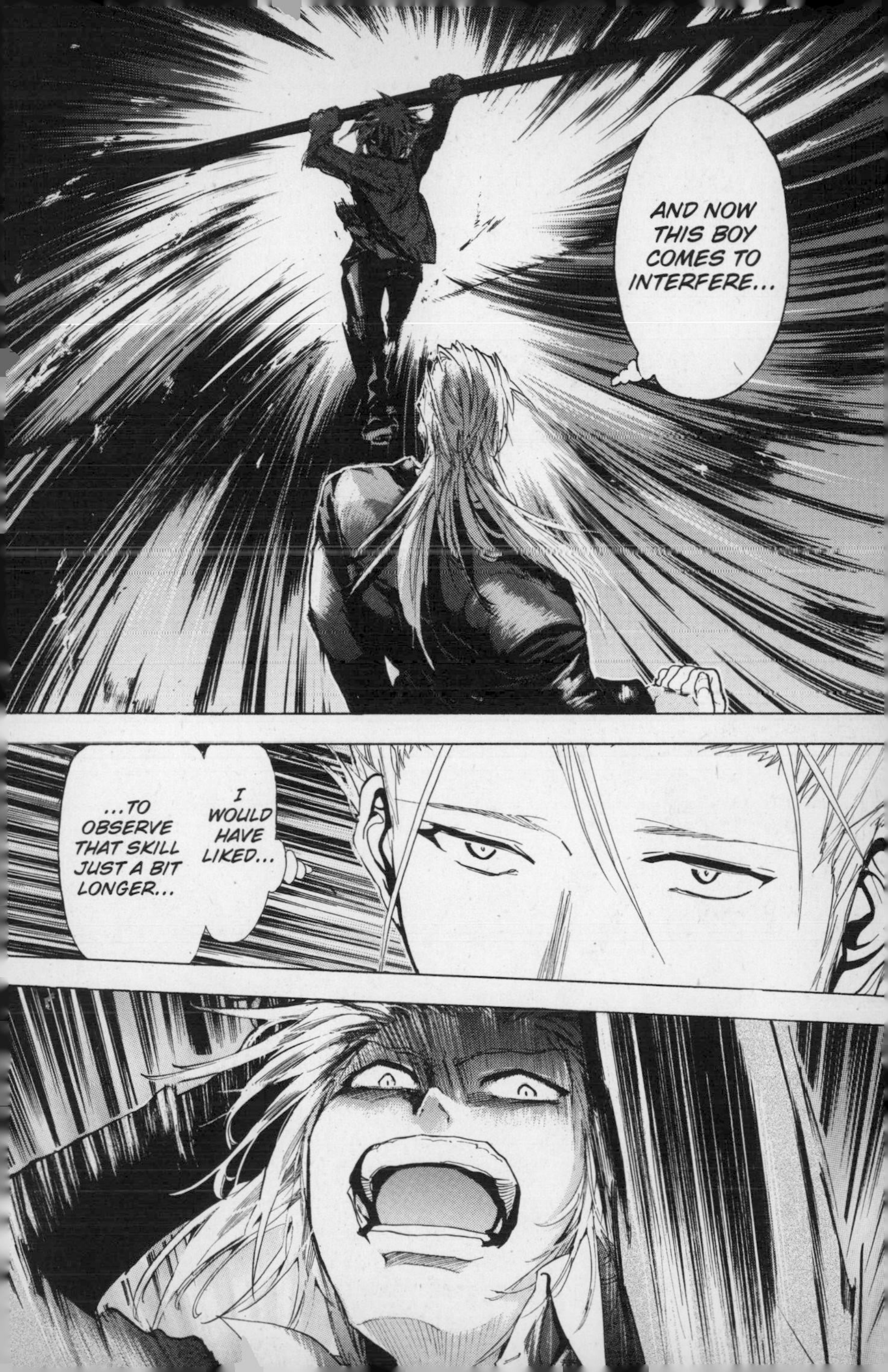
AND NOW THIS BOY COMES TO INTERFERE...
I WOULD HAVE LIKED...
...TO OBSERVE THAT SKILL JUST A BIT LONGER...

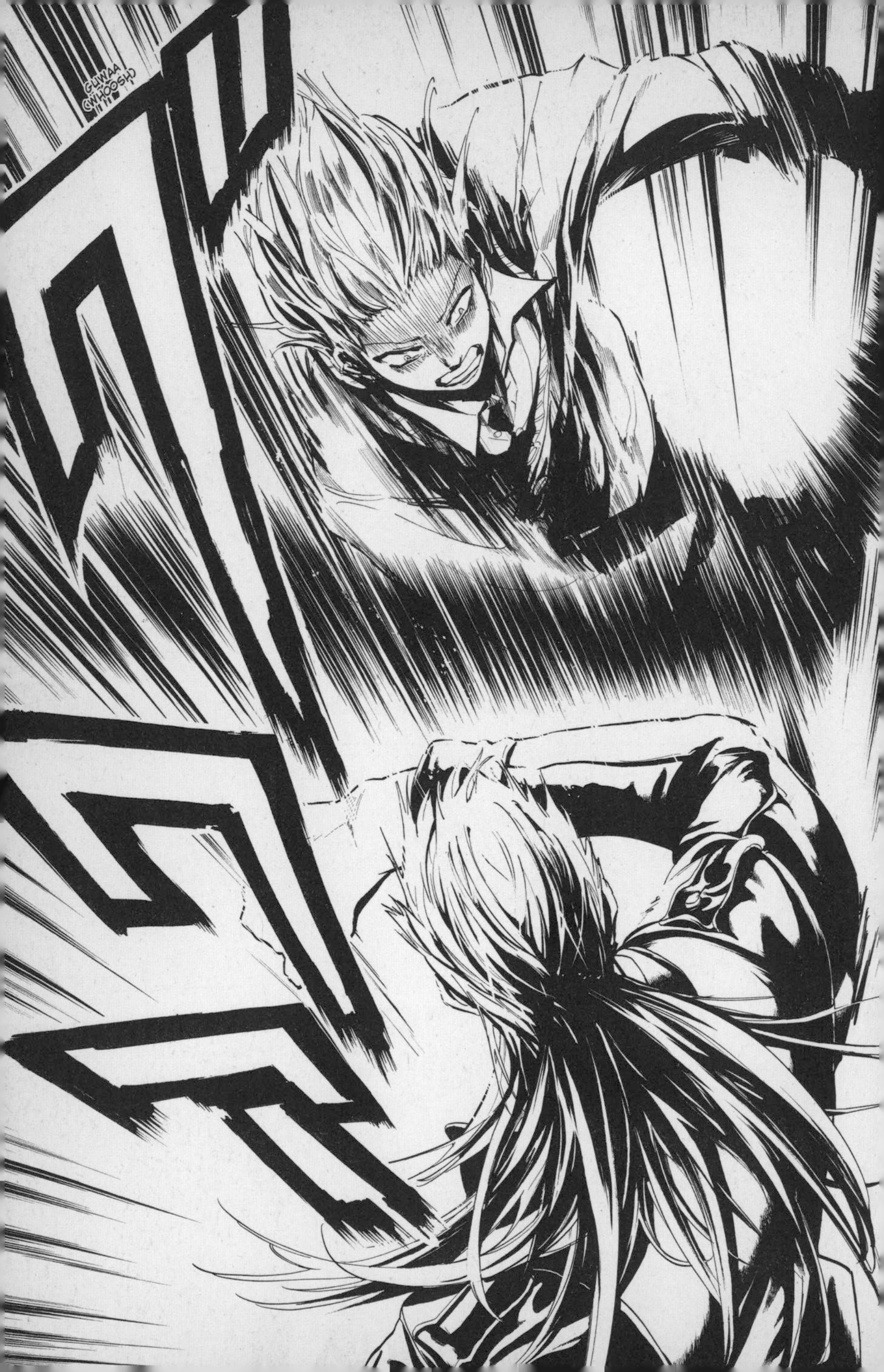
GUWAA (WHOOSH)

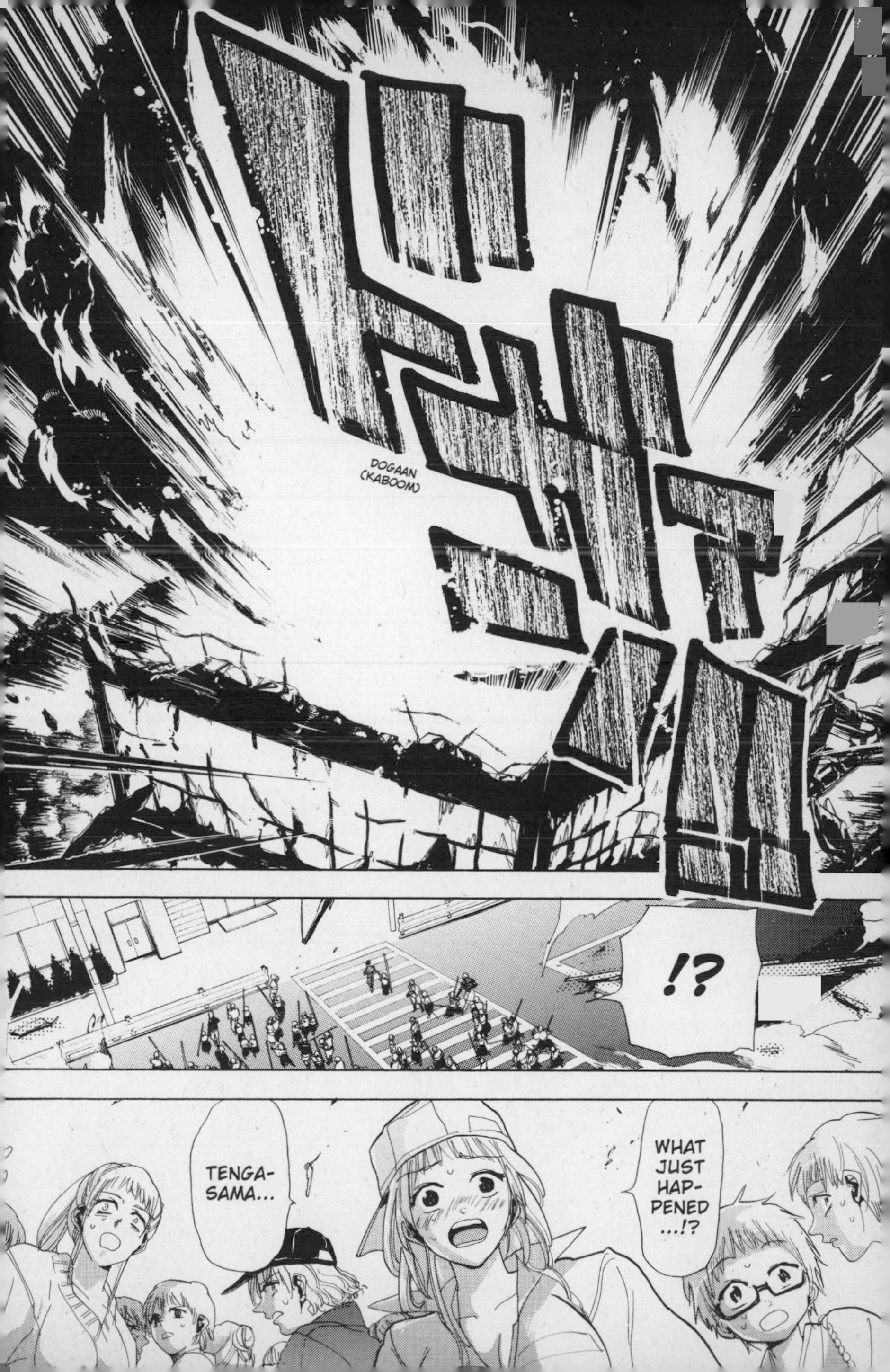
DOGAAN
(KABOOM)
!?
WHAT JUST HAP-PENED ...!?
TENGA-SAMA...

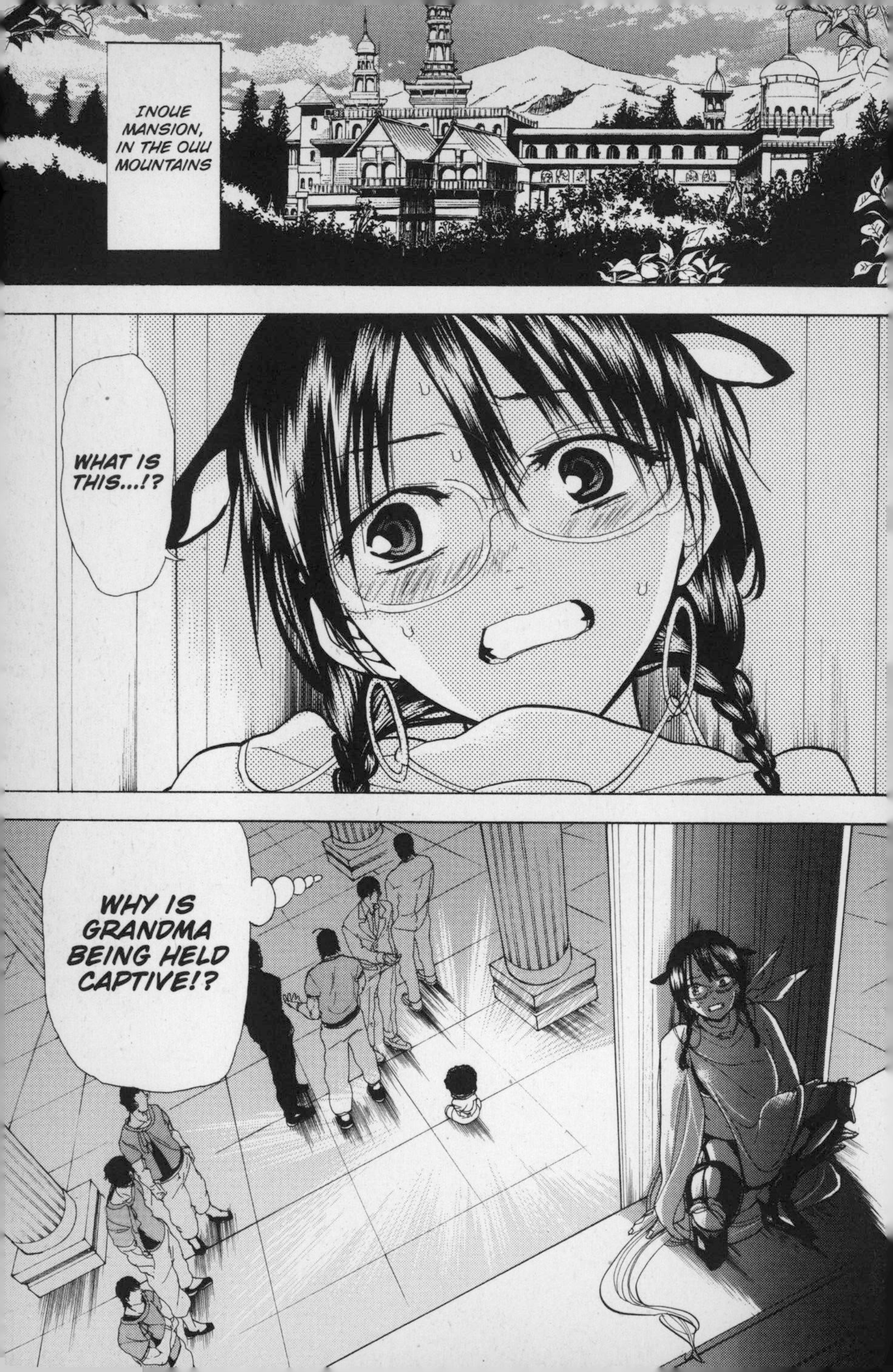
INOUE MANSION, IN THE OUU MOUNTAINS
WHAT IS THIS...!?
WHY IS GRANDMA BEING HELD CAPTIVE!?

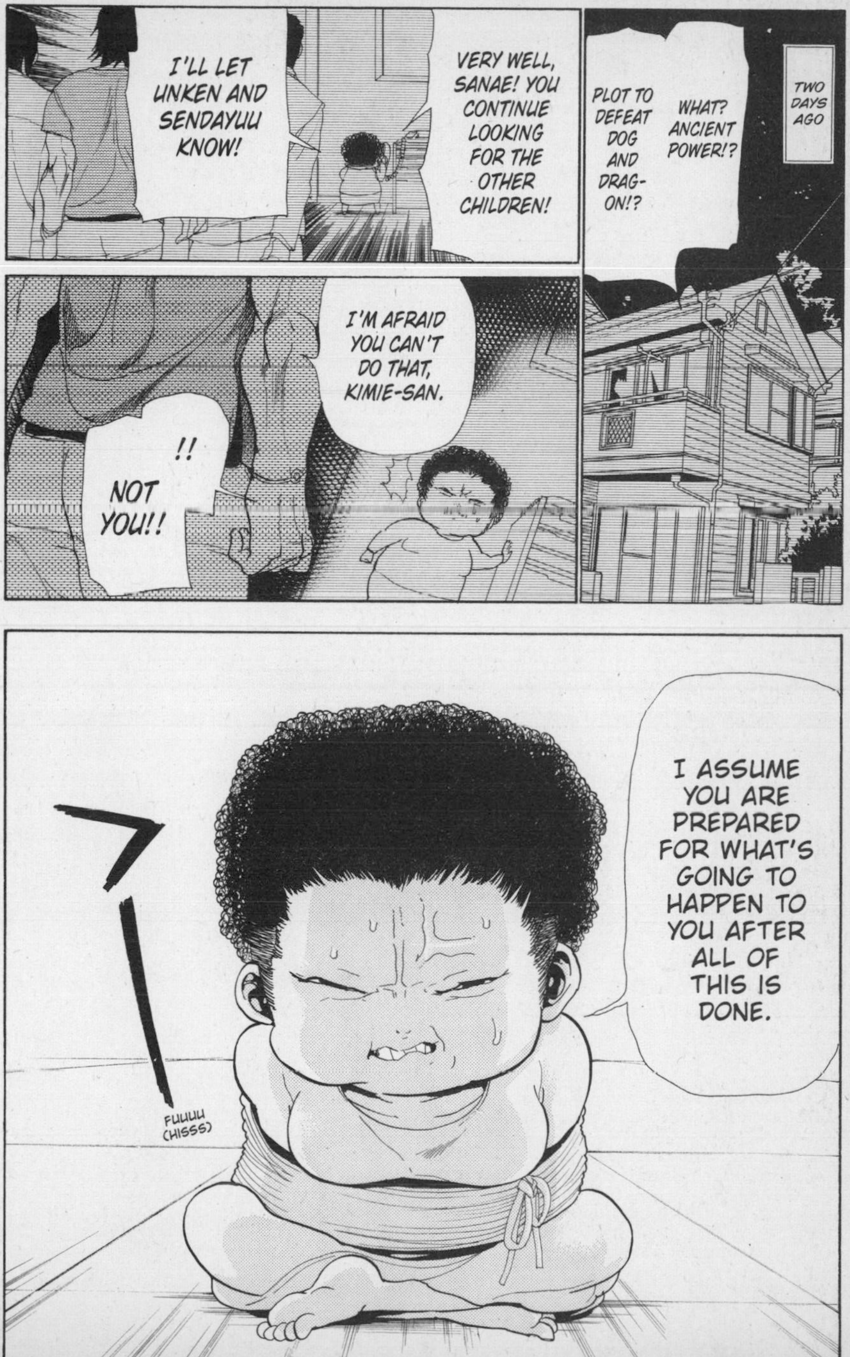
TWO DAYS AGO
WHAT? ANCIENT POWER!?
PLOT TO DEFEAT DOG AND DRAG-ON!?
VERY WELL, SANAE! YOU CONTINUE LOOKING FOR THE OTHER CHILDREN!
I'LL LET UNKEN AND SENDAYUU KNOW!
I'M AFRAID YOU CAN'T DO THAT, KIMIE-SAN.
!!
NOT YOU!!
I ASSUME YOU ARE PREPARED FOR WHAT'S GOING TO HAPPEN TO YOU AFTER ALL OF THIS IS DONE.
FUUUU (HISSS)

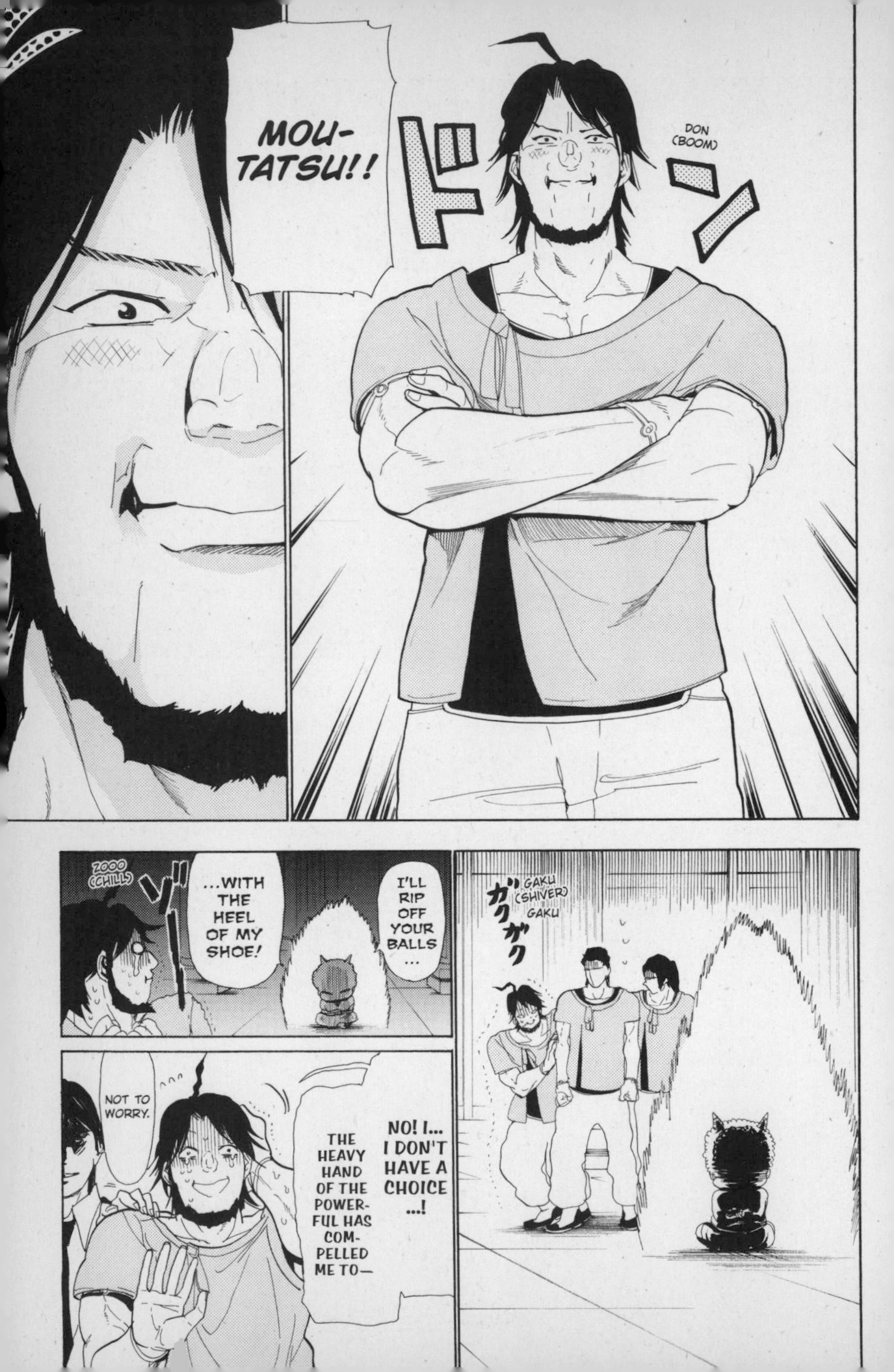
DON (BOOM)
MOU-TATSU!!
GAKU (SHIVER) GAKU
I'LL RIP OFF YOUR BALLS...
...WITH THE HEEL OF MY SHOE!
ZOOO (CHILL)
NO! I... I DON'T HAVE A CHOICE...!
THE HEAVY HAND OF THE POWERFUL HAS COMPELLED ME TO—
NOT TO WORRY.

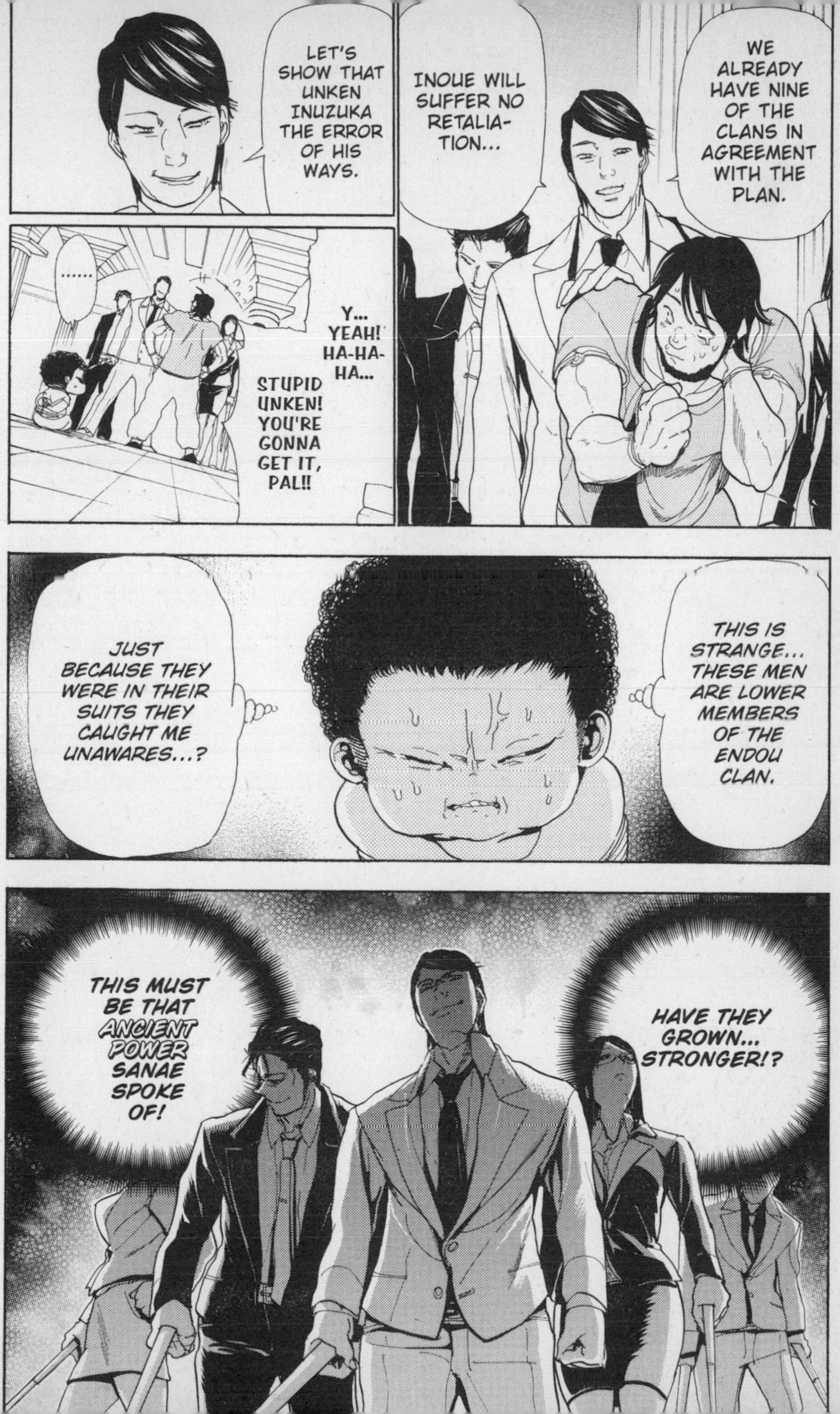

WE ALREADY HAVE NINE OF THE CLANS IN AGREEMENT WITH THE PLAN.
INOUE WILL SUFFER NO RETALIATION...
LET'S SHOW THAT UNKEN INUZUKA THE ERROR OF HIS WAYS.
Y... YEAH! HA-HA-HA...
STUPID UNKEN! YOU'RE GONNA GET IT, PAL!!
......
THIS IS STRANGE... THESE MEN ARE LOWER MEMBERS OF THE ENDOU CLAN.
JUST BECAUSE THEY WERE IN THEIR SUITS THEY CAUGHT ME UNAWARES...?
HAVE THEY GROWN... STRONGER!?
THIS MUST BE THAT ANCIENT POWER SANAE SPOKE OF!

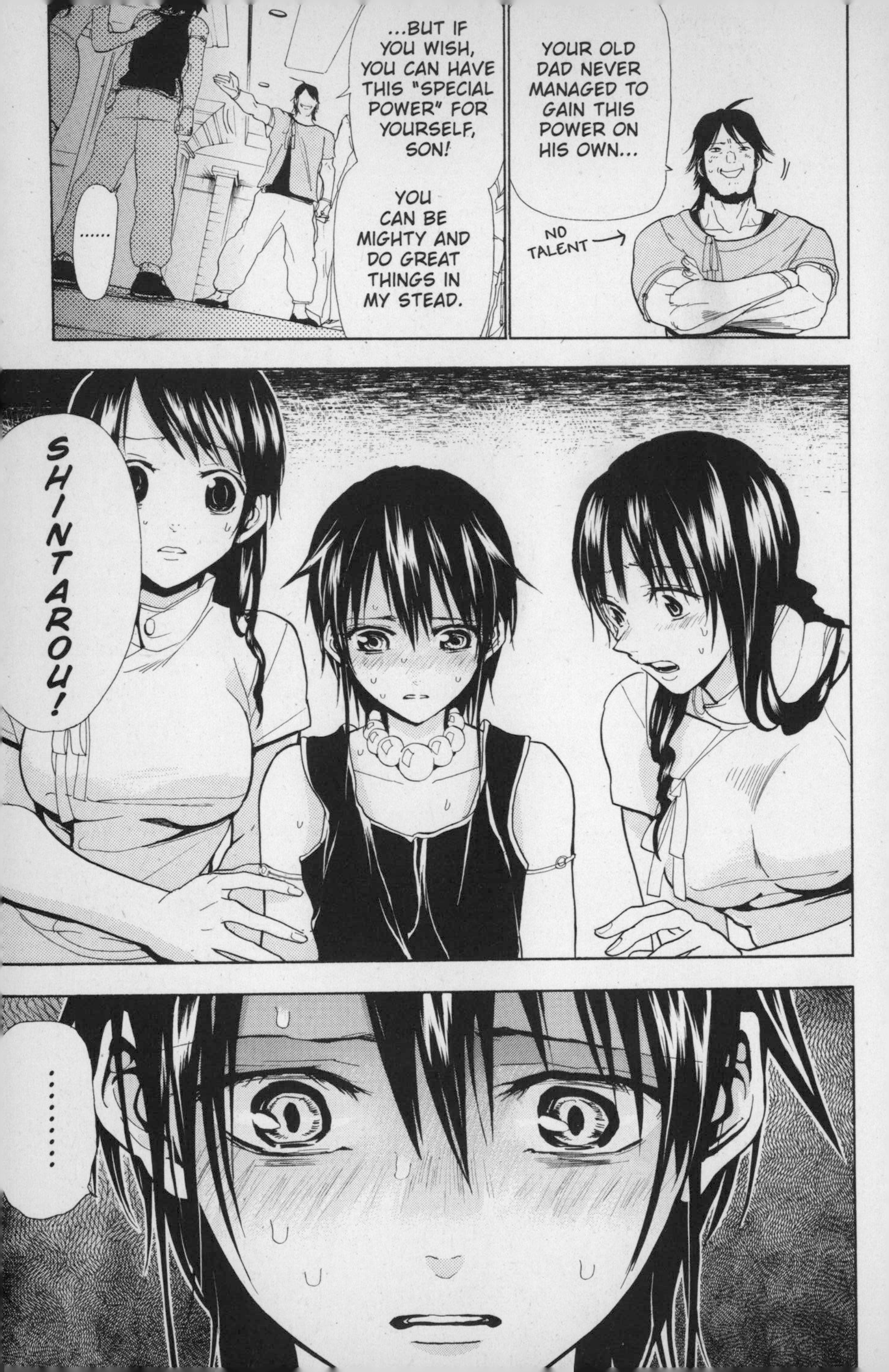
YOUR OLD DAD NEVER MANAGED TO GAIN THIS POWER ON HIS OWN...
NO TALENT
...BUT IF YOU WISH, YOU CAN HAVE THIS "SPECIAL POWER" FOR YOURSELF, SON!
YOU CAN BE MIGHTY AND DO GREAT THINGS IN MY STEAD.
......
SHINTAROU!
....

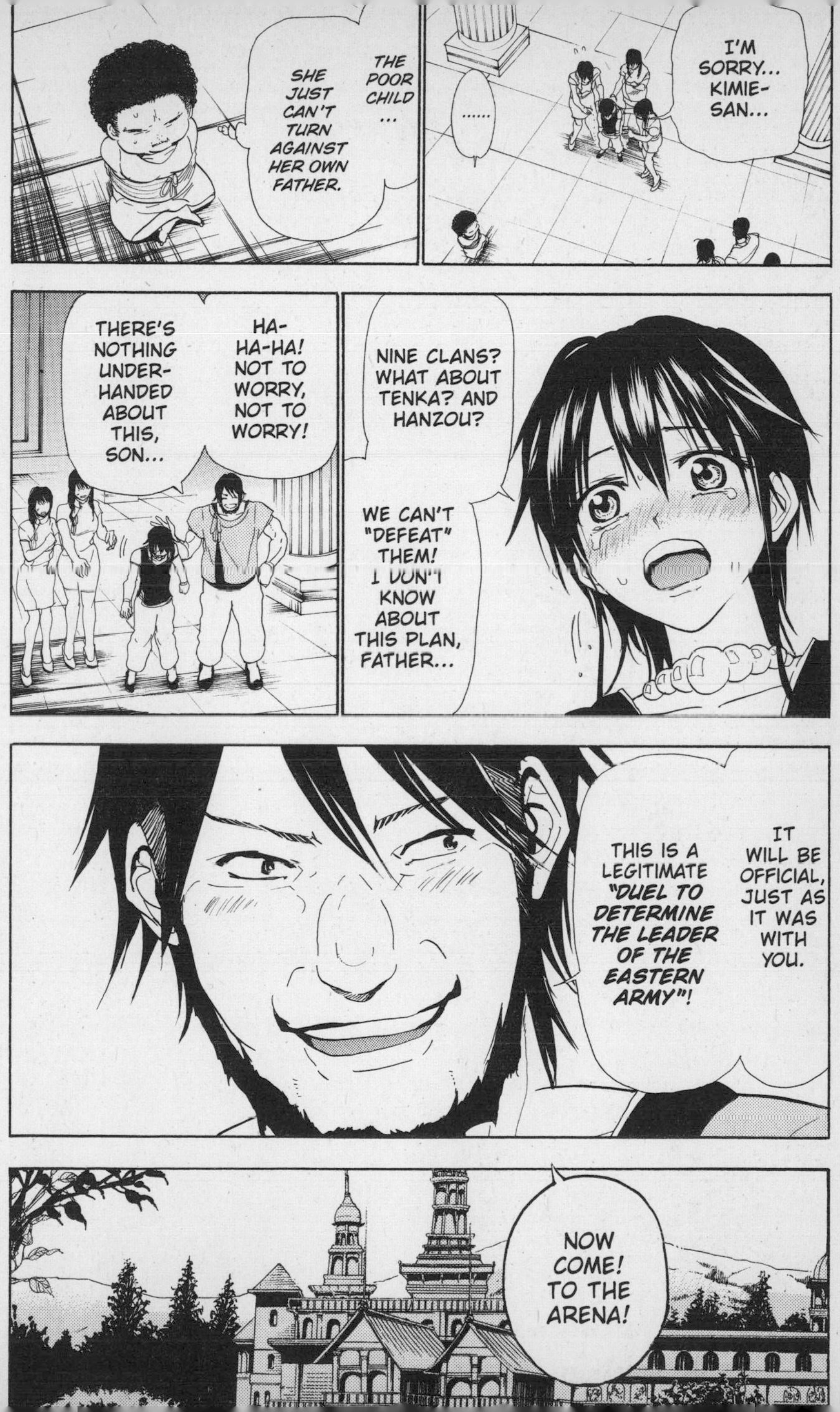
I'M SORRY... KIMIE-SAN...
......
THE POOR CHILD...
SHE JUST CAN'T TURN AGAINST HER OWN FATHER.
NINE CLANS? WHAT ABOUT TENKA? AND HANZOU?
WE CAN'T "DEFEAT" THEM! I DON'T KNOW ABOUT THIS PLAN, FATHER...
HA-HA-HA! NOT TO WORRY, NOT TO WORRY!
THERE'S NOTHING UNDER-HANDED ABOUT THIS, SON...
IT WILL BE OFFICIAL, JUST AS IT WAS WITH YOU.
THIS IS A LEGITIMATE "DUEL TO DETERMINE THE LEADER OF THE EASTERN ARMY"!
NOW COME! TO THE ARENA!

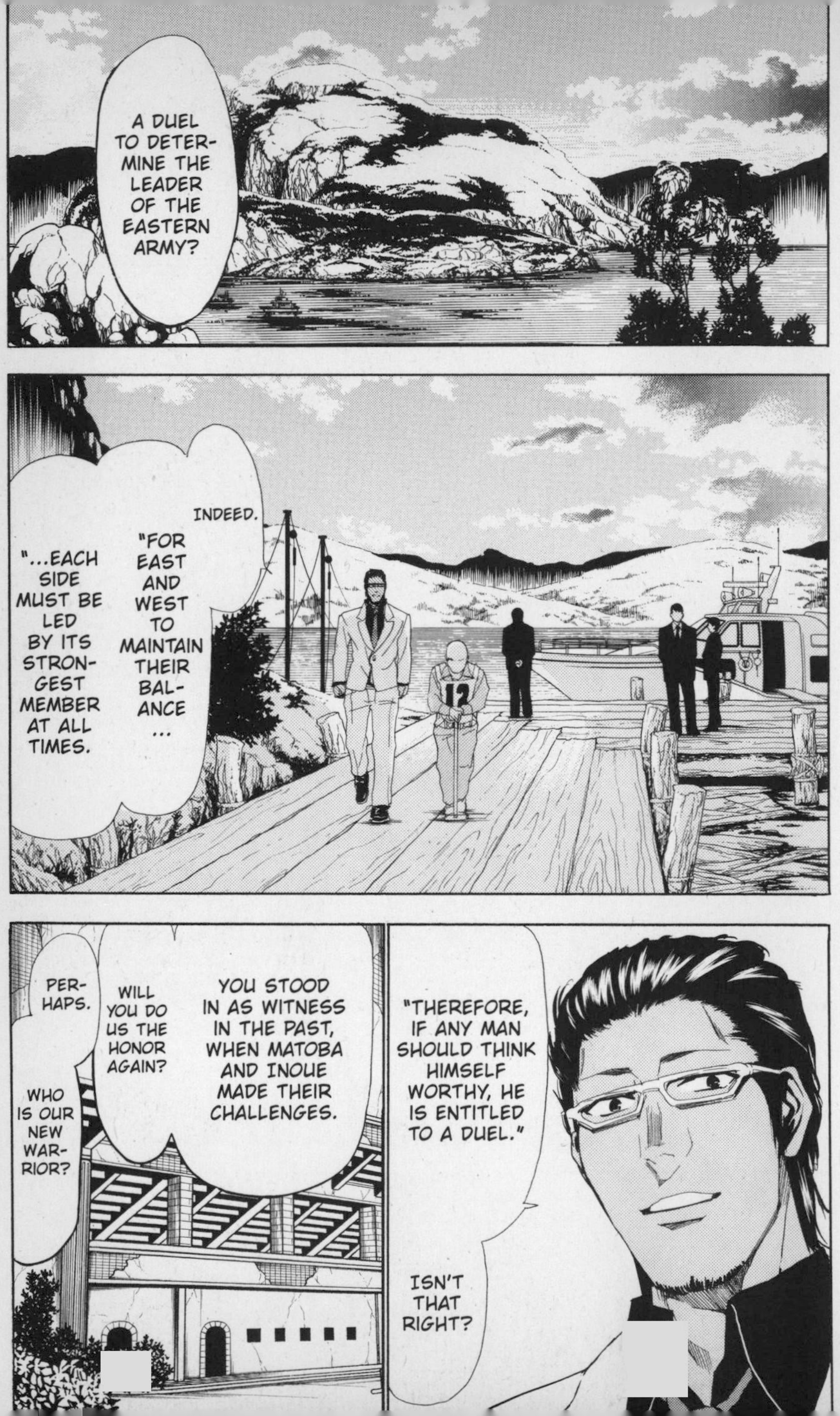
A DUEL TO DETERMINE THE LEADER OF THE EASTERN ARMY?
INDEED.
"FOR EAST AND WEST TO MAINTAIN THEIR BALANCE...
"...EACH SIDE MUST BE LED BY ITS STRONGEST MEMBER AT ALL TIMES.
"THEREFORE, IF ANY MAN SHOULD THINK HIMSELF WORTHY, HE IS ENTITLED TO A DUEL."
ISN'T THAT RIGHT?
YOU STOOD IN AS WITNESS IN THE PAST, WHEN MATOBA AND INOUE MADE THEIR CHALLENGES.
WILL YOU DO US THE HONOR AGAIN?
PERHAPS.
WHO IS OUR NEW WARRIOR?

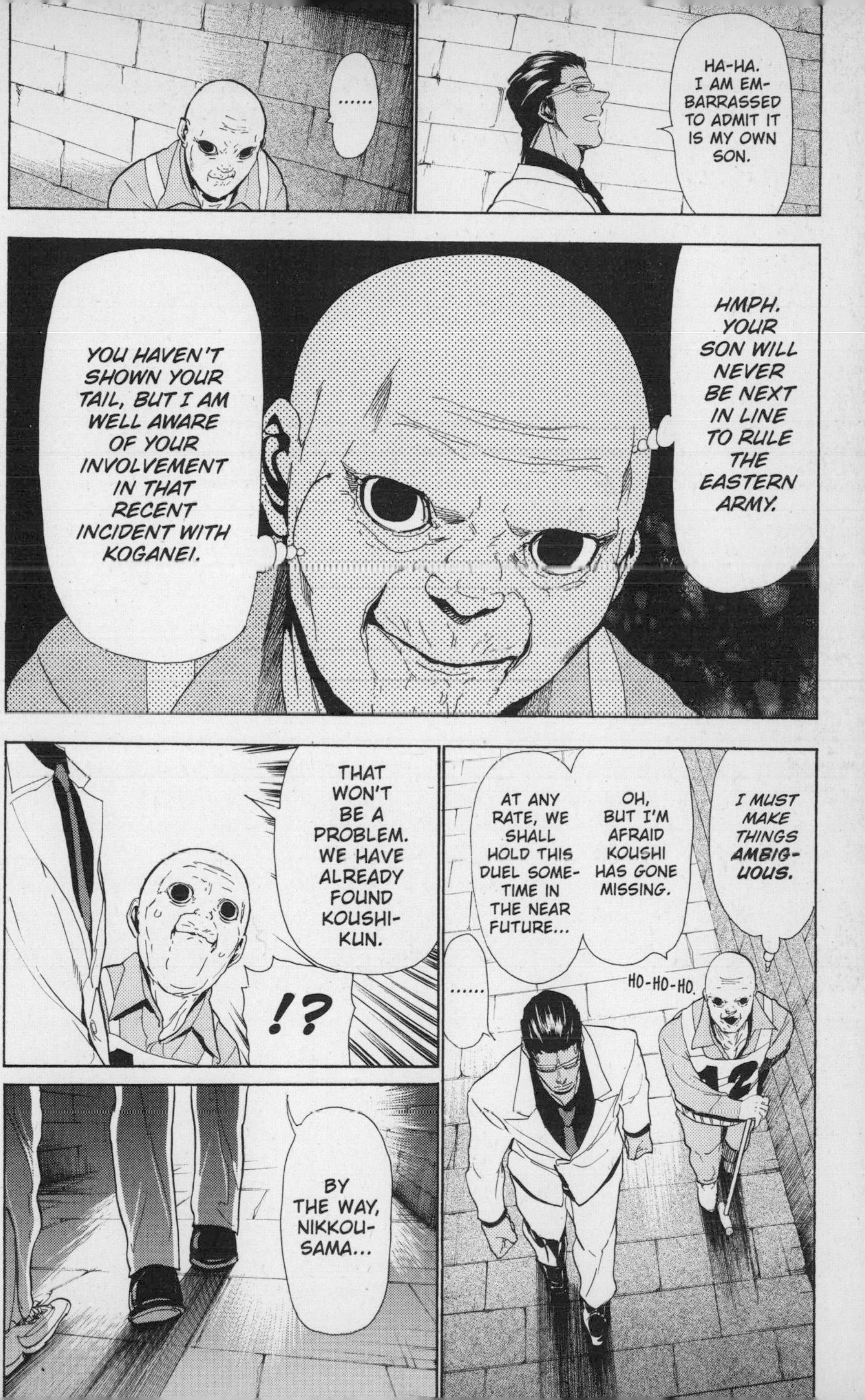
HA-HA. I AM EMBARRASSED TO ADMIT IT IS MY OWN SON.
......
HMPH. YOUR SON WILL NEVER BE NEXT IN LINE TO RULE THE EASTERN ARMY.
YOU HAVEN'T SHOWN YOUR TAIL, BUT I AM WELL AWARE OF YOUR INVOLVEMENT IN THAT RECENT INCIDENT WITH KOGANEI.
I MUST MAKE THINGS AMBIGUOUS.
OH, BUT I'M AFRAID KOUSHI HAS GONE MISSING.
AT ANY RATE, WE SHALL HOLD THIS DUEL SOMETIME IN THE NEAR FUTURE...
HO-HO-HO.
......
THAT WON'T BE A PROBLEM. WE HAVE ALREADY FOUND KOUSHI-KUN.
!?
BY THE WAY, NIKKOU-SAMA...

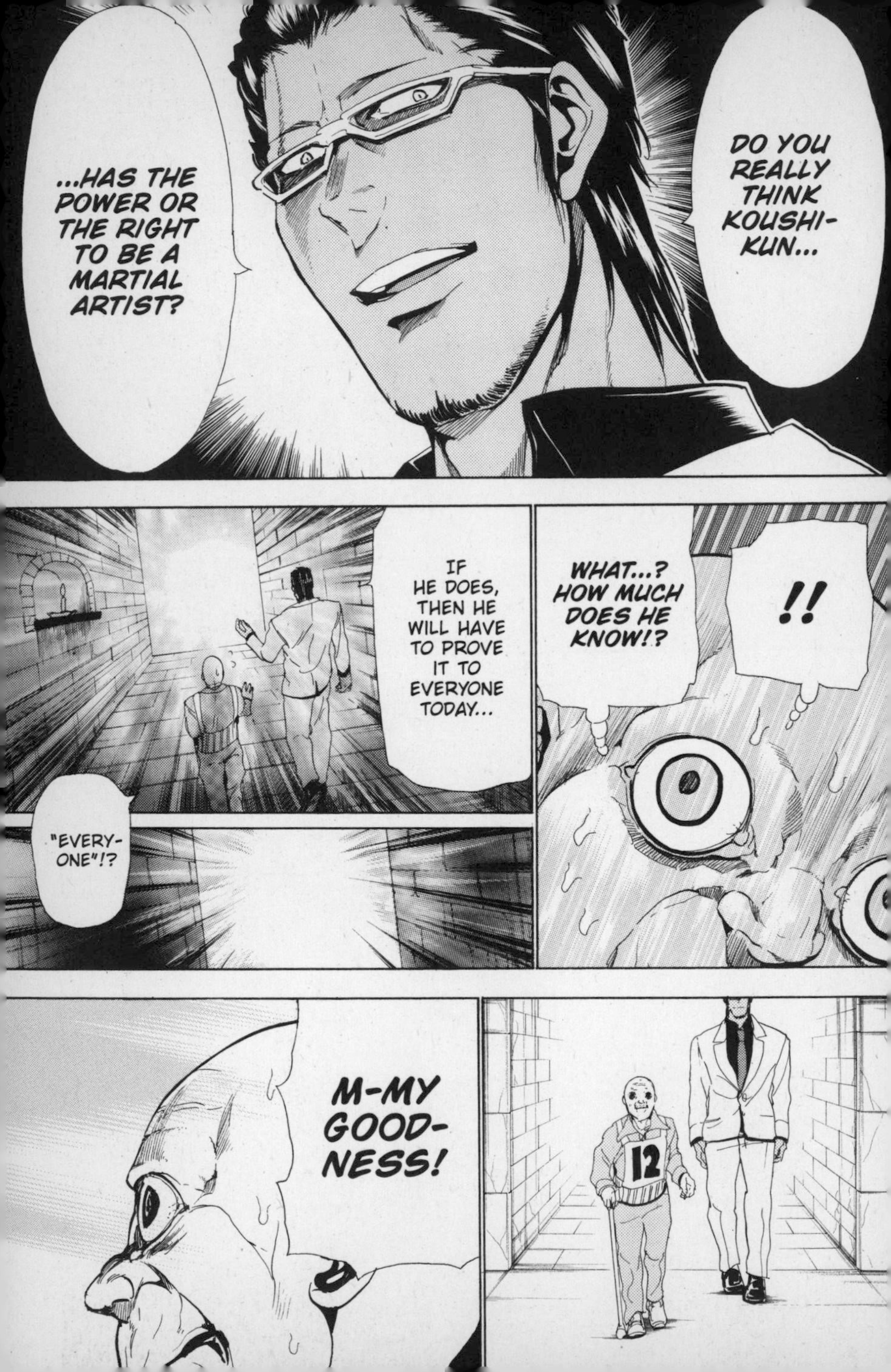
DO YOU REALLY THINK KOUSHI-KUN...
...HAS THE POWER OR THE RIGHT TO BE A MARTIAL ARTIST?
!!
WHAT...? HOW MUCH DOES HE KNOW!?
IF HE DOES, THEN HE WILL HAVE TO PROVE IT TO EVERYONE TODAY...
"EVERY-ONE"!?
12
M-MY GOOD-NESS!

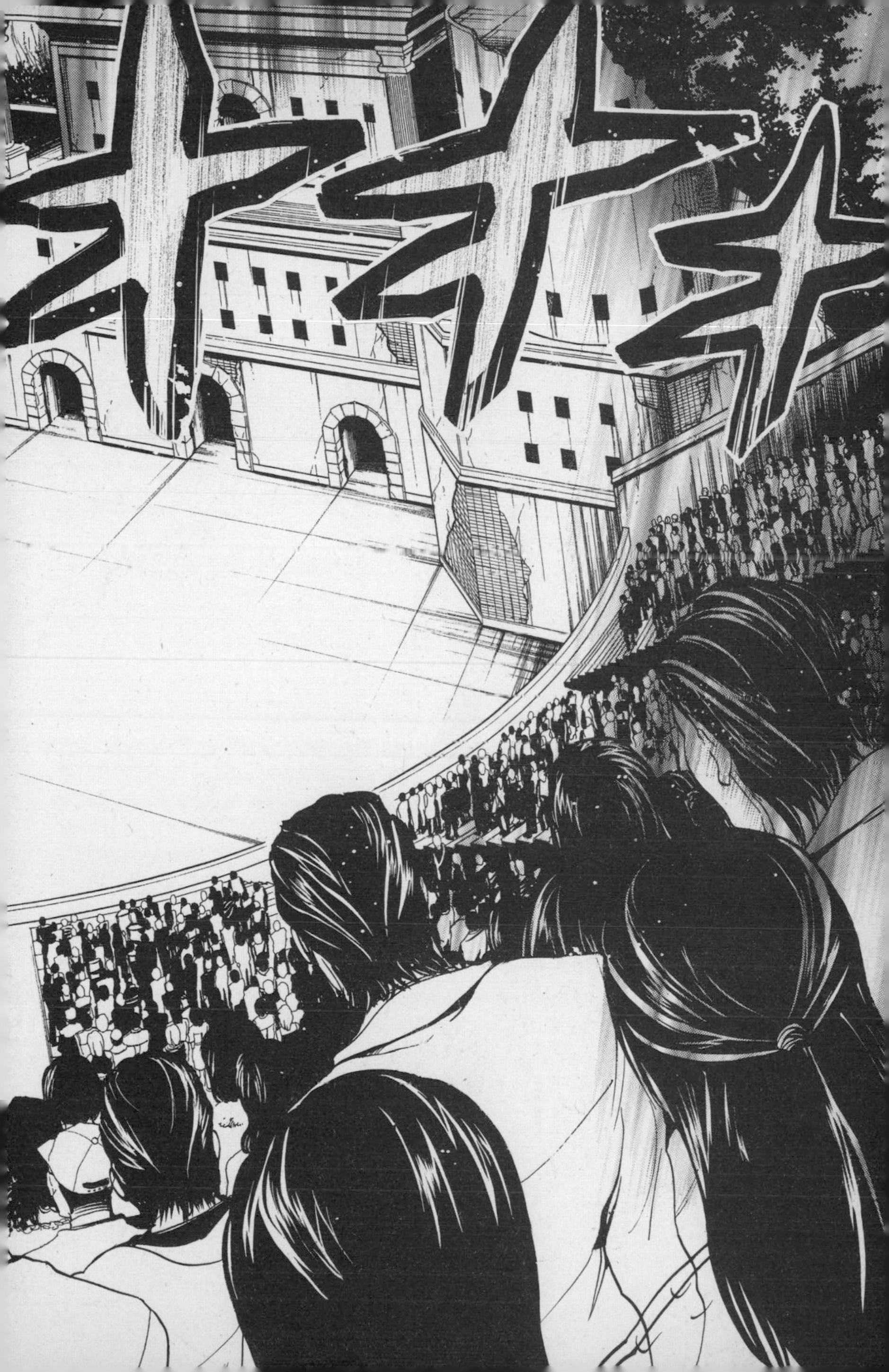

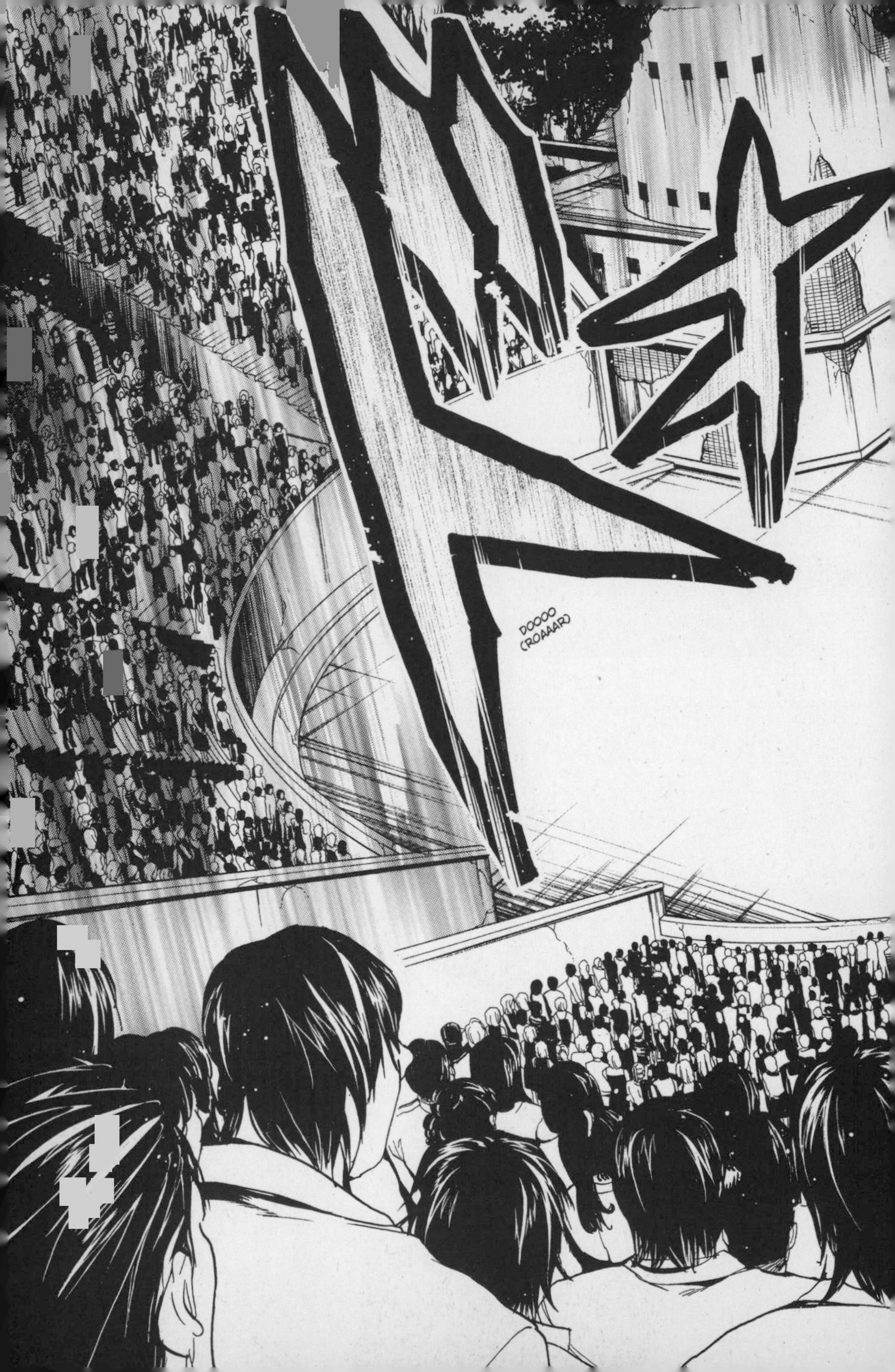
DOOOO
(ROAAAR)

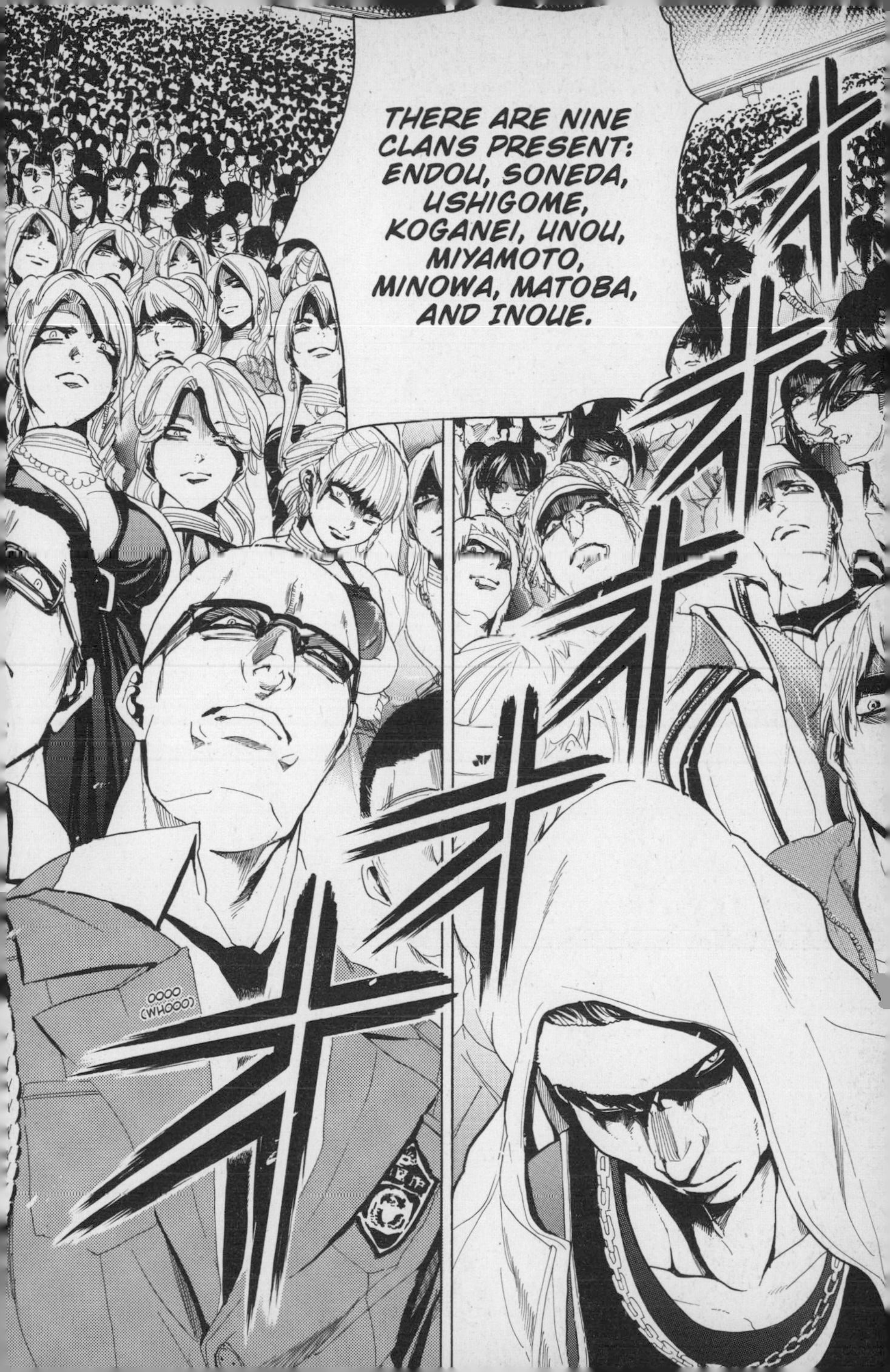
THERE ARE NINE CLANS PRESENT: ENDOU, SONEDA, USHIGOME, KOGANEI, UNOU, MIYAMOTO, MINOWA, MATOBA, AND INOUE.
OOOO (WHOOO)

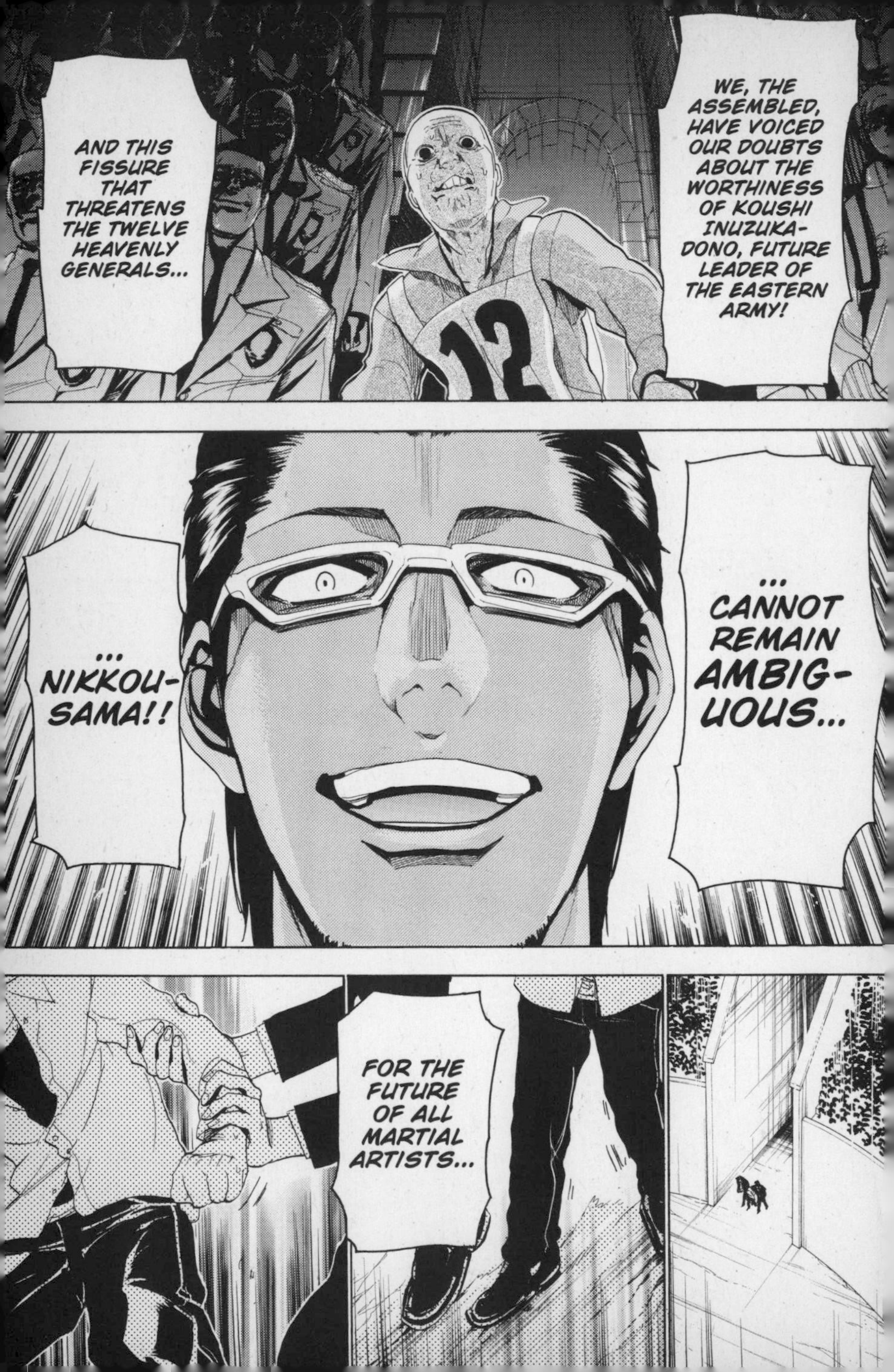
WE, THE ASSEMBLED, HAVE VOICED OUR DOUBTS ABOUT THE WORTHINESS OF KOUSHI INUZUKA-DONO, FUTURE LEADER OF THE EASTERN ARMY!
AND THIS FISSURE THAT THREATENS THE TWELVE HEAVENLY GENERALS...
12
...CANNOT REMAIN AMBIG-UOUS...
...NIKKOU-SAMA!!
FOR THE FUTURE OF ALL MARTIAL ARTISTS...

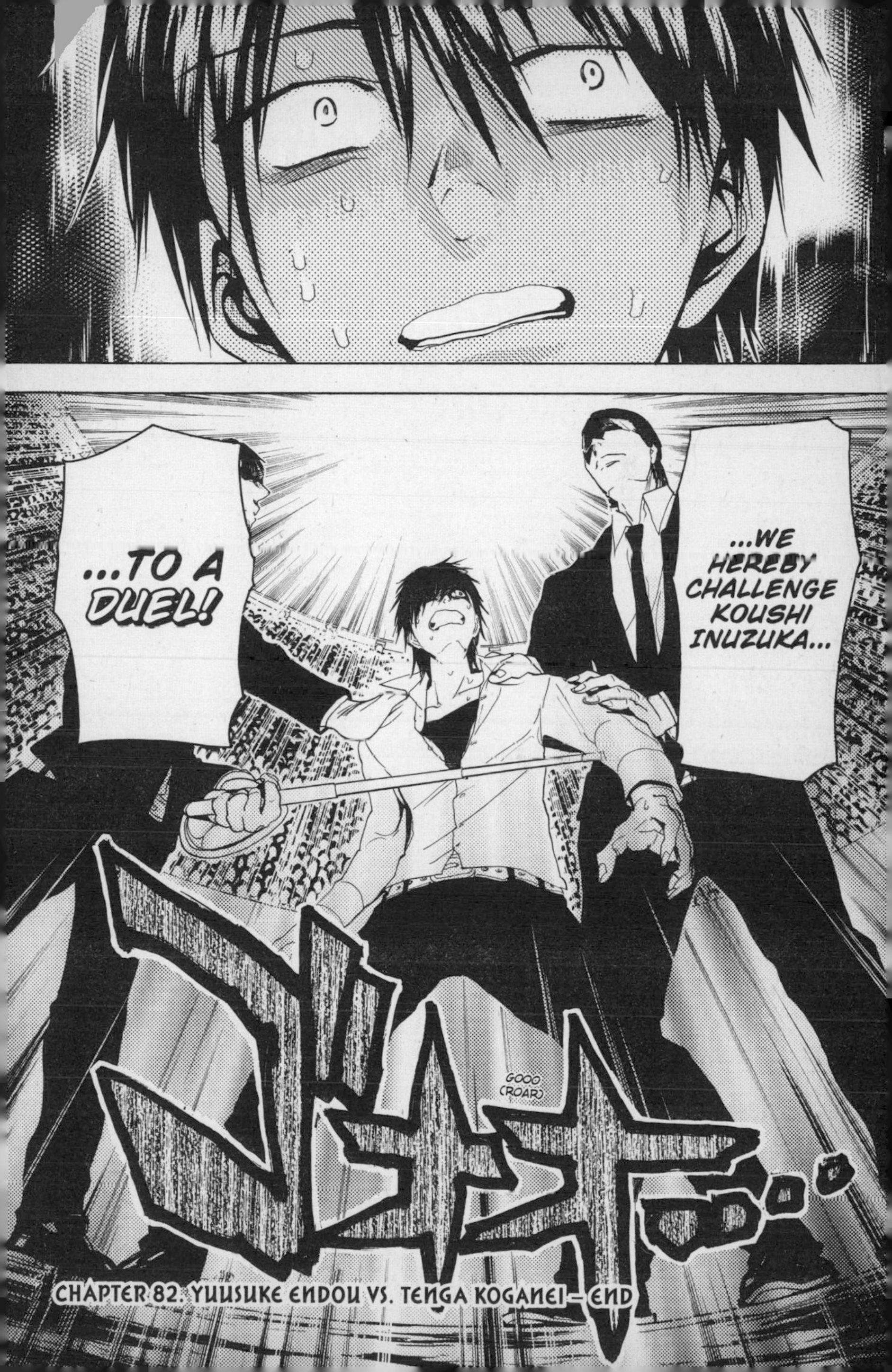
...WE HEREBY CHALLENGE KOUSHI INUZUKA...
...TO A DUEL!
GOOO (ROAR)
CHAPTER 82. YUUSUKE ENDOU VS. TENGA KOGANEI – END

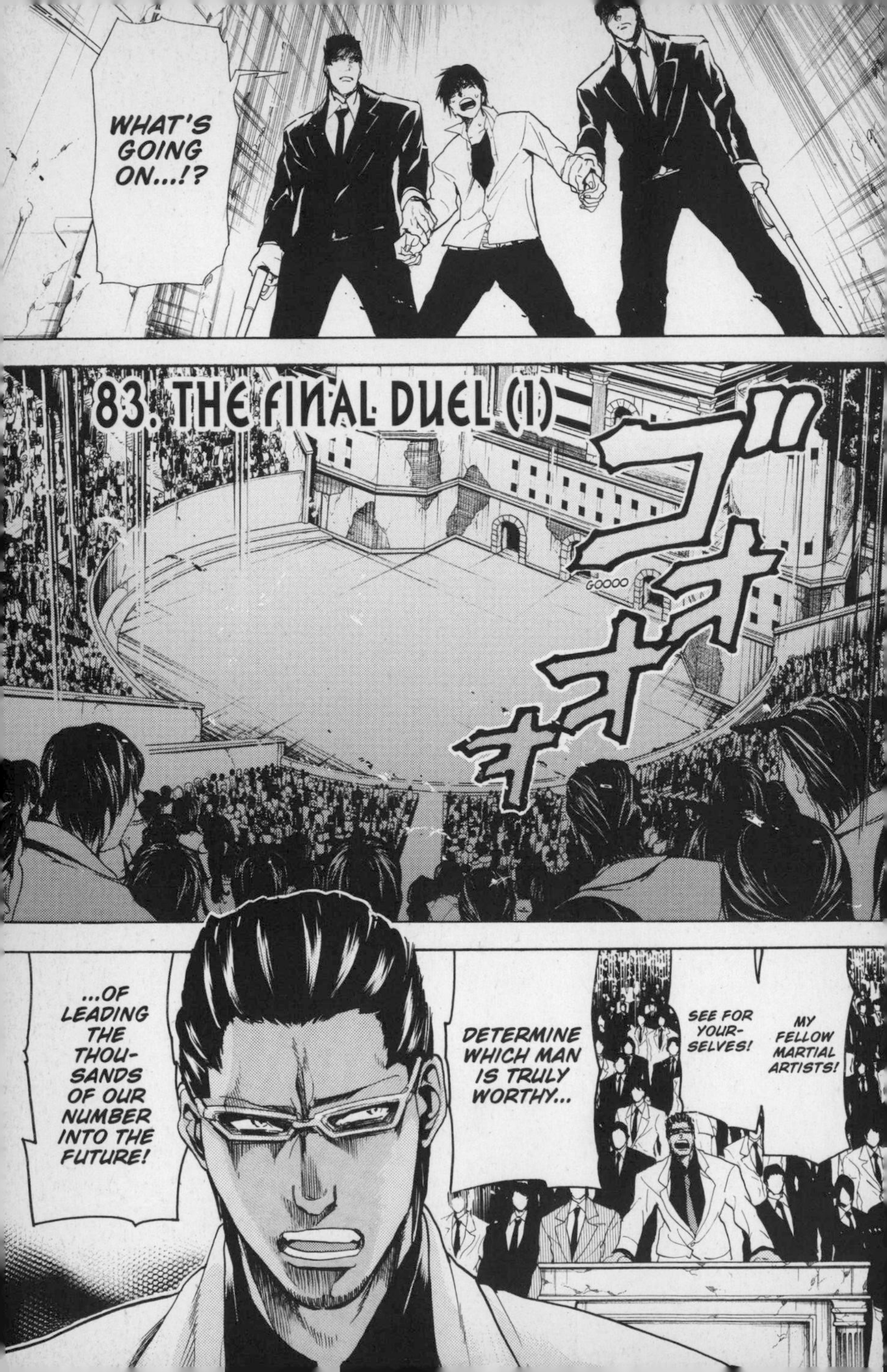
WHAT'S GOING ON...!?
83. THE FINAL DUEL (1)
ゴオオオ
GOOOO
MY FELLOW MARTIAL ARTISTS!
SEE FOR YOUR-SELVES!
DETERMINE WHICH MAN IS TRULY WORTHY...
...OF LEADING THE THOU-SANDS OF OUR NUMBER INTO THE FUTURE!

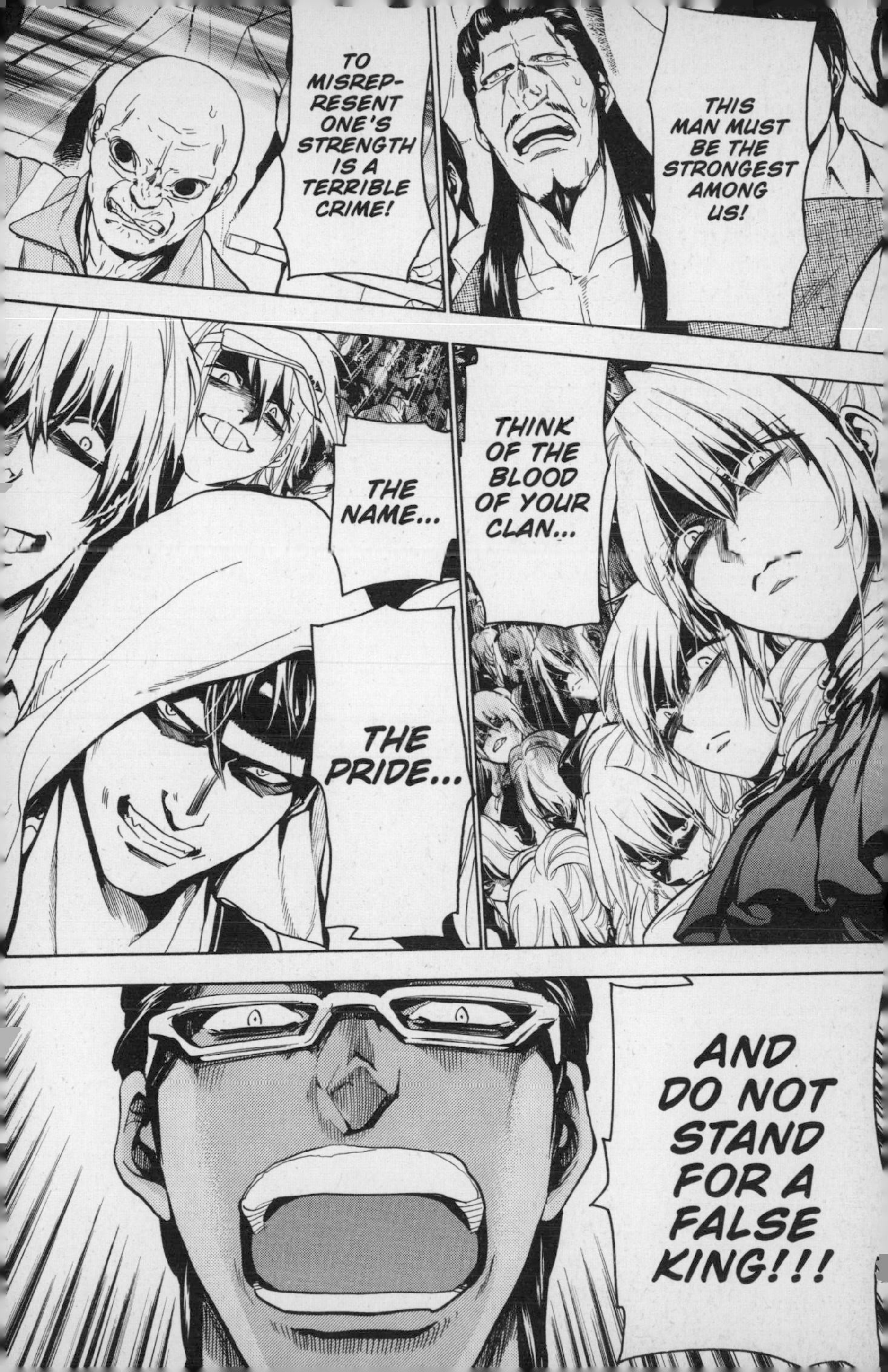
THIS MAN MUST BE THE STRONGEST AMONG US!
TO MISREP-RESENT ONE'S STRENGTH IS A TERRIBLE CRIME!
THINK OF THE BLOOD OF YOUR CLAN...
THE NAME...
THE PRIDE...
AND DO NOT STAND FOR A FALSE KING!!!

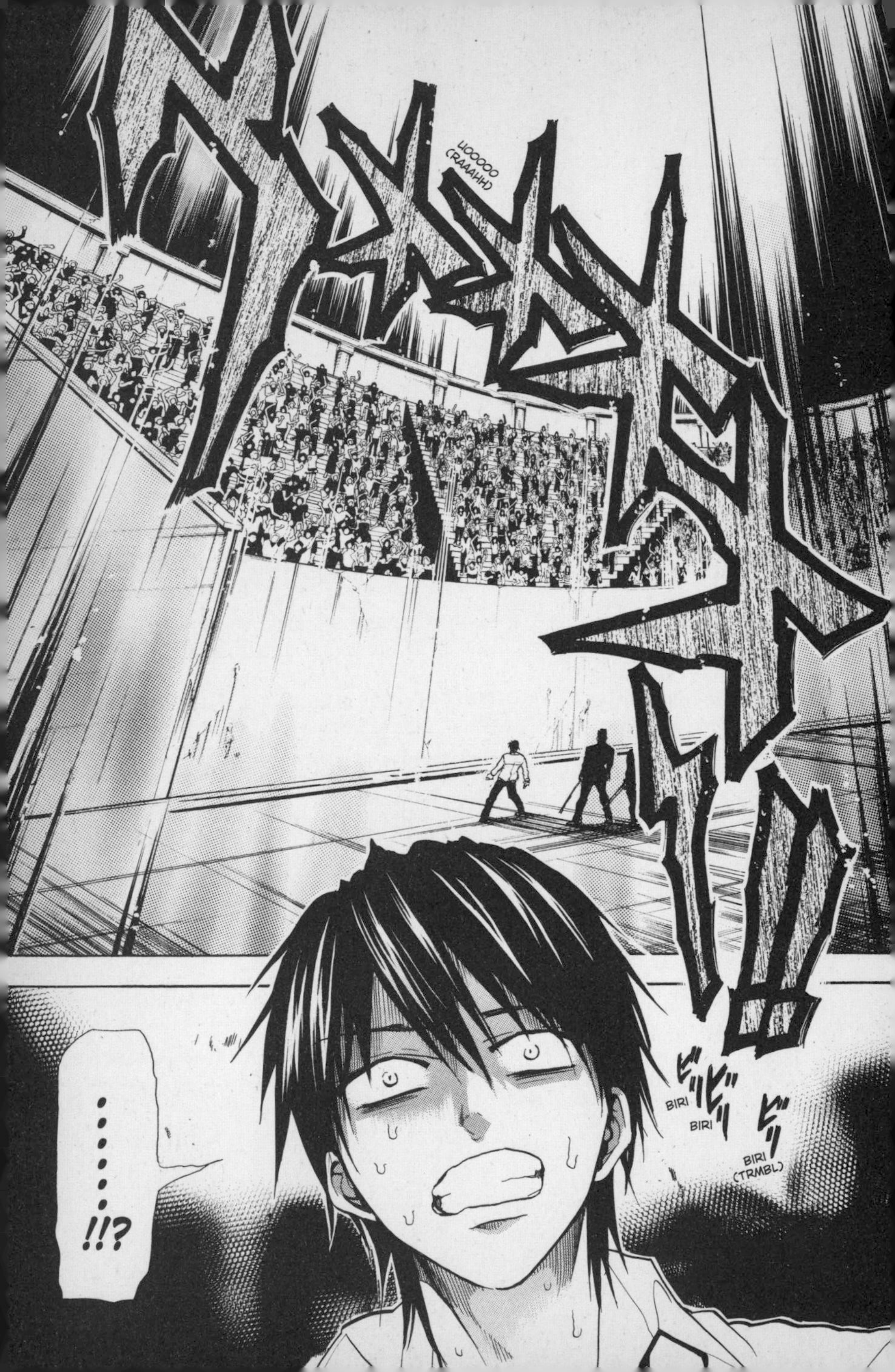
UOOOOO
(RAAAHH)
BIRI
BIRI
BIRI
(TRMBL)
......!!?

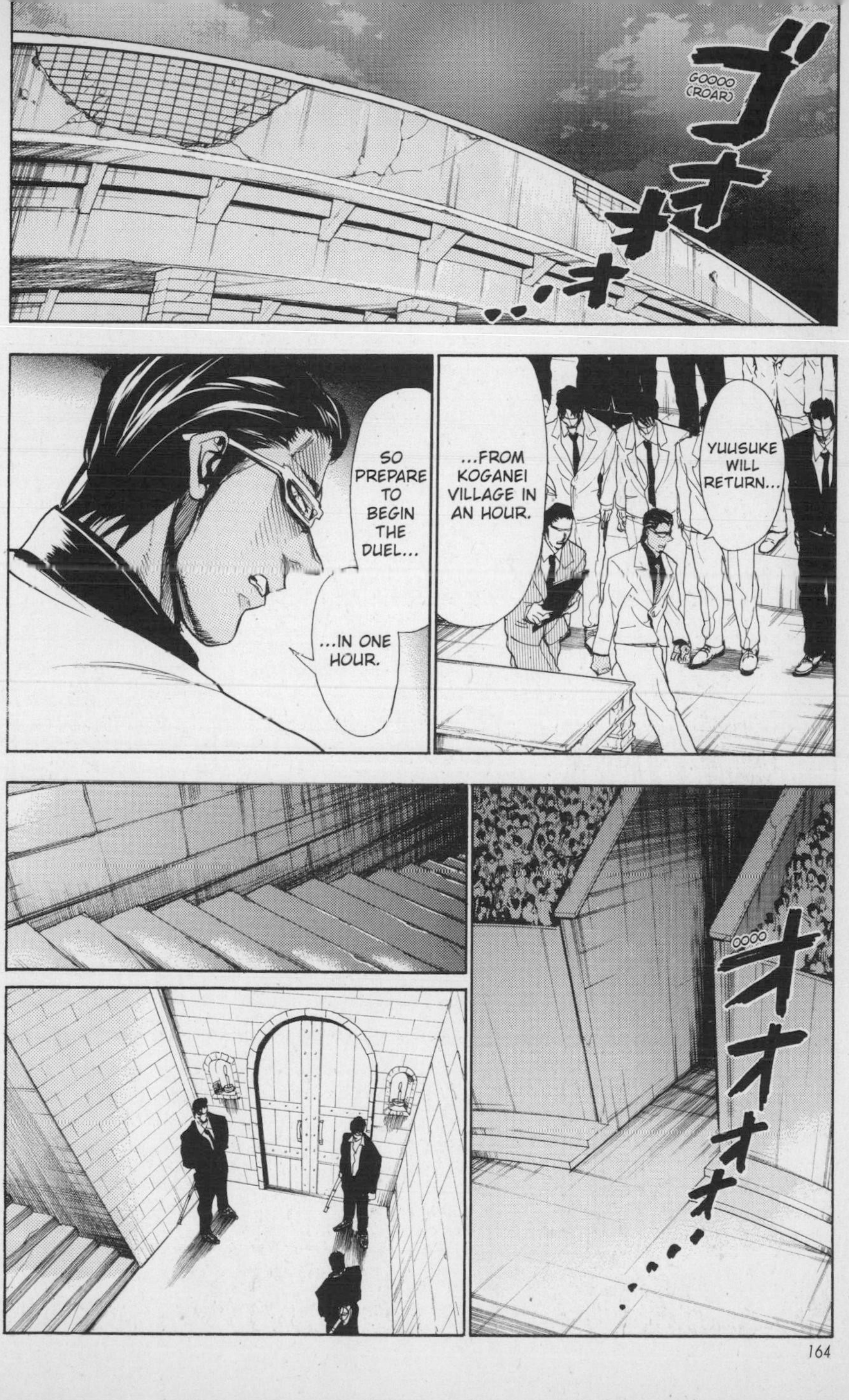
GOOOO (ROAR)
YUUSUKE WILL RETURN...
...FROM KOGANEI VILLAGE IN AN HOUR.
SO PREPARE TO BEGIN THE DUEL...
...IN ONE HOUR.
OOOO

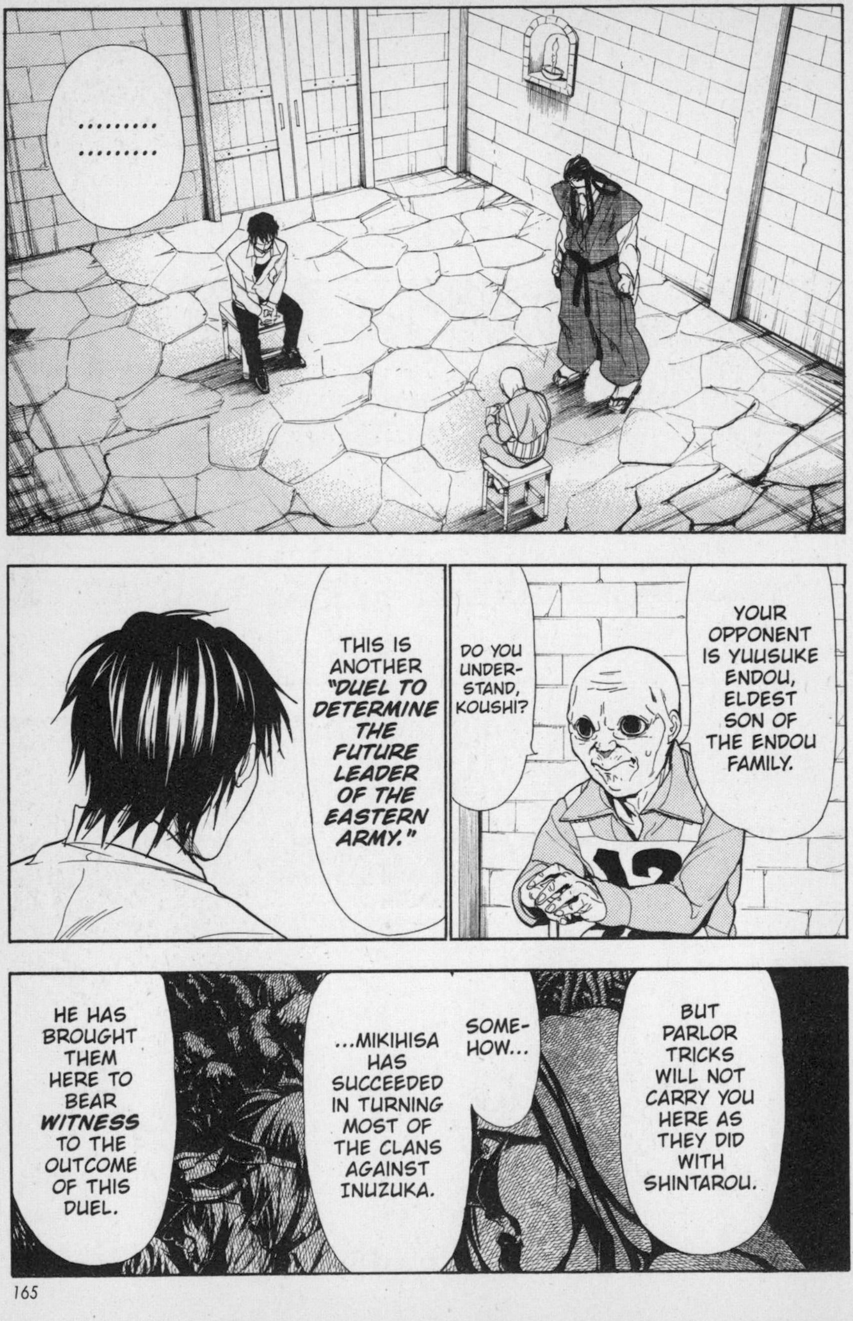
....
....
YOUR OPPONENT IS YUUSUKE ENDOU, ELDEST SON OF THE ENDOU FAMILY.
DO YOU UNDER-STAND, KOUSHI?
THIS IS ANOTHER "DUEL TO DETERMINE THE FUTURE LEADER OF THE EASTERN ARMY."
BUT PARLOR TRICKS WILL NOT CARRY YOU HERE AS THEY DID WITH SHINTAROU.
SOME-HOW...
...MIKIHISA HAS SUCCEEDED IN TURNING MOST OF THE CLANS AGAINST INUZUKA.
HE HAS BROUGHT THEM HERE TO BEAR WITNESS TO THE OUTCOME OF THIS DUEL.

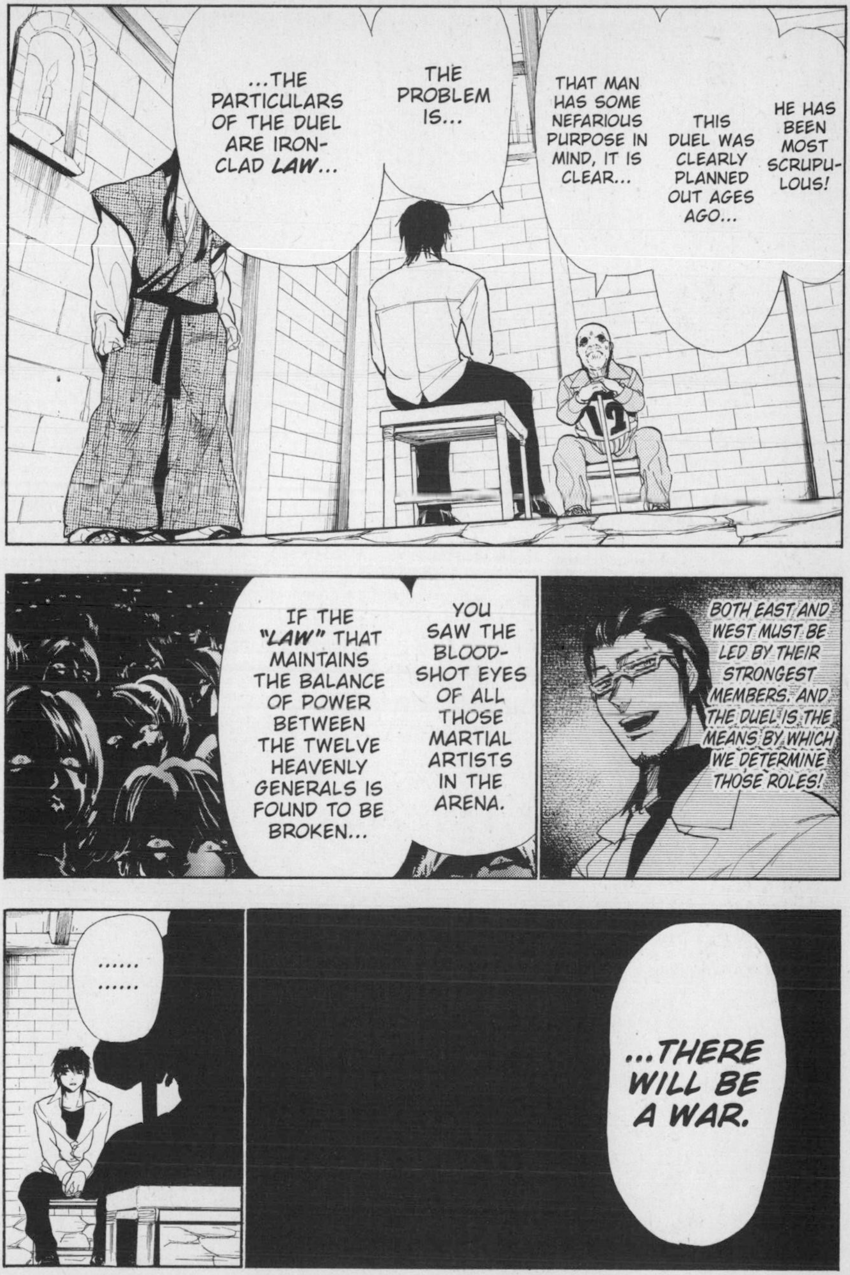
HE HAS BEEN MOST SCRUPULOUS!
THIS DUEL WAS CLEARLY PLANNED OUT AGES AGO...
THAT MAN HAS SOME NEFARIOUS PURPOSE IN MIND, IT IS CLEAR...
THE PROBLEM IS...
...THE PARTICULARS OF THE DUEL ARE IRON-CLAD *LAW*...
BOTH EAST AND WEST MUST BE LED BY THEIR STRONGEST MEMBERS. AND THE DUEL IS THE MEANS BY WHICH WE DETERMINE THOSE ROLES!
YOU SAW THE BLOODSHOT EYES OF ALL THOSE MARTIAL ARTISTS IN THE ARENA.
IF THE *"LAW"* THAT MAINTAINS THE BALANCE OF POWER BETWEEN THE TWELVE HEAVENLY GENERALS IS FOUND TO BE BROKEN...
...THERE WILL BE A WAR.
......
......

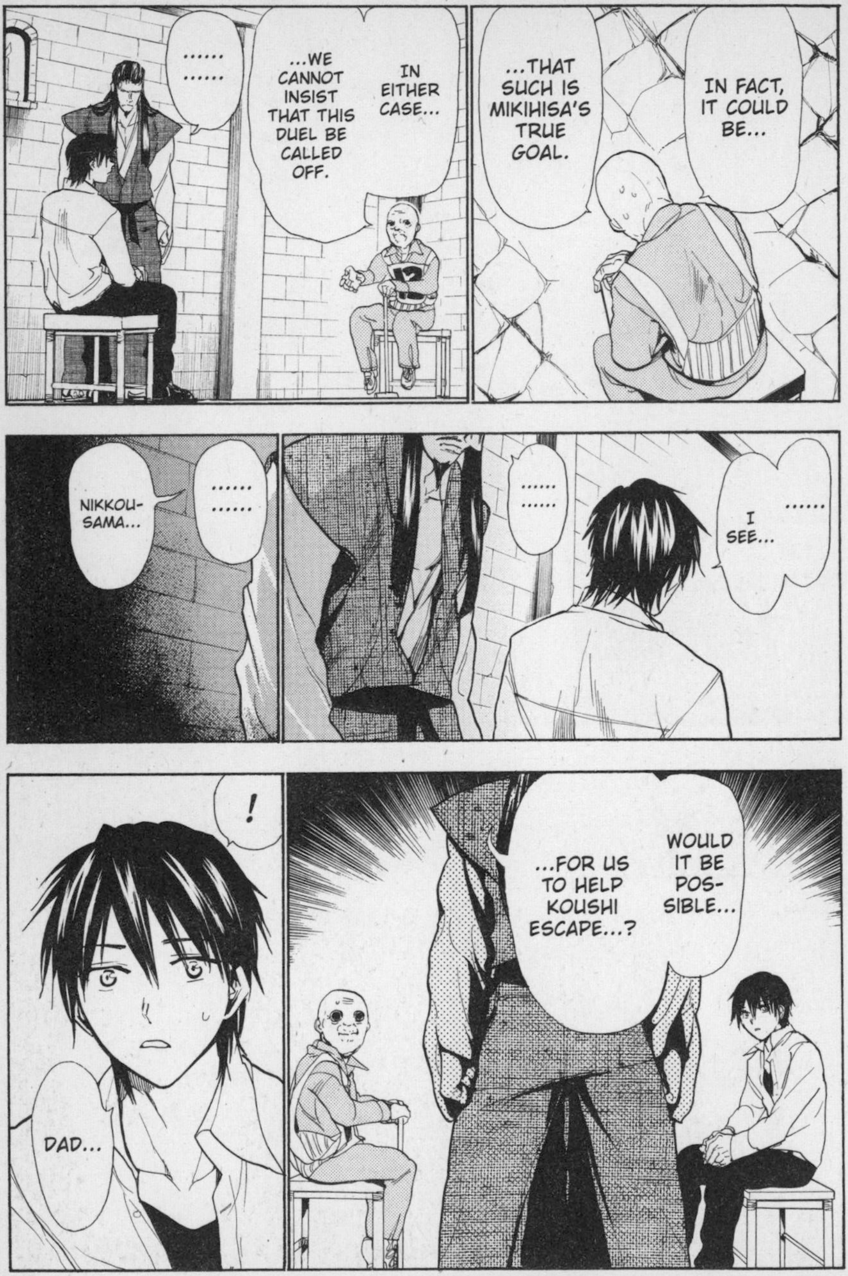
IN FACT, IT COULD BE...
...THAT SUCH IS MIKIHISA'S TRUE GOAL.
IN EITHER CASE...
...WE CANNOT INSIST THAT THIS DUEL BE CALLED OFF.
......
......
...... I SEE...
......
......
......
NIKKOU-SAMA...
WOULD IT BE POS-SIBLE...
...FOR US TO HELP KOUSHI ESCAPE...?
!
DAD...

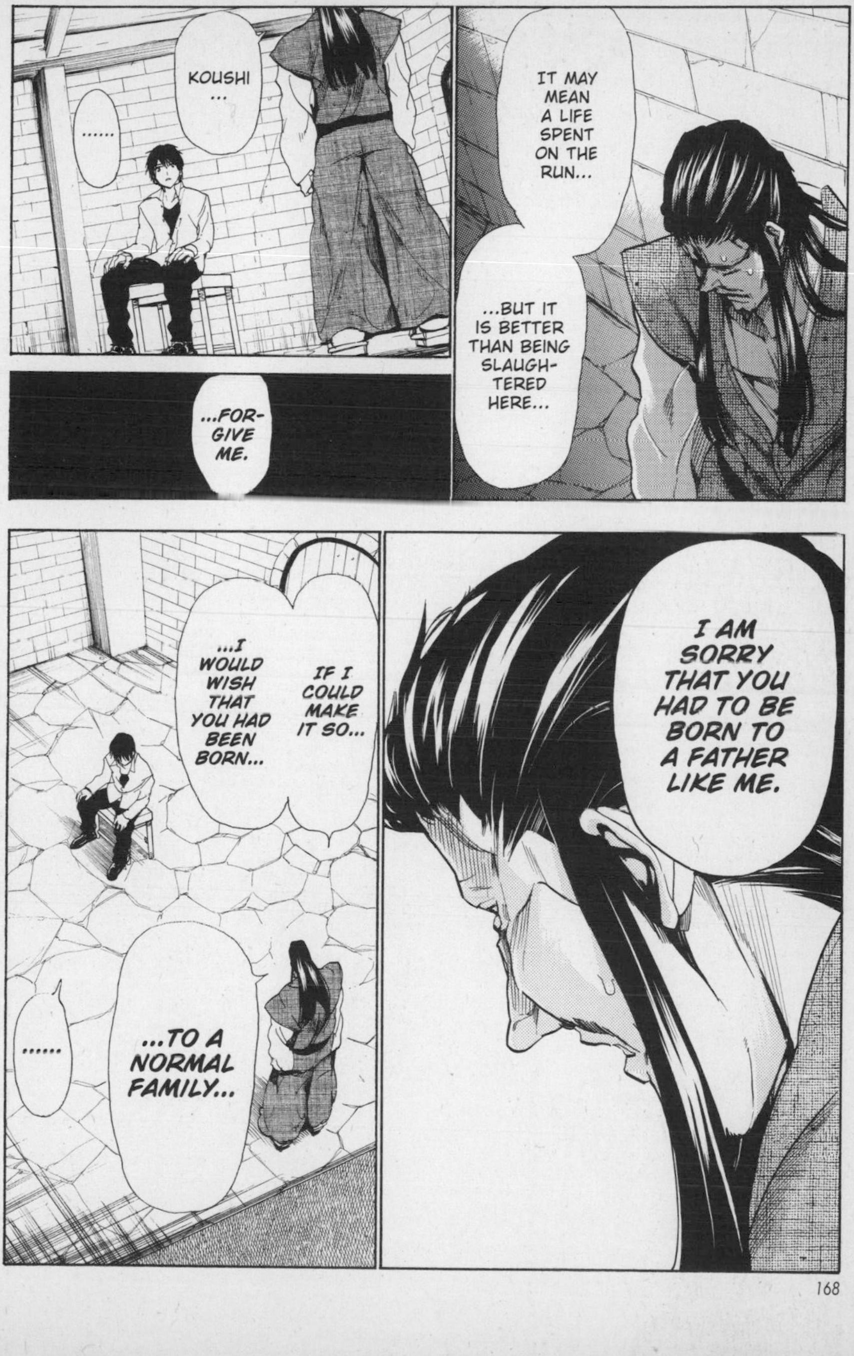
IT MAY MEAN A LIFE SPENT ON THE RUN...
...BUT IT IS BETTER THAN BEING SLAUGH-TERED HERE...
KOUSHI ...
......
...FOR-GIVE ME.
I AM SORRY THAT YOU HAD TO BE BORN TO A FATHER LIKE ME.
IF I COULD MAKE IT SO...
...I WOULD WISH THAT YOU HAD BEEN BORN...
...TO A NORMAL FAMILY...
......

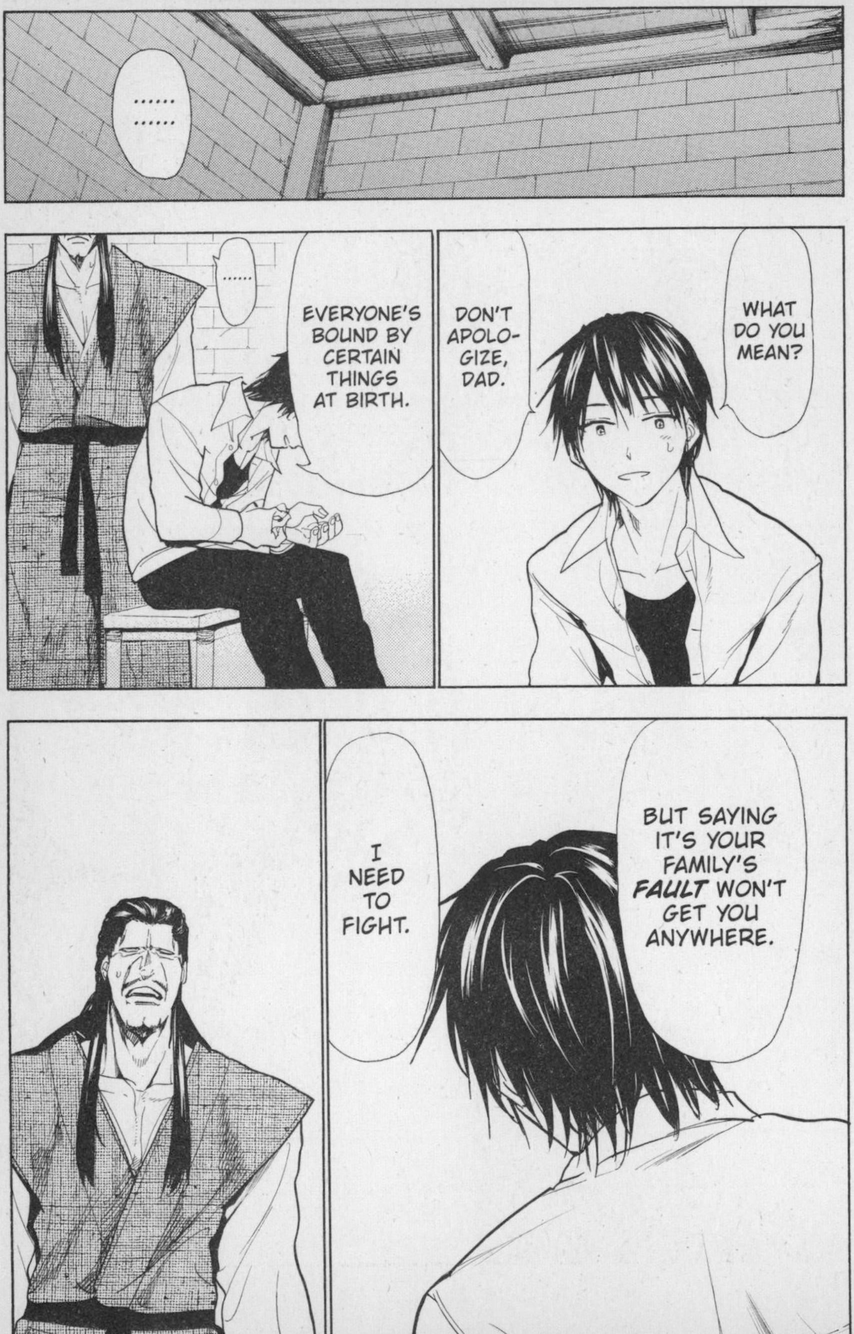
......
......
WHAT DO YOU MEAN?
DON'T APOLOGIZE, DAD.
EVERYONE'S BOUND BY CERTAIN THINGS AT BIRTH.
......
BUT SAYING IT'S YOUR FAMILY'S *FAULT* WON'T GET YOU ANYWHERE.
I NEED TO FIGHT.

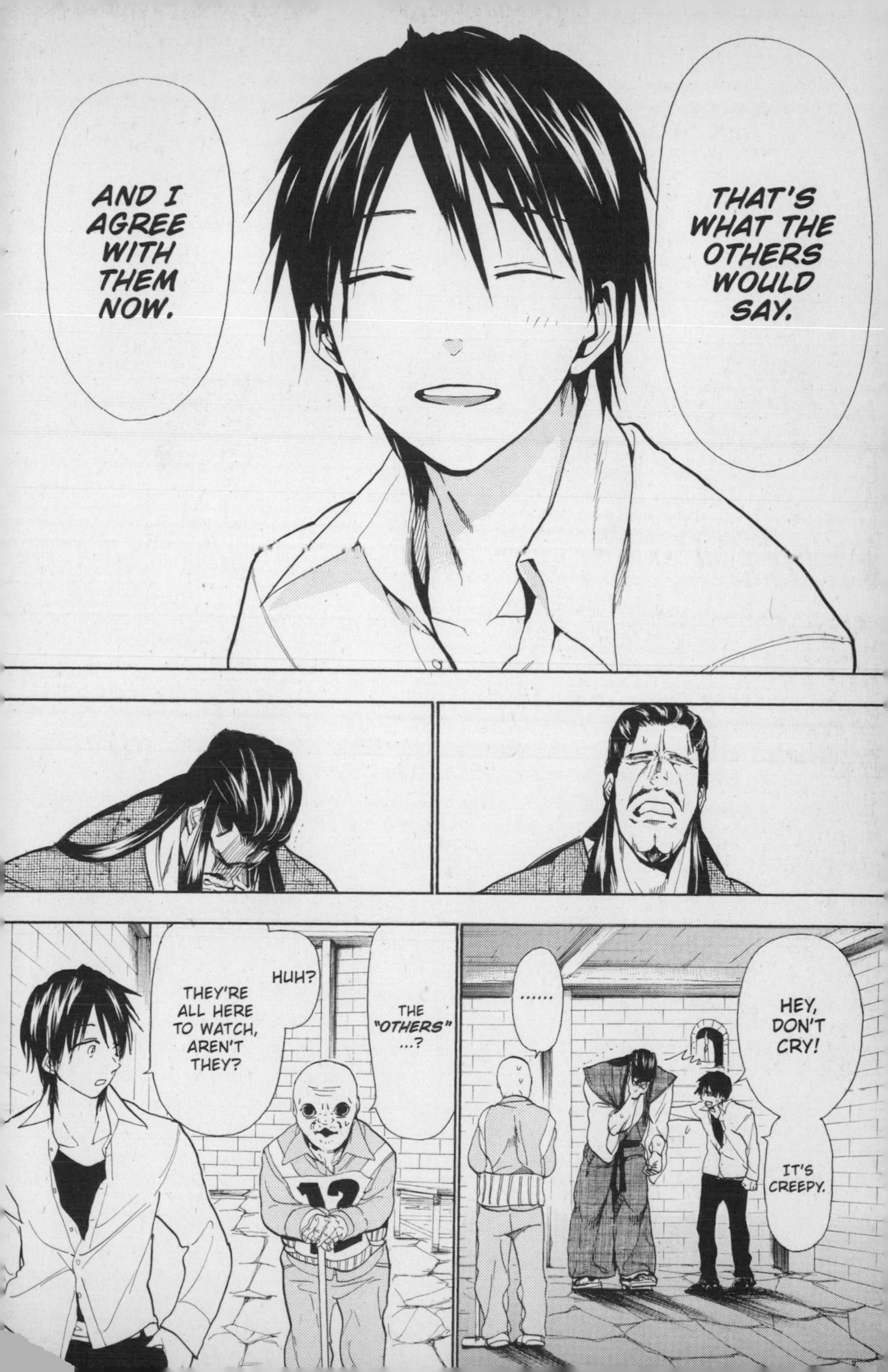
THAT'S WHAT THE OTHERS WOULD SAY.
AND I AGREE WITH THEM NOW.
HEY, DON'T CRY!
IT'S CREEPY.
......
THE "OTHERS" ...?
HUH?
THEY'RE ALL HERE TO WATCH, AREN'T THEY?

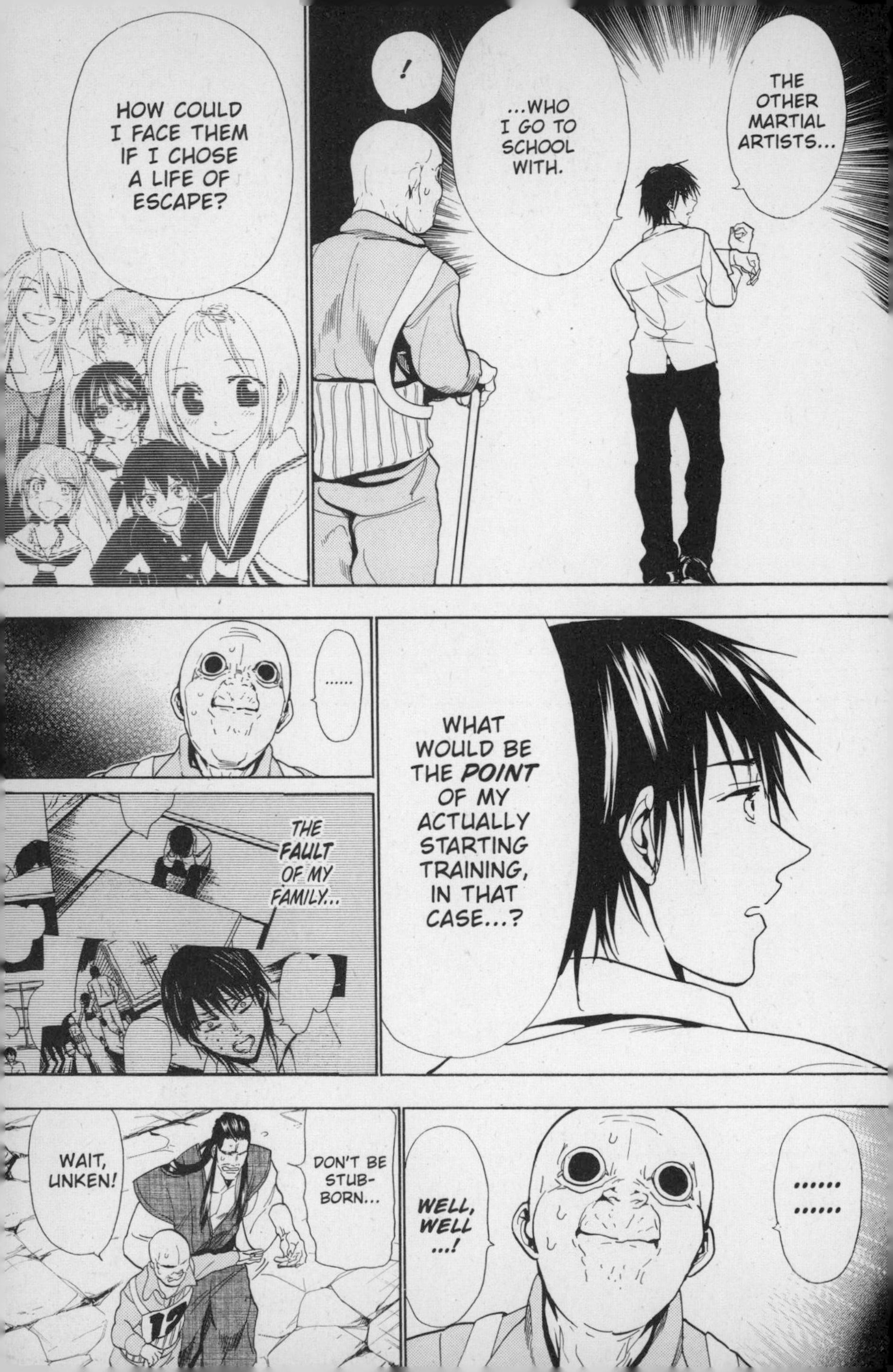
THE OTHER MARTIAL ARTISTS...
...WHO I GO TO SCHOOL WITH.
!
HOW COULD I FACE THEM IF I CHOSE A LIFE OF ESCAPE?
WHAT WOULD BE THE *POINT* OF MY ACTUALLY STARTING TRAINING, IN THAT CASE...?
......
THE FAULT OF MY FAMILY...
....
WELL, WELL ...!
DON'T BE STUB-BORN...
WAIT, UNKEN!

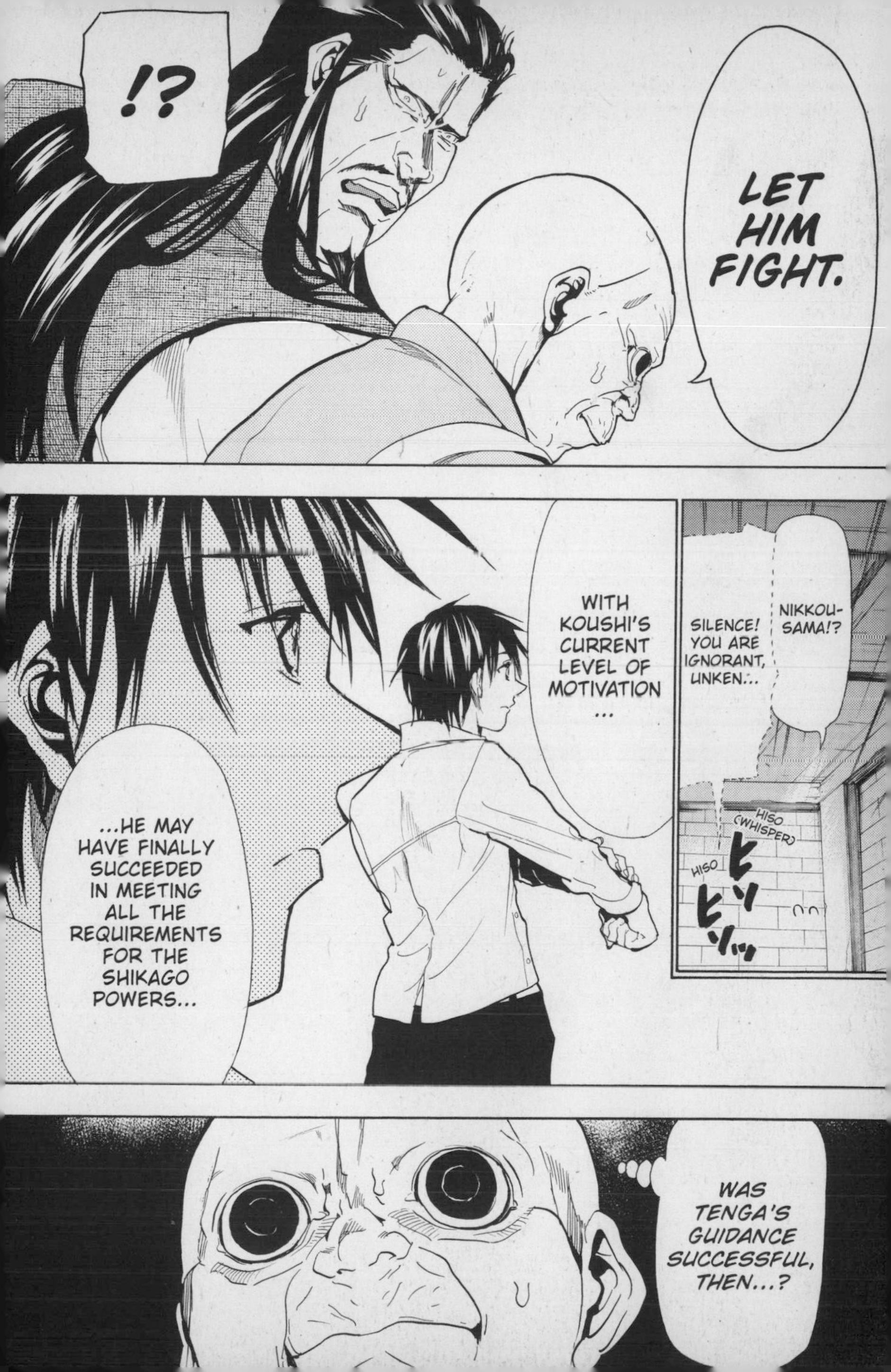
LET HIM FIGHT.
!?
NIKKOU-SAMA!?
SILENCE! YOU ARE IGNORANT, UNKEN...
HISO (WHISPER)
HISO
WITH KOUSHI'S CURRENT LEVEL OF MOTIVATION...
...HE MAY HAVE FINALLY SUCCEEDED IN MEETING ALL THE REQUIREMENTS FOR THE SHIKAGO POWERS...
WAS TENGA'S GUIDANCE SUCCESSFUL, THEN...?

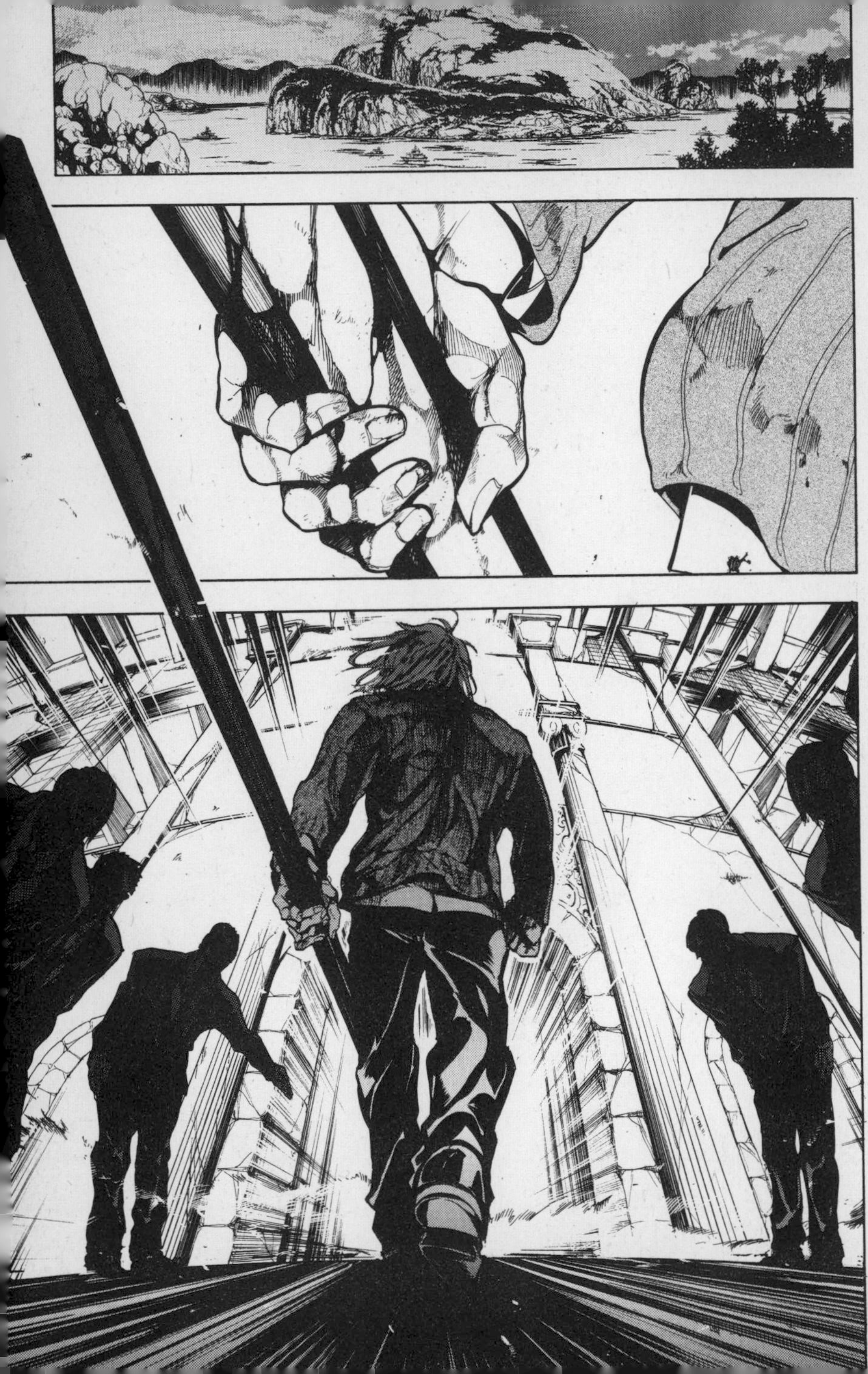

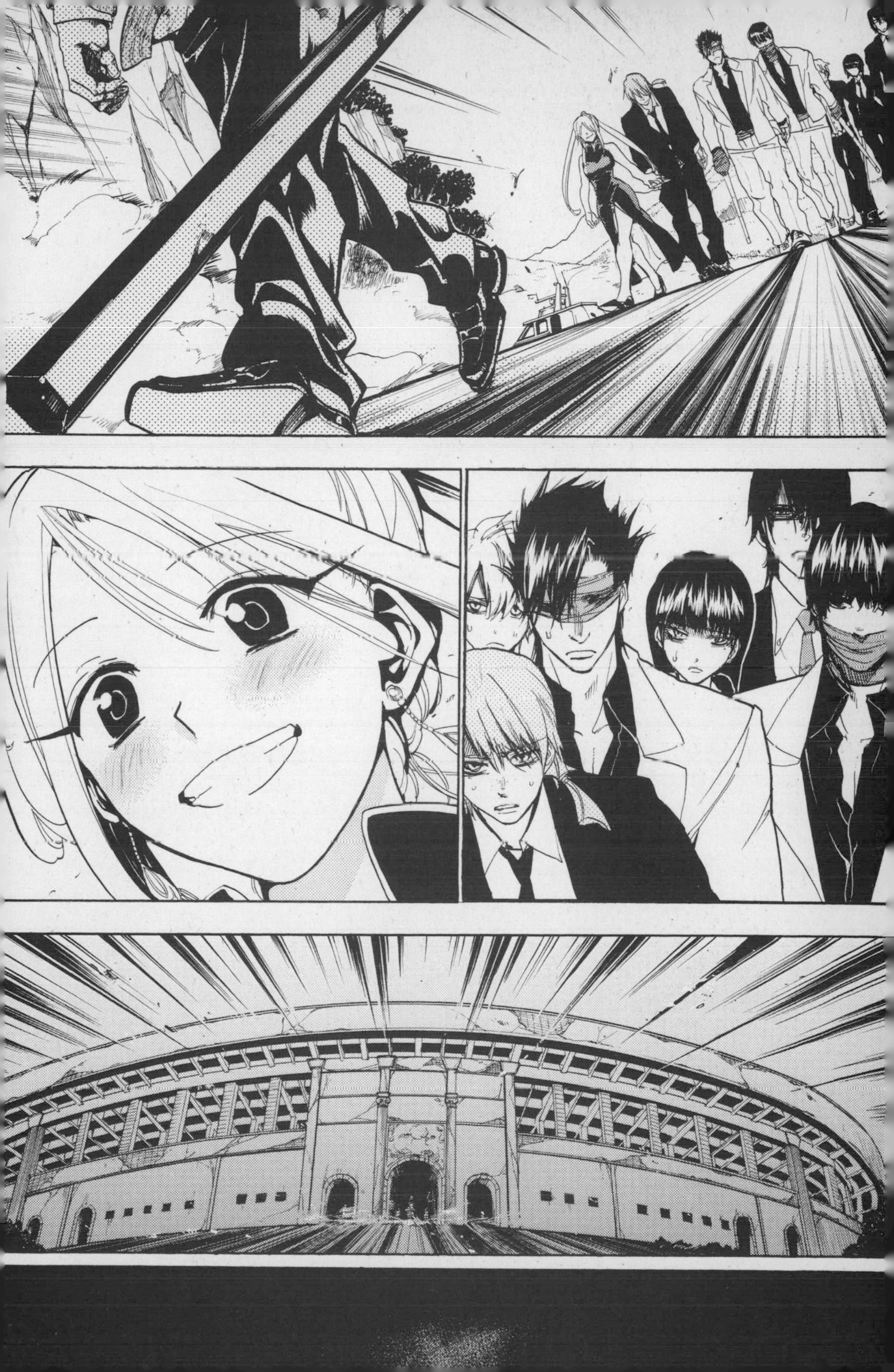

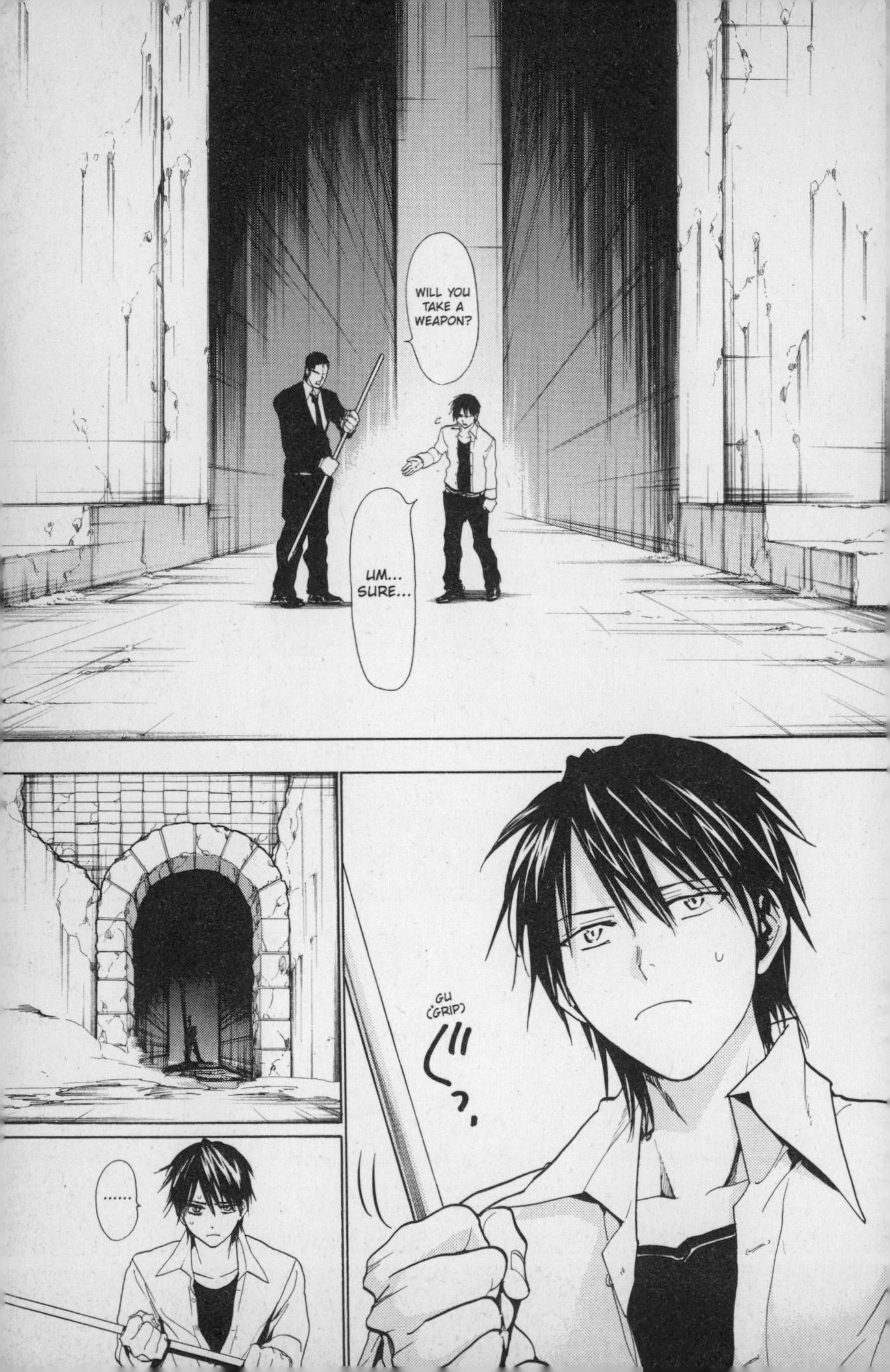
WILL YOU TAKE A WEAPON?
UM... SURE...
GU (GRIP)
......

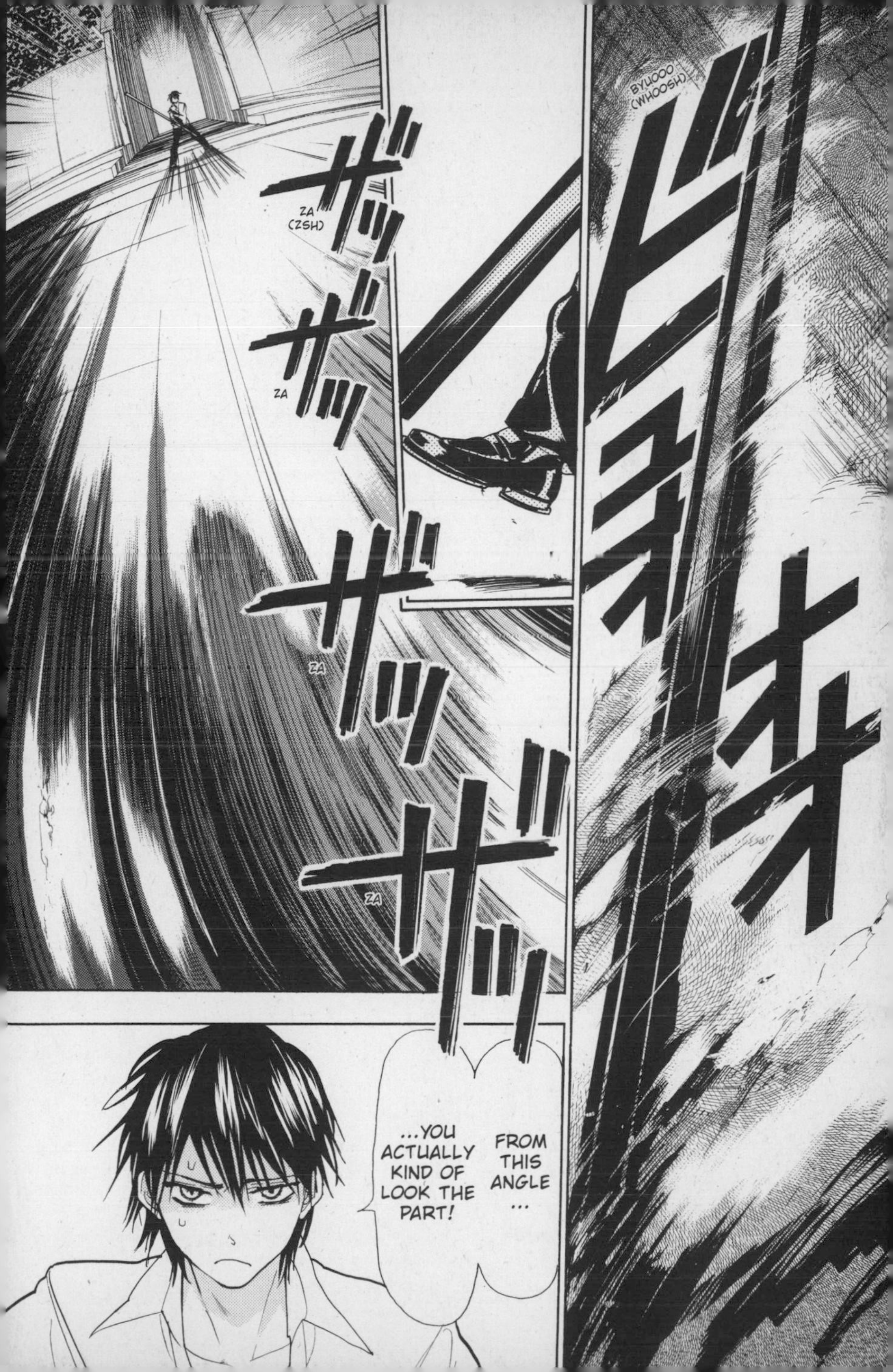
BYUOOO (WHOOSH)
ZA (ZSH)
ZA
ZA
ZA
FROM THIS ANGLE...
...YOU ACTUALLY KIND OF LOOK THE PART!

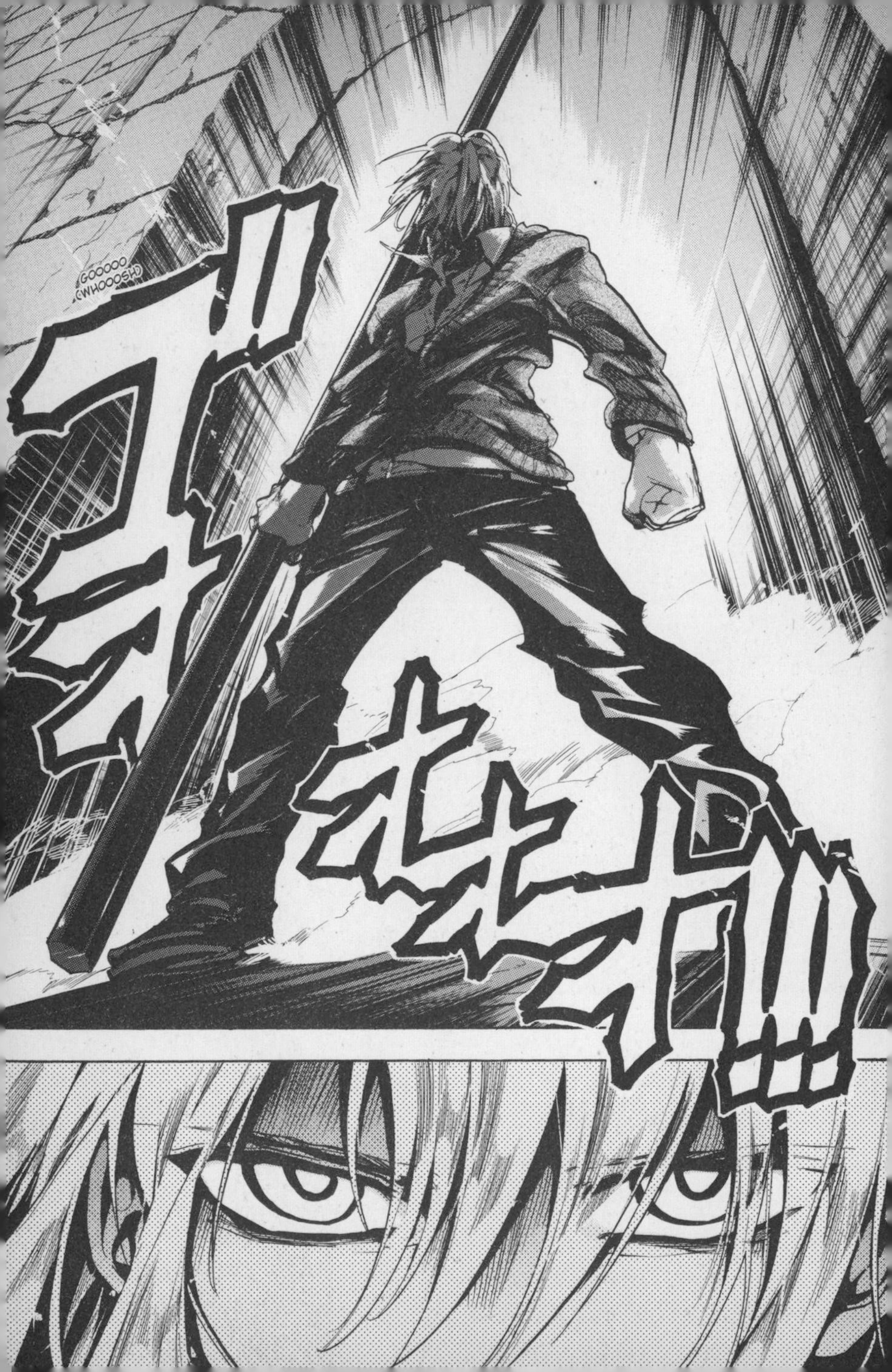

ゴオオオ!!
GOOOOO (WHOOOSH)

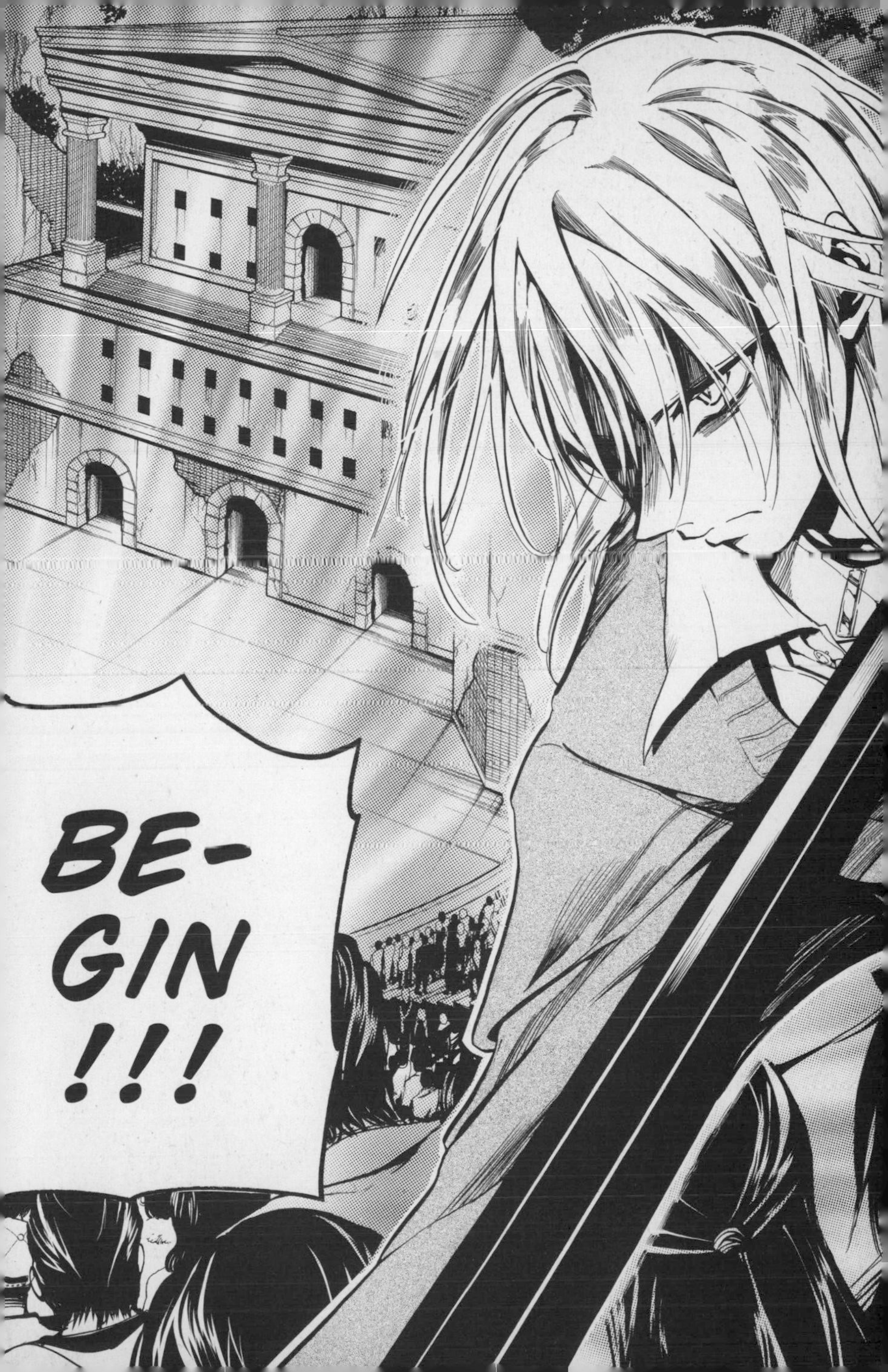
BE-
GIN
!!!

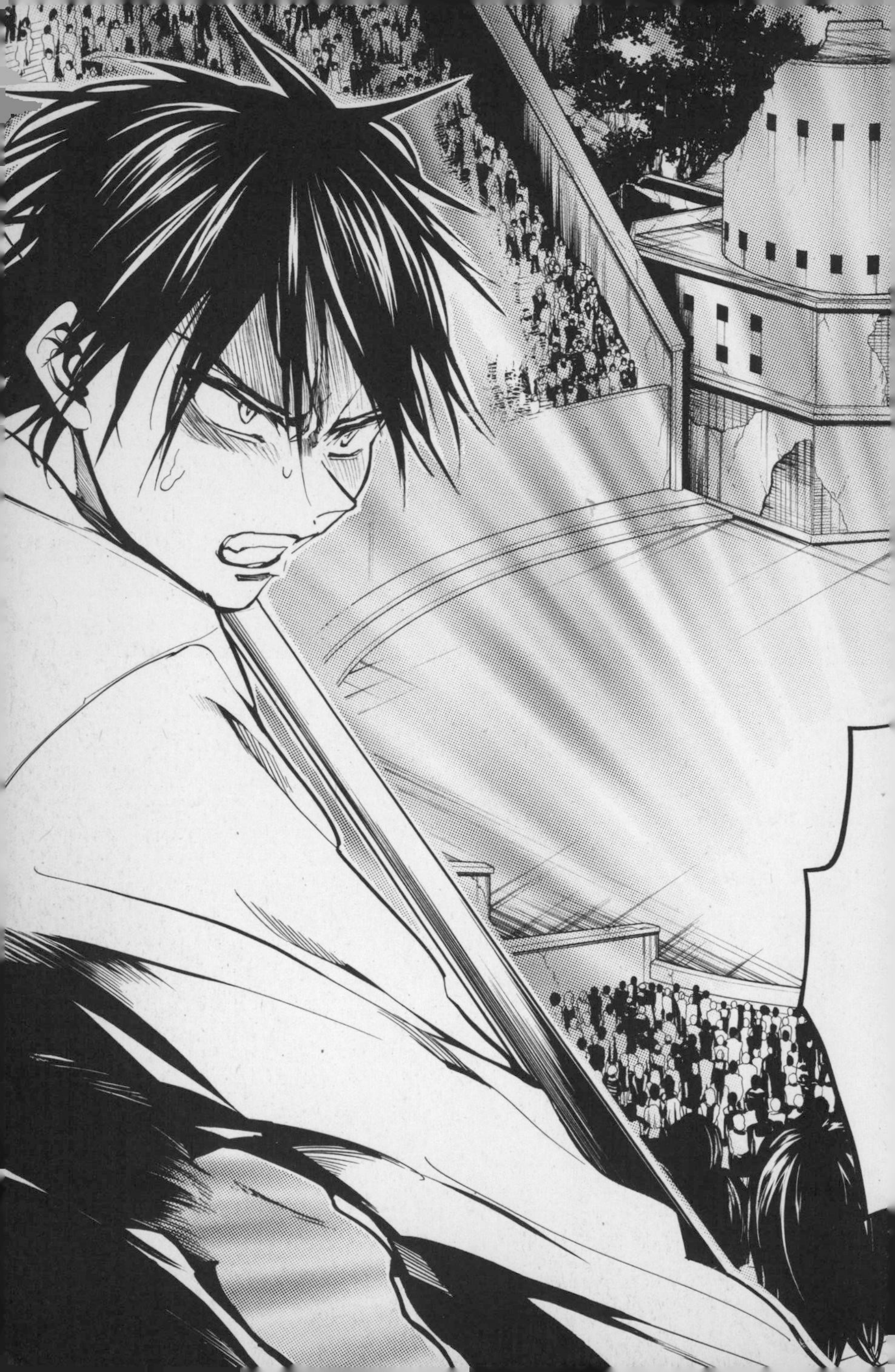

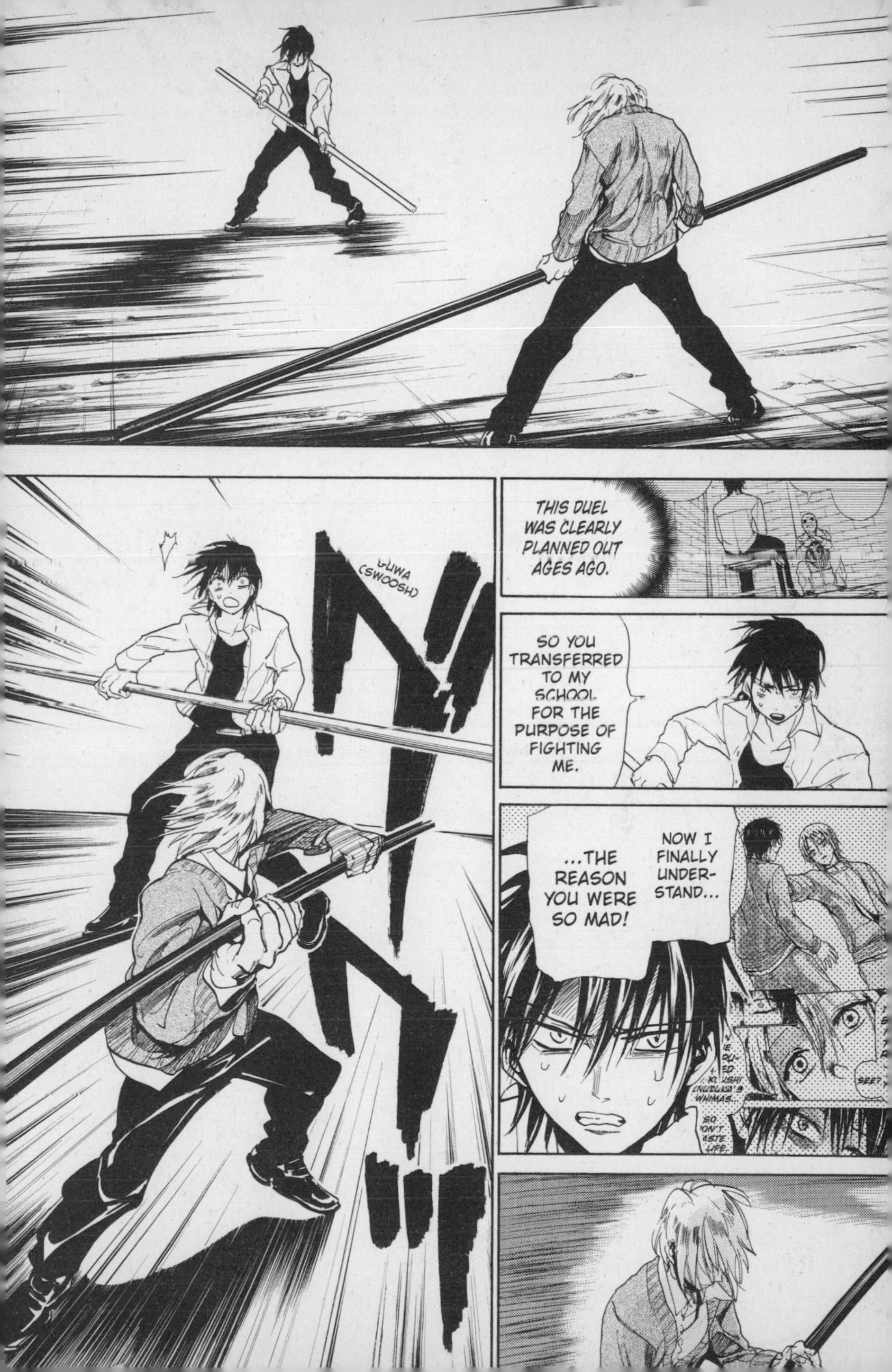
THIS DUEL WAS CLEARLY PLANNED OUT AGES AGO.
SO YOU TRANSFERRED TO MY SCHOOL FOR THE PURPOSE OF FIGHTING ME.
NOW I FINALLY UNDER-STAND...
...THE REASON YOU WERE SO MAD!
GUWA (SWOOSH)

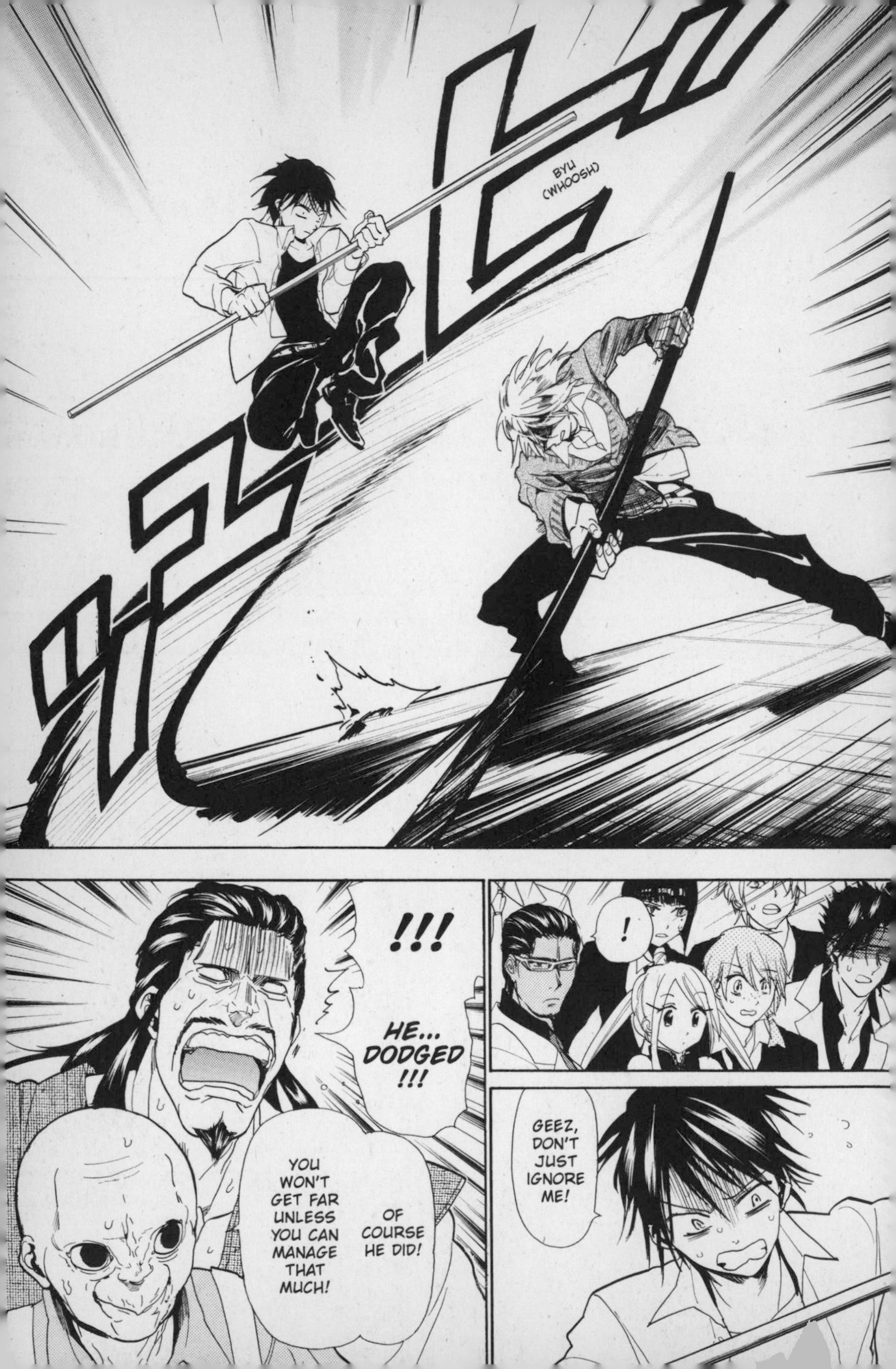
BYU (WHOOSH)
!
GEEZ, DON'T JUST IGNORE ME!
!!!
HE... DODGED!!!
OF COURSE HE DID!
YOU WON'T GET FAR UNLESS YOU CAN MANAGE THAT MUCH!

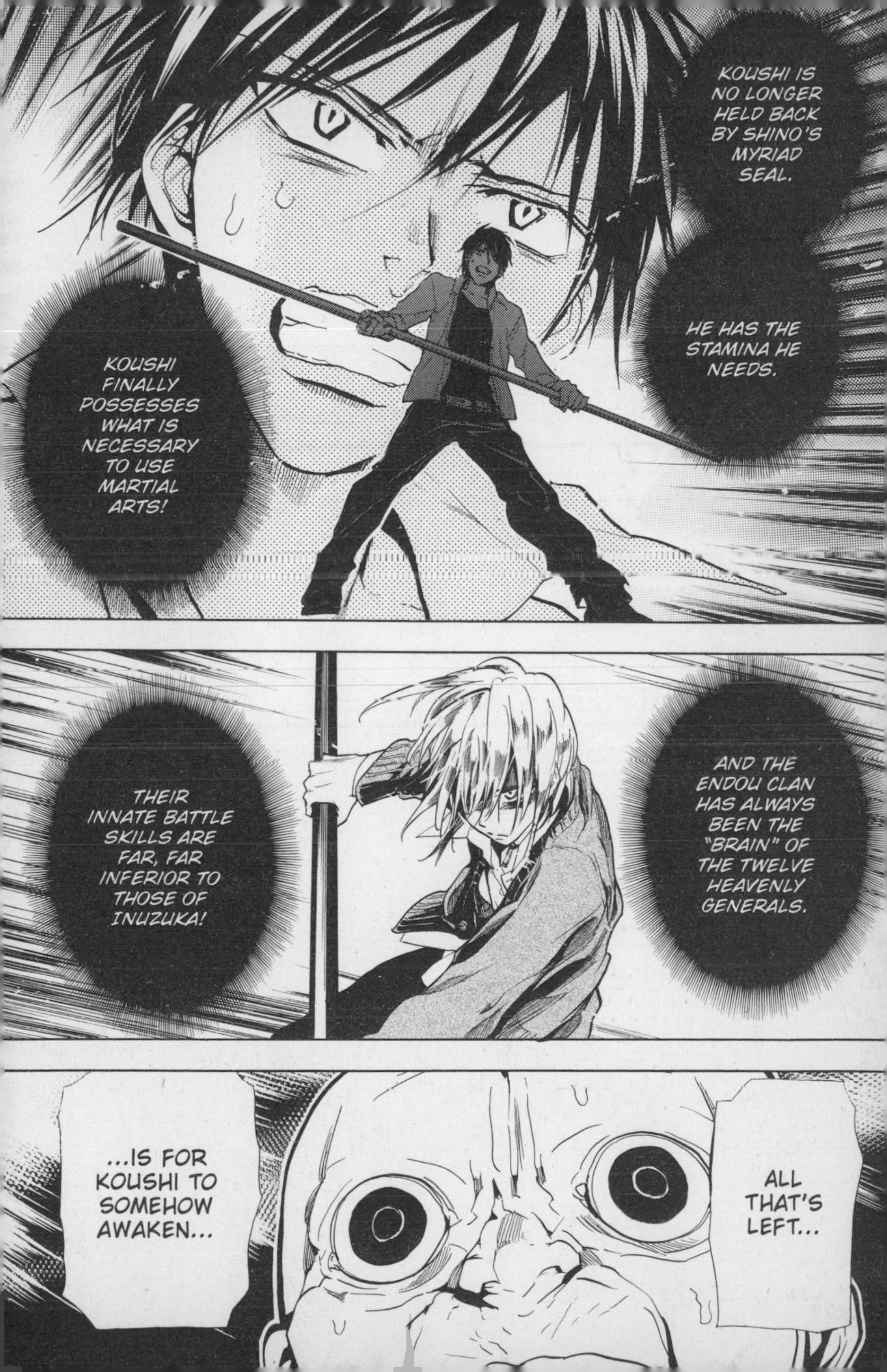
KOUSHI IS NO LONGER HELD BACK BY SHINO'S MYRIAD SEAL.
HE HAS THE STAMINA HE NEEDS.
KOUSHI FINALLY POSSESSES WHAT IS NECESSARY TO USE MARTIAL ARTS!
AND THE ENDOU CLAN HAS ALWAYS BEEN THE "BRAIN" OF THE TWELVE HEAVENLY GENERALS.
THEIR INNATE BATTLE SKILLS ARE FAR, FAR INFERIOR TO THOSE OF INUZUKA!
ALL THAT'S LEFT...
...IS FOR KOUSHI TO SOMEHOW AWAKEN...

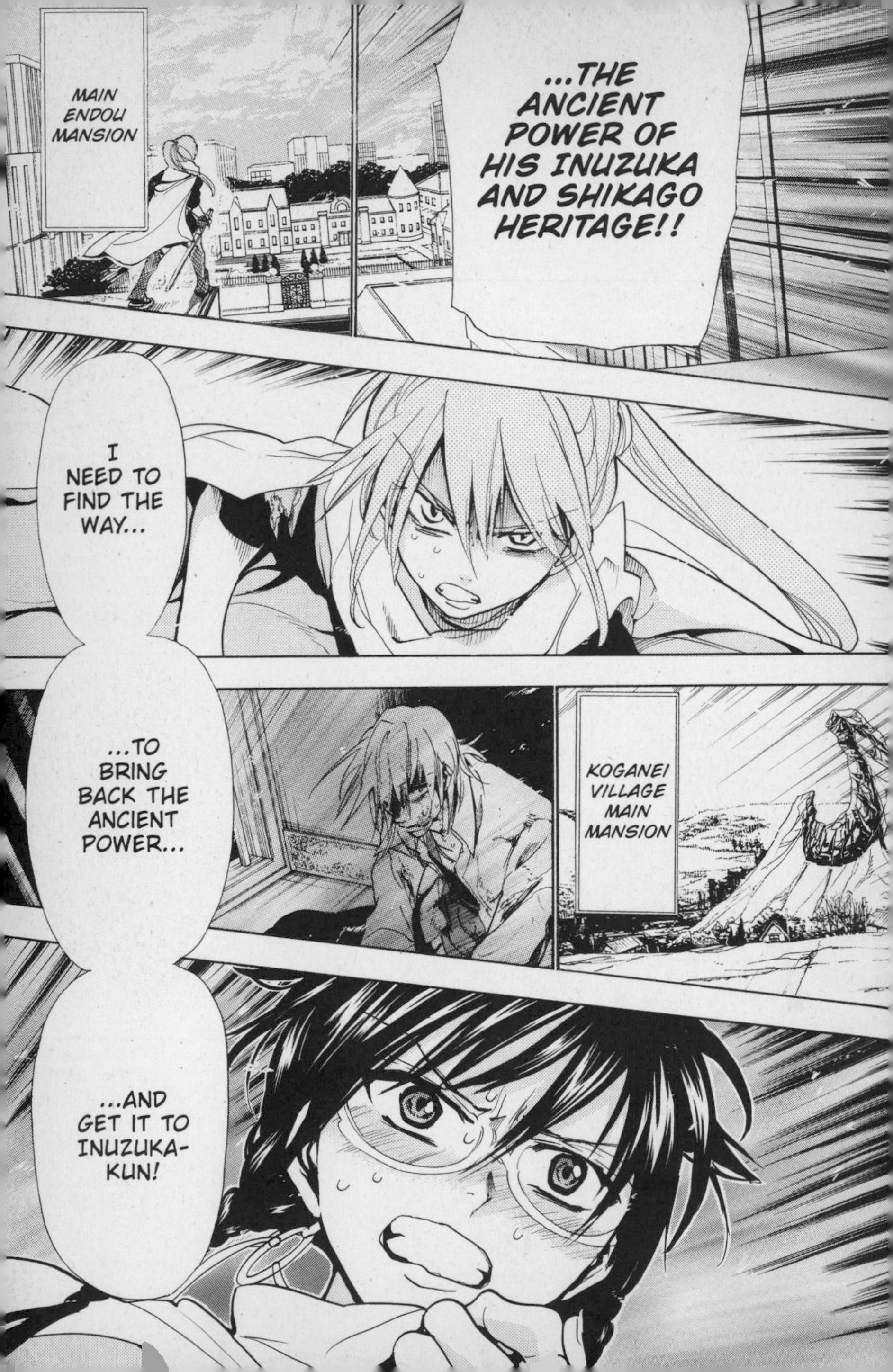
...THE ANCIENT POWER OF HIS INUZUKA AND SHIKAGO HERITAGE!!
MAIN ENDOU MANSION
I NEED TO FIND THE WAY...
KOGANEI VILLAGE MAIN MANSION
...TO BRING BACK THE ANCIENT POWER...
...AND GET IT TO INUZUKA-KUN!

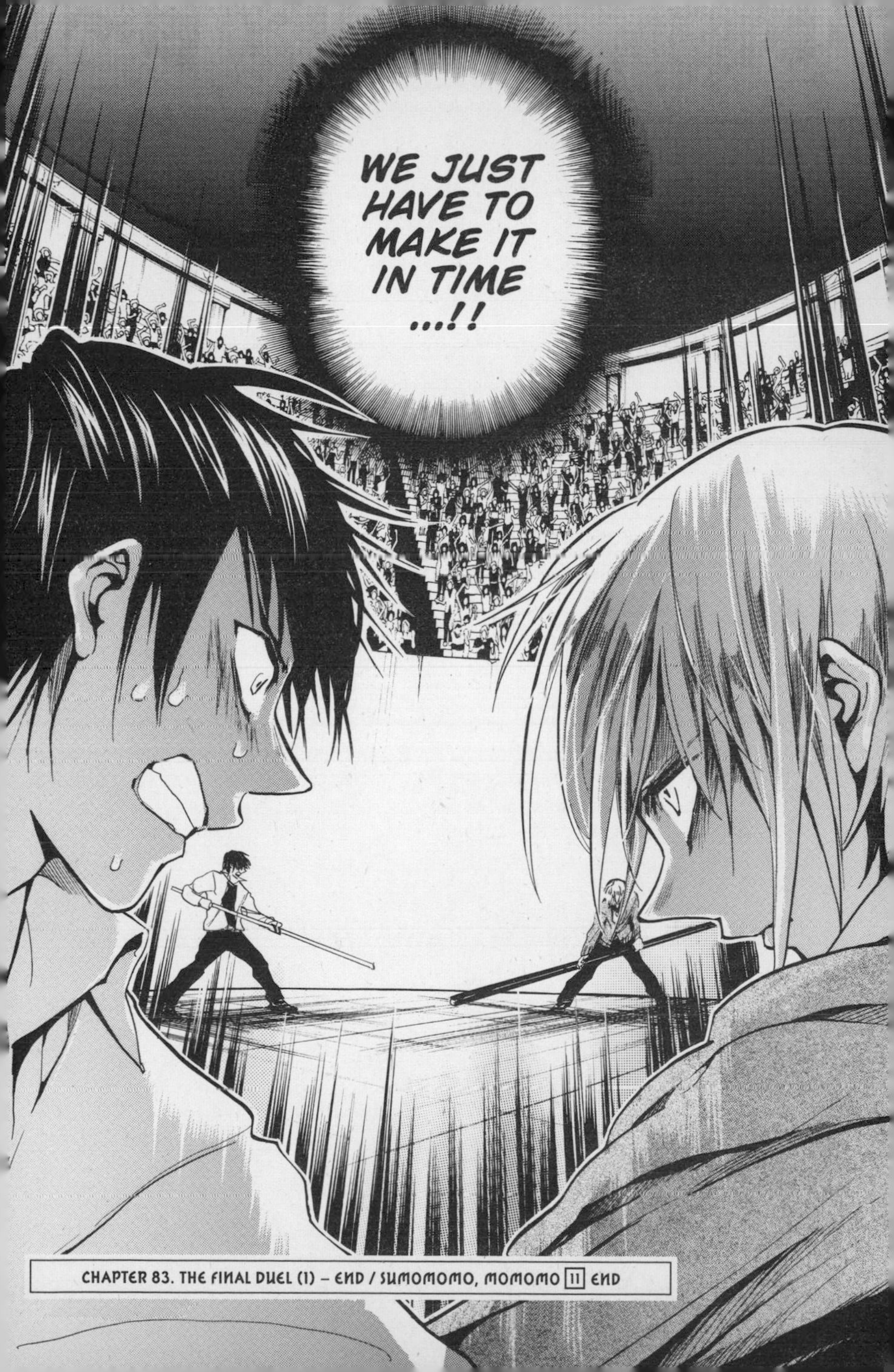
WE JUST HAVE TO MAKE IT IN TIME ...!!

CHAPTER 83. THE FINAL DUEL (1) – END / SUMOMOMO, MOMOMO 11 END

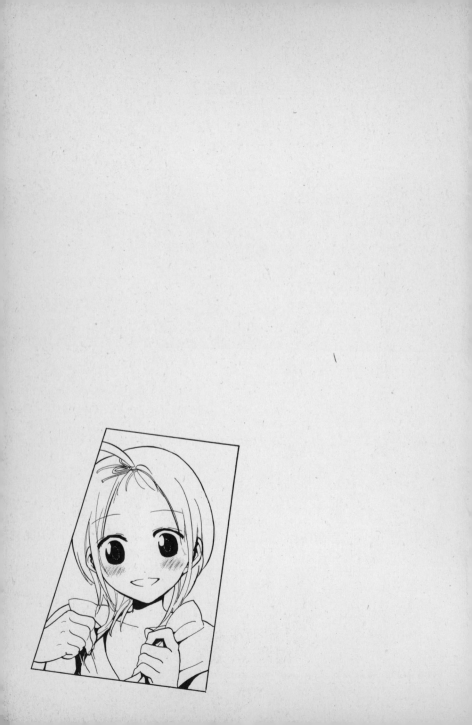

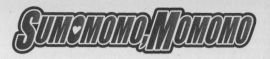

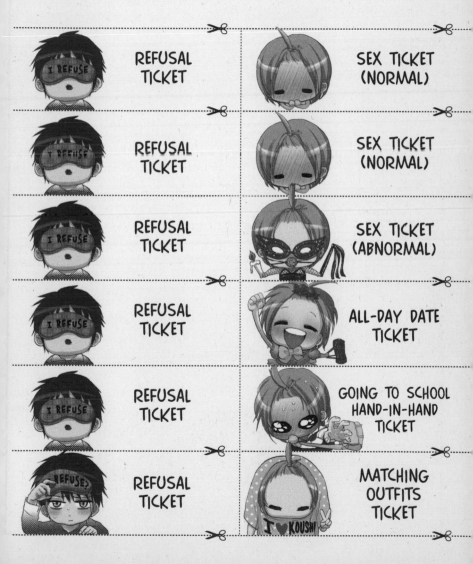

REFUSAL TICKET		SEX TICKET (NORMAL)	
REFUSAL TICKET		SEX TICKET (NORMAL)	
REFUSAL TICKET		SEX TICKET (ABNORMAL)	
REFUSAL TICKET		ALL-DAY DATE TICKET	
REFUSAL TICKET		GOING TO SCHOOL HAND-IN-HAND TICKET	
REFUSAL TICKET		MATCHING OUTFITS TICKET	

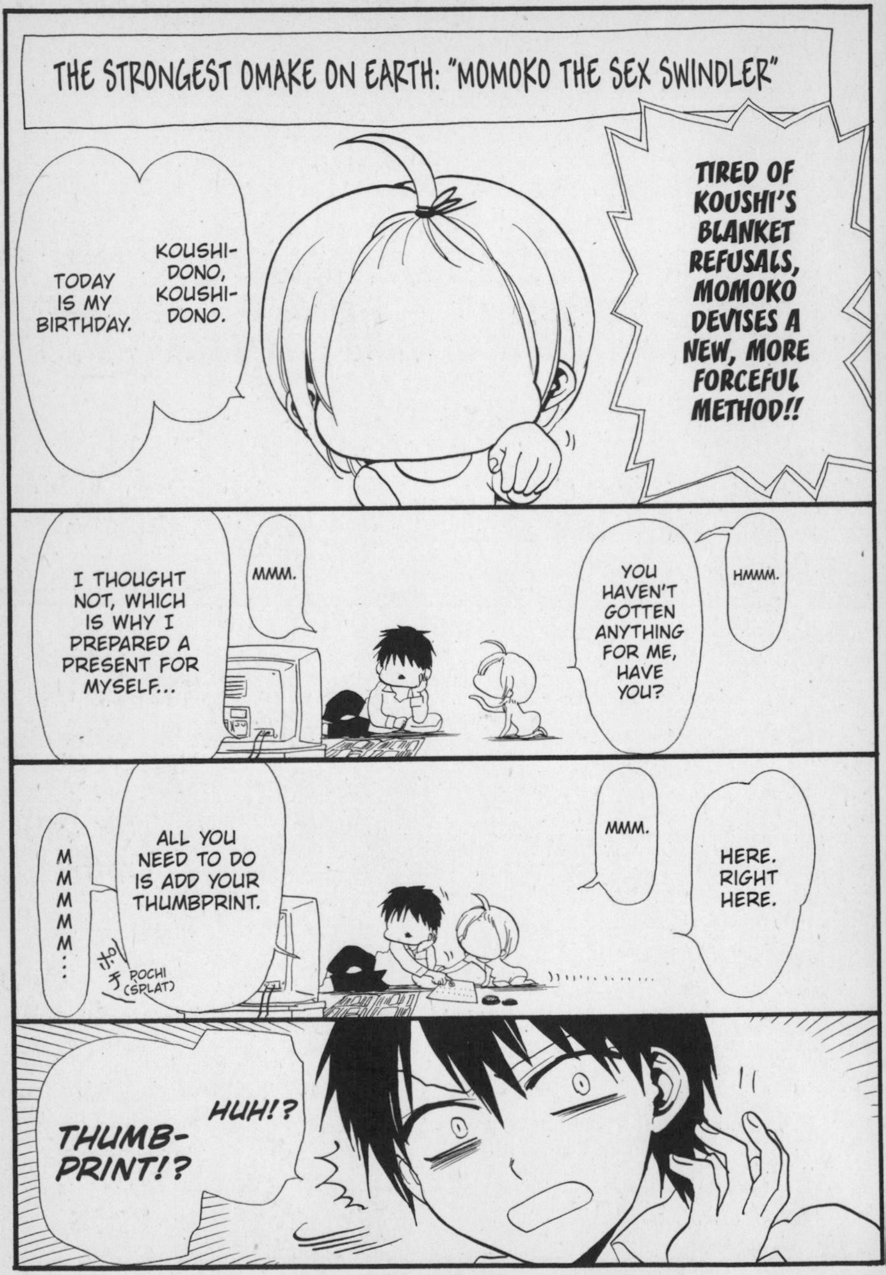
THE STRONGEST OMAKE ON EARTH: "MOMOKO THE SEX SWINDLER"
TIRED OF KOUSHI'S BLANKET REFUSALS, MOMOKO DEVISES A NEW, MORE FORCEFUL METHOD!!
KOUSHI-DONO, KOUSHI-DONO.
TODAY IS MY BIRTHDAY.
HMMM.
YOU HAVEN'T GOTTEN ANYTHING FOR ME, HAVE YOU?
MMM.
I THOUGHT NOT, WHICH IS WHY I PREPARED A PRESENT FOR MYSELF...
HERE. RIGHT HERE.
MMM.
ALL YOU NEED TO DO IS ADD YOUR THUMBPRINT.
MMMMM...
ポチ POCHI (SPLAT)
HUH!?
THUMB-PRINT!?

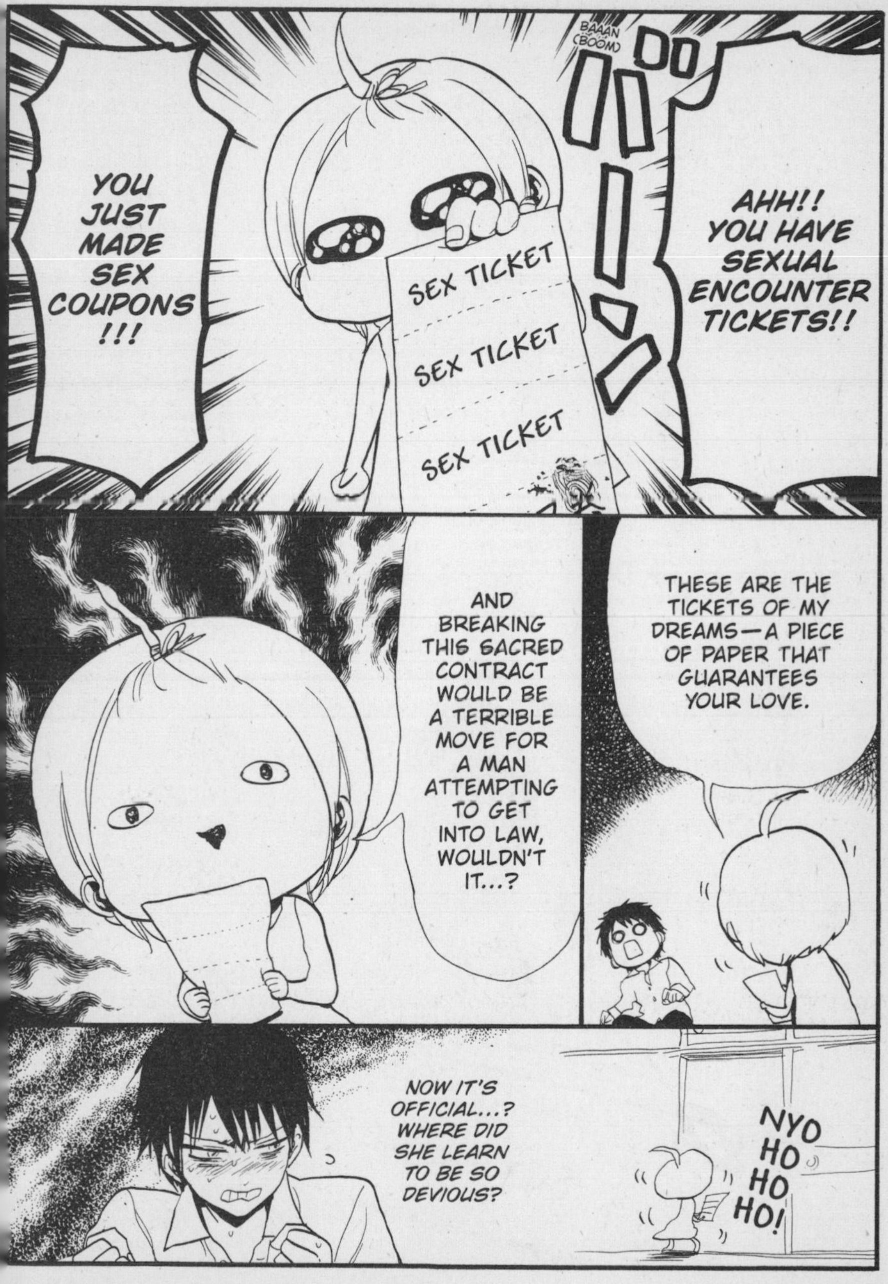
BAAAN (BOOM)
AHH!! YOU HAVE SEXUAL ENCOUNTER TICKETS!!
SEX TICKET
SEX TICKET
SEX TICKET
YOU JUST MADE SEX COUPONS!!!
THESE ARE THE TICKETS OF MY DREAMS—A PIECE OF PAPER THAT GUARANTEES YOUR LOVE.
AND BREAKING THIS SACRED CONTRACT WOULD BE A TERRIBLE MOVE FOR A MAN ATTEMPTING TO GET INTO LAW, WOULDN'T IT...?
NYO HO HO HO!
NOW IT'S OFFICIAL...? WHERE DID SHE LEARN TO BE SO DEVIOUS?

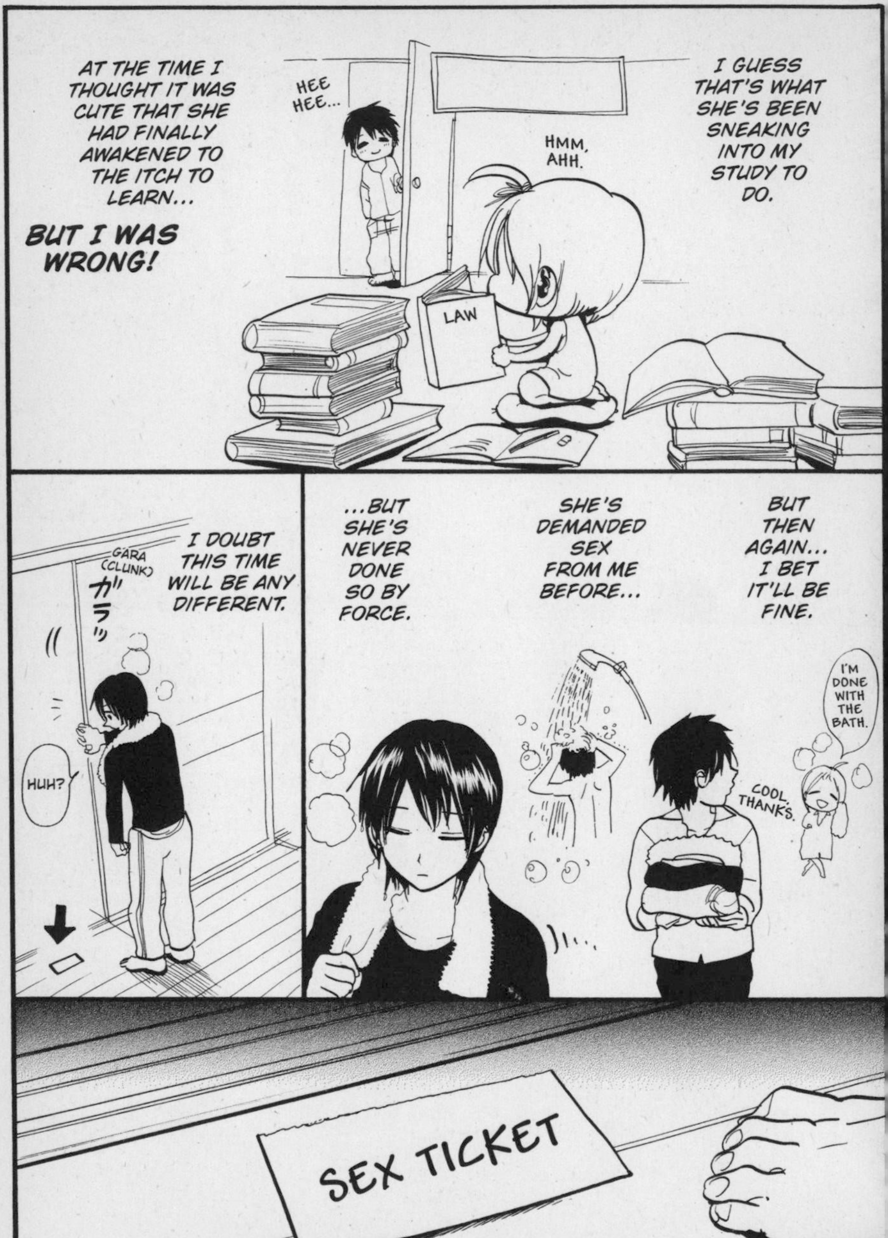
I GUESS THAT'S WHAT SHE'S BEEN SNEAKING INTO MY STUDY TO DO.
HMM, AHH.
HEE HEE...
LAW
AT THE TIME I THOUGHT IT WAS CUTE THAT SHE HAD FINALLY AWAKENED TO THE ITCH TO LEARN...
BUT I WAS WRONG!
BUT THEN AGAIN... I BET IT'LL BE FINE.
I'M DONE WITH THE BATH.
COOL. THANKS.
SHE'S DEMANDED SEX FROM ME BEFORE...
...BUT SHE'S NEVER DONE SO BY FORCE.
I DOUBT THIS TIME WILL BE ANY DIFFERENT.
GARA (CLUNK)
ガラッ
HUH?
SEX TICKET

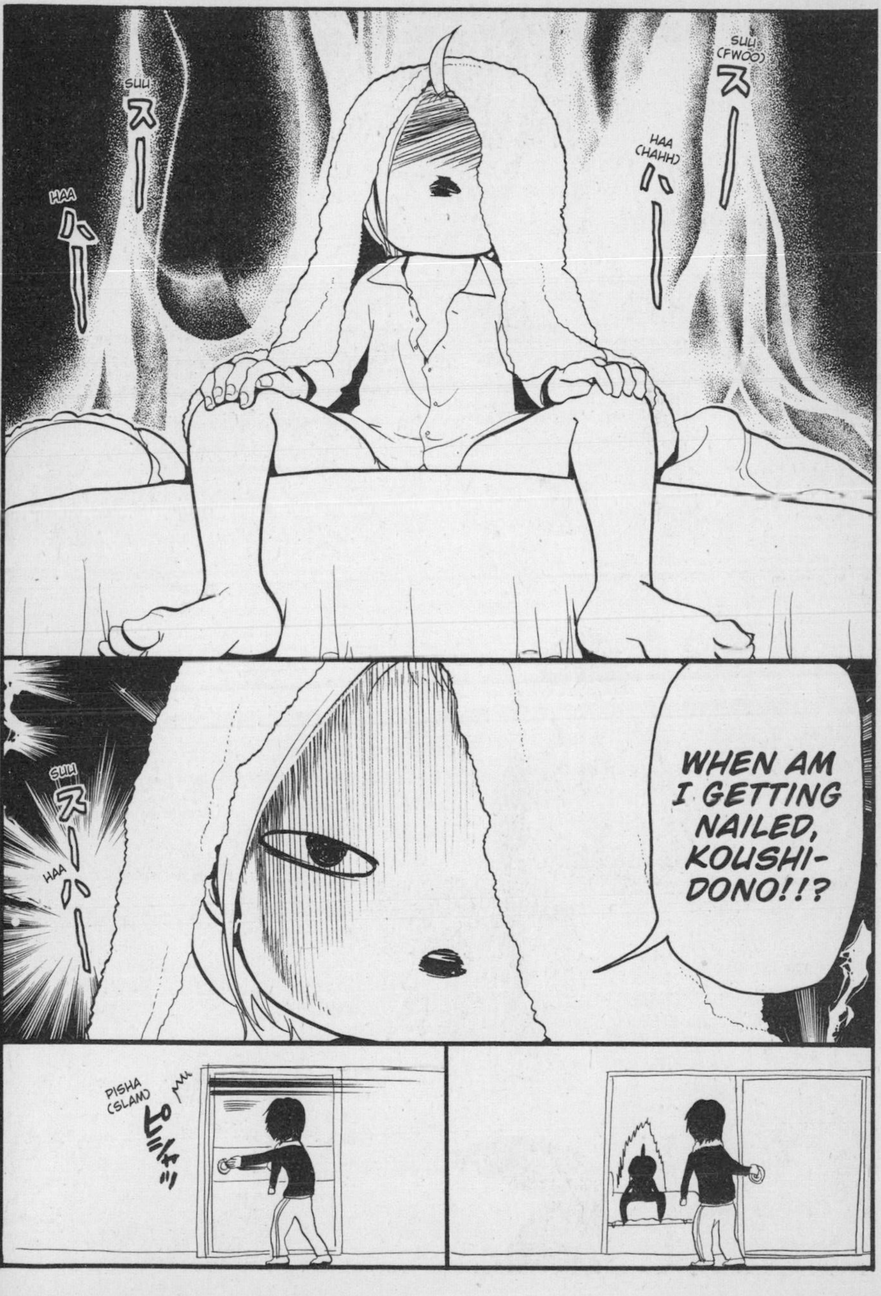
SUU (FWOO)
スー
HAA (HAHH)
ハー
SUU
スー
HAA
ハー
WHEN AM I GETTING NAILED, KOUSHI-DONO!!?
SUU
スー
HAA
ハー
PISHA (SLAM)
ピシャッ

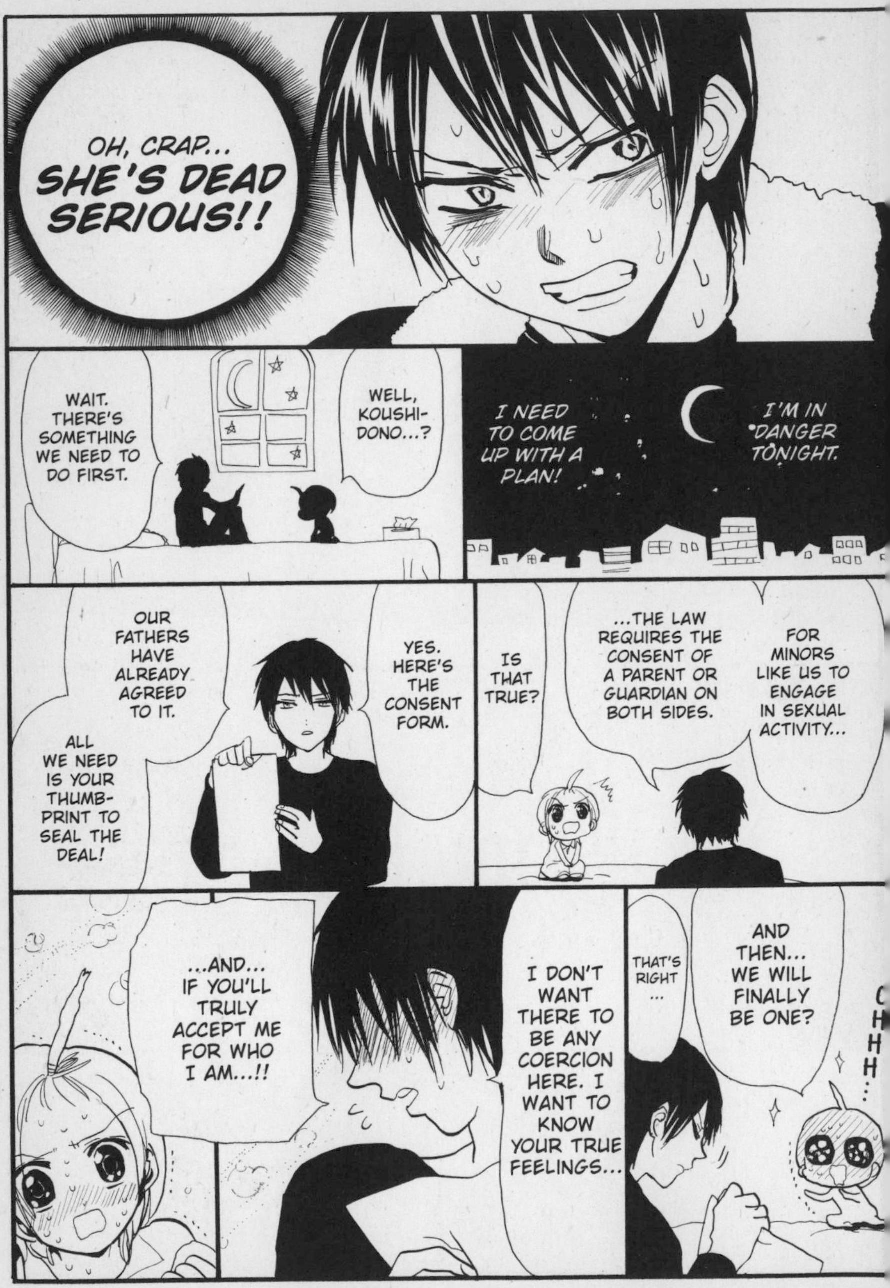
OH, CRAP... SHE'S DEAD SERIOUS!!
I'M IN DANGER TONIGHT.
I NEED TO COME UP WITH A PLAN!
WELL, KOUSHI-DONO...?
WAIT. THERE'S SOMETHING WE NEED TO DO FIRST.
FOR MINORS LIKE US TO ENGAGE IN SEXUAL ACTIVITY...
...THE LAW REQUIRES THE CONSENT OF A PARENT OR GUARDIAN ON BOTH SIDES.
IS THAT TRUE?
YES. HERE'S THE CONSENT FORM.
OUR FATHERS HAVE ALREADY AGREED TO IT.
ALL WE NEED IS YOUR THUMB-PRINT TO SEAL THE DEAL!
AND THEN... WE WILL FINALLY BE ONE?
THAT'S RIGHT...
I DON'T WANT THERE TO BE ANY COERCION HERE. I WANT TO KNOW YOUR TRUE FEELINGS...
...AND... IF YOU'LL TRULY ACCEPT ME FOR WHO I AM...!!

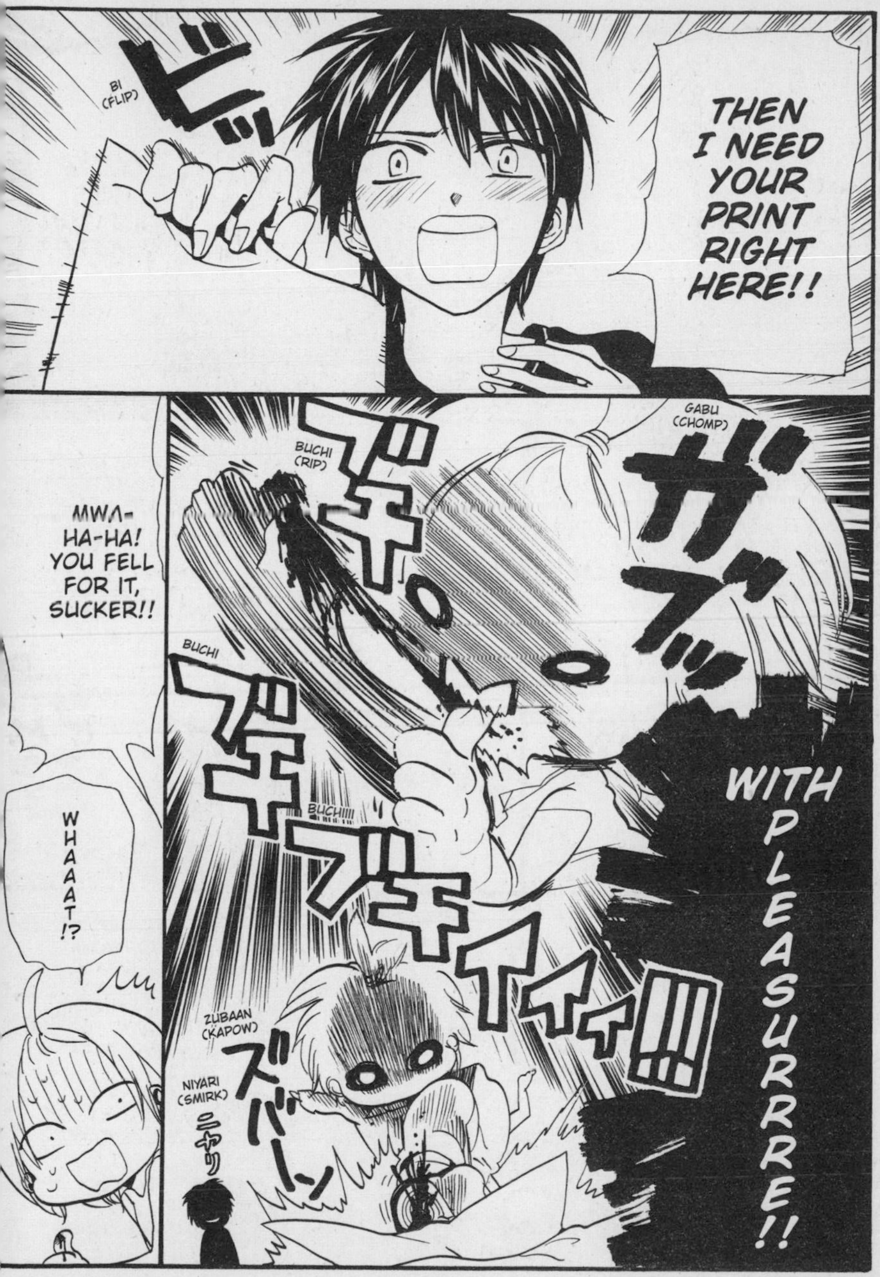
THEN I NEED YOUR PRINT RIGHT HERE!!
BI (FLIP)
GABU (CHOMP)
BUCHI (RIP)
BUCHI
WITH PLEASURRRE!!
BUCHI!!!!
ZUBAAN (KAPOW)
NIYARI (SMIRK)
MWA-HA-HA! YOU FELL FOR IT, SUCKER!!
WHAAAAT!?

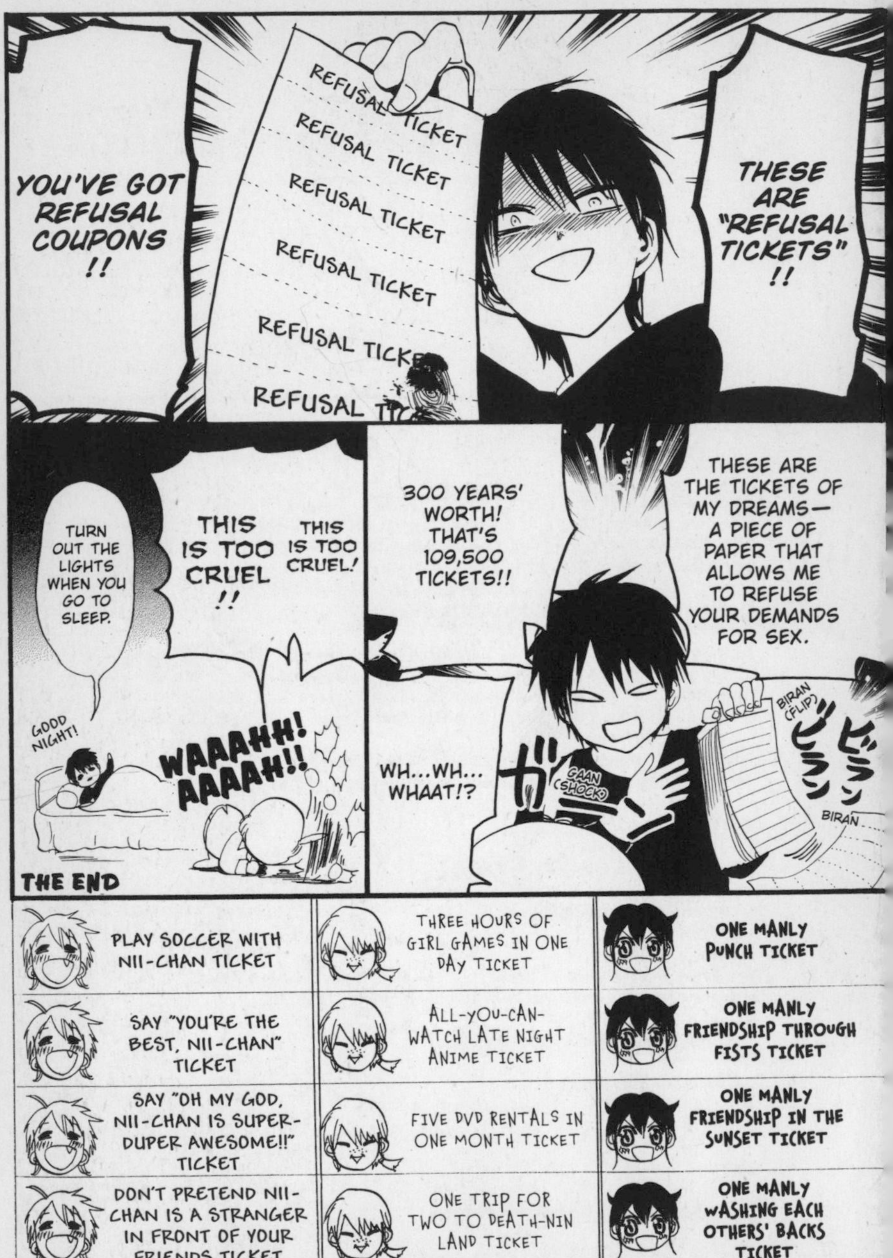
THESE ARE "REFUSAL TICKETS"!!
REFUSAL TICKET
REFUSAL TICKET
REFUSAL TICKET
REFUSAL TICKET
REFUSAL TICK
REFUSAL
YOU'VE GOT REFUSAL COUPONS!!
THESE ARE THE TICKETS OF MY DREAMS—A PIECE OF PAPER THAT ALLOWS ME TO REFUSE YOUR DEMANDS FOR SEX.
300 YEARS' WORTH! THAT'S 109,500 TICKETS!!
ビラン BIRAN (FLIP)
ビラン BIRAN
ガ GAAN (SHOCK)
WH...WH... WHAAT!?
THIS IS TOO CRUEL!
THIS IS TOO CRUEL!!
TURN OUT THE LIGHTS WHEN YOU GO TO SLEEP.
WAAAHH! AAAAH!!
GOOD NIGHT!
THE END
ONE MANLY PUNCH TICKET
ONE MANLY FRIENDSHIP THROUGH FISTS TICKET
ONE MANLY FRIENDSHIP IN THE SUNSET TICKET
ONE MANLY WASHING EACH OTHERS' BACKS TICKET
THREE HOURS OF GIRL GAMES IN ONE DAY TICKET
ALL-YOU-CAN-WATCH LATE NIGHT ANIME TICKET
FIVE DVD RENTALS IN ONE MONTH TICKET
ONE TRIP FOR TWO TO DEATH-NIN LAND TICKET
PLAY SOCCER WITH NII-CHAN TICKET
SAY "YOU'RE THE BEST, NII-CHAN" TICKET
SAY "OH MY GOD, NII-CHAN IS SUPER-DUPER AWESOME!!" TICKET
DON'T PRETEND NII-CHAN IS A STRANGER IN FRONT OF YOUR FRIENDS TICKET

SUMOMOMO MOMOMO ⑪

SHINOBU OHTAKA

Translation: Stephen Paul

Lettering: Terri Delgado

SUMOMOMO MOMOMO Vol. 11 © 2008 Shinobu Ohtaka / SQUARE ENIX.
All rights reserved. First published in Japan in 2008 by SQUARE ENIX CO.,
LTD. English translation rights arranged with SQUARE ENIX CO., LTD.
and Hachette Book Group through Tuttle-Mori Agency, Inc.

Translation © 2012 by SQUARE ENIX CO., LTD.

Yen Press
Hachette Book Group
237 Park Avenue, New York, NY 10017

www.HachetteBookGroup.com
www.YenPress.com

Yen Press is an imprint of Hachette Book Group, Inc. The Yen Press
name and logo are trademarks of Hachette Book Group, Inc.

First Yen Press Edition: February 2012

ISBN: 978-0-316-20469-9

10 9 8 7 6 5 4 3 2 1

BVG

Printed in the United States of America